TOTAL QUALITY DEVELOPMENT

ASME PRESS SERIES ON INTERNATIONAL ADVANCES IN DESIGN PRODUCTIVITY

Editor:
K. M. Ragsdell, University of Missouri–Rolla, Rolla, Missouri, U.S.A.

Advisory Board:
Don P. Clausing, Massachusetts Institute of Technology, Cambridge, Massachusetts, U.S.A.

Stuart Pugh, University of Strathclyde, Glasgow, Scotland

Genichi Taguchi, Okhen Associates, Tokyo, Japan

Intelligent Engineering Systems Through Artificial Neural Networks, Volume 1, edited by Cihan H. Dagli, Soundar R. T. Kumara, and Yung C. Shin, 1991

Intelligent Engineering Systems Through Artificial Neural Networks, Volume 2, edited by Cihan H. Dagli, Laura I. Burke, and Yung C. Shin, 1992

Taguchi on Robust Technology Development: Bringing Quality Engineering Upstream, by Genichi Taguchi, 1993

Total Quality Development: A Step-by-Step Guide to World-Class Concurrent Engineering, by Don P. Clausing, 1994

TOTAL QUALITY DEVELOPMENT

A Step-By-Step Guide to World-Class Concurrent Engineering

by

DON CLAUSING

NEW YORK   ASME PRESS   1994

© 1994 by The American Society of Mechanical Engineers
345 East 47th Street, New York, NY 10017-2392

2nd printing, 1994
3rd printing, 1995

Library of Congress Cataloging-in-Publication Data

Clausing, Don.
        Total quality development: a step-by-step guide to world-class
    concurrent engineering / Don Clausing.
                p.   cm.
        Includes bibliographical references and index.
        ISBN 0-7918-0035-0
        1. Concurrent engineering.   2. Quality control.   I. Title.
    TS176.C5371993
    658.5'75 — dc20

                                                        94-73
                                                        CIP

ISBN   0-7918-0035-0

To my wife Ruth,
whose patience helped me to have
the concentration to write this book

To the late Professor Stuart Pugh
and Dr. Genichi Taguchi
whose examples helped to inspire this book

To Mr. Bernard M. Gordon
whose generosity to MIT provided me
with the opportunity to write this book

Table of Contents

Foreword

This book stands alone, as the first truly cogent effort to integrate the very latest tools and practices for modern product development. Years from now it will be regarded as a benchmark for similar efforts which are sure to follow. *Total Quality Development* gives an easy-to-apply, step-by-step prescription for the development of high-quality, low-cost products. The author synergistically integrates the latest methods—including enhanced quality function deployment, Pugh's concept selection, Taguchi's system of quality engineering, and total quality management. In addition, the book is organized in a fashion that maximizes its utility to designers, engineers and managers in every phase of the product realization process. The many examples and references to actual industrial experience greatly enhance the book, and should allow the reader to tailor the presented tools and methods to his or her particular situation and environment.

I met Don Clausing during one of my many consulting trips to Xerox Corporation in Webster, New York, in 1980. Don invited me to lunch to "pick my brain about design and development engineering." We talked for quite some time, and I soon learned that I was the pupil, not the teacher; I have been learning from Dr. Clausing ever since. Students of engineering design in academe and practice will find this book of long-lasting value.

KEN RAGSDELL

Preface

This book is for all product people who wish to make major improvements in the development of new products—whether their "products" are actual devices or are production processes or services. Faster time to market, product variety to satisfy a broad range of customers, best-in-class quality, and reduced costs—the processes to achieve these goals are described. The integrated approach in this book—based on personal experience and searching out best practices—is required for success in product development in the modern, competitive global economy.

This book will help you attain many benefits, from better product planning to a smoother transition to production. Rapid time to market is accelerated by giving attention to several principles: listening to the voice of the customer, developing robust technology, planning for reusability of technological ideas, employing basic concurrent engineering, and following a disciplined process overall. These same elements, combined with integrated planning of products, technologies, and basic strengths, provide product variety together with control over spending for acquisition and over risks. Quality is achieved by systematic deployment of the voice of the customer throughout the organization and by the application of quality engineering to provide products that remain very close to ideal performance. Costs are minimized by employing basic concurrent engineering, robust design, competitive benchmarking, and careful consideration of the cost of providing each benefit to the customer.

The aim of this book is to span both engineering and management. It has more breadth than the typical engineering viewpoint on product development, and more depth than the typical management book. Much of this book, in fact, is quite applicable to the development of products not ordinarily thought of as engineered—from greeting cards to health services. It appears that this book is, so far, unique in its combination of breadth and depth, and in its application to a wide variety of development activities. Many elements that until now have been described in specialized writings are integrated here to form a unified approach to development.

The primary purpose of this book is to improve industrial performance. In order to do this it is aimed at product people who are working in industry. The book addresses the major concerns and needs of all levels of people doing product work, from entry level to the top managers. This book is for everyone who wishes to improve product development. Although the cases and illustrations used are from the world of engineered products, the book can also be applied to packaged consumer goods, production capability, and services. Its primary audience may be in industry, but the book can also be used in a university course on product development. It has grown out of the product development course that I have taught at MIT for seven years. There are very few such courses in the United States at this time, but this book is written with the hope of helping others to get started. Thus, it is aimed at all product people, primarily in industry, but also at university students who intend to do product work in industry.

The book is meant to be an overview of all aspects of development, far beyond the partial design that is the content of university design courses. The emphasis is on the integrated processes and teamwork that are essential to success with products. The scope is very broad, from technical subjects such as Dr. Genichi Taguchi's quality engineering to people-oriented topics such as the changes that may be needed in the corporate culture to bring about improved development. The only criterion for including a subject is that it be essential to success with products.

This book takes the reader through product development from the voice of the customer to the factory floor. It includes technology development, strategy, and management, including the necessary change in the corporate culture. The content is independent of discipline, not restricted to mechanical engineering or electrical engineering or any other engineering specialty. In fact, much of the book is not restricted to engineered products. For example, the basic approach to bringing in the voice of the customer does not depend on the specific nature of the product. Thus, this book can be applied to all products. Its contents will guide readers toward achieving excellent performance in the higher-level tasks that determine the specific responsibilities of their own discipline. For example, the voice of the customer and the House of Quality lead to concept work using the Pugh concept selection process, but the concepts themselves—the ideas for specific products—will be dependent on one's specific discipline. This book is for readers who are already familiar with a specific discipline and who wish to leverage their competence in their own discipline to achieve success with products.

A feature of this book is effective systems engineering—the integration of quality function deployment (QFD) and Taguchi's quality engineering. Integration both of QFD and quality engineering, first of all, and of the two of them into the total development process—is crucial. Although QFD and quality engineering are now being applied in more and more situations, their effectiveness has been limited by the proverbial syndrome of the blind men and the elephant: there has been a tendency to grab one element and think that it is the whole thing. Also, there has been a tendency to treat QFD and quality engineering as activities that are added to normal development work. This is ineffective or worse. The emphasis in this book is on the *integration* of QFD and quality engineering into total development. Then they form a very effective type of systems engineering, which can be applied in the heat of product development to make better decisions—a key to successful products.

This book has been written to address many problems that have plagued product development; these cover a range encompassing disregard of the voice of the customer, lack of teamwork, premature concept selection, and a lack of robust functionality. They are summarized in Chapter 1 as the 10 cash drains. Vigorous international economic competition has led people in industry to find many opportunities for improvement. This book describes those improvements that are most crucial to success with products.

This book has two primary sources—my personal experience during 29 years in industry, and benchmarking of the best practices around the world. In evaluating improved practices as they have come to my attention, I have used a single criterion: Would they have improved success in projects in which I have been involved during my career? When the answer has been yes, the improved practice has been incorporated into the total development process and included in this book. It has been my good fortune to have had a long career in industry and then to have taken early retirement from industry to accept a position at MIT. Both phases of my career have been essential in making this book possible. Industrial experience and academic teaching and research give very different viewpoints. This book has grown out of the synthesis of the two viewpoints. My position at MIT has been half-time, allowing me to continue to work in industry applying the teachings in this book. My hope is that this book will represent the best of both worlds.

The book is organized into 10 chapters and 3 appendixes. Product development is an activity, and the only way to fully learn this material is to practice it. Therefore, the book is organized in accordance with the development activity. The first chapter outlines the problems and opportunities. The second chapter describes basic concurrent engineering, which is the first level of improved product development and permeates all of the subsequent improvements. Chapter 3 is an overview of and introduction to better decision making, emphasizing the effective systems engineering that is formed by the integration of QFD and Taguchi's quality engineering. Chapters 4 through 6 describe the product development process—concept, design, and production preparation. Then Chapter 7 describes technology development and Chapter 8 describes strategy. In actual practice, strategy comes first; then technology development follows, and then product development is the culmination of the work that has started with strategic planning and technology development. However, the sequence of the chapters allows a more natural evolution of the material. Chapter 9 describes the role of management in total quality development, including the importance of cultural change; and Chapter 10 describes the benefits. Appendix A expands upon the important subject of the best metric for the robustness of functionality: the signal-to-noise (SN) ratio.

Special attention is called to Appendixes B and C, which are "road maps" for your easy reference. Appendix B is a concise diagrammatic summary of the development processes for technologies and products. Thus, it is a summary of the major connections throughout the activities that are described in Chapters 4 through 7. As you read the detailed descriptions of activities in those chapters, a quick look at Appendix B will reveal the relationship of any one activity to the overall process. This is very helpful in developing an integrated image of the total set of activities. Appendix C is a diagrammatic road map through the same material from the viewpoint of effective systems engineering. It provides a ready bird's-eye view of the connections among the elements of QFD and quality engineering that integrate them together into effective systems engineering. This will help you overcome the typical tendency toward the blind-men-and-the-elephant syndrome—the tendency to see each element only in isolation. In summary, the view from 30,000 feet that is provided by Appendixes B and C will reward your frequent reference to them with a more comprehensive grasp of total quality development.

As with most books, a partial reading will suffice for some purposes. Chapters 1, 2, and 3 provide an overview that introduces total quality development. For awareness of the subject, these chapters are sufficient. A management course can be based on Chapters 1, 2, 3, 8, 9, and 10, with the addition of some material on SN ratio from Chapter 5 and Appendix A. Those who want an introduction to Taguchi's quality engineering, with emphasis on its integration with QFD and into product development, can read Chapter 3, the relevant portion of Chapter 5, and Appendix A. However, for those who wish to fully transform product development, a reading of the entire book is essential.

Some readers may prefer to read selected chapters in an individualized order—for example, Chapter 8, Chapter 7, then Chapter 4. In this way, the reading will be in the same sequence as the practice. To do this, the reader will need a good prior knowledge of the subject. Also, it may help in this approach if the material on robust design in Chapter 5 is read at the same time as Chapter 7. This sequence of reading may be particularly effective for readers who are especially interested in strategy and technology development.

The objective of this book is to transform product development to achieve competitiveness in the global economy. Learning the improved process and teamwork is essential, but the critical factor is implementation. This is covered in Chapter 9. Some readers may find this the most valuable part of the book. It is essential to master implementation, including cultural change, in order to reap the full benefits of the improvements that are described in this book.

I owe a debt to many people—first, to all product people with whom I have worked and from whom I have learned. When I was a young engineer I had the good fortune to work with Dr. Robert C. Dean, Jr., who inspired me to become a much better engineer than I then was and started me on the path to improvement that has culminated in this book. During the past 10 years, it has been my good fortune to work cooperatively with two of the giants of product development improvement—Professor Stuart Pugh and Dr. Genichi Taguchi. It is interesting to note that one lived in the United Kingdom and the other lives in Japan—indicative of the global scope of improved product development.

The global community of product developers, and myself personally, experienced a great loss in the passing of Professor Pugh. He was not only a good personal friend and professional collaborator, but also a great leader in improving product development. Another valued colleague is Mr. Maurice Holmes, now the president of the Office Document Systems Division of Xerox. We worked together for many years; at one time he was to some extent my pupil. Now I watch in appreciation and some awe at his success in implementing improvements in product development.

With regard to this book in particular, I appreciate the helpful comments I have received from many people. I would like to explicitly acknowledge Ron Andrade, Chris Argyris, Joel Moses, Frank Pipp, and Preston Smith. Dr. Andrade of the engineering faculty of the Federal University of Rio de Janeiro, is currently my colleague as he serves a term of two years as a visiting scholar at MIT. He reviewed the entire book as it was being written and made many helpful comments. Chris Argyris, Joel Moses, and Frank Pipp kindly reviewed those portions of the book that deal with their work and made comments that led to improvements. Preston Smith reviewed the final manuscript and recommended a road map—which took the form of Appendixes B and C and some improvements in clarity in the main body that made it compatible with the two appendixes. Finally, I thank the several students from my 1992 class whose detailed comments led to clarifications and improvements.

To you the reader, I hope that this book meets your needs and expectations. It is my fervent hope that it will help to make significant improvements in product development.

DON CLAUSING

CHAPTER

1

Building Better Products

Total *quality development* is the modern way of developing new products that will be competitive in the global economy. It combines the best engineering, the best management, the best strategy, and, especially, the best teamwork—far beyond traditional product development practices. The resulting improvements are greatly reduced development time, a reduction in all costs, higher quality, and increased product variety. Combined, these improvements greatly increase customer satisfaction. But let us begin at the beginning.

BASIC ENGINEERING—THE FOUNDATION

At the core of all development work is concept creation. Without new concepts a corporation's new products degenerate into mere rearrangements of the old. It is as if somebody had thought to rearrange the deck chairs on the *Titanic* to prevent it from sinking. Eventually the corporation's product portfolio sinks because potential customers regard the products as stale and passé. Aggressive competitors overtake the corporation. Products that are truly new, on the other hand, start with outstanding creative work. Although specialized knowledge and experience are not required to create very simple concepts, technologically complex products require a basic engineering foundation.

We create new technological concepts by combining our knowledge of engineering science (the study of physics and materials) with technological insights to achieve a new idea, what we might describe as a creative rearrangement of physics and materials (Figure 1.1). For an example of such a rearrangement, consider the internal combustion engine. The older steam engine employed a slow-burning fire outside a cylinder. Placing a fast-burning fire *inside* the cylinder—rearranging the physics—gave us the appropriately named internal combustion engine. We cannot rearrange the physics, chemistry, and materials, however, unless we understand them. Thus, a sound grounding in the engineering sciences is required. Likewise, we cannot invent a new mechanism if we have never seen a

PHYSICS

Maxwell's Equations

$$\nabla \cdot \mathbf{E} = \frac{\rho}{\epsilon_0}$$

$$\nabla \times \mathbf{E} = -\frac{\partial \mathbf{B}}{\partial t}$$

$$\nabla \cdot \mathbf{B} = 0$$

$$c^2 \nabla \times \mathbf{B} = \frac{\mathbf{j}}{\epsilon_0} + \frac{\partial \mathbf{E}}{\partial t}$$

Charge Conservation

$$\nabla \cdot \mathbf{j} = -\frac{\partial \rho}{\partial t}$$

Force Law

$$\mathbf{F} = q(\mathbf{E} + \partial \times \mathbf{B})$$

Law of Motion

$$\frac{d\mathbf{P}}{dt} = \mathbf{F}$$

Gravitation

$$\mathbf{F} = -G \frac{m_1 m_2}{r^2} \mathbf{e}_r$$

+

MATERIALS

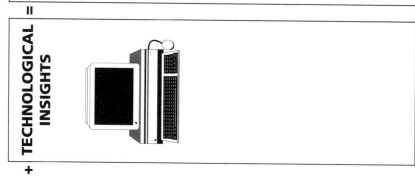

+

TECHNOLOGICAL INSIGHTS

=

INVENTIONS

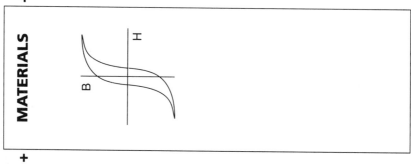

FIGURE 1.1 Concept creation process.

mechanism. Our education and experience, then, provide the technological insights that are the springboard to new technology. These are the fundamentals that engineers learn in engineering school and during their first few years in industrial practice. They enable the creation of concepts.

However, concept creation is not enough for success. Many concepts are just not feasible. When design is in conflict with physics, physics always wins. This is the overwhelming case for the engineering sciences as the required foundation for all product development. If the inertial forces, Poynting vectors, and entropy changes are not carefully planned in concert with nature, then the product is doomed to failure. Perpetual motion machines are the classic example.

Anyone who has had the opportunity to evaluate many proposed devices will have observed many concepts that were in conflict with physics. One example of a defective concept is thinking in terms of almost static operation. A device that might work well at 1 Hz has a response time that is 10 times the available cycle period. Because of its inadequate dynamic response, such a concept will do little except add to the cost. We cannot defeat physics.

Although dysfunctional devices are still a problem, the severity of that problem has been greatly reduced during the past 30 years by the strong emphasis upon engineering fundamentals. Also, it appears that competency in engineering fundamentals is not a major discriminator in the vigorous trade competition among nations. The spectrum of competencies in engineering fundamentals is roughly the same throughout the leading industrial countries.

The engineering sciences, which are the core of the basic engineering curriculum, are the foundation for success in product development. Newtonian mechanics, electromagnetic theory (Maxwell's equations), and thermodynamics, the mathematics to succinctly summarize and apply the knowledge learned from these disciplines must be at the core of all device development. The undergraduate engineering curriculum typically also includes one or two design courses. These concentrate on creative concepts and feasibility, the assurance of a first-order compatibility with the laws of nature. Let us call this *partial* design. A person's initial design assignments in industry further hone his or her partial design capability. After a few years of design experience in industry the engineer is competent in partial design. The breakdown of the engineering sciences into specialized fields for mechanisms, circuits, and energy converters, along with competence in partial design, enables the development of simple devices that *function* well, at least under limited operating conditions.

Undergraduate engineering education today is both very successful and plagued by a major problem. Undergraduates are very well trained in the basic engineering sciences that must underlie all successful engineering work, and in partial design. The problem is that after four or more years it is easy for the students to believe that the engineering sciences and partial design are all there is to engineering, and that after four years they have become engineers. In reality, the B.S. degree prepares the student to start *learning to practice* engineering. Still to be learned are the disciplines that will make the difference between successful products and failures, between a corporation's or a nation's economic success and its slow demise. The great challenge to undergraduate engineering education is to fan the fires of desire for engineering practice during the long learning time of the engineering basics. Then the student must be prepared to learn the disciplined practice that distinguishes between success and failure. That practice is the subject of this book.

Getting the engineering fundamentals right is the foundation for a good product. However, two products can both have very competently designed mechanisms and circuits and yet differ greatly in their success. The difference between success and failure can originate in their responsiveness to customer needs, the viability of the core concepts, the producibility of their design, the robustness of their functional quality, the economical precision of their production, their success of integration, their effective reusability, and their strategic impact. Total quality development includes all of these factors. In contrast, they are not much considered in partial design, which concentrates on creativity and feasibility.

This book is for the reader who already knows the engineering fundamentals, including the partial design that is the beginning of product development. This book describes the structured, disciplined practices that build on the fundamentals to make the critical difference between success and failure in product development. These practices are essentially independent of the specific type of product, applying to mechanisms, circuits, energy converters, and structures alike, although for each application the "plain vanilla" principles will benefit from tailoring to the specific product and organizational culture. This book describes the basic principles for product success.

BEYOND THE BASICS—SUCCESS WITH PRODUCTS

Beyond the basics—engineering science and partial design—success with products is achieved by total quality development. This improved total development process builds on the engineering sciences and partial design by incorporating the successful approaches that address customer needs, concept selection, functional robustness, integration into the total system, beneficial reusability, producibility and maintainability, problem prevention, teamwork, good management, and strategic coherence, all combined to achieve corporate success.

Success with products requires total quality development for bringing new products into being, starting with consideration of customer needs and ending with production of the product and its sale and service in the field. Figure 1.2 displays the major activities of product people. The engineering sciences, partial design, and partial production, along with

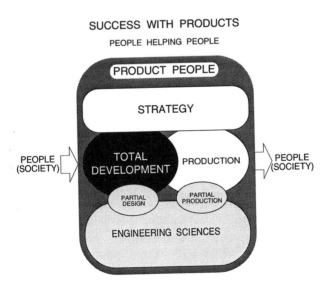

FIGURE 1.2. Roles of product people.

courses in the humanities, social sciences, and management, constitute the basic training for engineers. They form the foundation in Figure 1.2. Total development builds on the foundation to provide the context and style that enables success in partial design to be leveraged into success with products. Strategy is the overall plan that links different product programs with one another, products with technology, and products with business success.

This book builds on partial design, as learned in basic design courses and in the first few years of experience the engineer traditionally gets in industry. Total quality development includes the areas of Figure 1.2 labeled *total development, strategy, partial design*, and *engineering sciences*. This book concentrates on total development, strategy, and management. Partial design and the engineering sciences are already well covered in many books, and are usually practiced well in industry. Total development and strategy determine the many partial design tasks that have to be included within a product development program. In traditional product development the partial design tasks are done well enough. However, the definition of these tasks is not sufficient to ensure product success. Total quality development defines the partial design tasks so that task success leads to product success.

Total quality development and production operations are the linked activities in which product people help all people (society). The needs of society are the input to the total development activity (left side of Figure 1.2); the output that should result is new products that will benefit society (right side of Figure 1.2). Total quality development incorporates the application of the engineering sciences and partial design, and goes beyond them to successfully address customer needs, concept selection, robust functionality, integration, reusability, producibility, and strategy. This is the story that will unfold in this book, which concentrates on selecting the best practices from around the world and showing how they can be integrated together in total quality development.

First, let us examine the problems that have frequently plagued traditional product development. The total quality development that this book describes has evolved to overcome these problems.

PROBLEMS IN THE PRODUCT DEVELOPMENT HEARTLAND

After a few years of design experience in industry, the young engineer has mastered partial design. Unfortunately, many product development activities have moved only a short distance beyond partial design. The product development process has not been the subject of much study. There is much opportunity to improve it.

The MIT Commission on Industrial Productivity, in its report *Made in America* (Dertouzos et al., 1989), found that six weaknesses hamper American manufacturing industries. The two weaknesses that are most relevant to product development are (1) technological weaknesses in development and production and (2) failures of cooperation. Technological weakness seems paradoxical, since the United States is widely believed to be the technological leader of the world. However, the technological strength of the United States is in research and advanced development activities—creating new technological concepts. Sustained commercial success requires excellence in rapid development of those concepts into high-quality, low-cost product designs. It is this development that has become a weakness in the United States. Ralph Gomory, formerly senior vice president for science and technology at IBM and more recently the president of the Sloan Foundation, observed, "You do not have to be the science leader to be the best consumer of science; and you do not have to be the best consumer of science to be the best product manufacturer" (Gomory and Shapiro, 1988).

The MIT Commission noted, "In the United States outstanding successes in basic science and in defense research have left the product-realization process a poor cousin." Product realization is another term for total development. Let us define the traditional product development process as that which was dominant in the 1950s and 1960s, and which remained in widespread use in the early 1990s. Often it is little more than partial design, structured for complex products by phased program planning, and encumbered with a management bureaucracy that adds insufficient value. With respect to the shortcomings of the traditional process, the findings of the MIT Commission are consistent with a large body of other literature. Much of this writing is couched in terms of recent inferiority of companies in the United States versus the superiority of Japanese companies. This book concentrates on the superiority of total quality development relative to the problems of the traditional development process.

According to an old proverb, if we do not change our direction, we might end up where we are headed. Thus, we gain insight by being aware of the problems with the traditional process, so that we can overcome them for the future. The remainder of this introduction to the problems in the heartland is based on the findings of the MIT Commission, which in turn received much help from the work of Kim Clark and Takahiro Fujimoto, which has since been published as a book (Clark and Fujimoto, 1991).

Clark and Fujimoto cite many problems with the traditional process: difficulty in designing for simplicity and reliability, failure to pay enough attention at the design stage to the likely quality of the manufactured product, excessive development times, weak design for producibility, inadequate attention to customers, weak links with suppliers, and neglect of continuous improvement. The process and its management may suffer from a lightweight program manager, fuzzy objectives and roles at the outset, and serial development. Lightweight program managers have insufficient authority relative to the functional "silos" in the organization,[1] with the result that there is inadequate concentration on the specific products and decisions are slow in being made. Inadequate consensus at the outset leads to considerable divergence and chaos as the work progresses. Serial development has been caricatured as the "throw-it-over-the-wall" style. A group does work and makes decisions, and throws them over the wall to the next group. This creates great problems of wasted time, weak understanding, and inadequate commitment to earlier decisions.

Technological progress rests on a foundation of both incremental improvements and radical breakthroughs, and finding the right balance between them is a constant challenge. The traditional approach has

---

[1]We often speak of "functional silos" and the "cloistered groups" of specialists inhabiting them as a way of pointing out some weaknesses of the traditional organization—both its vertical orientation and its tendency to isolate. Such shortcomings will be described in more detail in Chapter 2, under the heading Avoid Dysfunctional Specialization.

relied excessively on the radical breakthrough, with companies attempting to leverage the strength they have in creative research and advanced development, but balance is required. Frequently, developing several products with incremental improvements will be a better approach than trying to create one product that represents a breakthrough.

The MIT Commission (Dertouzos et al., 1989) observed:

> The key to major additional reductions in product-development time will be to make further progress in what manufacturing specialists term "design for quality" techniques. The challenge here is for product-development teams to arrive at a product design that has been systematically optimized to meet customers' needs as early as possible in the development project. The design must be robust enough to ensure that the product will provide customer satisfaction even when subject to the real conditions of the factory and customer use. The more problems prevented early on through careful design, the fewer problems that have to be corrected later through a time-consuming and often confusing process of prototype iterations.

Inadequate attention to customers' needs and weak development of robust functionality are major shortcomings of the traditional process.

The traditional approach emphasizes specialized excellence, all too often at the expense of overall success. Cloistered groups of technical specialists looking inward within their own specialty can appear overwhelmingly competent at a conference among other specialists, but a product development program that relies excessively on the expertise of specialists usually lacks integration and often focuses only on suboptimal objectives. Brilliant results are of little value if, within the receiving group to which the work is passed on, they are little noted and not long remembered.

Also, the brilliant results are often answers to the wrong question. High-bay, automated inventory storage and retrieval systems were a brilliant solution to the objective of the materials management specialty, the improved storage and retrieval of inventory. A much better approach was to redefine the objective: minimization of inventory, which led to just-in-time (JIT) production. Although this example is from production operations, the same type of problem is prevalent in product development. One product development example is reliability. The traditional product development objective is to quantify the expected reliability in the field. A much better objective is to maximize the improvement in reliability. The two are incompatible; we must choose between them. Precise quantification of the expected reliability requires extensive testing of one product configuration. Improvement is achieved by many systematic changes to the configuration. The traditional quantification of reliability has developed sophisticated analyses and methodology—specialized brilliance in answering the wrong question. The reader is encouraged to think of other examples from his or her experience.

In reflecting upon this litany of shortcomings in the traditional process, it becomes clear that they largely constitute the difference between partial design and total quality development. A simple summation is that the traditional process has not moved far enough beyond partial design.

Another perspective is to reduce the situation to two problems: (1) failure of process, and (2) failure of cooperation. During the same time that the MIT Commission was doing its work, the CEO of a Japanese company said, "In the United States you have all-star teams, but you keep losing all of the games." Why do all-star teams lose games? If a championship team plays an all-star team—for example, if the Super Bowl winner were to play the NFL all-stars—the championship team would normally win because it has a better game plan and better teamwork. The findings of the MIT Commission and the sports metaphor give the same message: the traditional approach suffers from a weak development process and weak teamwork.

SOLVING PROBLEMS VERSUS PREVENTING PROBLEMS: A TALE OF TWO TEAMS

To better understand some of the problems, let us look over the shoulders of two teams, A and B, and observe their contrasting approaches to the development of a low-cost paper feeder, such as is used in a desktop copier.

When we place a stack of blank paper sheets (Figure 1.3) into the tray, our fundamental requirements for the paper feeder are:

(1) Feed one sheet of paper.
(2) Do not feed two or more sheets of paper.

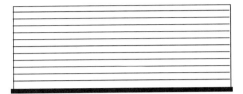

FIGURE 1.3. Paper stack.

An example of a paper feeder concept is the flipper feeder that is shown in Figure 1.4. A rubber flipper periodically strikes the top of the paper stack and flips the top sheet into the main part of the office machine. The rubber–paper friction is large enough to accelerate the first sheet into the downstream transport within the limited time that is available. The paper–paper friction is inadequate to accelerate the second sheet into the transport within the allowed time. These are the basic principles by which the two fundamental requirements are met (most of the time).

The tray in Figure 1.4 is of sheet steel and has rectangular strips stamped to all three sides and bent (pivoted downward) about the fourth

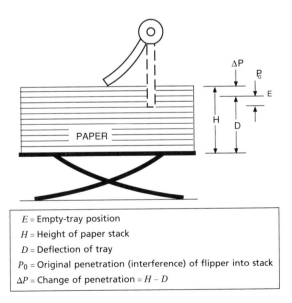

E = Empty-tray position
H = Height of paper stack
D = Deflection of tray
P_0 = Original penetration (interference) of flipper into stack
ΔP = Change of penetration = $H - D$

FIGURE 1.4. Flipper feeder; example of an innovative concept.

side to form spring legs. The principle is the same as in the plate dispensers that are commonly seen in cafeterias. As the top of the stack is gradually removed, the reduced weight allows the springs to push the trays up so that the top of the stack remains in a fixed position. This gives the flipper a fixed target. Of course, this principle will not always be perfectly achieved in practice, so Figure 1.4 recognizes that the top of the stack will change position by an amount ΔP. Now let us examine two fictional case studies in the development of the flipper feeder. These contrasting case studies are composites from real case studies.

Team A consisted of heavy hitters with much partial design experience, but little diversity in background. They were known for their ability to solve problems. They demonstrated their experience by quickly completing detailed drawings and having experimental units made.

Team A operated its experimental units with great enthusiasm and solved many problems. They found that with a full stack the tray moved down excessively so that the top of the stack was below its intended position. They tried shortening the legs to make them stiffer, and that helped but didn't solve the problem. Then they had new trays made from thicker steel and solved the problem. They operated the flipper at different speeds, and in one narrow speed range they observed that the tray bounced too much. They set the speed just below the bouncing range, and solved the problem. The Team A members were especially diligent in searching for the right rubber material for the flipper. Their first choice was isoprene, which worked very well initially. However, after a few months it had trouble flipping the sheet from the stack reliably. They tried flippers made from many different elastomers until they found a room-temperature-vulcanizing (RTV) silicon rubber that fed paper reliably after three months of operation.

After one year the vice president of engineering was scheduled to visit Team A's lab. Since they wanted to make a good impression, they prepared industriously. On the day that the vice president of engineering was coming at 10:00 a.m., Team A and its manager came in at 7:00 a.m. to ensure that everything was ready. The feeder was working very well. Then the manager's manager came in to see the feeder operate. After a few minutes he said, "I have noticed that the VP likes to ask us to feed coated paper, the glossy kind used in advertising." After some searching, the team found coated paper, and it would not feed. It just sat there as the flipper whacked it, moving slowly if at all. Bill noticed that the top of the stack was low, so he bent the legs downward to raise the stack. Tom bent the flipper with his hand, and noticed that it didn't feel as stiff as the flippers that they had used three months earlier. He taped a thin Mylar strip to the back of the flipper to make it stiffer. Now the coated paper fed beautifully. Five minutes later the vice president of engineering walked in. After a short discussion about the feeder, it was demonstrated feeding ordinary copier paper. Then the VP pulled coated paper from his case, and of course, the feeder fed it beautifully again. The VP congratulated Team A for their excellent work.

Six months went by with Team A solving all problems as they arose. Some observers did note that new problems kept occurring at a moderately high rate. Then the feeder was ready to go into production. The vice president of manufacturing angrily told the vice president of engineering that he couldn't afford to buy sheet steel with a thickness tolerance of ±0.0025 mm. Also, the RTV silicon rubber took 24 hours to cure, which greatly increased the cost. The vice president of engineering explained that these were decisions that his team had been forced to make to solve functional problems. They reached a compromise, and the feeder went into production. Was it a success? Well, it was not a failure, but problems kept occurring. The problems were solved, but then new problems occurred.

Next we turn to the contrasting style of Team B. Team B was multifunctional. It included a design engineer, a materials specialist, an applied mechanician, and a production engineer. The team carried out two simultaneous activities: (1) production-intent design and (2) applied mechanics and materials development experiments and analyses to develop functionality over the anticipated range of conditions. Equation 1.1 was one of many equations it wrote:

$$ma_2 = \mu_{12}(F_N + mg) - \mu_{23}(F_N + 2mg) + F_{B,12} - F_{B,23} \qquad (1.1)$$

where

m = mass of one sheet of paper
a_2 = acceleration of second sheet
g = acceleration of gravity
μ = coefficient of friction
F_N = normal force between flipper and stack
F_B = parasitic bonding force between two adjacent sheets (e.g., force caused by "welding" of edges when fibers were tangled together during cutting at the paper mill)
12, 23 = subscripts denoting interfaces (e.g., subscript 12 is the interface between sheets 1 and 2)

The team recognized that if the acceleration of the second sheet, a_2, could be kept small enough, multifeeding would not occur. This led to much investigation of the friction coefficient as a function of normal force (or pressure) and slip velocity. Measurements were made using a three-dimensional piezoelectric load cell. The team made analyses of the nonlinear bending of the flipper, the vibration of a paper stack, frictional sliding as a thermally activated process, and other pertinent aspects of the physical phenomena. Although the team gained much insight, it was never sufficient to make all of the critical design decisions.

Eventually graphs such as Figure 1.5 were recognized as the key to success. In the range of F_N from 0.2 N (newton) to 0.55 N, the feeder worked well with the anticipated range of papers (including the coated paper). This gave an operating range of 5 mm (from 1 mm to 6 mm) in the penetration (interference) of the flipper with respect to the stack. The team recognized from the shape of the curves in Figure 1.5 that a thinner flipper (to reduce the slope in Figure 1.5) would increase the penetration operating range from 5 mm to 9 mm.

Meanwhile, the production-intent design activity had developed the relationships shown in Figure 1.6. Curves are shown for nine different conditions. The extreme conditions are (1) small paper, fluffy stack, strong springs, which raises the top of the stack; and (2) large paper, dense stack, weak springs, which depresses the top of the stack.

After $1\frac{1}{2}$ years of development, the maximum range of variation in position of the stack top, ΔP in Figure 1.6, was brought down to 6 mm. Since the flipper could tolerate a ΔP, or variation, of 9 mm, the design was ensured of avoiding any major functional problems, despite the nor-

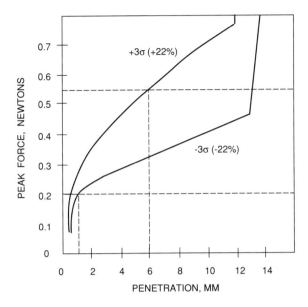

FIGURE 1.5. Critical functional parameters.

mal variations of parts and operating conditions. This is called *robust design*. The product has robust functionality; it functions well over the range of conditions that are likely to be met.

When the vice president of engineering and manufacturing (the traditional two jobs were combined into one) came to visit Team B, the team showed him Figures 1.5 and 1.6 and described how their design prevented all potential major failure modes over the anticipated range of production and field conditions. They pointed out that by being able to tolerate 9 mm of variation in the position of the stack top, an unusually tight tolerance on the sheet metal thickness had been avoided. This design was placed in production and was a big success.

Now, what should we conclude about the different styles of Teams A and B? The major conclusion is that solving problems is not good enough. Team A solved problems, but Team B prevented problems. Team A was constantly adjusting the design and could always solve any specific problem. However, Team A did not increase the variation of penetration that could be tolerated (Figure 1.5), nor did it reduce the variation that would occur in actual practice (Figure 1.6). Therefore, Team A was

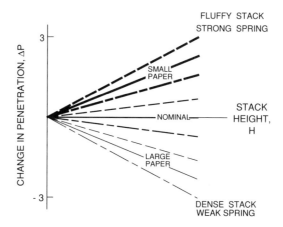

FIGURE 1.6. Critical variations; noises to paper feeder.

constantly adjusting away from one problem and into another problem. It did not develop robust functional quality. Therefore, Team A's paper feeding reliability was poor, its design was expensive to produce, and its development time was excessive. In summary, Team A showed some of the inadequacies of partial design.

Team B did much better, but after it successfully completed the development of the flipper feeder, it recognized that its approach, although much faster than that of Team A, had taken longer than necessary. Team B initially emphasized the research approach of understanding all of the phenomena. When that proved too difficult to achieve in a time span that was compatible with the opening in the market window, the team found that the information provided in Figures 1.5 and 1.6 was sufficient for making the design decisions. Earlier use of a direct approach to design decisions would have resulted in capturing the problem-prevention advantages of Team B's approach in a much shorter time. Team B did well, but initially depended too much on a *research* style.

Team B used some of the main features of *total quality development:* a multifunctional team, undertaking simultaneous development for functionality and producibility; and an emphasis on functional robustness (the ability to work well over a wide range of conditions). Once this team becomes skilled at making disciplined decisions based on the existing understanding of nature, it will have a successful development style.

Team A dramatizes some of the shortcomings of the traditional process, which is little more than partial design. Team B initially tended toward another pitfall, a research style in development. The time frame for development work is much shorter than for research. Decisions must be based on the existing understanding of nature. We take needs for major advances in knowledge back into research, and unlock the secrets over a time period that is much too long for the typical development project. In other respects Team B did very well, skillfully benefiting from some of the key elements of total quality development.

TEN CASH DRAINS OF TRADITIONAL PRODUCT DEVELOPMENT

After reflecting upon the experiences of many teams, I formulated 10 cash drains that plague traditional product development. I first presented the idea in the summer of 1986 as part of my consulting work at Saturn, the new GM company. There, and subsequently in roughly 100 other presentations to industrial audiences, the 10 cash drains were received with knowing recognition as a good summary of the problems that cause new products to be too slow in development, too expensive, lacking in quality, and not satisfactory to the customer. Attempts to improve product development can be brought into better focus if all of the cash drains are kept in mind. They are described in the following section.

Cash Drain 1—Technology Push, but Where's the Pull?

Inherent strengths in technology development are often dissipated by three problems. (1) Clever technology is developed that does not satisfy any significant customer need. (2) There are strong customer needs for which technology generation activities are lacking. (3) Good concepts are developed for which there are clear customer needs, but the new technological concepts are inadequately transferred into the development of a specific product.

Technology push leads to many "one but" concepts. These concepts are great, but—they fail dismally to meet some important customer need. Often the cleverness of a concept, or its attractiveness in meeting some customer needs, results in draining much money into its development before there is full recognition that the concept has no potential—that it is inherently incapable of fulfilling yet other important customer requirements and therefore the product will not be purchased.

At the other extreme, there are often major customer needs for which there are no technology development projects. This has often led to the development of new technology during the concept design of a specific new product. Usually this has caused disaster. The resulting concepts are too technologically immature to be developed on the short schedules that are necessary for the competitive development of specific new products. It is a strong operating principle that significantly different new concepts are not selected during the system design of a new product unless the new technology has reached some level of maturity.

Often, good new concepts are generated that have the potential to meet customer needs but are only poorly transferred into the product system design activity. These concepts often go down a technology drain and never make it to the market. This has frequently led to prolonged blame giving between the technology organization and the product development organization.

Technology must be responsive to the customer and effectively implemented in products.

Cash Drain 2—Disregard for the Voice of the Customer

The first step in the development of a specific new product is the determination of the customer's needs. In traditional product development the product has often been doomed to mediocrity before the completion of the needs activity. The biggest culprit has been the deployment of the voices of corporate specialists, rather than the voice of the customer. This further aggravates technology push, or cash drain 1. Frequently the concept selection criteria have already caused the voice of the customer to be largely lost or distorted.

High fidelity to the voice of the customer is a key success factor.

Cash Drain 3—The Eureka Concept

The light bulb flashes on over the inventor's head, and the cry is heard, "Eureka, I have this great new concept!" Often it becomes the only concept that is given serious consideration. Alas, all too often it does not stand the test of time. Many concepts look good in the first flush of creation. However, six months after they are rushed into prototypes they are found to be vulnerable. It is a tremendous cash drain to waste development resources on a concept that then becomes recognized as highly vulnerable even before the product reaches the market.

Concepts should stand the test of competitive evaluation before a company bets a new product on them.

Cash Drain 4—Pretend Design

"How many of you have seen a pretend design?" This question is asked in a seminar of 25 people from industry, and one cautiously raises a hand. The other 24 look as though they think that they have seen one, but they wait to hear the definition. Pretend designs, you say, are (1) new and different, but not better, and (2) not production-intent designs. Now almost everyone in the seminar audience is grinning in recognition. Yes indeed, they have seen many pretend designs.

The pretend design comes as if by default to have as its objective the building of prototypes, rather than the achievement of the best possible design that the factory can produce for the marketplace. Pretend designs are motivated by a strong cultural desire to be new and different, but all too often the result is demonstrably inferior to a design that is already in the field. The lack of production intent leads to the attitude, "Oh well, this is just the first design—we'll fix this later." This is a sure road to disaster.

Producibility and competitive superiority must be designed in from the beginning.

Cash Drain 5—Pampered Product

Team A pampered their product so that it looked good in the demonstration for the vice president. They did this by tuning the feeder for one operating condition. Most products work well under some particular operating condition. The traditional approach to product development is to pamper the product to make it look good. The product is not seriously challenged, but rather is pampered by special tuning and tinkering so that it puts on a good demonstration.

The usual partial compensation for the shortcomings of the pampered-product approach has been rigorous application of reliability growth and problem-solving methodology. However, reliability growth and problem-solving methodology are not enough for optimizing the vital few design parameters in order to achieve good performance over a wide range of conditions (robust performance). The reliability growth and problem-solving process consists of inspection of the design, which has all of the faults of inspection of actual units during production (see cash drain 9). In this approach of identifying and solving problems to increase reliability, purposeful improvements are not made until the product has been found defective. The result is that countermeasures are brought to bear too late, when they are very expensive, and often not all of the problems are detected before the product is in the hands of the customer. This approach is very ineffective in optimizing the critical (vital few) design parameters, which control the unique aspects of the new design and control its most important performance characteristics.

The inadequacy of the problem-solving approach to optimization is that it is incapable of detecting situations in which a problem is very close to surfacing but is not brought out in the specific test conditions. Therefore, performance that is about to go over the cliff will not be detected. However, if further improvement is not made, the performance will be disappointing over the full range of production and field-use conditions. Therefore, it is very important to have a problem-prevention approach in the optimization of the vital few design parameters that will ensure that the design is not only performing well in some limited test, but is far away from any problem-causing cliff. Under the wide range of realistic conditions, the performance will remain close to ideal customer satisfaction. This is called *robust functionality*.

Lack of systematic optimization to achieve robust functionality not only reduces customer satisfaction but is also a major cause of long product development times. The traditional approach deals with the symptoms of the lack of robustness by using many iterations of build-test-fix cycles with prototypes. This greatly extends the development time.

The problem-solving process is very satisfactory for correcting simple mistakes in the design. However, a systematic optimization process is required to achieve robust performance by finding the best values for the critical design parameters.

Cash Drain 6—Hardware Swamps

Hardware swamps occur when the prototype iterations are so numerous and so overlapping in time that the entire team becomes swamped by the chores of debugging and maintaining the experimental hardware. The hardware swamp can become so severe that no time remains to improve the design. The prototype hardware has become an end unto itself, rather than simply a means to improve the design. A hardware swamp can be recognized by laboratories packed full of prototypes, and a team's inability to complete any organized experiments because of the voracious appetite of the hardware for debugging and maintenance.

Early optimization of robust functionality avoids the excessive numbers of prototypes and thus prevents the occurrence of hardware swamps.

Cash Drain 7—Here's the Product. Where's the Factory?

In the traditional approach a product has been developed to an almost final stage before anyone looks at how it might be produced. This is a sure road to failure. The production capability must be developed along with the product design. It is not a design if we do not know how to make it.

The production capability and the product design must be developed concurrently and in close coordination. If the design of the production capability starts only a few months before actual production, many severe problems are likely to be encountered. Similarly, field operations must also be developed concurrently with the product design.

Cash Drain 8—We've Always Made It This Way

"We've always made it this way, and it works." Yes, but has the production capability been optimized to achieve minimum cycle time and maximum quality? For example, the process operating points (for example, speeds, depths of cut, feed rates, pressures, temperatures) are specified on process sheets or numerically controlled (NC) programs. The values for the process parameters have often been fixed for a long time. Even originally, there has often been little process development. The critical processes must be optimized to achieve customer satisfaction, and to increase throughput.

Cash Drain 9—Inspection

Inspection in the factory means sorting the good from the bad after the completion of production. This is now widely recognized as a poor process for most products, largely through the efforts of Dr. W. Edwards Deming. The third of his famous 14 points (Deming, 1986) is, "Cease dependence on inspection to achieve quality. Eliminate the need for inspection on a mass basis by building quality into the product in the first place."

Cash Drain 10—Give Me My Targets, Let Me Do My Thing

Targets seem good. However, Deming has pointed out that they tend to limit improvement. Also, the allocation of targets down to a detailed level tends to destroy teamwork. The writing of "contracts" so that each person (or tiny group) can work in isolation may seem attractive. However, it leads to subsystems that cannot be integrated, products that cannot be produced, and many other problems. Overspecialization has led to poor definitions of the many design tasks. Often the tasks are done very well according to the definition, but the definitions are not compatible and are not sufficiently directed toward customer satisfaction and the business needs of the corporation. Teamwork and better management practices are needed.

The 10 cash drains prevent an organization from being competitive. They are the shortcomings of partial design. Partial design, learned in engineering school and during one's first few years of employment in industry, is satisfactory for designing small units that will have good functionality under limited operating conditions. However, partial design is plagued by the 10 cash drains.

Total quality development goes beyond partial design to overcome the 10 cash drains. The emphasis is on increasing the scope of the activity to better define the many partial design tasks. Then the team members, with their ever-present skill at partial design, can complete all of the necessary work.

This book is directed toward overcoming the 10 cash drains. Chapter 2, Basic Concurrent Engineering, partially addresses cash drains 2, 4, 7, 8, 9, and 10. Chapter 3, Better Decisions, is an overview that addresses all of the cash drains. Then the cash drains are explicitly addressed in the rest of the book as follows:

Cash Drain	Chapter
1	7, Technology Development; 8, Successful Strategy
2	4, In the Beginning—Customer to Concept
3	4, In the Beginning—Customer to Concept
4	5, The Design
5	5, The Design; 7, Technology Development
6	5, The Design; 7, Technology Development
7	5, The Design
8	6, Getting Ready for Production
9	6, Getting Ready for Production
10	9, Managing for Success

TOTAL QUALITY DEVELOPMENT—AN OVERVIEW

This book is about product development, which is simply diagramed in Figure 1.7. The numbers in Figure 1.7 are the chapters in this book that describe the activity. Products are developed through the phases of *concept, design,* and *production preparation.* This development of a specific new product is supported by new technologies from the technology stream. The specific new product is in the context of the total corporate strategy, which determines when the development of a product will start and when, after the product has been produced, its life cycle will be terminated through withdrawal.

This book describes improvements in carrying out these activities. Basic improvements are described in Chapter 2. Enhanced improvements for better decision making are overviewed in Chapter 3. Chapters

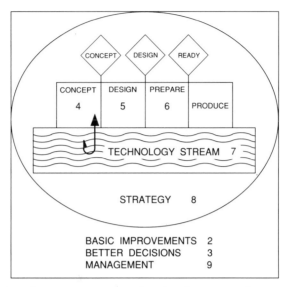

FIGURE 1.7. Development process. The development of new products is supported by new technologies "fished out" of the technology stream.

4 through 7 describe the enhanced improvements in more detail in the context of their application to the four major development activities. The product development activities are undertaken in the context of corporate strategy, which is described in Chapter 8. Further improvement is achieved by better management (Chapter 9), which includes the implementation of the transition into total quality development.

Total quality development has three major elements:

(1) Basic improvements in clarity and unity (basic concurrent engineering)
(2) Enhanced quality function deployment (EQFD)
(3) Quality engineering using robust design

The latter two improvements integrated together provide better decision making that goes beyond the basic improvements.

There is little agreement in the field about nomenclature. The first major element of the three just given is usually called *concurrent engineering*, although some prefer the synonym *simultaneous engineering*, or another name such as *integrated product and process development*. As Shakespeare said, "A rose by any other name would smell as sweet." In this book the terms *total quality development, improved total development process*, and *world-class concurrent engineering* will be considered to be synonyms for the entire subject matter. The basic improvements in clarity and unity will be known as *basic concurrent engineering*; this was implemented by many American companies during the 1980s and has become the subject of many conferences and seminars. Although it has commonly been referred to simply as concurrent engineering, here it will be referred to as *basic concurrent engineering* to distinguish it from *world-class concurrent engineering*, which is the subject of this book. Most of the companies that have implemented basic concurrent engineering are not nearly as far along in their practice of enhanced quality function deployment (EQFD) and quality engineering using robust design. Therefore, their results have been both very promising and somewhat disappointing. *All* elements of total quality development are needed for success in the global economy.

Basic concurrent engineering consists of two elements: (1) improved process (better game plan), which provides greater clarity to the activities, and (2) closer cooperation (better teamwork), which creates greater unity within the team that does the work. Thus, basic concurrent engineering addresses the problems that were found by the MIT Commission on Industrial Productivity, and which were supported by the sports metaphor of all-star teams losing games.

The improved process (better game plan) that provides improved clarity has four primary features: (1) concurrent process, (2) focus on quality, cost, and delivery (QCD), (3) emphasis on customer satisfaction, and (4) emphasis on competitive benchmarking. In the concurrent process, key activities are carried out at the same time, a big improvement over the traditional sequential, throw-it-over-the-wall style. As an example, process engineering to prepare for production is done concurrently (simultaneously) with the design of the product.

The closer cooperation (better teamwork) that improves unity consists of (1) integrated organization (multifunctional teams, such as Team B in the section A Tale of Two Teams), (2) employee involvement (participative management), and (3) strategic relations with suppliers. The key is empowered teams, with the inclusion of suppliers as much as is feasible.

Basic concurrent engineering is summarized in Table 1.1. Many partial design tasks are embedded within the total development activity—for example, designing mechanisms and circuits, which are not described in this book. Engineers tend to perform the partial design tasks well, but in the traditional process the partial design tasks are often poorly defined with objectives that will not lead to product success. Basic concurrent engineering provides better objectives for the partial design tasks, considers related decisions together, brings more of the relevant information to bear at the opportune time, achieves a stronger commitment to decisions, and emphasizes awareness of the best in the world. Basic concurrent engineering addresses part of the gap between partial design and total quality development.

Table 1.2 provides further insights into new-product work. The engineering fundamentals—engineering sciences and partial design—are sufficient for the first two steps, creativity and feasibility. Basic concurrent engineering includes the third step by using the concurrent process carried out by a multifunctional (including design and production) team. Basic concurrent engineering makes a start on step 4 by emphasizing customer satisfaction and competitive benchmarking. Customer satisfaction receives the full attention that it deserves through the use of enhanced quality function deployment (EQFD), the second primary component of total quality development. Step 5, the consistent functionality of the new product—which is not much helped by basic concurrent engineering—is provided by robust design, the third primary com-

---

TABLE 1.1 Basic Concurrent Engineering

A. Improved process (better game plan), improved clarity
   1. Concurrent process
   2. Focus on quality, cost, and delivery
   3. Emphasis on customer satisfaction
   4. Emphasis on competitive benchmarking
B. Closer cooperation (better teamwork), improved unity
   1. Integrated organization
   2. Employee involvement, empowerment
   3. Strategic relations with suppliers

TABLE 1.2 New-Product Work

Critical Steps	Activity
1. Create concept.	Fundamental engineering
2. Will it work?	Fundamental engineering
3. Can it be made?	Basic concurrent engineering
4. Satisfy customer needs?	EQFD
5. Consistently?	Robust design
6. Profitable?	Strategy

Efficient and Coordinated?

Efficient process—clarity
Cooperation—unity

ponent of total quality development. Those aspects of strategy that are most relevant to product development are described in Chapter 8. The management of product development to make it efficient and coordinated is described in Chapter 9.

Basic concurrent engineering is described more completely in the next chapter. Beyond basic concurrent engineering we need a strengthened approach to decision making that emphasizes two objectives: the satisfaction of customer needs and the consistency of the product's performance. Enhanced quality function deployment (EQFD) and quality engineering using robust design provide dramatic enhancement by including these objectives. Together they help the teams to practice more vigilant information processing that provides strong responsiveness to the voice of the customer and helps ensure the viability of the core concepts, the robustness of functional quality (consistency of product performance), the economical precision of production, the success of integration, and effective reusability.

In summary, EQFD and quality engineering using robust design fill in most of the gap between basic concurrent engineering and the approach that enables success in the global economy, total quality development. Chapter 3 is an overview of these two major enhancements, and they are described more fully in the context of the total quality development process in Chapters 4 through 7.

THE BENEFITS OF TOTAL QUALITY DEVELOPMENT

The benefits are the entire rationale for this book. Starkly stated, total quality development enables success in the global economy. Anything substantially short of the total quality development that this book describes leads inexorably to a bedraggled economic condition—either corporate demise or increasing dependence on an ever-declining standard of living as the primary basis for marginal competitiveness. Total quality development provides a buoyancy that separates the swimmers from those who must resort to cries to politicians to save them from drowning.

The benefits of total quality development are enhanced customer satisfaction, reduced costs, and shorter time to market; combined, they provide international competitiveness. The ability to complete more product cycles than the competition provides greater product variety and increased corporate learning. The lead rapidly grows over the companies that are still stuck in the rut of the traditional process.

Total quality development brings competitiveness in civilian industries and in defense industries, in mature industries and in dynamic industries, in industries with complex products and in industries with simple products, and in high-volume industries as well as those making low-volume products. Companies that do not practice total quality development will continue to have technological weaknesses in development, which will prevent international competitiveness. Total quality development appears to be the only modern way effectively to develop products and processes.

The benefits will be explored further in Chapter 10. Now let us turn to a panoramic view of basic concurrent engineering.

Basic Concurrent Engineering

- ■ **Concurrent Process**
- ■ **Multifunctional Product Development Team**
- ■ **Other Elements of Basic Concurrent Engineering**
- ■ **Better, But Not Enough**

B asic concurrent engineering has received much attention and application since about 1980, and the attention given it has intensified since about 1988. It makes a strong start on overcoming some of the 10 cash drains and has been a major element of many leading companies' improved competitiveness.

Basic concurrent engineering has two essential characteristics: (1) it is a concurrent process, and (2) it is carried out by a multifunctional product development team (PDT). Product design, production-process engineering, field-support development, and all other elements of product success are addressed from the beginning as an integrated set of activities and objectives. The ideal is simple: to have one team working on one system in one total development activity, all focused on benefit to the customer. The system is the product, the production capability, and the field-support capability. The design parameters, production parameters, and field-support parameters all integrated together define the unified system. It is the responsibility of the PDT to define and quantify all of the parameters in one total development activity.

The major benefits of basic concurrent engineering stem from a few principles:

(1) Start all tasks as early as possible.
(2) Utilize all relevant information as early as possible.
(3) Empower individuals and teams to participate in defining the objectives of their work.
(4) Achieve operational understanding for all relevant information.
(5) Adhere to decisions and utilize all previous relevant work.
(6) Make decisions in a single trade-off space; that is, treat design, production, and field support as a single system within which trade-offs can be made.
(7) Make lasting decisions, overcoming a natural tendency to be quick and novel.
(8) Develop trust among teammates.

(9) Strive for team consensus.
(10) Use a visible concurrent process.

All of these principles may seem to be unexceptionable. However, relative to traditional product development, they are major improvements.

The essence of the concurrent process and the multifunctional PDT is both simple and subtle. The mind literally cannot work on two tasks concurrently (at least not consciously). In the concurrent process, frequent information exchanges occur at the level of the small unit design tasks. In the traditional process the work blocks are huge before information transfer occurs. At the micro level the tasks in the concurrent process are sequential or iterative, but from the macro perspective the effect is the concurrent process. The rugby image of cooperatively moving the scrum downfield is appropriate (Nonaka and Takeuchi, 1986).

It may seem a small difference whether two people are members of the PDT or, alternatively, are assigned to the same project but remain in separate organizations, but that difference is critical. If the two people are not members of the same PDT, the probability is greatly increased that some of the 10 principles will be violated, with a very detrimental effect on the development program. When an individual's primary allegiance is to a cloistered group of functional specialists, the performance within the specialty may be elegant, but there is usually inadequate benefit to the overall development program. This is suboptimization.

When an individual is a member of the PDT, he or she is much more likely to participate in defining the objectives of the PDT's work, and thus the objectives are likely to be both more relevant to the program and better understood by the participants. Often, definition of the objectives is the most difficult part of any task; a PDT is much more likely to succeed at this than separate groups of specialists.

Membership in a team also greatly improves the exchange of information. Specialists like to communicate in terms that are dear to their own specialty but not fully understood by other people. Membership in the PDT greatly increases the probability that individuals and small groups will help others to effectively use the output from their work, going beyond a perfunctory communication. This greatly improves understanding of and commitment to the decisions that they make, which are vital success factors.

The next section describes the concurrent process, the first key success factor of basic concurrent engineering. Then the section following describes the multifunctional product development team (PDT), the other key factor in enabling the success of basic concurrent engineering.

CONCURRENT PROCESS

In the best form of concurrent engineering, the design of the production system and of the field-support system starts early, concurrently with the design of the product; see Figure 2.1. This has five major benefits:

(1) The development of the production and field-support systems has an early start.
(2) Trade-offs occur among design, production, and logistics concurrently, as one system.
(3) Good design for manufacturability and field supportability is facilitated.
(4) The production and field-support people gain a clear understanding of the design, and are committed to its success.
(5) Prototype iterations are reduced, because the design is more mature before the first full-system prototypes are built.

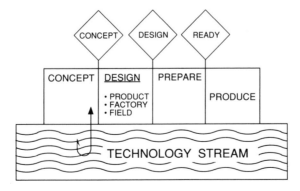

FIGURE 2.1. Concurrent process.

Although Figure 2.1 emphasizes the concurrent process during the *design phase*, it is used throughout the development of the new product.

CONCURRENT CONCEPT DEVELOPMENT

The concurrent process is first used during the development of the system concept. In the past it was common for market research to determine customer or user needs and throw its conclusions over the wall to planning, which in turn outlined the requirements for the product and then threw its results over the wall to product design engineering. This sequence of first determining users' requirements and then developing the system concept made it unlikely that the needs of the customer or user were adequately considered in choosing the system. These activities are now in the best practice combined and carried out by one multifunctional team.

This is the early application of the basic principles of concurrent engineering.

DEGREE OF CONCURRENCE

Clark and Fujimoto (1991), in their excellent study of product development in the global automotive industry, identified five levels of increasing concurrence between upstream and downstream activities:

(1) The traditional sequential approach
(2) High-bandwidth technology transfer (that is, a high rate and large total amount of information exchange)
(3) Overlapping with preliminary information transfer
(4) Overlapping with mutual adjustment
(5) Overlapping with early downstream involvement

Clearly, moving in the direction of level 5 will bring progressively improved benefits. However, even at the fifth level, product engineering is still a distinct upstream activity and process engineering a distinct downstream activity. Merging the two activities (and field-support development with them) into one activity provides still more benefit.

The best concurrent process, envisioned in Figure 2.1, treats development as one activity that incorporates product, production system, and field-support system. There are no upstream and downstream activities in the traditional sense. Of course, in the natural flow of the work some things are done before others. Concepts are selected before detailed design, and production tools are designed before they are built, for example. However, the best concurrent process avoids the unnatural separation of work into upstream and downstream in accordance with organizational rigidities.

In the traditional process, tasks were clearly labeled product development, production-capability development, or field-support development, and tasks of the first type (upstream) were completed before tasks of the other two types (downstream) were started. In the best concurrent process the tasks are not defined in this divisive style. All tasks now incorporate the product view, the production view, and the field-support view. Subtasks may still remain "pure." For example, the finite-element analysis (FEA) is still usually done by a specialist. However, the results of the analysis can now be put to much better and more immediate use. The FEA specialist works closely with a subsystem design team—for an automobile frame, for example. In the concurrent process, producibility and functionality are optimized together. We combine the FEA with the design of the production process to minimize the deflection of the frame and the cost of producing it at the same time. The FEA specialist works closely with the subsystem team to define the objectives of the FEA and then presents the results to the team in a form they can easily use. The FEA specialist further works with the team to help in the application of the results, probably as electronic data. For the duration of this task the FEA specialist is effectively a member of the team.

Contrast this with the dysfunctions of the traditional process. The FEA specialist received drawings of the preliminary frame design, did the FEA, and tossed the printout over the wall to the frame design engineer— there was no team, so producibility was not considered. Commonly, the design engineer put the FEA results on the shelf to collect dust, occasionally pulling them out to be used as a talisman to ward off "evil" managers and other status seekers (people whose main job was to roam about seeking the status of all activities). Even when the design engineer wanted to use the FEA, it was difficult because the format was inconvenient. If this barrier was overcome, the FEA was typically used in a limited way to ensure that some deflection specification was not exceeded. The design was not optimized, and producibility (downstream activity) was not considered. Multiply this vignette by a thousand, and the contrasting superiority of the concurrent process is apparent.

HOLISTIC DEVELOPMENT

The ideal process is to have one activity that addresses all parameters in the total system. In traditional product development the total set of parameters that must be defined and quantified is decomposed in three ways: by program phase, subsystem, and discipline. We can visualize this as a three-dimensional structure, with each cell defined by a single phase, subsystem, and discipline. In a complex system this easily creates several hundred cells, each with its dedicated set of parameters. Suboptimization is done within each cell, with very inadequate attention given to parameters that lie outside that cell.

The best concurrent process eliminates this kind of partitioning into cells. All parameters that are relevant to a decision are considered in making the decision. (Which parameters are considered relevant is determined in part by their function in satisfying customer needs; this is one of the main subjects of this book.) The objective is to make the process seamless. In basic concurrent engineering we achieve a seamless process by forming the multifunctional product development team and strongly motivating it to use a seamless process. (This is not completely sufficient; vigilant information processing requires enhanced quality function deployment—or EQFD—and quality engineering using robust design, as described in Chapter 3.)

PROBLEM PREVENTION

The problem-prevention approach emphasizes considering all parameters as early as possible and thus provides a shift of activity level to the earlier part of the program. Frank Pipp (1990), who led the implementation of basic concurrent engineering within the Xerox Corporation from 1980 to 1983, cautions, "Don't yield to the temptation to save money in the early stages of a product program. Invest enough time and money to be sure customer requirements are known and faithfully translated to specifications. Passing on immature technology will surely cost you more money eventually than properly completing and engineering new technologies. One thing we have learned is that bad engineering and design go all the way to the customer; it never seems to get fixed along the way."

The concurrent process is a major improvement over the serial, throw-it-over-the-wall traditional process. It is most effectively implemented by a multifunctional product development team.

MULTIFUNCTIONAL PRODUCT DEVELOPMENT TEAM

In the best form of basic concurrent engineering, each product is developed by a multifunctional product development team (PDT). The PDT makes all decisions about the product design, production system, and field-support system. Although the PDT must grow and then later shrink in size and, in so doing, change its composition somewhat, there is never any sudden change. In particular, at the transitions in process phases, represented by the vertical lines in Figure 2.1, there are not any sudden changes in the PDT. Continuity is maintained; throwing results over the wall is avoided. All decisions are made with the full participation of the people who have all of the relevant knowledge.

TEAMING FOR SUCCESS

Basic concurrent engineering is best carried out by a multifunctional product development team (PDT) led by a strong product manager. All functions of the corporation should participate. People who are doing significant work for the specific product development program should be part of the PDT while they are doing the program's work. There is a vast psychological difference between performing a task within a support group and performing it as a member of the PDT. As a PDT member, the contributor will (1) understand the specific requirements, (2) have the necessary close communications with other members of the PDT, and (3) be dedicated to the utilization of the task results to make design decisions. All three of these benefits are much less likely to materialize if the contributor remains outside the PDT.

It is important that the people on the PDT from each function be able to (1) represent the knowledge of that function and (2) gain the commitment of that function to the decisions that are made. Dysfunctions will occur if the information is not provided or is wrong, or if the function subsequently disowns the decisions and wants major changes. For example, if the PDT decides to use an aluminum die casting and if later, when the product enters into production, the production operations people want a fiber-reinforced polymer part, then rework of the development will become rampant. The strong, complete multifunctional product development team is essential for success.

Some people will stay on the PDT throughout the development program, while others will be on the team only during the phase or task that requires their expertise. The important criterion is that there should not be any sudden changes in the composition or size of the PDT, since that would reduce teamwork and cause lack of continuity.

Even while a member of a team, the individual still does much independent work, but the work is done for the team. Membership in the team makes the goals of individual work more holistic. The individual's work is integrated into the team's activities and objectives. The individual's work contributes effectively to the overall development program.

Although we refer to *the* team, it is actually a team of teams of teams. The chief engineer who leads the PDT and the managers who report directly to him or her constitute one team. They are responsible for everything related to the product and its development program. They include the subsystem leaders, for each product subsystem has a team. Many critical interfaces have a dedicated team. Teams are formed wherever they are needed to achieve an integrated approach to the development of the new product. Although the complete PDT for a large, complex product may have several hundred members, it is rare for any one operational team to have more than 20 members. Many have only a few members. The formation of the best interlocking structure of teams is a key success factor.

AVOID DYSFUNCTIONAL SPECIALIZATION

The effectiveness of a PDT is strongly influenced by the spectrum of generalization and specialization that characterizes its capabilities and style.

Prior to 1940 most product development was done by generalists, as illustrated in Figure 2.2, and the problems of segmentalism were not usually severe. This approach sufficed for products that were not high in technical sophistication. However, during the period 1940–1960 the shortcomings of this approach became obvious, and the emphasis shifted to technical depth and sophistication. However, this led to segmentalism (see Figure 2.2), or cloistered groups of technical specialists looking inward within their own specialty. This caused tremendous problems that concurrent engineering is now overcoming.

The successful PDT uses a balanced modulation of specialization; see Figure 2.3. Even the most specialized people broaden themselves sufficiently to be able to communicate effectively with the in-house customers for their work. Most of the product development work is done by the core of the PDT, which consists of people who are not narrow specialists but combine a good combination of breadth and depth (curve 2 in Figure 2.3). Thus, the traditional product design engineers become quite knowledgeable about production, and traditional production-process engineers become knowledgeable about customer needs and product function. This enables them to function effectively as a team, to work on the complete set of parameters as one system to be developed in one activity.

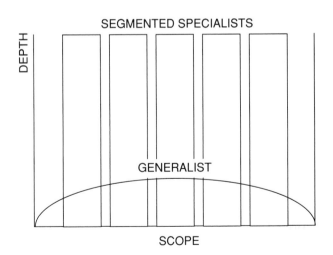

FIGURE 2.2. Dysfunctional specialization.

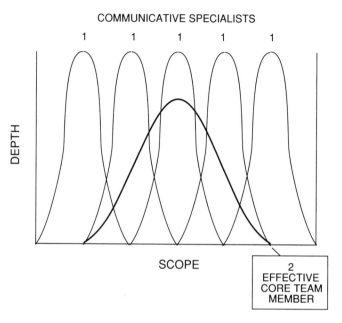

FIGURE 2.3. Successful breadth.

The FEA specialist, mentioned earlier, is a good example of the new model in specialization. In the days of dysfunctional specialization, the FEA specialist was an example of the segmented specialist in Figure 2.2. The FEA specialist did not understand design and production, and the design and production people did not understand FEA. Therefore, they often did not reach a common definition of objectives, and the FEA results were thrown over the wall in a format that the design and production people did not interact with effectively. Now, in the new model PDT, they have all broadened sufficiently to reach common objectives, and to use the FEA to quickly improve cost and quality early in the development process.

The example of FEA can be taken a step further. Should sophisticated design tasks be performed by specialists, or should they be moved into the work domain of the core PDT people? Should the design engineer do the FEA or go to a specialist? If the design engineer can do the FEA, that is preferred, because it sidesteps some of the inefficiencies of human interaction. As computers become more user-friendly, the design engineer can incorporate more and more specialized tasks into his or her portfolio of capabilities. Specialized knowledge is utilized both by bringing specialists into the PDT and by making the knowledge available to the core PDT people via user-friendly computers. The best balance between the two is constantly evolving in a process of continuous improvement. The same principle of broadened perspective to enable effective cooperative work applies here also. The specialists and the core PDT people must cooperate to produce computer systems that are effective in the PDT environment.

SUCCESSFUL PDT MANAGEMENT

Clark and Fujimoto (1991) identified four modes of development organization in the global automotive industry. In all four of these modes the people have functional "homes"; the modes differ in the degree of focus on a specific product. The modes are configurations employing (1) a functional structure, (2) a lightweight product manager, (3) a heavyweight product manager, and (4) a project execution team. Outside the automotive industry, and therefore not identified by Clark and Fujimoto, yet a fifth mode is used: (5) the independent PDT. The first two of these—the least product-focused of the five—may suffice for products characterized by high technical sophistication, low complexity, and relatively static concepts, but Clark and Fujimoto found that these modes had shortcomings in automobile development. In general, they will not offer a competitive advantage, so they will not be considered further.

Strong Managers for Success

In both of the more product-focused of the original four modes—heavyweight product manager and project execution team—the development people are managed by a strong product manager. In the project execution team the people are temporarily assigned (seconded) to the PDT. In the fifth mode, the independent PDT, which goes beyond the structure that was observed by Clark and Fujimoto (1991) in the automotive industry, the development people are members of the PDT only; they do not have a functional home, which makes the product manager even stronger. This is the organization that the Xerox Corporation started using in 1982; a very large improvement in product development effectiveness followed. Previously Xerox had been using a mode that was intermediate between a lightweight product manager and a heavyweight product manager, probably closer to the latter.

The independent PDT (which has no functional home) goes the furthest in adhering to the principles in this chapter. However, any of the three product-focused methods of organization (of the five) can undoubtedly be made to work well. All three product-focused modes, the heavyweight product manager, the project execution team, and the independent PDT, will work well if the other principles in this chapter are observed. The organizational structure is not the end objective, but rather a means to the end of implementing the principles of this chapter to make product development sufficiently holistic and focused on customers for the specific product.

Characteristics of Effective Product Leaders

Clark and Fujimoto compiled a list of characteristics of effective product leaders. These are valid for all three types of product-focused organization, and are restated here with some modifications. The product leader:

- Has responsibility that is broad in scope (for which he or she has the requisite broad knowledge) and endures over the entire duration of the development program
- Has responsibility for specifications, product concept, costs, and schedule
- Has responsibility for ensuring that the product concept is accurately translated into technical detail
- Has frequent and direct communication with PDT people at the working level
- Maintains direct contact with customers
- Has enough knowledge and experience in a variety of disciplines to communicate effectively with all relevant people
- Takes an active role in managing conflict; may initiate conflicts to prevent deviation from the original product concept
- Possesses market imagination, and the ability to lead in discerning the true voice of the customer

- Circulates among PDT people, and leads in achieving the winning product concept, rather than doing paperwork and conducting formal meetings

By following these guidelines and the other principles in this chapter, a corporation can achieve success with any of the three product-focused modes: heavyweight product manager, project execution team, or independent PDT. The choice will often depend in the short run on ease of implementation, which in turn will depend strongly on the local culture (that of the corporation, the division, or even the PDT).

THE TEAM IS NOT ENOUGH

The formation of the multifunctional PDT is a good start, but teams can go wrong, with disastrous results. The planning for the Bay of Pigs invasion is often cited in the social psychology literature as an example of groupthink, the downside of team potential. Although the planning of a military invasion may seem far from product development, the same things can go wrong. The team can develop a hubris, a strong desire to please each other and demonstrate their loyalty to the team, and a feeling of omnipotence, all of which can lead to disaster. The social psychologist Ian Morley, who has studied design teams in collaboration with the engineering design leader Stuart Pugh, has found that groups can go wrong by having too much confidence and afterward be unable to understand what happened (Hosking and Morley, 1991).

Morley, very largely on the basis of the work of Irving Janis, has analyzed the nature of the problem: (1) "stress generates strong need for affiliation within the group.... People who have misgivings keep silent and increasingly give the benefit of the doubt to the emerging group consensus." (2) The team members seek to "avoid the stress of actively open minded thinking." They tend to focus on the popular option, and use "non-vigilant information processing" to downplay the risks that later become all too obvious (Hosking and Morley, 1991).

Overcoming the possible dysfunctions of teams is straightforward but not easy. Successful teams use the vigilant information processing that is included within *total quality development*. Also, teams can help themselves by simply being on guard against problems, to realize that teams are not a panacea. Total quality development helps the team to be vigilant in processing information, as will be described in Chapter 3. The successful team runs down a clear path between facile consensus on the one hand and egocentric, disputatious behavior on the other.

TEN PRINCIPLES OF SUCCESSFUL TEAMS

Ian Morley (1990) has developed 10 principles of teamwork in doing total development work:

(1) Select cohesive teams, based on sentiments of mutual liking and respect for each other's expertise.
(2) Bring specialists from all major functional areas into the PDT.
(3) Ensure a common vision of the concurrent process.
(4) Organize controlled convergence to solutions that everyone understands and everyone accepts.
(5) Organize vigilant information processing and encourage actively open-minded thinking. Avoid the facile, premature consensus.
(6) Maintain the best balance between individual and group work. Let individuals do the things that individuals do best—for example, the initial generation of new concepts.
(7) Use systematic methods.
(8) Use both formal and informal communication.
(9) Select at least some of the members according to how well suited they are to the specific type of development work. One example is how static or dynamic the concepts underlying the work are. A person who is proficient in applying standards to rapidly complete static designs may have difficulty with dynamic conceptual work. The opposite is also true.
(10) Provide principled leadership. The leader must emphasize the improved process, making it visible to the team. He or she must take the primary responsibility for helping to empower members of the team.

The organization and leadership that were described earlier in this section on the multifunctional product development team help to develop the successful practice of Morley's 10 principles. If these and the principles that were stated earlier in this chapter are practiced, then any of the three product-focused modes can be successful—heavyweight product manager, project execution team, or independent PDT.

EARLY OUTSTANDING SUCCESSES

Two of the early, outstanding successes with basic concurrent engineering in the United States were at Ford and Xerox. At Ford the development of the new Ford Taurus was done by Team Taurus, led by Lewis Veraldi, from 1980 to 1985. The organizational mode was the heavyweight product manager mode; it was judged far more successful than the previous lightweight product manager mode. According to Veraldi (1988), "Teamwork was a major factor in the success of Taurus and Sable. Early and dedicated involvement by all members of the team was key."

At Xerox the change was even more radical. Implemented by Frank Pipp when he became manager of copier development and production, the change in 1982 was to the independent PDT. This has been highly successful in completing the development of the 10 series (Marathon) copiers, and in developing the more recent 50 series.

At Xerox the independent PDT is led by a chief engineer, and the PDT has been given a large degree of autonomy. As recounted by Pipp (1990):

> To implement the concurrent engineering approach a new position, called Chief Engineer, was created. The Chief Engineer was responsible for taking the product concept and the technology, engineering, designing and testing the product before turning it over for volume manufacturing. Testing included not only design verification tests, field machine tests, alpha and beta tests but also in their own pilot facilities the chief engineers were responsible for building sufficient pilot and pre-production models to prove that the production process would meet their design intent. This phase included meeting with major suppliers to ensure that they understood drawing specifications and could produce parts on soft and hard tools to meet quality and volume requirements. The Chief Engineer also was responsible for delivering the product in accordance with the quality, schedule and cost goals contained in the business plan and to accomplish this following the formal guidelines contained in the Xerox Product Delivery Process.

The next steps were the ones that truly allowed a concurrent engineering approach to work, namely the transfer of advanced manufacturing engineers, quality control engineers, quality assurance engineers, procurement specialists and field service engineers to the Chief Engineer.

At the same time personnel from departments we called Shared Resources were assigned to the Chief Engineer's team on a dotted line basis. These shared resource activities included: Industrial Design and Human Factors, Competitive Analysis Laboratory, Software and Electronics Division and our Supplies Group which developed the necessary toners, developers and photoreceptors.

The Xerox chief engineer and independent PDT do the pilot production. Of course, production operations people are seconded into the PDT for this purpose. The principle is that the chief engineer is responsible for all developmental problem solving. When the fully developed system is transferred to production operations, the seconded people return along with some of the core PDT people.

PDT PITFALLS TO AVOID

The independent PDT, as utilized at Xerox, is clearly very successful, at least in the short run. In the long run there are potential problems to guard against: (1) functional obsolescence, (2) weak organizational learning, and (3) stale technology. Without a functional home, the core PDT people may remain strongly focused on their product and gradually fall behind in functional competence. Organizational learning is hindered because each PDT tends to be isolated; learning does not spread easily between PDTs. The PDTs focus on their current product, not on developing new technologies. In summary, the independent PDT is susceptible to the parochialism that was observed as a weakness by the MIT Commission on Industrial Productivity.

One approach to avoiding these problems is to have a shared resource organization that is responsible for the three problem areas. This group, often titled "advanced development" or some similar name, has as its primary mission the development of new technology. The advanced development group is usually functionally organized and is charged with also maintaining the functional competence of the PDTs. A companion role is to facilitate the transfer of learning among the PDTs. This has been successfully accomplished by forming functional users' groups, networks of advisers, and a design institute, all of which extend across the full scope of technical activities.

No matter what form the organization takes, there will still be boundaries that must not be allowed to create a throw-it-over-the-wall style. The modes that focus on the product have been the most successful. The product-oriented PDT using the concurrent process has been found to be much more successful than functional groups using a sequential process. The switch to the multifunctional PDT using the concurrent process can be made in less than a year with strong leadership. Examples are Veraldi and Team Taurus, and Pipp and the Xerox PDTs, both in the early 1980s.

OTHER ELEMENTS OF BASIC CONCURRENT ENGINEERING

In addition to (1) being the practice of the concurrent process and (2) being carried out by a multifunctional PDT, basic concurrent engineering includes other improvements over traditional product development that reinforce these two major thrusts. These additional enablers are described next.

BETTER GAME PLAN

The game-plan improvements are:

(1) The concurrent process (already described)
(2) Focus on quality, cost, and delivery (QCD)
(3) Emphasis on customer satisfaction
(4) Emphasis on competitive benchmarking

Focus on Quality, Cost, and Delivery (QCD)

The second aspect of the better game plan—after the concurrent process already described—is the focus of all activities on the quality, cost, and delivery (development schedule) of the new product. This overcomes many fragmented bits of game plans with other, more local objectives, which often have adverse effects on quality, cost, and delivery (QCD). In the past, much work that appeared very elegant by some functional criteria was eventually found to add little to the QCD of the product, and in many cases was actually dysfunctional. The focus on QCD is part of the general approach of utilizing all relevant information to make decisions that satisfy all of the relevant objectives.

Emphasis on Customer Satisfaction

The third aspect of the better game plan is the emphasis on customer satisfaction. Inward-looking corporate metrics are deemphasized and are replaced by responses from customers. The emphasis on customer satisfaction extends throughout all of product development, and all other corporate activities. All objectives are put to the test of the effect upon the customer. The team devotes much effort to learning and understanding the opinions of customers. In developing the Taurus in the early 1980s, Ford developed a list of 1401 features that car buyers were looking for. The team's interest in the customers' views extends from the customers' needs at the start of a new development to the reactions from the users of the finished product.

Emphasis on Competitive Benchmarking

The fourth aspect of the better game plan is the emphasis on competitive benchmarking (CBM). Not only are the products benchmarked against the best of the competition, but also all processes are subject to being benchmarked. Concurrent engineering itself is to a considerable extent the result of competitive benchmarking, which is applied to many detailed subprocesses within concurrent engineering and is important for continuous improvement. The MIT Commission found that parochialism was a major weakness of American companies. It is very unlikely that a large percentage of all improvements around the globe will occur within one organization. Therefore, an important element of success is vigilance in finding, understanding, bringing in, and implementing major improvements. To a large extent this book is the result of benchmarking.

REINFORCING THE TEAMS

The improvements to cooperation are:

(1) The multifunctional PDT (already described)
(2) Employee involvement and participative management
(3) Strategic relationships with suppliers

Employee Involvement and Participative Management

The second aspect of closer cooperation, reinforcing the multifunctional PDT, is employee involvement and participative management. The full talents of all people are utilized, and responsibility is decentralized to empowered teams in their local areas of expertise and action. The ultimate form is layered organizational and communication networks. Communications occur horizontally and diagonally, on a need basis, not excessively constrained by the vertical orientation of treelike organization charts. Sometimes the lament is heard, Just tell me what to do and I will do it. Often, however, determining the right objectives is the most difficult part of the task. The principle is that the people who have the relevant information set the objectives, unconstrained by any ideology that says that objectives should be set by some particular segment or layer of the organization. Similarly, communications should occur in natural patterns as required for effectiveness in doing the work, unconstrained by the formal organizational chart or traditional culture. QCD to satisfy the customer is always the guiding light, and anyone who can contribute effectively should participate.

Strategic Supplier Relationships

The third aspect of closer cooperation is strategic relationships with suppliers. In addition to bringing the corporation's own production and field-support people upstream to work concurrently with the product design engineers, it is also an essential element of concurrent engineering to bring in suppliers to play a major role in the design of the new product. In the old, serial form of product development, suppliers were usually brought in very late, at which time they could only respond to designs that were already completed and compete with other potential suppliers primarily on the basis of lowest quoted cost. This led to a proliferation of a company's suppliers, none of whom were contributing significantly to the design of new products. As a result, designs were often ill suited to the capabilities of suppliers.

When a company employs concurrent engineering, the number of its suppliers tends to be much smaller, and participating suppliers are treated insofar as possible as full members of a design team. In many cases the number of suppliers has been reduced substantially—at Xerox, for example, from more than 3000 in the early 1980s to fewer than 400 in the late 1980s. This enables beneficial strategic relationships with suppliers.

In his excellent study of the interactions of higher-level (more integrative) manufacturers and their suppliers, Toshihiro Nishiguchi (1989) observed the effect of strategic relationships with suppliers as it emerged with new interfirm practices:

> Institutionally, there emerged a range of new inter-firm practices that were designed to ensure the continuous output of high-quality, low-cost products. Principally these practices were based on "problem solving" commitments between customer and subcontractor. Examples include joint price determination based on objective value analysis (VA), joint design based on value engineering (VE), the "target cost" (or "cost planning") method of product development, "profit sharing" rules, subcontractor proposals, "black box" design, "resident engineers," subcontractor "grading," quality assurance through "self-certified" subcontractors, and just-in-time (JIT) delivery circumscribed by "bonus-penalty" programmes. Along with these institutional changes, the main purchasing function of the customer shifted from downstream price negotiation to the assessment of subcontractor performance and the coordination of various intra- and inter-firm functions.
>
> The most important outcome from this evolution of subcontracting in Japanese manufacturing was a transformation in the underlying logic of contractual relations. The basis for these relationships shifted from the notion of classical exploitation onto a new view of collaborative manufacturing, in the sense that both purchasers and subcontractors came to benefit, under newly established rules, from the synergistic effects of an orientation to bilateral problem-solving.

In his comparative study of electronics suppliers in the United Kingdom and in Japan, Nishiguchi (1989) observed:

Japanese subcontractors also noted their customers' readiness to help improve product quality and reduce costs. Subsequent case studies, of Hitachi's subcontractor improvement programmes and of the interesting interactions between British subcontractors and their Japanese "transplant" customers in the U.K., then indicated an important conclusion. Japanese subcontracting relations have institutional attributes that promote *continuous improvement* in quality and cost reduction through "problem-solving" oriented commitments between customer and subcontractor. This contrasted with the "bargaining" orientation of U.K. subcontracting relations, which tended to produce adverse effects.

Although this was a comparison between the United Kingdom and Japan, it does not appear to be primarily a result of culture. The distinction is of the new-model strategic relationships with suppliers versus the traditional arms-length relationships.

Suppliers on the Team

The principle is simple: make the suppliers members of the PDT. There are two impediments to implementation: (1) collocation is difficult, if not impossible; and (2) residues of traditional practices may linger—for example, the supplier participates in the design but then does not receive the production business. The second problem is straightforward to solve. A strategic relationship means that the supplier will receive the production business. Usually there is a long-term (several years) contract that provides guidance and an infrastructure for the specific purchases.

Collocation

The first problem is more difficult, especially in the modern global economy. As an American materials management specialist said in 1981, "It is difficult to arrange supplier involvement in the design when the directions to find the supplier are to go up the Yangtze 200 miles and turn left." This may suggest that the supplier network should not be so widely dispersed. Other approaches are frequent meetings, a few supplier people collocated on a temporary basis, and computers.

Computers are tantalizing. Enthusiasts have suggested that the need for collocation can be eliminated by the use of electronic networks. However, this seems to overlook the psychological advantages of face-to-face collaboration. Electronic systems may ameliorate the advantages of collocation in the future, but much development is still needed. Today, physical collocation has great advantages.

A related problem is the splitting of the PDT itself between two major sites. For example, the system engineering and electromechanical design may be in New York, and the electronic and software development in California. To make this work successfully, the chief engineer spends much time on a frequent basis at both sites. Also, the other enablers of collaborative work that were mentioned—meetings, temporary collocation, and computers—are fully used.

In 1982, when Xerox switched to the independent PDT, the people were scattered at various sites in the Rochester, New York, area. Great effort was made to collocate the teams. This facilitated the informal communications that greatly improve the effectiveness of the PDT.

Strategic relationships with suppliers are a great extension of the multifunctional PDT. They are an essential element of basic concurrent engineering.

BETTER, BUT NOT ENOUGH

Basic concurrent engineering is a significant improvement in game plan and teamwork relative to the traditional functional, serial process. The better game plan is the concurrent process, reinforced by emphasis on quality, cost, and delivery; customer satisfaction; and competitive benchmarking. Better teamwork is achieved by the multifunctional product development team (PDT), reinforced by participative management and strategic relationships with suppliers.

Basic concurrent engineering makes large improvements; Ford and Xerox made major comebacks in the early 1980s by switching to it. However, even more vigilant information processing is needed for global competitiveness in today's international economy. Basic concurrent engineering is elevated to world-class concurrent engineering by enhanced quality function deployment (EQFD) and quality engineering using robust design. These vigilant information processes are introduced in the overview found in the next chapter.

CHAPTER

3

Better Decisions

- **Enhanced Quality Function Deployment**
- **Robust Quality — When Experience is Not Enough**
- **Disciplined Decisions**
- **The Right Decision Style**

Global competitiveness requires vigilant information processing that goes beyond basic concurrent engineering. A complex product requires millions of decisions to carry it into production and into the marketplace. The development program starts with broad goals, which are then focused by customer needs. Decision making in total quality development has five improvements over the traditional process:

- Team decisions (utilize collective experience, and develop commitment)
- Visual, connective methods, usually employing large displays on paper (focus team, and reveal interrelationships in data)
- Customer focus
- Optimization of critical decisions
- Problem prevention

There is a hierarchy of decisions. Individuals make most product development decisions, on the basis of experience—their own and others'. For decision makers, the body of available experience includes analyses, the most concise records of experience. It also includes handbooks, computerized records, and other repositories of experience. In developing a complex product, there may be 10 million decisions; most of them are within the grasp of individuals equipped with these tools.

Although individuals can make most decisions, the most critical decisions (roughly 1000 to 10,000 for large, complex products) require more attention, and most of them do not lie entirely within the experience or group of any individual. However, collective experience properly concentrated is sufficient. The right multifunctional team using a disciplined approach can make good decisions. The primary approach for these decisions is quality function deployment (QFD; Hauser and Clausing, 1988), now expanded into enhanced QFD (EQFD; Clausing and Pugh, 1991).

Still fewer decisions, typically several hundred for a large, complex product, are truly critical and cannot be made successfully on the basis of even the collective team experience. These decisions must be arrived at by systematic optimization. The process that has been found most broadly useful in total development work is Dr. Genichi Taguchi's *system of quality engineering using robust design* (Taguchi and Clausing, 1990; Phadke, 1989). This process also often uses teams, and EQFD can be effectively used to lead into Taguchi's optimization system.

Basic concurrent engineering by itself overcomes the problems of the traditional process to some degree. EQFD greatly adds to the vigilance of the information processing. The use of visual, connective team methods greatly increases the vigilance and effectiveness of the information processing. EQFD provides a good entrance into the optimization by Taguchi's quality engineering. The two are most effective when integrated together (as described in Appendix C).

In summary, individuals make most decisions. This is especially true in *partial design*, which is a key foundation element within total quality development. To provide much stronger definition of the partial-design tasks, we use EQFD to effectively utilize team experience, and Taguchi's quality engineering when experience alone is not enough. This decision-making process is displayed in Figure 3.1. It is critical to make each decision in the right style. EQFD and Taguchi's quality engineering are much more powerful than individual decision making, but they take more time. Therefore, they are to be used only on the most important decisions, where the extra time spent early in the development process will save even more time later by avoiding rework of the design. Constant assessment of priorities will reserve these powerful processes for the most important decisions.

In basic concurrent engineering a key feature is team decision making using simple team problem-solving methods. EQFD takes this much farther by using strong visual, connective methods. These methods use large visual displays (explained near the beginning of the next section), usually on a wall, to help the team to interact and to concentrate on the decision and the relevant information. Usually these displays are on paper, and vary from a few feet in both dimensions to as large as 5 feet by 15 feet. Many of them also illustrate connections between stages; the output from one activity becomes the input to the next.

In the traditional process there has been insufficient attention to the customer. Instead the work has often focused on satisfying the professional standards of cloistered groups of technical specialists, to the detriment of customer satisfaction. Basic concurrent engineering improves

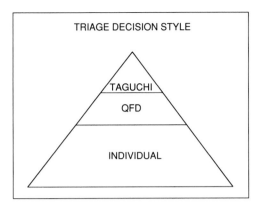

Figure 3.1. Select the right decision style for each decision.

this by emphasizing customer satisfaction, and QFD further greatly improves the effectiveness of meeting customer needs.

In 1984 while visiting Japan, the author was told by the vice president in charge of development and production for a Japanese company that there are three levels of competence in addressing problems:

(1) Problems are found. Wishful thinking allows many to be swept downstream. A large number end up in the marketplace.

(2) Problems are found. The total quality control approach is used to find and correct the root causes of the problem. The information is fed upstream so that the same problem is not introduced on a later development program.

(3) Problems are prevented. Potential problems and their root causes are identified before they occur. Optimization positions the design as far as possible from all potential problems. The information is fed downstream to ensure that the problem-prevention decisions are understood and maintained, to avoid the inadvertent later introduction of the problem.

It is a key principle of total quality development to emphasize problem prevention, rather than depend primarily on reaction to problems.

Total quality development, or world-class concurrent engineering, (1) focuses on benefits to the customer, (2) with a problem-prevention style that (3) uses team experience to make decisions, with the help of (4)

TABLE 3.1   Summary of Design-Decision Processes

	Traditional	Basic Concurrent Engineering	EQFD	Taguchi's Quality Engineering
Beneficiary	Specialist	Customer	Customer	Customer
Style	Reaction	Prevention	Prevention	Prevention
Who	Individual	Team	Team	Team
Communication	Over the wall	Verbal	Visual, connected	Uses EQFD
Source	Specialized experience	Team experience	Team experience	Optimization

visual, connective methods, which also lead into (5) systematic optimization for the most difficult and critical decisions. The roles of the major elements of total quality development in achieving these improvements over traditional product development are summarized in Table 3.1.

EQFD and Taguchi's quality engineering are critical to success with products. They emphasize team decisions, optimization of the most critical decisions, customer focus, problem prevention, and visual, connective team problem-solving methods. These two highly beneficial decision-making processes are introduced in overview in the remainder of this chapter. Operational details are described in the next four chapters in the context of the total quality development process.

ENHANCED QUALITY FUNCTION DEPLOYMENT

Quality function deployment (QFD) is a visual, connective process that helps teams focus on the needs of customers throughout total development. Enhanced QFD (EQFD) builds on QFD to make it more relevant to complex products that are conceptually dynamic.

QFD is a systematic process that helps identify customer desires and deploy them throughout all functions and activities of the corporation, remaining faithful to the voice of the customer. It is a combination of total quality management (TQM) process elements that multifunctional teams use to act effectively in response to the voice of the customer. Four of the seven management tools of TQM—affinity diagram, relation diagram, tree diagram, and matrix diagram—are combined and focused on the customer to form QFD. These are formatted as large displays to:

- Focus the decision-making interactions of the multifunctional teams
- Visually display the relevant information for ready reference
- Document the decisions in a visual corporate memory

As an additional advantage, the output from one large display becomes the input to the next matrix. This establishes a visual track from the customer's needs to the factory floor.

OVERCOMING MAJOR PROBLEMS

QFD has been evolved by product development people in response to these major problems in the traditional process:

- Disregard for the voice of the customer
- Disregard of competition
- Concentration on each specification in isolation
- Low expectations
- Little input from design and production people into product planning
- Divergent interpretations of the specifications
- Lack of structure
- Lost information
- Weak commitment to previous decisions

We can better understand the source of these problems with the help of the communication circle, an old party game also used as an exercise in communication classes. Joe in Seattle tells a story to Bill in Los Angeles, who passes it along to Jane in Dallas, who shares it with Nancy in Atlanta, who repeats it to Sam in New York, who passes it along to Jill in Boston, who returns it to Joe in Seattle; of course, Jill is unaware that Joe is the

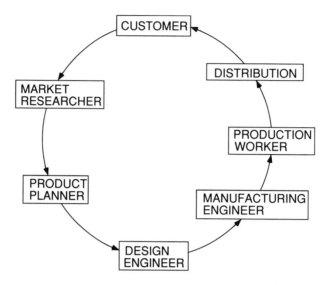

FIGURE 3.2. Corporate communication circle.

original source of the story. Does Joe receive back the same story that he originally told to Bill? Of course not!

In developing new products we have a similar corporate communication circle (Figure 3.2). We receive the story from the customer, pass it around the corporate communication circle, and eventually return it to the customer in the form of the new product. In the traditional process the story has been much changed; the product has not adequately satisfied the customer's desires. It is human nature to change the story; we all tend to embellish the part that appeals to us and to deemphasize the remainder. QFD is a disciplined, systematic process to overcome the degradation of the story and remain faithful to the voice of the customer.

To get another insight into the nature of the problem, observe the strong vertical orientation of the traditional organization in Figure 3.3. The analogy with vertical fibers in a fabric has been emphasized by the late Professor Kaoru Ishikawa, one of the founders of total quality management. A fabric with strong fibers in only one direction will be very weak in the face of general stresses from all directions. We also speak of the strong vertical fibers as *silos* or *chimneys*. Each vertical fiber—or chimney or silo—contains cloistered groups of specialists, looking inward within their specialties. The vertical cloisters of

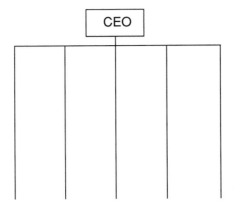

FIGURE 3.3. Vertical orientation.

specialists are good for deploying the voice of the executives vertically, for enabling fast-trackers to rise quickly, and for polishing specialties to a brilliant luster.

Unfortunately, new products do not move through the organization vertically. They must move through the organization horizontally, starting with the customers and returning to the customers. QFD is a strong weaver of horizontal threads to provide a strong organizational fabric, overcoming the traditional weaknesses of the vertical orientation; see Figure 3.4.

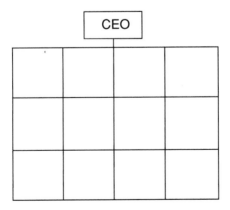

FIGURE 3.4. Strong organizational fabric.

FROM CUSTOMER TO FACTORY FLOOR—BASIC QFD

QFD helps the multifunctional team to deploy from the voice of the customer into production operations on the factory floor. To start this process, QFD uses a matrix form that is known as the House of Quality to do the planning for the new product.

House of Quality

The House of Quality is a large visual format that the multifunctional team uses to plan the new product. It is the first of a series of matrix diagrams used in the visually connected communication chain. Like all the matrices in the chain, it has rows in which inputs are entered and columns from which results are outputted. The inputs in this case represent the voice of the customer. The diagram has eight fields, each representing a different facet of product planning, which can be regarded as the rooms of a house (hence the name). The House of Quality is considered "built" when the rows and columns have been filled with all the necessary inputs and outputs.

The House of Quality is not an activity that is new to product development. Rather it is a much more effective way of doing the traditional activity of product planning. By eliminating much rework that has traditionally been done later in the development process, the House of Quality greatly reduces the development time. It also provides greater customer satisfaction as a result of the much sharper concentration on the voice of the customer. In the House of Quality, the multifunctional team *deploys* (thus the D in QFD) from the voice of the customer to the corporate expectations for the new product. This is the first step in the communication circle, and the House of Quality helps the team to maintain a high fidelity to the voice of the customer.

The House of Quality format is shown schematically in Figure 3.5. Room 1 is the voice of the customer, in the customer's language—the needs and desires of customers. An example, from a famous QFD project that was completed at Toyota Autobody in 1979, is, "The van will not rust while carrying fresh fruit," nor will it rust "as a result of being washed in an automatic car wash." These needs are clearly from the customer's perspective, in the voice of the customer. These voices tend to be subjective,

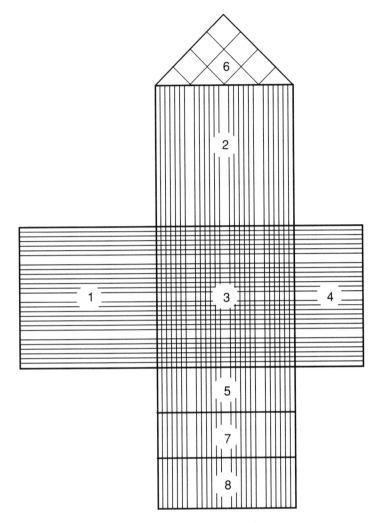

FIGURE 3.5. House of Quality schematic.

qualitative, and nontechnical. To develop the new product, it is essential that the team translate customers' needs into corporate language, which is more quantitative and technical, and has a very different perspective.

It is critically important to capture the customers' perspective in the corporate language; this is the work that is done in room 2 of the House of Quality. An example from the Toyota Autobody QFD project is, "will not rust at the edges of the sheet metal," a well-known site for severe rusting to start. Note the very great difference in perspective between the engineers, who thought about technology, and the customers, who thought about uses of the product. It is one of the great strengths of QFD that it helps to connect technology with uses.

To overcome the traditionally poor translation from the customer's language to the corporate language, the House of Quality includes a relationship matrix (room 3). This is where the team verifies and improves the fidelity of the translation. Once the multifunctional team has reached consensus in the first three rooms, it has made an excellent start on improved product planning. The customers' needs are clearly stated in corporate terms that are well understood in the same way by all the members of the team.

It is essential that the new product be not only new and different, but also better. To help achieve superiority, the House of Quality has the benchmarking rooms 4 and 5. Room 4 is for benchmarking from the perspective of the customer, while room 5 is for technical benchmarking using standard corporate tests. Typically three products are benchmarked: the company's own product, if one already exists in the market segment, and two products from competitors. (If the product is radically new, these benchmarks will not be available. However, potential customers will have been meeting the need in some way. Careful evaluation of the existing satisfaction of the need will give good insights.) The team surveys customers to obtain their opinions about the products they are using—specifically, whether the products are satisfying the needs recorded in room 1. The same products are subjected to the same tests that will quantify whether the new product satisfies the expectations recorded in room 2. The results of the survey of customers are plotted in room 4, and the results of the corporate tests are plotted in room 5.

The team compares the two sets of benchmarks for consistency, and performs further iterations until the sets are consistent. Commonly, traditional tests—which have not been sufficiently tuned to customers' perspectives—have to be redesigned at this point. The completion of consistent benchmarking further strengthens the team's understanding of the customers' perspective, and creates a sound basis for the goals of the new product.

Room 6, the attic, can be thought of as the conflict-of-interests room. Traditionally failure has resulted because specifications have been treated in isolation. Then, after considerable work, some specifications are found to conflict, and rework is required. In room 6, the team examines each pair of specifications for interference or reinforcement (synergy). This early identification of interactions among the specifications enables early planning to overcome inherent conflicts—much better than rework.

In room 7 the team does much of the planning of the project. Typically, room 7 is at least the place where the importance of each corporate expectation is weighed with the expected difficulty in achieving it. If two expectations are both very important and both very difficult and room 6 shows that they are conflicting, then the team plans the strongest development effort for those expectations.

Room 8 is the final objective for the entire House of Quality activity: the quantification of the corporate expectations for the new product. The team bases its numbers on the output from room 5, the technical benchmarks, which provide strong guidance on the values that will characterize a superior product. The multifunctional team reaches consensus about the values that will bring success. What is more important, there will be consistent understanding of the definition of each corporate expectation, and a common commitment to achieving the goals for success that the team has worked so hard to define in the House of Quality.

The House of Quality will be described in operational detail in Chapter 4. A good case study of a House of Quality (Hauser, 1993) was published as this book was being completed.

Now the remainder of QFD will be surveyed.

Transferring Customer Needs to the Factory Floor

After completing the House of Quality, the multifunctional team uses QFD (and its visual, connective methods) to deploy into design and production-process engineering, and thus into production operations planning, which defines the operations on the factory floor. The output from each matrix is in the columns. This output then becomes the input in the rows of the next matrix; see Figure 3.6, in which the first matrix on

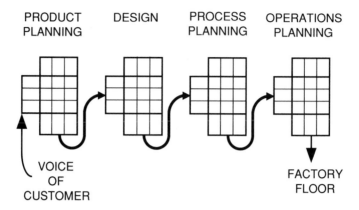

FIGURE 3.6. Structure of basic QFD.

the left is the House of Quality. The matrices of QFD provide connections. Production operations can be traced back to the customers' needs driving them, by retracing a course back through the design and process engineering decisions that responded to the needs and led to the specific production operations.

QFD has the advantages of visual, connective methods:

(1) Relevant information is found and used.
(2) The large, visual formats focus the team discussion on the objectives of the work session.
(3) The large displays allow the eye to rove over the relevant information, and logical connections are observed that otherwise would remain hidden.
(4) The different types of decisions are connected; for example, product design and process engineering decisions are consistent and compatible.
(5) The team members develop a common understanding about the decisions, their rationales, and their implications.
(6) The team members become committed to the common enterprise of implementing the decisions.

In addition, QFD provides the added specific advantage of focusing all decisions on the voice of the customer. For these reasons QFD provides a very large increase in the vigilance of the information processing. When holistically integrated into total quality development, QFD provides very large benefits. Of course, QFD is not a magical incantation. If QFD is treated as an add-on activity to fill in some spaces on a chart, then little will be accomplished. Once the team becomes adept at capturing the spirit of QFD, it becomes a tremendous organizational capability, which provides a strong competitive advantage.

ENHANCEMENTS TO BASIC QFD

QFD provides strong capability beyond basic concurrent engineering. However, in its basic form (Figure 3.6) the total system expectations are directly deployed into piece-part characteristics. This procedure is straightforward for simple products that are conceptually static. However, for conceptually dynamic products the total system concept must be selected before piece parts can be considered. For example, when cars were first invented, the total system had to be selected to have three wheels or four before the design of the wheels could be addressed. Now that the total system concept is well known to have four wheels (making it a static concept), the design of the wheels can be directly addressed. Concept selection is the most important enhancement in EQFD. Also, for complex products, the total system expectations must be deployed down to the subsystem level and then to the piece-part level. This is the second enhancement in EQFD. Enhanced QFD (EQFD) has been developed to extend the applicability of QFD to dynamic, complex products. It also contains three additional enhancements to strengthen product planning, which are woven into the description in Chapter 4.

Pugh Concept Selection Process

The most important of the enhancements is the Pugh concept selection process (Pugh, 1981). Although originally developed completely independently from QFD, it too is a visual, connective process and therefore has proven very easy to integrate into QFD. As shown in Figure 3.7, the Pugh concept selection process can be used to develop the total system architecture, subsystem concepts, and piece-part concepts. It is also used to select production concepts. Although referred to as a selection process, it

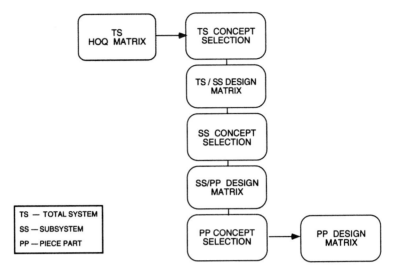

FIGURE 3.7. The two primary enhancements in EQFD: concept selection, and deployment through the levels.

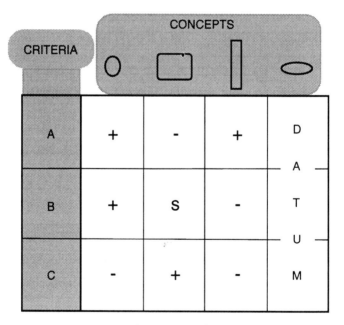

FIGURE 3.8. Pugh concept selection matrix.

almost always leads to the generation of new concepts that did not previously exist. The criteria for the concept development and selection are based on the House of Quality, so that the concepts are responsive to the needs of customers. The criteria are entered as the row headings, A, B, and C in the schematic of the concept selection matrix, Figure 3.8. Typically 15 to 20 criteria are used. The concepts are posted as the column headings. Often there are more than 15 concepts, indicative of vigorous concept generation.

The team chooses one concept as the initial datum with which all of the other concepts will be compared. If there is an existing dominant concept in the marketplace, then it is usually used as the initial datum. Otherwise, the team makes a quick judgment to pick a concept that seems to be very good, and it becomes the datum.

Then the team judges each concept relative to the datum in its ability to satisfy criterion A. If a concept is clearly superior, then it is given a plus mark. If clearly inferior, it is given a minus mark. If it is neither clearly superior nor clearly inferior, then it is given an S for "the same." The team judges all concepts on the basis of criterion A, and then proceeds to criterion B. As this evaluation is being done, the team members develop much new insight. Commonly there are differing initial perceptions about the evaluations, and the ensuing brief discussions add greatly to clear understanding of the concepts and the criteria. Frequently a team member will observe that the combination of, say, concepts 2 and 13 is a superior concept. This hybrid is added to the matrix as a new concept.

After several hours, the matrix evaluations are complete. Then the team computes the total score for each concept. However, the scores are not nearly as important as the insight that has been gained by the team. The team now has a much clearer understanding of the types of concept features that will be responsive to the customer.

The team agrees on additional work, and comes back together to "run" the matrix again in a few weeks. Typically the team has dropped roughly half of the original concepts, but new and better concepts have been generated and added to the matrix. The team iterates in this fashion until it converges on the dominant concept (Figure 3.9). The Pugh concept selection process greatly improves the capability of the team to move forward with a strong concept and thus avoid much rework later in the development process. It is described in operational detail in Chapter 4.

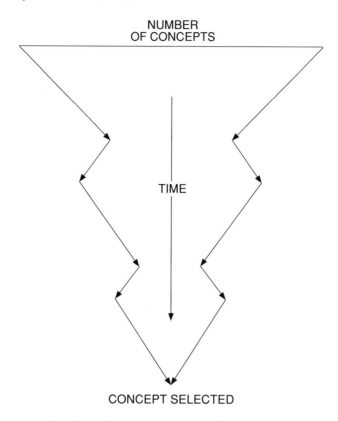

FIGURE 3.9. Iterative convergence to dominant concept.

Deployment through the Levels

The second enhancement in EQFD, deployment down through the levels of the product, also displayed in Figure 3.7, is done in matrices that are essentially the same as the basic design and process engineering matrices. Instead of deploying forward in the direction of the factory, the total system/subsystem (TS/SS) matrix and the subsystem/piece-part (SS/PP) matrix deploy downward from the total system level to the piece-part level. Again the columns from one matrix become the rows of the next matrix.

All five enhancements, the two that have just been introduced plus three enhancements to product planning, will be described in operational detail in the context of the total quality development process in Chapters

4 to 7. In addition, functional analyses that have long been used to some extent have been integrated into EQFD. Fault tree analysis (FTA), failure modes and effects analysis (FMEA), and functional trees (functional analysis system technique, or FAST diagrams, known in Japan as reverse FTA, or R-FTA) are closely related to each other and fit directly into the structure of EQFD. To a considerable extent QFD grew out of value analysis/value engineering (VA/VE), so one way to view QFD is that it is an extended form of VA/VE. The functional analyses and related good practices that have been developed during the use of VA/VE can be readily integrated into EQFD. Improved understanding and optimization of the functions of the product are a key element of total quality development. In the remainder of this book the acronym EQFD is used to include basic QFD, the enhancements, and the extensions that integrate functional analysis.

In summary, *EQFD is an extensive corporate capability that integrates the corporation holistically with a concentrated focus on customer satisfaction.* The visual, connective process greatly improves the team decision making that is based on collective experience.

ROBUST QUALITY—WHEN EXPERIENCE IS NOT ENOUGH

The disciplined practice of EQFD goes far beyond basic concurrent engineering in integrating the organization together in a holistic pursuit of customer satisfaction, based on collective experience. However, some of the most critical decisions must go beyond the limitations of experience. Then systematic optimization is used to select the values for the critical design parameters that will most consistently achieve customer satisfaction. EQFD marshals the team's experience to identify the most critical parameters, and to judge the range that will be best. For example, on the basis of its collective experience, a team identifies a friction coefficient as critical. The collective team experience teaches that the best value is probably between 1.5 and 2.0. Then systematic evaluations of performance in the range between 1.5 and 2.0 determine the best value. This is traditional good engineering.

However, the real problem is more difficult. The team may identify 13 critical parameters for a subsystem. It seems to be prudent to evaluate three values for each parameter: the ends of the range, and the middle point. This creates 3^{13} (1,594,323) options, a number that would be impossible to evaluate experimentally and difficult to evaluate for many analyses. A second difficulty is the objective. What metric, to be evaluated early in the development process, will best represent eventual customer satisfaction? Customers want robust products—products that go beyond mere feasibility to work well under actual conditions of use, maintaining performance close to ideal customer satisfaction even under adverse conditions. *Quality engineering using robust design* builds on EQFD to make still better decisions by optimizing sets of critical parameters to achieve robustness, products that consistently satisfy the customers.

CHARACTERISTICS OF ROBUSTNESS

Robust products work well—close to ideal customer satisfaction—even when produced in real factories and used by real customers under real conditions of use. All products look good when they are precisely made in a model shop and are tested under carefully controlled laboratory conditions. Only robust products provide consistent customer satisfaction. Robustness also greatly shortens the development time by eliminating much of the rework that is known as *build, test, and fix*.

Robustness is small variation in performance. For example, Sam and John go to the target range, and each shoots an initial round of 10 shots (Figure 3.10). Sam has his shots in a tight cluster, which lies outside the

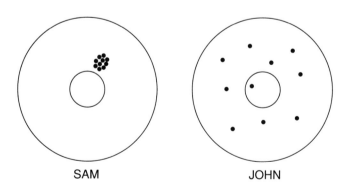

SAM   JOHN

FIGURE 3.10. Example of robustness.

bull's-eye. John actually has one shot in the bull's-eye, but his success results only from his hit-or-miss pattern. In this initial round John has one more bull's-eye than Sam, but Sam is the robust shooter. By a simple adjustment of his sights, Sam will move his tight cluster into the bull's-eye for the next round. John faces a much more difficult task. He must improve his control altogether, systematically optimizing his arm position, the tension of his sling, and other critical parameters.

Several facts about this example reveal important characteristics of robustness:

(1) The application of the ultimate performance metrics to initial performance is often misleading; Sam had no bull's-eyes even though he is an excellent marksman.
(2) Adjustment to the target is usually a simple secondary step.
(3) Reduction of variation is the difficult step.
(4) A metric is needed that recognizes that Sam is a good marksman and that measures his expected performance after he adjusts his sights to the target.

Automobiles give further insight into robustness. Customers do not want a car that is a lemon. They want one that is robust against production variations. A lemon is a car that has excessive production variations that cause great customer dissatisfaction. To overcome this, the production processes have to be more robust so that they produce less variation, and the car design has to be more robust so that its performance is less sensitive to production variations. The customers also want a car that will start readily in northern Canada in the winter and will not overheat in southern Arizona during the summer; that is, they want a car that is robust with respect to the variations of customer use conditions. Customers would also prefer cars that are as good at 50,000 miles as when new, that are robust against time and wear.

This example reveals the three sources of undesirable variation (also called noises) in products:

(1) Variations in conditions of use
(2) Production variations
(3) Deterioration (variation with time and use)

The three types of noises inevitably cause some degradation of performance, some deviation away from ideal customer satisfaction. The optimization of robustness minimizes these deviations, keeping performance economically close to ideal customer satisfaction.

Once the team defines the critical parameters as far as possible by experience, then the systematic optimization of robustness quickly determines the best values. In our previous example, the team determined, on the basis of its collective experience and assisted by EQFD, that the friction coefficient should fall in the range 1.5 to 2.0. It would then use Taguchi's quality engineering to optimize the value—say, at 1.7.

Robustness is the objective. For efficient optimization it is essential to define the best metrics for robustness. The exact metrics will depend upon the definition of ideal performance—analog or digital, static or dynamic, for example. Robustness goes far beyond mere feasibility, which simply requires one satisfactory operating point. Robustness expands upon this by developing a large region of satisfactory operating points, a region in which the product will nearly always lie, thus consistently providing customer satisfaction. Better decisions require clear statements of the objectives. The metrics of robustness when applied early during the development process are powerful in achieving problem prevention.

DR. TAGUCHI'S SYSTEM OF QUALITY ENGINEERING

Although there have been many independent approaches to robustness, by far the most complete and powerful approach has been developed by Dr. Genichi Taguchi starting in the late 1940s. His system of quality engineering using robust design is summarized in Figure 3.11. Lack of robustness causes the *performance degradations* in the output from the *product system*[1] to be excessive, producing large *quality loss*, the financial loss after the product is in the hands of the customer. Performance variations are caused by the three types of *noises* that afflict the product. These important aspects of quality are represented by the four lower left

---

[1]The term *product system* is commonly used, particularly in the Taguchi literature, to emphasize that most products are systems of smaller units.

boxes in Figure 3.11. They are the challenge to the activities of *quality engineering.*

Four activities are involved in reducing the total cost (quality loss plus manufacturing cost):

(1) Product parameter design, the systematic optimization of the robustness of the product design
(2) Tolerance design, to select the economical precision levels around the nominal (target) design values
(3) Process parameter design, the systematic optimization of the most important production processes so that they will inherently produce more consistent products
(4) On-line quality control, prudent intervention on the factory floor to further improve production consistency

The activities are represented by the four upper right boxes in Figure 3.11, the three design activities and the quality control activity in the factory.

The first activity, product parameter design, is the most powerful because it provides protection against all three kinds of noises. The remaining three activities all economically reduce production variations, one of the three types of noise that afflict the product. Although they are very valuable, these activities cannot help overcome the problems that are caused by the variations in the conditions of customer use, nor can they prevent the problems that stem from wear and other forms of deterioration. The rapid, early optimization of the robustness of the product system is the most important activity in Taguchi's quality engineering.

Now we will look in more detail at each of the eight elements of the system displayed in Figure 3.11.

Quality Loss

Quality loss is the financial loss after the product is in the hands of the customer. It is caused by deviations from ideal performance. Of course, customer dissatisfaction can also result because the "ideal" performance is not what the customer wanted; product planning in this case has not

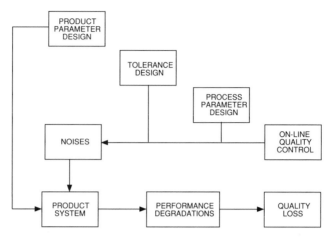

FIGURE 3.11. Dr. Taguchi's system of quality engineering.

followed the voice of the customer. In working on robustness we do not reconsider the product planning; our objective now is to avoid excessive quality loss that is the result of deviations from the ideal performance that was defined during product planning. A car with air conditioning might be said to be higher in quality for having this feature, but it is not therefore more robust. Its ideal quality has simply been chosen during product planning to be improved by the inclusion of air conditioning. Obviously there is more than one dimension to the customers' total image of quality. When dealing with robustness, we are considering one particular dimension: the discrepancy between actual performance and the ideal performance arrived at during product planning. Robust products minimize quality loss by keeping actual performance close to the ideal performance.

Two products that both meet their respective corporate specifications—as opposed to meeting customer needs—can exhibit very different degrees of quality loss. Therefore, meeting specifications is a poor measure of quality. This is counter to the tradition that zero defects is sufficient. Zero defects is simply an interesting and sometimes useful, rather arbitrary milepost on the road to quality improvement. Ideal performance is unobtainable, but it is a constant beacon that shows the direction for quality improvement. If we settle for lesser quality as the objective, then achieving that quality will tend to stop all improvement, leaving us more vulnerable to being surpassed by the competition. Robust products reduce quality loss.

Performance Degradations

Performance variations cause quality loss. Customers are completely satisfied only by ideal performance. We gain insight into the relationship between performance variation and quality loss by considering a case study that is based on a report about Sony color television sets that was published in the *Asahi* newspaper in the late 1970s.

The top half of Figure 3.12 shows the production variation in color density from the Sony factories in San Diego and Tokyo, the design of the television sets being the same. The curves that are plotted are probability density functions, smoothed out histograms of the measurements of color density from the actual sets that were shipped. T represents the target color density that provides ideal customer satisfaction. The corporate specification limits are at $T \pm 5$. All of the sets that were shipped from San Diego were within the corporate specification limits; in other words, the shipment had zero defects. The probability density function for the Tokyo factory is the normal (Gaussian) distribution with six standard deviations within the specification range of $10 (\pm5)$. From standard probability tables, we can read that the small tails that lie outside the corporate specification limits contain 0.3% of the total sets; three out of every thousand sets that were shipped were "defective"—that is, they did not satisfy the corporation's definition of acceptability. Thus, San Diego was shipping zero defects, while Tokyo was shipping 0.3% defective. On the basis of percentage defects, San Diego was doing better.

However, grades are also placed on Figure 3.12; grade A is within one standard deviation of the target, grade B is within the second standard deviation, and grade C is within the third standard deviation. We see that Tokyo had about twice as many A sets as San Diego, and many fewer C sets. The customers really wanted A sets, so the Tokyo sets were pleasing twice as many customers. Which should we prefer, then: zero defects, or twice as many pleased customers?

Let us further analyze the comparison. Taguchi developed the quality loss function, a quadratic curve displayed in the bottom half of Figure 3.12. The abscissa is color density, as in the top half of the figure. The

A TALE OF TWO FACTORIES

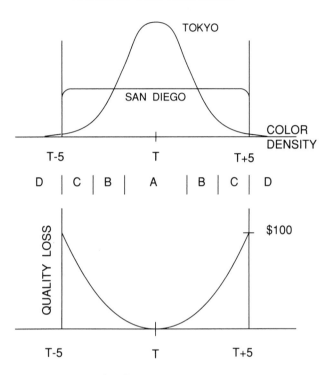

FIGURE **3.12.** Quality loss: the modern quality paradigm.

ordinate is the average quality loss per set. For example, if we ship 1000 sets with color densities between 1.95 and 2.05 and their total quality loss is $16,000, then the average quality loss per set of $16 would be plotted at 2.

Now there are two key observations that provide us with great insight. First, we must associate a dollar value with the specification limit of $T \pm 5$. The corporation has defined this to be the limit of acceptability, so the expected quality loss from sets that are at $T \pm 5$ must be unacceptably high. We can estimate the dollar value as the cost of the countermeasure the company must take to bring customers' sets up to standard. At the specification limit, many customers will demand service. We know fairly accurately the average cost of such service—say $100—and enter this as the ordinate at $T + 5$. We also expect this to be symmetrical, and we therefore also enter $100 at $T - 5$. Of course, at the customer satisfaction target T, we expect the quality loss to be zero, so now we have three points on the quality loss curve.

Next, what shape do we expect the curve to have between zero and the specification limits? A second observation will give us the needed insight. The second key observation is of two sets near a specification limit. Suppose we pick two sets from the assembly line and measure their color densities to be $T + 4.99$ and $T + 5.01$, one just inside the corporate specification limit, and the other just outside the corporate specification limit. Now let us position the sets in adjacent rooms and walk back and forth between the two sets. Can we tell any difference between the two pictures? Of course not! The corporate specification limit is completely unnoticed by the customers. This means that the expected quality loss does not jump at the specification limit, but is continuous. The average quality loss at 4.99 is only slightly less that at 5.01. This is different from the concept of zero defects, which lumps all products within the corporate specification limits together as nondefective. From this it might be inferred that the expected quality loss is zero within the specification limits and then jumps to a large value at the specification limits. Instead, it seems reasonable that the expected quality loss will increase slowly at first—that anything in the A range will be considered good and there will be little quality loss. Then the curve of expected quality loss will swing upward with increasing slope to the value of $100 at $T \pm 5$.

After considering these simple commonsense observations, Taguchi proposed that the simplest approximation that conforms to reality is the quadratic quality loss curve that is shown in the bottom half of Figure 3.12. Actual quality loss curves undoubtedly differ somewhat, but the quadratic curve powerfully changes our thinking and is sufficiently accurate for nearly all purposes. Furthermore, it is relatively easy to determine, while the actual curve would be very difficult to determine.

Now let us apply Taguchi's quality loss function to the Sony production example. We see that the Tokyo factory had about two-thirds of its shipments in the A range, where the quality loss per set is very small. In contrast, the San Diego factory had nearly one-third of its production in the C range, where the quality loss per set is very high. If we simplify by assuming that the San Diego straight line extends all the way to the specification limits, multiply the probability density functions by the quadratic quality loss function, and then integrate over all of the sets that were shipped, the result is that the expected quality loss from the Tokyo sets was one-third of that from the sets that were shipped from San Diego.

A major conclusion is that it is more important to keep performance close to the ideal customer satisfaction target than it is to avoid a few defects. The fact that the factories were in San Diego and Tokyo is incidental. Even the normal distribution curve is not the important message. The objective must be to reduce the variance from the ideal customer satisfaction target. The quality loss L_a averaged over the entire population of products that are shipped is proportional to the variance V (square of the standard deviation): $L_a = kV$. This assumes that the mean value for all of the sets is equal to the target value. More completely, $L_a = k[(m - T)^2 + V]$, where m = mean value and T = target value. Good quality is a mean value that is near the target, together with a small variance. The value of k is directly determined from the value of L at the specification limit. Thus, $100 at 5 gives a k value of $4(100 \div 25)$.

One of the great advantages of this understanding of quality is that it always provides a goal for continuous improvement. The value of the variance will never become zero, so we can always evaluate it and make improvements if the cost is justified. One of the problems with intermediate quality goals, such as zero defects, is that they can be achieved but then there is not any motivation for further improvement. However, a competitor may then greatly further reduce the variance and gain a competitive advantage. By concentrating on the variance and the deviation of the mean from the target, we always know our exact position and can determine the most productive areas for our quality improvement activities.

A little reflection about how the probability density function for the San Diego factory got its shape leads to the conclusion that San Diego was inspecting the sets after the final assembly and shipping only the sets that were within the corporate specification limits. Sets that were outside the limits had to be reworked. The inspection and rework cost money, increasing the unit manufacturing cost (UMC). Tokyo was obviously not inspecting; its inherent quality was good enough that it did not have to inspect, thus reducing the manufacturing cost. This is another lesson: robustness reduces the manufacturing cost.

Learning about performance is a key element of better decisions. The reduction of performance variance is an essential goal.

Noises

Noises are the causes of the performance variations. When all conditions are nominal, then the performance is on target. Three types of noises afflict products:

(1) The most important noise is the variations in the conditions of use by customers. The product will be used at high temperatures and low temperatures, at high humidity and in dry conditions, at high power line voltage and low, and in many other varying conditions that challenge the product. We product people have very little control over these conditions. Sometimes in exasperation we may exclaim that customers should not have used the product the way they have, but customers are going to use the products as they see fit. Competitive advantage comes to the robust products that can best withstand the varying conditions of use.

(2) The second type of noise is production variations. The Sony case is an example.

(3) The third type of noise is wear and other forms of deterioration. This is similar to production variations; the critical part characteristics deviate from their nominal values.

Thus, the second and third types of noise are really the same, except that one occurs in the initial condition, while the other is time-dependent. We do have control over the production variations, and during design we have some control over the rate of wear and other deterioration.

The Product System

The *product system* is afflicted by the noises, which cause its output performance to vary. We want the product to be robust, to dampen the effects of the noises, not passing them through to the output. Once the system concept is selected, robustness is achieved by finding and operating on the flat part of the response curve. This provides little change in

performance as the values of the principal causal factors change. Therefore, the performance remains very close to the ideal customer satisfaction value under the wide range of actual conditions.

Figure 3.13 is the voltage from a power supply as a function of the
value of a resistor. The target output voltage is 115. The initial design
value for the resistor was 200 ohms, which gave a voltage of 100, far
below the target. The simplistic next iteration would be to change the
resistance to 250, which does give an output of 115 volts. However, it is
still on the steep part of the response curve. The vertical dashed lines
represent the tolerances of low-cost resistors whose nominal values are
represented by the solid lines at A_2. The resulting variation of the output voltage is excessive. The robust design is at 350 ohms (A_3), where
the curve is flat and the variation of the resistor causes little variation of
the output voltage. Of course, this throws the voltage to a high value,
but remember Sam the marksman. It is usually easy to adjust to the
target after we have reduced the variation. For the power supply there
is another resistor, B, that does not provide opportunity for robustness
improvement; this can be used to adjust the output voltage to the target
value of 115.

Thus, we see that in products that have a target performance value
(115 volts in Figure 3.13), robustness is simply operating on the flat part

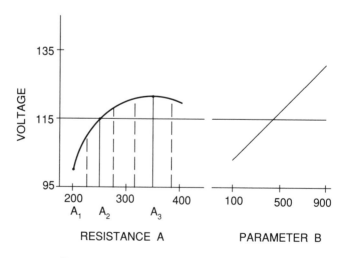

FIGURE 3.13. Basic concept of robustness.

of the curve, a simple aspect of traditional engineering. However, in real systems there are many critical design parameters, not just one resistor, and plotting response curves is not feasible. We need a direct engineering approach to find the robust part of the curve for the many-dimensional curves (surfaces) that represent realistic systems.

Product Parameter Design

Product parameter design is the optimization of the nominal values of the critical design parameters to achieve robustness in a short time. In the previous example the resistance of 350 ohms is the optimized nominal value of a critical design parameter. For one critical parameter, finding the optimized nominal value was easy, but real systems and subsystems have many more critical parameters. The process for robustness optimization is:

(1) Define objective, in terms of the best functional metric.
(2) Define feasible alternative values for each critical design parameter.
(3) Select some alternatives for evaluation.
(4) Impose noises.
(5) Evaluate performance of selected alternatives.
(6) Select the best design values.
(7) Confirm robust performance.

The most important guideline is to accomplish the robustness optimization early so that problems are prevented.

Define Objective: Best Functional Metric

We start by defining the best functional metric to concisely measure robust functionality. For a product with a target value, such as 115 volts for the power supply, this is the performance variation (standard deviation) after the mean value has been adjusted to the target. This is by far the most important step in the optimization of robustness. The best metrics have been given the name *signal-to-noise ratio*. *Signal* refers to the performance that we want, and *noise* refers to the variation of performance away from the ideal customer satisfaction value, which we do not want. Thus, we want a high signal-to-noise (SN) ratio. The terms *signal* and *noise* are used for both inputs and outputs. Earlier the three types of input noises were described. Now the noise in the performance output has been introduced as part of the SN ratio. Usually it is clear from the context which SN ratio is intended.

For a television set the picture from the station is the input signal and lightning and other electromagnetic disturbances are the principal input noises. The picture on the screen is the performance signal, and snow and other forms of picture degradation are the noises in the performance. The SN ratio measures the ratio of good performance to undesirable performance for fixed values of the input signal and noises. Thus, in comparing different designs it is important to keep the input signal and noises fixed in magnitude, or else the comparison of the performance SN ratios will not be valid.

Define Feasible Alternative Design Values

We define feasible alternative design values for the critical design parameters, chosen primarily on the basis of engineering judgment. The multifunctional team uses EQFD, especially fault trees, to select the critical parameters. For a subsystem the team may prioritize the 20 most important parameters and then decide to use the top 13 in the initial optimization. The best judgment about the nominal value, based on experience including analyses, has already been exercised in the normal course of design. Now it seems prudent also to try a larger value and a smaller value, seeking improvement. Thus, commonly we use three feasible alternative values for each critical design parameter. For 13 critical design parameters, we have 3^{13}, or 1,594,323, combinations. It is easy to comprehend that the traditional poke-and-hope approaches are unlikely to find the needle in such a big haystack.

Select Some Alternatives for Evaluation

The team chooses some alternatives for evaluation so that a combination that is close to the optimum will quickly be found. It is better to have 95% of optimum performance in two months than to obtain 98% of optimum performance in one year.

When each critical design parameter has three levels, there are two increments of variation, a total of 26 for the 13 parameters. Thus we need

26 data points to evaluate the effects of the 26 variations. In addition to variation, we also need to evaluate the mean value of performance, which requires another data point. Therefore, a minimum of 27 evaluations (degrees of freedom; see any statistical text) are necessary for 13 critical design parameters at three levels each.

It seems simple prudence to evaluate each level of each critical parameter nine times; we do not have any basis for preferring one level over another. Likewise, in considering pairs of critical design parameters, it seems prudent to select each combination an equal number of times. For three levels there are nine combinations of pairs, 1-1, 1-2, ..., 3-3, so for 27 evaluations each is selected three times. Finding 27 combinations that obey these commonsense guidelines seems as though it might be quite difficult. Fortunately it has been done for us and tabulated in ready references. Combinations that obey our simple guidelines are called *orthogonal arrays*.

For three levels of 13 parameters, the orthogonal array is referred to as the L_{27} orthogonal array. The L stands for *Latin*, a term for such arrays whose derivation is rooted in their history. The 27 refers to the number of evaluations that are defined by the array. The L_{27} array in Figure 3.14 obeys our prudent guidelines. Each column has nine 1s, nine 2s, and nine 3s. Each pair of columns has each pair of numbers present three times. The numbers 1, 2, and 3 in the table refer to the three levels of each critical design parameter. Thus, in the first evaluation (the first row) each of the critical design parameters has 1 as its level. Each row defines a different design combination for evaluation. The team evaluates the performance of each of the 27 design combinations. If a good computer simulation—a finite-element analysis, for example—is available, then it can be used to evaluate the performance. Otherwise the team performs experimental evaluation.

Impose Noises

Noises are imposed on the product during the evaluations to simulate real conditions so that the comparisons of the 27 options will be realistic, not merely reflecting laboratory comparisons under ideal conditions. If the winning combination is chosen under ideal operating conditions, it is not likely to be successful in the real operating conditions of the marketplace. Therefore, the multifunctional team carefully identifies the

	1	2	3	4	5	6	7	8	9	10	11	12	13
1	1	1	1	1	1	1	1	1	1	1	1	1	1
2	1	1	1	1	2	2	2	2	2	2	2	2	2
3	1	1	1	1	3	3	3	3	3	3	3	3	3
4	1	2	2	2	1	1	1	2	2	2	3	3	3
5	1	2	2	2	2	2	2	3	3	3	1	1	1
6	1	2	2	2	3	3	3	1	1	1	2	2	2
7	1	3	3	3	1	1	1	3	3	3	2	2	2
8	1	3	3	3	2	2	2	1	1	1	3	3	3
9	1	3	3	3	3	3	3	2	2	2	1	1	1
10	2	1	2	3	1	2	3	1	2	3	1	2	3
11	2	1	2	3	2	3	1	2	3	1	2	3	1
12	2	1	2	3	3	1	2	3	1	2	3	1	2
13	2	2	3	1	1	2	3	2	3	1	3	1	2
14	2	2	3	1	2	3	1	3	1	2	1	2	3
15	2	2	3	1	3	1	2	1	2	3	2	3	1
16	2	3	1	2	1	2	3	3	1	2	2	3	1
17	2	3	1	2	2	3	1	1	2	3	3	1	2
18	2	3	1	2	3	1	2	2	3	1	1	2	3
19	3	1	3	2	1	3	2	1	3	2	1	3	2
20	3	1	3	2	2	1	3	2	1	3	2	1	3
21	3	1	3	2	3	2	1	3	2	1	3	2	1
22	3	2	1	3	1	3	2	2	1	3	3	2	1
23	3	2	1	3	2	1	3	3	2	1	1	3	2·
24	3	2	1	3	3	2	1	1	3	2	2	1	3
25	3	3	2	1	1	3	2	3	2	1	2	1	3
26	3	3	2	1	2	1	3	1	3	2	3	2	1
27	3	3	2	1	3	2	1	2	1	3	1	3	2

FIGURE 3.14 L_{27} orthogonal array for 27 evaluations of 13 critical design parameters.

most important noises in the actual use of the product. EQFD, including fault trees, is again very helpful here. Then each option, each row of the orthogonal array, is subjected to the same array of noises, and the performance is evaluated for each noise combination.

In the simplest approach, two combinations of noise are used. If high temperature, high humidity, and low input voltage are known to place stress on the performance in one direction, then these noises are taken to reasonable extremes, based on customers' conditions, and then the performance is evaluated. Then the noises are taken to their opposite extremes, and then the performance of each of the 27 options is again tested. This gives a total of 54 evaluations—two performance evaluations for each of the 27 design points, just enough to test the sensitivity to noises for each design point. The exact amount of stress in the values of the noises is not too important; we are not going to use these performance values to predict the field performance, but simply to compare the 27 options. As long as the values of the noises that we select are roughly the same as in the field, then the comparison will be valid, and the combination that we select will be robust in the marketplace.

Alternatively, if each performance evaluation is quick and simple, then the team uses more noise combinations. For example, we might identify the seven most important noises and decide to test each of them at their two extreme values. This gives 2^7, or 128, combinations. We might decide that 128 is too many to evaluate and use an orthogonal array to select a representative sample. Typically we would use an L_8 orthogonal array to select eight combinations of noise for actual evaluation. Then each of the design points, 27 in the example, is subjected to the eight different noise combinations, a total of 216 performance evaluations. When computer simulations that take only a very short time to run are available, then it is common to use more performance evaluations. It is common to use the L_{36} orthogonal array to select 36 design points and then also to use the L_{36} orthogonal array to select 36 noise combinations, a total of 1296 performance evaluations.

Thus we see that the number of noise combinations that we select is strongly influenced by the ease and time to perform the evaluations. For experimental evaluations it is common to take two noise combinations, and rare to use more than eight.

Evaluate Performance of Selected Alternatives

The next stage of the process is straightforward engineering work, using either experimental or computer determination. For each design point (row of the design orthogonal array), the team evaluates the performance. The evaluation is done at each of the appropriate noise conditions, enabling the effect of noises to be evaluated in the SN ratio. Thus, an SN ratio is calculated for each design point. When the team uses the L_{27} orthogonal array to select the design options for comparison, then it calculates 27 SN ratios, one for each row (design option). Thus, each design option that is evaluated is characterized by its SN ratio.

Select the Best Design Values

By comparing the SN values, the team quickly identifies the best of the 27 options. However, there were a total of 1,594,323 options, so it is improbable that the best overall option was in the 27 that were selected for initial evaluation. Therefore, the team must interpolate from its data to select the best point from among the 1,594,323 options. Taking column 1 of the L_{27} as an example, the first nine rows were tested with this critical design parameter at its first level. Therefore, the average of these nine SN ratios characterizes the performance that is associated with level 1 of the critical design parameter that was assigned to the first column. Likewise, the average of the second set of nine SN ratios characterizes the second level of the critical design parameter, and the average of the third set of nine SN ratios characterizes the third level.

Then the team chooses the level that has the highest average SN ratio as the best level. The same type of analysis is done for the other critical design parameters, and the best level is chosen for each. A little reflection will lead to the insight that this analysis opens the door to each of the options. Any of the 1,594,323 could be the winner. If level 1 was best for critical parameter 1 (first column of the design array), level 3 was best for the second critical parameter, level 2 was best for the third parameter, etc., then the best combination can be written in the form 1323312113223, for instance, each number giving the best level for the critical parameter corresponding to its digit position. It is the team's prediction that this combination will give the best performance, the best SN ratio, of all of the 1,594,323 design options.

Next we need to verify the performance of the selected winner.

Confirm Robust Performance

The team evaluates the performance of the selected winner and calculates its SN ratio. Usually it will be significantly better than the best of the 27 design options that were originally evaluated, and much better than the original design point. The robustness of the product or subsystem has been optimized, with tremendous benefit.

Of course, using 27 data points to estimate the most likely best design point out of 1,594,323 options cannot be a precise process. The design point that is selected by the simple process that has been described will usually be close to the best, but not actually the best. To find the best would require 1,594,323 evaluations, and even then the team could not be absolutely certain it had found the best. Therefore, the goal is simply to get close to the best in a short time.

There are also two other types of uncertainty in the optimization. First, the 13 design parameters that were selected may not have been the most critical. Second, the best value of SN ratio for each parameter probably did not lie exactly on one of the three values initially selected. Therefore, one or two more iterations are usually in order. Initially, 20 critical design parameters were selected in prioritized order, on the basis of the team's collective experience. In the first iteration of evaluations, the team evaluated the top 13 on the list. Typically some of these are found to actually have little effect on the SN ratio and can be dropped from the second iteration of evaluations. They are replaced by some of the design parameters that were lower on the original list, in the 14th to 20th positions.

To overcome the second uncertainty, the team plots the SN values from the first iteration against the three levels of each design parameter to enable interpolation. For example, if the curve appears to have a peak between the second and third levels, then in the second iteration the three values are selected in this range, thus providing a fine tuning of the optimization.

Commonly the team judges that a third iteration has captured most of the potential gain in a short time, and the optimization of product robustness is complete. The benefits in improved customer satisfaction, reduced costs, and shorter development time are tremendous.

Product parameter design is described in operational detail in Chapter 5.

Tolerance Design

After the team selects the nominal values of the critical design parameters, it selects the economical precision levels. The nominal values are the target for production, whether by the factory or its suppliers. However, production will always vary, and during product development there is some choice about the amount of precision that will be achieved. Product parameter design is often all benefit, but tolerance design always involves a trade-off. If we want more precision, we must pay for it.

In the traditional process, tolerances have often been determined in a concurrence meeting. To exaggerate only slightly, the design engineers sit on one side of the conference table and chant "tighter tolerance, tighter tolerance," while the production engineers sit on the opposite side of the conference table and chant "looser tolerance, looser tolerance." After much acrimony, they tire and settle on some value for the tolerance. The production engineers know that tighter tolerances cost more during production, and the design engineers know that tighter tolerances will provide operation that is closer to the ideal function of the product and will reduce the quality loss in the field. Usually the increase in unit manufacturing cost (UMC) to provide tighter tolerances is well known, but the reduction in the expected quality loss in the field is not known; hence, the irrational concurrence meetings.

Now during tolerance design the team uses the quadratic quality loss function to estimate the expected quality loss in the field, and it makes a quantitative trade-off. During product development the primary precision decision to be made is the selection of the production process. For example, a shaft can be turned or it can be turned and ground. The second option provides much better precision but also costs much more. Is it worth it? If the expected quality loss is reduced enough, then the extra manufacturing cost will be justified.

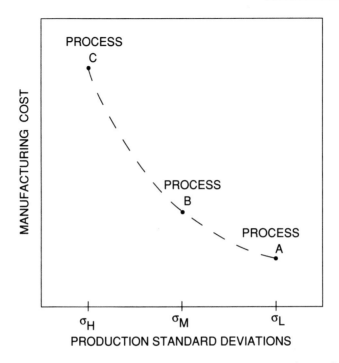

FIGURE 3.15. Tolerance design: choosing among process alternatives.

The options are shown in Figure 3.15. There are the low-UMC, low-precision option; the high-UMC, high-precision option; and usually a few options in between. The basic tolerance design procedure is to add the UMC to the expected quality loss for each production-process option and to pick the process with the least total cost. Of course, for many common situations the appropriate precision has been determined by long experience, and formal tolerance design is not necessary. The trade-off with the use of the quadratic quality loss function is reserved for critical new situations that will have a high impact on the total cost.

Tolerance design is described in operational detail in Chapter 5.

Process Parameter Design

Process parameter design optimizes the robustness of the production processes, thus reducing production variations, the second type of noise to the product. Production variations are caused by factory noises such as the variations in the properties of raw materials, variations in the ambient temperature and humidity, vibrations, variations in the values of the critical process parameters, variations in the maintenance of the production equipment, and variations in the practices of the workers. Optimization of the robustness of the processes makes the production more uniform despite these noises. This improves both customer-perceived quality and the manufacturing cost.

The process for optimizing the robustness of the production processes is the same as that for robustness of the product, with one exception. For production optimization, it is usually not necessary to explicitly control and impose realistic values of the noises. Instead the production processes are operated in their normal way, without taking special care, and appropriate samples of the production are taken for measurement. The SN ratio is calculated from the measurements, and the entire optimization proceeds as for the product. As long as the environment is similar to that during actual production, the comparisons of the different process settings will be valid. (The same is not true for products; laboratory conditions are usually much nicer than customers' conditions, so we must explicitly simulate the customers' conditions of use.) In process parameter design we optimize the values of the critical production-process parameters, such as feeds, speeds, and depth of cut. This has often been applied to existing processes, frequently with very large improvements that have brought substantial cost reductions.

On-Line Quality Control (QC)

On-line quality control further reduces variations during actual production. No matter how robust the production processes are, if there is never any intervention during production, then the values will soon deviate substantially from the target. The time nature of these variations can be classified as drift, shift, and random. In all cases, if we can predict the value of the next unit of production from the measurement of the previous unit of production, then we have a good basis for on-line QC.

For example, we might measure the outside diameter (OD) of a shaft as 0.001 inch over the target. Usually we are justified in expecting that the value of the next shaft will also be approximately 0.001

inch over the target unless we intervene. On this basis we do intervene, and we turn the cross-slide leadscrew enough to move the cutting tool in by 0.0005 inch, a diameter reduction of 0.001 inch. We are cautious, because there may be a component of variation that is random even during the short interval from one unit of production until the next. Then our prediction for the next unit will have some error, and it will turn out that we should have adjusted the process by something less than the full discrepancy measured, 0.001 inch. Normally, however, adjustment of the process by the full magnitude of the measured discrepancy is satisfactory.

The primary remaining question is the frequency of intervention. If we never intervene, the quality loss will be excessive. If we intervene too frequently, the reduction in quality loss will not compensate for the immediate cost of the excessive frequency of intervention. This is another trade-off, similar to tolerance design. We add the cost of intervention (measurement cost plus adjustment cost) to the expected quality loss because of the deviation from the target and choose the frequency of intervention that minimizes the total cost.

On-line QC is described in operational detail in Chapter 6.

Summary of Taguchi's Quality Engineering

Dr. Taguchi's system of quality engineering using robust design has four improvement activities. Product parameter design is the most important improvement activity, since it provides protection against all three types of noises. This keeps *performance* close to the ideal customer satisfaction value, which is our real objective. The last three of the improvement activities—tolerance design, process parameter design, and on-line QC—all reduce production variations, the second type of noise to afflict the product. This is very beneficial, but these activities provide no protection against customer-use noises, and very little protection against the deterioration noises.

In traditional product work, quality was a factory activity to make parts conform to corporate specification limits. In the new quality paradigm, quality is primarily a design activity to make performance adhere closely to the ideal customer satisfaction value. This paradigm shift is an essential element of total quality development.

The primary features of Taguchi's system of quality engineering are

- Focus on robust performance
- Early optimization of robustness
- Best functional metrics (SN ratios)
- Integrated system of quality engineering (see Figure 3.11)
- Systematic design changes for efficient optimization

These are in descending order of importance. The systematic design changes, through the use of the orthogonal arrays, are an important feature, but they are the least important of the five primary features. When first introduced to Taguchi's system of quality engineering, some have perceived it as only a wrinkle in the design of experiments (DOE), but DOE is actually the least important of the significant features. Rather, it is the emphasis on robustness that is the most important feature. At Xerox during the 1970s, for example, we achieved great success by using the first two of the five features, combined with a good approach to the third feature.

Quality engineering using robust design greatly improves customer satisfaction, reduces costs, and most important of all greatly shortens the development time. The early optimization of robustness eliminates great amounts of rework later in the development process, and thus gets the product to market much sooner with much less confusion during production start-up.

DISCIPLINED DECISIONS

After making better decisions, it is essential that we maintain constancy of purpose. In traditional product development there has been an unfortunate tendency to revisit decisions. This has stemmed from several causes:

- Lack of confidence in decisions, which reflects poor decision style
- Long development times, which allow external conditions to change
- Dysfunctional iteration

- The notion that changing decisions creates an aura of dynamic creativity

Total quality development brings a much better decision style, the best that we know how to practice. After making each decision by using the best approach, we can have confidence in the result. Instead of agonizing about the decisions that were just completed, we move on to the next decisions. Our commitment to the decisions provides a firm foundation for the ongoing work.

Long development times and the reconsideration of decisions have a chicken-and-egg effect. Because the development times have been so long, we felt that we had to reconsider the decisions so that they did not lose touch with the market. However, the constant reconsideration of the decisions has greatly lengthened the development time. A high-level executive complained to Taguchi of having some trouble with product planning. Taguchi replied to the executive that his company would always have trouble with product planning as long as it took five years to develop new products. In total quality development, we do the best possible job of understanding the market at the beginning of each specific development program. Then we depend on our fast time to market to keep the product current.

Some iteration is good and necessary. However, much of the iteration in traditional product development has been the dysfunctional result of organizational rigidities and serial development. We need discipline to stick with our decisions and deliver the new product to the market quickly. Creativity is good, but very few of the decision changes in traditional product development have anything to do with effective creativity.

The successful style emphasizes a progressive reduction in the number of remaining decisions.

PROGRESSIVE FREEZES

Total quality development emphasizes problem prevention. We make the decisions early, using the best approach to decision making. Then we stick with the decision. As we often say, *do it once and do it right*. This needs some refinement, as will be described in the next section, on iteration. However, we do want to progressively reduce the number of remaining decisions.

To avoid dysfunctional repetition, we use the progressive freezing of decisions. This leads to a profile that has the overall tendency that is shown in Figure 3.16. As the work progresses, the team freezes the decisions. At the end of each phase, it freezes the decisions that are appropriate for that time in the development process. Then it uses the frozen decisions as the basis for the next phase, not reconsidering the frozen decisions. This discipline is critical for success. More explicit understanding of disciplined decision making comes from the analysis of iteration in product development.

ITERATION

To iterate is defined in the dictionary as "to do again or repeatedly." In product development, some iteration aids creative decision making, while other types of iteration are dysfunctional repetition. Obviously, we want to keep the good iteration while throwing out the bad.

Creative Iteration

Iteration is an essential part of design activity. When I was a teenager my father taught me that a designer's best friend is an eraser. We put a design thought on paper, and then we consider it from many perspectives. The

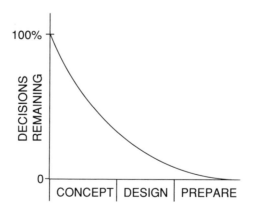

FIGURE **3.16.** Progressive freezes.

increased understanding leads us to modify the design. This iteration is inherent in human limitations. We cannot conceive an idea, consider it from all perspectives instantaneously, and draw the final design. We can only operate with approximately seven items in our short-term memory. Thus, we must iterate.

The Pugh concept selection process utilizes positive iteration. This was indicated graphically in Figure 3.9. The number of concepts that the team is working with increases and decreases, until the team converges on the dominant concept that has evolved as a result of the process. On a more micro scale, each member of the team uses the type of iteration that is described in the previous paragraph to generate new concepts. Also, the team uses this type of iteration in modifying concepts and creating hybrid concepts while working with the concept selection matrix.

Creative iteration needs to be nurtured by a creative environment.

Dysfunctional Iteration

In traditional product development much iteration has been the result of serial development that is reinforced by the functional silos. The most noted example is the initial development for function, which is then followed by development for production. The second iteration, which emphasizes production, naturally requires that many of the decisions that were made during the first iteration be redone.

In total quality development we avoid this dysfunction by doing both functional and production design concurrently. Of course, we cannot literally do them both during the same second. Therefore, the different perspectives are still addressed iteratively. In contrast to dysfunctional iteration, we complete the iteration loops in the shortest time that is compatible with human limitations. From a macro perspective, the different aspects are addressed concurrently by one team. This minimizes process loss.

Disciplined Iteration

The do-it-once-and-do-it-right attitude is basically the problem-prevention approach that we want to utilize. This would lead to making deci-

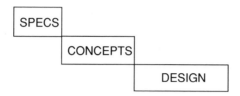

FIGURE 3.17. Rigid freezes.

sions in closed segments, as indicated by the example in Figure 3.17. If we followed this literally, then we would complete and freeze all decisions about the specifications before starting to work on concepts.

This is too rigid. We want concept generation to be motivated and started during the development of the House of Quality. Also, although the development of the specifications must be complete at the end of the *specs subphase*, it is best not to solidly freeze them yet. This is indicated in Figure 3.18. We want to encourage some creative iteration between the specifications and the concepts. However, we do want to select a concept that is responsive to the customer, so we cannot change the specifications very much after the completion of the specs subphase. This requires great discipline.

At the end of the specs subphase, the specifications are best thought of as being completed but not frozen. They are completed in the sense that the team is not going to revisit the excellent work it has just completed by again bringing in the voice of the customer and then deploying it into the corporate specifications for the new product. Thus, the team will not engage in further iteration that is internal to the primary activity of defining the specifications. That would tend to redefine

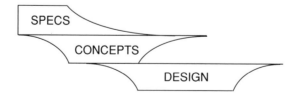

FIGURE 3.18. Progressive freezes.

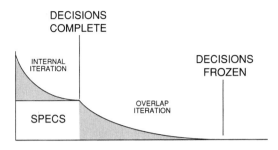

FIGURE 3.19. Completion and freezing of decisions.

the marketplace, negating the good work that was just completed. This is indicated in Figure 3.19. The internal iteration comes to an end at the completion of the specs subphase. On the other hand, the team can make some changes to the specifications that are based on opportunities identified during the overlap between the specifications subphase and the concept and design work. This is positive iteration. The team cannot totally envision the specifications that will represent the strongest product in the marketplace until some concept and design work have been done. Therefore, the overlap iteration will further strengthen the specifications in the context of the emerging product design. However, the team freezes the specifications before building the full-system prototypes. Later changes would be disruptive, causing chaos and confusion.

Any changes to the specifications during overlap iteration must not reintroduce disregard for the customer. The changes should be compatible with the voice of the customer, as verified in the House of Quality. In some circumstances it is good to verify the changes with customers. However, this can easily become the camel's nose in the tent door. It must not lead to dysfunctional iteration, the revisiting of the internal iteration that was completed during the specs subphase.

The example that has been described for specifications applies to all activities. First the internal iterations within each activity are completed. The activity is kept slightly open to enable creative iteration during the overlap with the next activities. When creative overlap iteration has achieved all that it can and further changes would be disruptive to the ongoing work, then the decisions are frozen.

The team can follow the best path of disciplined decisions by being aware of a pair of twin dangers:

- Disruptive revisiting of decisions that have been completed
- Premature rigid freezes (not taking advantage of overlap iteration)

THE RIGHT DECISION STYLE

Individuals make most decisions with only informal interactions with their colleagues. However, important and critical decisions require intensified vigilant information processing to achieve world-class concurrent engineering. This is provided by enhanced QFD and quality engineering using robust design. EQFD is a visual, connected methodology that helps teams to reach the best decisions when individual decision making is not adequate. When the team finds that even its collective experience is insufficient to complete the decision, then it branches out of EQFD into the systematic optimization of robust design.

The most critical decisions are those that most strongly influence customer satisfaction, including costs. Starting with the voice of the customer, the application of EQFD and quality engineering using robust design leads the team to identify the critical parameters and make the best decisions.

It is important that these vigilant information-processing methodologies be tightly integrated into total quality development. Then the excellent decisions that are made are maintained by disciplined convergence to the final definition of the product. The beginning, starting with the voice of the customer, is described in the next chapter.

CHAPTER

4

In the Beginning — Customer to Concept

- **House of Quality — Planning a Successful Product**
- **Selecting a Winning Concept**
- **Deployment to the Subsystems (SS)**
- **Progress Check**
- **43 Steps for the Successful Concept Phase — A Summary**

Chapters 4 through 7 describe the heart of the total quality development process. The chapters and what they cover are as follows:

Chapter 4 In the Beginning—Customer to Concept
Chapter 5 The Design
Chapter 6 Getting Ready for Production
Chapter 7 Technology Development

The relationships among these activities were displayed in Figure 1.7. In Figure 4.1, the core of Figure 1.7 is repeated, with emphasis on the subject of this chapter, the *concept phase*.

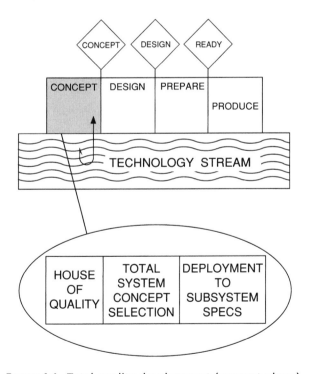

FIGURE 4.1. Total quality development (concept phase).

Chapters 4 through 6 describe the development of a new product from the voice of the customer to readiness for production. This description is based on the assumption that any new technologies are developed within the product program. Many products are developed this way. It is usually most productive to develop a stream of generic technologies that provide the technological foundation for new products. When the concept for a specific product is developed, the mature winning technologies are "fished out" of the technology stream for integration into the new product concept. Usually the new technologies are eventually used in more than one product, thereby improving productivity. Chapter 7 describes the development of new technologies, the major improvements for new products.

Even before the concept phase begins, we make some major strategic decisions:

- What is the business plan for our new product?
- How does this product relate to all of our products (product strategy)?
- What degree of reusability of existing designs are we planning?
- When is the product needed in the marketplace?
- How long do we plan to keep it in production?
- How many units do we plan to make?
- Where will the new product be manufactured?
- What regulations, standards, and safety requirements (beyond the compulsory ones) will be met?

Many of these decisions will be updated as we progress through the development of the new product. The strategic context for the new product, which is very important, is described in Chapter 8. Now we turn to the development of the selected product.

In the beginning of product development, in the concept phase, there are three primary steps:

(1) Bring in the voice of the customer, in the context of the product strategy.

(2) Develop the product concept (including appropriate new technology).
(3) Deploy to design requirements that are responsive to the customer and to the corporate strategy.

The voice of the customer is brought into the House of Quality, and there we (the multifunctional team) deploy (translate) it into product expectations and extend these expectations into specifications, which become the design requirements. These requirements are the criteria for selecting a winning product concept, including the new technologies that provide substantial cost and performance improvement. The *Pugh concept selection process* gives the team strong help in selecting the winning total system concept. Then *enhanced quality function deployment* (*EQFD*) is used to deploy the requirements from the total system level to the level of the subsystems. The *concept review* refines the consensus of the multifunctional product development team (PDT) and the entire corporation, making small adjustments to ensure that the concept phase has been cleanly concluded. The consensus around the product concept and the subsystem requirements provides a strong start into the design phase.

The concept phase of total quality development overcomes 2 of the 10 cash drains of the traditional product development process, which were described in Chapter 1:

- Disregard for the voice of the customer (cash drain 2)
- Eureka concepts (not winners) (cash drain 3)

The House of Quality, the Pugh concept selection process, and the systematic deployment from the total system expectations to the subsystem requirements (all part of EQFD) combine to overcome cash drains 2 and 3, and to make a good start on cash drain 4, which is "pretend" designs. As practiced by the multifunctional PDT, these improved practices enable a successful transition from the customer to the product concept, and a strong basis for successful design during the ensuing design phase.

HOUSE OF QUALITY—PLANNING A SUCCESSFUL PRODUCT

The first step in developing a new product is product planning, as diagramed in Figure 4.2. The product's capabilities, features, and costs are planned in response to the customers who are in the specific market segment for which the product is intended. Primary problems with traditional product planning are

(1) Disregard for the voice of the customer
(2) Lack of consensus about the specifications

QFD strongly helps to overcome these problems by emphasizing

(1) Formats that guide careful deployment from the voice of the customer to the corporate expectations (specifications)
(2) Multifunctional teams that work to achieve consensus

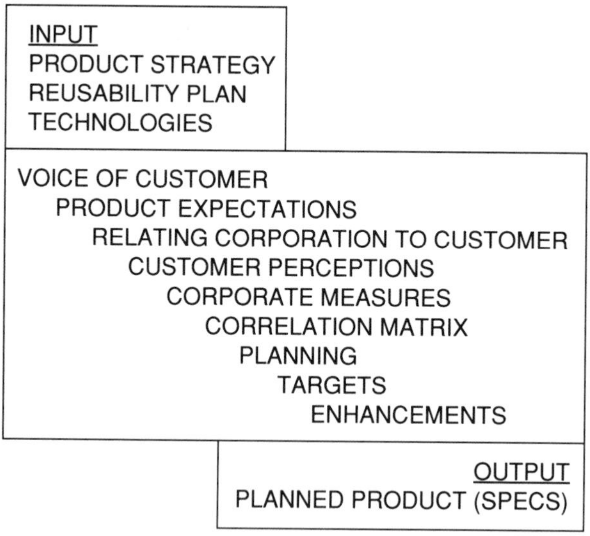

INPUT
PRODUCT STRATEGY
REUSABILITY PLAN
TECHNOLOGIES

VOICE OF CUSTOMER
   PRODUCT EXPECTATIONS
      RELATING CORPORATION TO CUSTOMER
        CUSTOMER PERCEPTIONS
          CORPORATE MEASURES
            CORRELATION MATRIX
            PLANNING
              TARGETS
                ENHANCEMENTS

OUTPUT
PLANNED PRODUCT (SPECS)

FIGURE 4.2. House of Quality subphase of the concept phase.

In QFD (product planning), the voice of the customer is carefully and systematically deployed into the product expectations specifications with the strong help of the House of Quality (Hauser and Clausing, 1988). QFD depends strongly for success upon our having complete multifunctional teams (Pandey and Clausing, 1991). Although in this book the format and steps for this deployment are described in detail, a successful result depends greatly on effective teamwork.

The House of Quality is a matrix diagram with eight fields; we say that it contains eight "rooms." A total of 20 steps are carried out in the eight rooms. The eight rooms and 20 steps are listed as follows:

Room 1—Voice of the customer

(1) Plan.
(2) Interact with customers.
(3) Develop an image of the customers.
(4) Scrub the data to achieve clarity.
(5) Select significant voices.
(6) Structure the needs.
(7) Characterize customer needs.

Room 2—Product expectations

(8) Develop product (corporate) expectations (responsive to the voice of the customer).
(9) Organize product expectations.
(10) Define tests for corporate expectations.

Room 3—Relating the corporation to the customer

(11) Complete the relationship matrix.
(12) Verify the fidelity of the product expectations.

Room 4—Customer perceptions: benchmarking

(13) Complete the customer competitive survey.

Room 5—Corporate measures: benchmarking

(14) Perform competitive technical tests.
(15) Check customer perceptions, objective measures, and the relationship matrix for consistency.

Room 6—Correlation matrix: evaluate specs together

(16) Complete the correlation matrix (the triangular attic of the house).

Room 7—Planning: concentrate on the crucial few expectations

(17) Calculate design requirements' importance ratings.
(18) Evaluate the technical difficulty of meeting the product expectations.

Room 8—Targets: quantified expectations

(19) Determine specification values for the new product.

Review

(20) Analyze the quality planning table (HoQ) and select areas for concentrated effort.

These eight rooms and 20 steps for successful product planning will now be described.

VOICE OF THE CUSTOMER—ROOM 1

Other ways of thinking of the voice of the customer include

- Customer needs
- Customer requirements
- Customer desires
- Customer attributes

Customers' needs are typically obtained in qualitative interviews. The interviews develop and identify the needs of customers in prose statements. Typically, each need is a short phrase. In room 1 it is important to stay close to customers' own language, not modifying it to achieve closer conformity to corporate standards. Some examples of the customers' voice for a copier are shown in Figure 4.3.

Obtaining the voice of the customer requires four generic activities, which will be described here in seven steps, following closely on the Ph.D. thesis of Gary Burchill (1993):

Generic Activity	Steps
Immerse in context and obtain voice	1, 2, and 3
Clarify	4 and 5
Structure	6
Characterize	7

The team can choose one of several successful approaches, some of which have different numbers of steps.

Step 1 is actually somewhat broader, since the team can use it to plan all seven steps, or even its entire House of Quality development. After the completion of tasks in room 1, the team will have knowledge of the clarified, structured, and characterized voices of the customers, grounded in the context of the customers' use of the product and feelings about it.

	VOICE OF CUSTOMER
1	ALWAYS GET A COPY
2	NO BLANK SHEETS
3	NO JAMS TO CLEAR
4	MEDIUM SPEED
5	COPIES ON CHEAP PAPER
6	COPIES ON HEAVY PAPER
7	COPIES ON LIGHT PAPER
8	EASY TO CLEAR JAMS
9	NO PAPER DAMAGE
10	LOW COST

FIGURE 4.3. Examples of voices of customers.

The seven steps in the process for bringing in the voice of the customer will be described sequentially. In actual practice there will be many small iteration loops. We cycle back to earlier steps in light of new perceptions that have emerged from later steps. Also, we may develop a slightly different path through the steps. The important objective is to develop the same sort of detailed guidance that is provided by the following seven steps.

Step 1—Plan

The team plans the interactions with customers—and to some extent, it plans the entire House of Quality activity at this point. It is important at the outset to ensure that the success factors are in place. Pandey and Clausing (1991) found that the following factors were related to successful implementation of QFD:

- Completeness of multifunctional teams
- Management support (both top and middle management)
- Integration of QFD into total quality development
- Flexibility in adapting QFD

Top management support can be made real by the formation of a steering committee. After the success factors are in place, the team starts to plan for bringing in the voice of the customer.

We are immediately confronted with a major question: *Who are the customers?* Consistent with corporate strategies (Chapter 8), we define the market segment that will be explored. The level of abstraction is important: Are we going to search out the most important customer needs for a

- Black Lexus 400?
- Lexus?
- Luxury car?
- Car?
- Road vehicle?
- Means of transportation?

In addition to the market segment, we must make decisions about the type of user:

- Lead user, or first to try new concepts (von Hippel, 1988)?
- Satisfied customer?
- Dissatisfied customer?
- Former customer?
- Customers who have never bought our products?

Also, purchasers and users have different needs. For many consumer products, purchasers and users are the same people. However, for many products we need to interact with separate users and purchasers. This includes purchasers at all levels. We may sell to a system integrator, who sells to a distributor, who sells to a retailer. We should regard all of them as our customers. For example, if we sell through retailers, good shelf space is important. What is the voice of the retailer?

Customers will not always say everything that is required. Some things are taken for granted. Thus, if we ask customers about an airplane trip, they may give much information about the needs for food, check-in, and baggage retrieval. They may not explicitly state that they need to be flown from Boston to Detroit; that is an implicit need. We have to be sure that they get on the plane for Detroit, not Atlanta. Most important, we have to ensure that the plane and crew have a high probability of arriving at the destination safely. The day-to-day application of this need has been implicitly turned over by our customers to the FAA, a regulatory agency.

Also, the customers will not usually give voice to latent needs right away. Bringing these out requires careful questioning. Why does the customer want something? How will that something be used? Understanding both customers' use of a product and the product's technological possibilities will uncover the latent needs.

An entire category of needs is addressed by regulation. Standards—governmental or otherwise—require that certain characteristics be present in the product. It is best simply to treat these as additional customer needs. They are customer needs that are so widely perceived in our society that they have been codified as societal requirements. Typically these would be represented in the House of Quality by a row, "regulatory requirements." Unless the QFD activity is aimed specifically at improving compliance with the regulatory requirements, the row is usually not further defined in more detail.

The team plans the number and types of interactions with customers. The number is typically in the range of 10 to 100. There are many different types of interaction. Some examples are

- Individual interviews
- Telephone interviews
- Mailed questionnaires
- Focus groups
- Contextual inquiry

The team attempts to obtain various types of information from potential customers:

- Images (scenes or emotions) related to the use of the product
- Role of the product in their lives
- Specific needs
- Importance of each need
- Characterization of each need—for example, the Kano characterization (see page 121 for a further explanation of Professor Kano's work):
  - This is something I must have.
  - The better it is, the better I like it.
  - That would delight me!

Typically, not all of these are addressed in one interaction with customers. Therefore, we plan the set of interactions to obtain all types of information.

The team takes all of these considerations into account while selecting the customers and planning the interactions. Questionnaires and interview guidelines are developed. The team practices using them to gain skill and confidence. Then the team is ready to interact with the customers.

Step 2—Interact with Customers

There are several types of beneficial interactions with customers. Here we describe individual interviews and contextual inquiry.

Interview

Typically, the interview is one to two hours in length. There are two primary styles:

- Two interviewers (one talks and the other transcribes)
- One interviewer with an audio recorder

The advocates of each style are effective in utilizing their favored approach.

We obtain essential understanding by probing underneath the immediate responses. Why does the customer want what he or she says? That the customer wants a product like the Lexus 400 does not help us very much. What is it about the Lexus 400 that appeals to the customer? Styling? What is it about the styling that is appealing? Focus on the customer's use of the product, not on technical details that are primarily interesting only to the product people. Keep probing for latent needs. "If you had feature X, how would you benefit?"

After each interview, a review or debriefing is helpful. What did the customer say? What was the customer's environment like? Make notes that capture your fresh reflections. Also, how can the interviewing technique be improved? Share observations with team members.

The leader of the team during this step of bringing in the voice of the customer may be a person with a market research background. However, it is highly beneficial for team members with diverse backgrounds to participate in the customer interviews and the other interactions with the customers. Many product developers have never met a customer. A little interaction will greatly enhance their perspective. One very informative type of activity is field calls. When I was at Xerox the product development people were encouraged to spend a day with a service person making calls. The protocol was that *we* carried the tool bag. That strongly discouraged new designs that would add to the number of required service tools.

The team usually obtains both specific needs and customer images in the first round of interactions. The record of the interview is reviewed, and each need and image is documented on a separate card or Post-it note, to be used in the next step. Several hundred separate notes are typically compiled.

Contextual Inquiry

Contextual inquiry is observation of the customer's needs as expressed in actions rather than words. Customers have been satisfying their needs by using one of the company's existing products or a competitor's product. The team will want to observe them using the product in their normal context. The team seeks data that will help it to *support, extend,* and *transform* the customer's activities. In order to achieve these goals, it focuses on what customers actually do, rather than on what they say they want. Ultimately the team wants to transform the customer's activity by making it more useful or attractive.

When we visit the customer "on site," we strive to be open and aware of all contextual aspects. The most important aspects of the context are the ones that differ most from our own experience and assumptions. Important aspects are location, people, culture, and values.

Once I was making the rounds with a Xerox service representative. While we had a copier apart and were immersed in parts and black toner, the building fire alarm sounded. The last thing that we wanted to do was leave our mess, but we had to exit the building. This helped me to understand *location* in the context of the service representative's workplace. We focus on the location in which our product is used.

Other important aspects of the context provide similar food for thought. A product that one is used to using alone may seem to work differently in the presence of other *people*. When coworkers, colleagues, friends, students, teachers, patients, clients, teammates, or antagonists look over your shoulder, you may find the product harder to use. Some people you share the product with may forget to turn off the power or close the lid.

In a *culture* where open shirts are the norm, neckties will not be a good product; we want to be sensitive to the effect of culture on the use of our product. *Values* on the other hand, refers to what is important to the customer; they determine the difference between success and failure in the mind of the customer.

In doing contextual inquiry we seek to become partners with our customer. We have special knowledge about our product; our customer has special knowledge about the use of our product. This is quite different from the asymmetrical relationship in an interview. The interviewer asks the question, the customer responds. Our roles are different. In contextual inquiry our roles are similar. We are both experts seeking to share and create an overlap between our areas of expertise.

As we continue our contextual inquiry with customers, we may develop some design ideas. By sharing them we give the customer the opportunity to validate the idea, or to suggest improvements.

The contextual inquiry interaction with the customer has three main stages:

- Introduction
- Observation
- Summary

In the introduction, we remind the customer of the purpose of our visit. Then we ask the customer to describe the activity of using our type of product. We seek information about the timing of the use. We ask open-ended questions about the environment, including location, people, culture, and values.

We ask the customer to show us the activity so that we can observe it. If the activity is too drawn out in time to observe in its entirety, we observe some segment of it that is of interest. Also, we ask to see tangible items that result from the activity. Examples are documents, models, work in progress, demonstrations, and diagrams.

At the end, we summarize what we have learned, and we show the customer a flow diagram of the activity. We ask the customer for clarification and correction.

Back at the office, we conclude in the same way as for the interview. We cull the record of our interaction with the customer, and document each need or image on a card or Post-it note.

Step 3—Develop an Image of the Customers

We organize the "image" notes—the notes recording the phrases that express the customers' images in relation to the use of our product. This forms an integrated image of the customer that will help us understand the context of the specific needs, which we will analyze next. We place the image notes on a table or wall so that the entire team can view them. Usually there will be too many. If the team tried to use all of them, it would soon be lost in a blizzard of notes. The team prioritizes the images, usually by some form of team voting. Then roughly the top 20 images are selected for further learning.

The selected images are then analyzed and organized so that the team can form a better impression of the mind-set of the customers. A very good method is for the team to form a KJ diagram of the images.[1] The complete set of notes is organized into what we might call "affinity groups," or families of ideas. The most detailed images are organized into fewer categories that represent a higher level of integration and abstraction. This organization of images is continued through as many levels as is useful, usually two or three. This is done by organizing the notes on a large sheet of paper. The affinity groups are named, highlighted, and related to each other with the use of colored pens. The large, colorful KJ diagram of images is a visual, connective focal point of attention for the team.

The preparation of the image KJ (which in the full process has 19 steps) gives the team great insight into the emotional side of customers' relationships with the product. An example of an image is "driving the car through a blizzard to get a mother in labor to the hospital." Another example is "fish jumping out of the water to grab the lure." The insights from the images are then used as the grounding context for the development of the final statement of customers' needs.

After the team has developed a better understanding of the customers' environment, including the more emotional and subjective reactions of customers to the product, this is then used as the basis for distilling from the raw data the specific customer needs that will be used to guide product development.

Step 4—Scrub the Data to Achieve Clarity

We can easily have several hundred specific statements of needs. In the raw data from the customers, there are many ambiguous phrases and duplications with not exactly the same wording. Therefore, we now have to "scrub" the data by editing the cards, clarifying ambiguities, separat-

---

[1] KJ stands for Kawakita, Jiro, the Japanese anthropologist who developed the method. A good explanation of KJ diagrams is found in Shiba, Graham, and Walden (1993).

ing composite thoughts, and bringing all statements to the same level of abstraction when appropriate. Duplications are identified, and the best wording is selected. The team quickly iterates through alternative compositions, until clear understanding and agreement on the best statement for each need is achieved.

The team associates each customer statement with the image KJ. This helps it to identify duplications. Also, it helps the team to understand customers' feelings and perspectives underlying a specific requirement. In some cases, specific statements that are not quite duplications are grouped together, and the higher-level category that includes them is carried forward. This helps to reduce the quantity of *needs* to a manageable number.

In scrubbing customers' statements of needs, the team strives for

- Clarity
- Statements styled so that they naturally lead to continuous variables
- Faithfulness to the voice of the customer

We are not yet trying to translate the voice of the customer. That comes in room 2. Now we strive for a clear statement that best captures all of the similar voices on one specific need in a way that reflects the images.

Clarity will help the team during the subsequent work. For a copier an example of poor communication is a statement such as:

The geometry of the surface of the copy shall not deviate from the vertical planar surface that is most nearly parallel to the major axis of the paper.

This statement should read:

Copy has little curl.

It is best to state needs in a way that implies a continuous variable: "little curl," rather than "shall not deviate." We understand that zero curl is the ideal. We need to think in terms of the customer's sensitivity, not absolute statements that do not provide useful guidance.

At the completion of step 4, the team has a well-stated set of customer needs. The total number of customer needs has been greatly reduced from the number of statements in the raw data. However, there will usually still be more needs than can be effectively used to guide the development of the new product.

Step 5—Select Significant Voices

The customers' needs are prioritized so that the team can concentrate on the vital few needs that will make the product successful. Working with too many needs has caused some early applications of the House of Quality to bog down.

It is often helpful to do a quick grouping of the needs. The total set of notes is divided among the team. One note is stuck onto the wall, and read aloud. Then any team member who has a note showing a similar need sticks it near the first one. Again, duplicates are identified and collapsed into one need if appropriate.

Then the team again uses team voting (as was done to select the images) to select the customer needs that will best guide product development. Before the vote is taken, the selection criteria are discussed. These are oriented toward the customers, with guidance from the images they have furnished. The corporation's strategic intent is also taken into account. If the primary strategic thrust of a new copier is better image quality, then customer needs in this area will be given priority.

Team voting is used to select a relatively small number of customer needs, often 15 to 30. These are the needs that will be carried forward to guide the concept selection and all aspects of the product development. In some cases the identification and clear understanding of only one customer need has had a major impact on the new product. The objective is not to satisfy large numbers of needs, but to develop strategic insights that will guide the new product to superior customer satisfaction.

Step 6—Structure the Needs

The team now prepares a KJ diagram for the customer needs. The organization of the needs into affinity groups gives great insight into the total set of needs. This insight is used further to refine the statement of needs.

In work that was done at Toyota Autobody in the late 1970s, more than 900 customer attributes were compiled and organized into a total of eight levels of customer attributes. The detailed phrases on separate cards or fliers were the eighth level. At the highest level, level 1, there were only four customer requirements. In other words, the more than 900 requirements had been grouped into only four categories. At the second level there were 13 categories. In one of the areas that was selected for concentrated effort—rust prevention—there were 53 detailed voices of the customer. At the sixth level these were organized into seven categories.

Although Toyota Autobody used more than 900 customer needs to select major improvement projects and then used 53 needs to guide its highly successful rust prevention developments, it is now more common to identify roughly 20 needs, which are organized into two or three levels. For some purposes the higher-level categories will be more useful than the detailed requirements. The needs, including the higher-level categories, are entered into room 1 of the House of Quality; an example was shown in Figure 4.3.

The team now has two KJ diagrams, one for images and the second for the specific needs. The team has also developed the connections between the two KJ diagrams. This gives the team the insights into the *customer needs* which enables it to receive guidance from the customers. Further insight is gained by characterizing the needs.

Step 7—Characterize Customer Needs

Characterization of the needs helps the team to concentrate its efforts in areas that will make the company's product more competitive. Two important characterizations are:

- Importance
- A Kano diagram

Kano Analysis

Professor N. Kano has developed a very useful diagram for characterizing customer needs (Figure 4.4). The abscissa is the degree of corporate

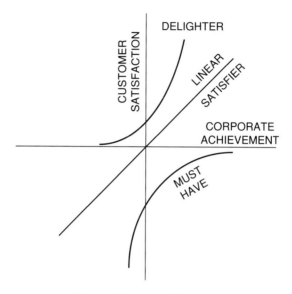

FIGURE 4.4. Kano diagram.

success in responding to the need. The ordinate measures customer satisfaction as a result of the corporate achievement.

There are three primary types of needs as perceived by customers:

- Must have
- Linear satisfier
- Delighter

The must-have requirements are represented by the bottom curve. No matter how well we do, the customer simply accepts it as something that is expected. However, if we do not meet the need sufficiently, the customer becomes very dissatisfied. In a car, for example, if the paint maintains its appearance, the customer accepts it with little increase in satisfaction. If the paint fades, however, the customer is very unhappy.

The second type of need is the linear satisfier. The better we do, the better the customer likes it. For a car, an example, is gas mileage. The customer might expect average mileage but his or her satisfaction increases as the mileage-per-gallon of gas increases.

The third type of customer attribute is the delighter. If we do not accomplish it, the customer in not unhappy. The delighter is not expected, so its absence does not cause dissatisfaction. Strong achievement in design delights the customer. For a car, a programmable suspension might be a delighter. For a copier, a paper feeder that automatically unwraps the paper could provide great delight to users, who would not have to struggle with the wrappers.

The latter example does represent a common problem. It already anticipates a design solution, the automatic unwrapper. Here, during product planning, we simply note the need not to struggle with wrappers. This leaves the solution open to creativity. For example, a paper wrapper that is much easier to open could be developed. Of course, any good concepts are discussed among the team members and noted for inclusion during concept generation and selection. It is one of the objectives of the preparation of the House of Quality to inspire the team to generate new concepts in response to customers' needs. However, in the House of Quality itself, we simply note needs, leaving the field open for creative solutions later on.

The data to prepare the Kano diagram are obtained through a questionnaire directed to customers. Two questions are asked for each customer need. The need is stated both positively and negatively. For example,

- Positive: If the copier delivers one sheet of paper, how do you feel?
- Negative: If the copier misfeeds or multifeeds, how do you feel?

For both versions of the question, the customer is given the same five options:

(1) I like it that way.
(2) It must be that way.
(3) I am neutral.
(4) I can live with it that way.
(5) I dislike it.

The answers are then interpreted by using the diagram in Table 4.1. For example, the answer to our positive question about misfeeds is number

TABLE 4.1 Kano Interpretation

		Negative statement				
		1	2	3	4	5
	1	Q	D	D	D	L
Positive	2	R	I	I	I	M
statement	3	R	I	I	I	M
	4	R	I	I	I	M
	5	R	R	R	R	Q

Numbers refer to the five options.
Customer requirement is: D—delighter; M—must have; R—reverse; L—linear satisfier; Q—questionable result; I—indifferent.

2, "It must be that way." The answer to the negative question is number 5, "I dislike it." Entering the matrix at the second row and fifth column, we find that the avoidance of misfeeds is a must-have characteristic.

Category I in the table means that the customers are neutral. Their satisfaction is not strongly affected by it. R and Q indicate a problem with the question or the data gathering.

Each cell in Table 4.1 will have a percentage number entered that represents the percentage of respondents who answered in that cell. Usually there is a dominant characterization.

The Kano characterizations are entered into the rows of room 1 in the House of Quality.

Importance

Customers are asked to rank the importance of each of their needs. There are many detailed methods for doing this. One that is frequently used is to give the customer three options:

Rating	Weight
1. Very important	9
2. Important	3
3. Somewhat important	1

Then one of the importance weights (9, 3, or 1) is entered alongside the customer need in the row of room 1 of the House of Quality. The weight that is chosen can be based on the mean, median, or mode of all the replies that are received.

An alternate approach to organizing the customer needs (step 6) and determining their importance is to let the customers do both together. Each need is noted on a card, and a full set of cards (roughly 100) is sent to approximately 100 customers. They are asked to group the cards in piles that seem similar. Then they pick the need (card) in each pile that seems to best represent that pile and put it on top. Next, each customer picks the pile that is most important to him or her and marks it 100. Then all of the other piles are marked with a number that represents its importance relative to the most important pile (the one marked 100). The customer is also asked to evaluate his or her current product relative to the need represented by each pile. The customer then returns the cards to be analyzed. Typically, the return rate is about 70%.

This approach is part of a commercial service, available under the name VOCALYST® (Klein, 1990) from Applied Marketing Science, Inc., in Waltham, Massachusetts. The data from the returned cards are entered into a computer program that performs a statistical clustering analysis. This determines the best clustering (affinity groups) from all of the returned sets of cards, the importance, and the best name for each group (from the top card on each pile). The VOCALYST® approach has the advantage that the customer's voice defines and rank-orders the affinity groups. The approach used in the KJ diagram has the advantage that the team generates great insight and commitment. Both approaches are excellent, and both can be used concurrently.

After completion of the seventh step, room 1 is complete. The team reviews all of the information, displayed visually on a big surface, to internalize the customers' viewpoint. After the voices of the customers have been thoroughly understood, the challenge is to translate them into corporate language that is objective, quantitative, and operational.

PRODUCT EXPECTATIONS—ROOM 2

Other names for product expectations are:

- Design requirements
- Corporate expectations
- Product requirements
- Product expectation characteristics
- Engineering characteristics
- Substitute quality characteristics

The columns in the House of Quality are the characteristics that are expected to be achieved in the new product. They are a restatement of the customer needs in corporate language. The customer needs will usually be stated in language that is somewhat subjective and qualitative. The product expectations are a restatement of the same needs in more objective, technical, and quantitative language.

Step 8—Develop the Product Expectations

In room 2 we begin to describe a product that we would really like to deliver, that we believe will be very responsive to the customer. We translate from the voice of the customer into clear statements of what we want the product to do and be.

As an example of the need for transformation from customer attributes to corporate product expectations, consider the cleaning of a kitchen blender. In the customer's voice, "The blender should be easy to clean." One engineer might think this means that the blender can be cleaned in 30 seconds with a damp cloth while the user is watching television. Another engineer might think that 4 minutes of undivided attention, with a damp cloth, brush, and cotton swab, is easy cleaning. Thus, our deployment must be specific and quantitative to ensure (1) that the product will have a competitive advantage and (2) that everyone will be working to fulfill the same requirement.

Broad categories of questions that need to be addressed in developing the product expectations are:

(1) What is the function of the product?
(2) What is the state (size, for example) of the product?
(3) What costs are involved?
(4) What sort of buying experience will customers encounter?

(5) What will be experienced in the field (in service, for example)?

Function of the Product

What is the product expected to do, and under what conditions of use is it expected to perform its functions? For a copier, the simple verb-noun functional description is MAKE COPY. What is the environment (*noises*, in robustness terminology) in which the copier is expected to make copies? What reliability and life are expected?

The functions of the product can be outlined in a functional tree. (This will be described in more detail in Chapter 5.) The top-level function for a copier is MAKE COPY. Below that will be many functions that contribute to the making of a copy, such as FEED SHEET. This is the top-level function for the copy-paper feeder.

Of course, when we say "feed sheet," we have much more in mind: types of paper, environment, misfeed rate, multifeed rate, avoidance of paper damage, safety. These are the characteristics that appear in the columns of the House of Quality, spelled out in room 2. We can think of these product expectation characteristics as amplifications of the functional requirements for the product. Thus, we can think of the corporate product expectations as having two sources:

(1) Deployed from the voice of the customer (room 1)
(2) Amplified from functional requirements

Using both views helps the team to develop the best set of characteristics.

State of the Product

Examples of variables that describe the state of the product are

- Weight
- Size
- Aesthetics (appearance, taste, smell, sound, feel)
- Ergonomics
- Corrosion resistance

Costs

Costs include manufacturing cost and service cost. Other costs will also have to be taken into account, such as distribution and selling costs.

Buying Experience

Will customers find and purchase the product easily? Will it be given shelf space and displayed attractively? Other aspects of the buying experience include shipping (distribution), packaging, and shelf life.

Field Experience

How will the product be installed? Who will maintain it? What tools will be available? How easy will it be to maintain? What documentation will be provided for installation, operation, and service? What tendency will it have to cause pollution? What will be the end-of-life disposal method? What political and social constraints will exist in the marketplace? An example of the latter would be the avoidance of a product that contains pork in a culture where the predominant religion rejects pork.

The team can review all the preceding elements of product expectations before beginning room 1, to help design the plan for bringing in the voice of the customer. Of course, these elements will not all be addressed in the House of Quality. Here we emphasize those crucial few that will guide us to competitive advantage. However, all of the elements need to be addressed by the team.

Usually we can take greatest advantage of the House of Quality methodology by concentrating on a few characteristics that will make our new product stand out from the competition, an attraction to customers. We avoid a tendency toward large numbers of characteristics. The most successful expectations emphasize a few characteristics that are very important to customers. The DC-3 airplane, one of the most successful products of all time, started with only one page of specifications (Allen, 1988). It contained only six items. At the next level of detail it still had only 16 items. The important characteristics of a new product reflect new or optional features, or address unmet needs and wishes of customers. If we can develop understanding of the customers' belief systems, major opportunities may become evident. For example, consumers tend to believe that a facial tissue cannot be both soft and strong. There-fore, if we can develop a tissue that is both soft and strong, our product can delight the customers.

The product expectations (room 2 of the House of Quality) define the requirements for the subsequent design activity. Usually they should not contain design decisions, since this would overly constrain creative design opportunities to satisfy the basic objective. For example, the per-centage of meat in a spaghetti sauce is a design decision and probably should not appear in the House of Quality. Instead, we should include the primary characteristics that create the response of the customers: taste, smell, feel, and appearance.

Occasionally, however, there are exceptions in which design decisions are included in room 2. If the standard for upholstery in luxury cars is leather, as in a Jaguar, then the product expectation can simply say that. However, since that would not provide competitive advantage, it is best omitted from the House of Quality. We prioritize to focus the House of Quality on those product expectations that will make our product a suc-cess.

We must be careful not to include only the characteristics that we know how to measure well. Our corporation may have laboratories full of test technicians, but if their traditional measurements are not sufficiently responsive to our new understanding of customer needs, then changes are required. In some cases this can mean significant changes in organi-zation and work practices. In the effective approach, technical specialists meet with customers and acquire better understanding of their needs. This practice tends to overcome unwarranted perpetuation of traditional measurements.

Step 9—Organize the Product Expectations

Once the product expectations have been compiled, the team organizes them into logical categories in a way that is similar to the structuring that was done for the customer needs (room 1). Again, techniques such as team voting and KJ diagrams can be used. Characteristics such as torque, speed, and gas mileage might be included as part of a higher-level attribute described as engine performance. For some of the subsequent work, the higher-level, more abstract (broader-scope) characteristics are used, while areas that require more attention are developed by using the detailed expectations.

Step 10—Define Tests for the Product Expectations

Each product expectation must be capable of being measured. Therefore, the team must ensure that for each characteristic there is a well-defined, appropriate test for measuring the value. Many tests are very technical tests in which a variable is measured on a continuous scale. Every effort should be made to develop metrics of continuous variables that correlate well with customer satisfaction. For continuous variables, it is now common practice to include symbols in the columns of room 2 to indicate that the characteristic is one of the following:

(1) Bigger is better.
(2) Smaller is better.
(3) Nominal is best.

An example of the latter is 24 volts for a power supply. The customer wants the nominal value (24 volts), not a bigger value, not a smaller value.

For some product expectations—the taste of a pizza, for example—there is no known technical characteristic that can be measured with a continuous variable. The characteristic depends on the complex reactions of human beings. In these cases the test is usually some kind of jury test. A jury of people is asked to undergo the experience—for example, tasting a pizza—and to rate it on a scale, from poor to excellent, for example. These qualitative categories may be given numbers such as 1 through 5, and then these numbers can be used in quantitative analysis.

Jury tests are one form of customer-simulated test. The pizza jury simulates a group of pizza customers. Customer-simulated tests can be used for many products. For example, temporary employees can be contracted to test copiers in a mode that is similar to normal office operation. However, in traditional product development, customer-simulated tests have been resorted to excessively, too early in the development program. Typically, these tests have not been conceived to measure variability, and so robust variability reduction is not achieved. The program is greatly accelerated by finding good technical measures that are the underlying causes for customer satisfaction and by early application of the measures, with quick improvement of the values.

Intermediate between the technical measurement of continuous variables by instrumentation and consumer juries, such as taste juries, are expert testers. For example, expert testers of cars provide highly developed evaluations of such handling characteristics as cornering confidence, roll control, ability to change lanes in an emergency, and torque steer (front-wheel drive).

Measurements of a continuous performance variable enable quick improvement. Therefore, we make every attempt to devise a test in which a continuous variable is measured. It is especially poor practice to measure a continuous variable and then simply divide it into categories such as good and bad. This is an extension of the basic concept (see Figure 3.12) that quality loss is a better metric than the number of defects. Once a continuous variable measurement is available, it should be *used* as the characteristic; dividing ranges of the variable into categories will only degrade the information.

For cleaning a kitchen blender, we will probably want to address both manual cleaning and the use of a dishwasher. For manual cleaning the specification would define the materials that are expected to be available—soft cloth, hot water, soap—and the maximum time to clean (which is included in the targets in room 8). Here we wish to define a good achievement; the design to achieve it will start taking form after the product specification is completed. In the product specification, we do not state that the product can be disassembled in three steps in less than 30 seconds, that it will incorporate PVC plastic because it is easy to clean, or that all gaps will be less than 0.1 mm. This would place excessive constraint on the design and would exclude some creative design approaches that might achieve very easy cleaning.

Writing a good product expectation requires walking a narrow path between too much constraint and insufficient specificity. The product expectation must constrain our expectation of the product so that the design that responds to the expectation will be competitive and everyone will work to the same requirements. However, we do not want to be so constraining as to shut out creative design approaches that might be very successful. The product expectation should usually not indicate a design approach, but should state a minimum expected achievement for the design approach that is eventually selected. Preparing clear product expectations that will guide us to success is very challenging and important work.

Examples of expectations for the total product system are shown in Figure 4.5 for a copier.

At our initial completion of room 2, we have a clear, quantifiable, and structured statement of our expectations for the new product. We have tried to make our expectations responsive to the customers. However, this has been such a serious problem that next we work to strengthen the responsiveness of our expectations to the customers' needs.

RELATING THE CORPORATION TO THE CUSTOMER—ROOM 3

In traditional product planning, product expectations have often not been highly responsive to the customers. To overcome this problem, the team uses the relationship matrix to ensure that corporate product expectations (room 2) are a high-fidelity translation of customer needs (room 1).

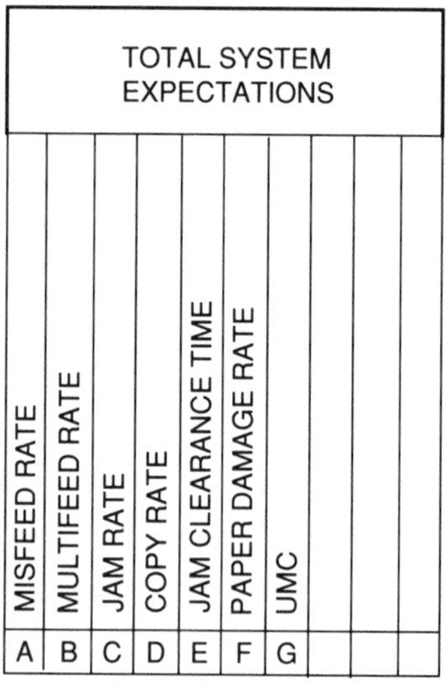

FIGURE 4.5. Examples of total system expectations.

Step 11—Evaluate the Relationship Matrix

In preparing the relationship matrix (room 3, in Figure 3.5), the team addresses each cell in the matrix. In addressing any one cell the question is asked, If the product expectation (column) is successfully achieved (during subsequent design), will there be a strong, moderate, weak, or negligible tendency to satisfy the customer requirement (row)? Here it is absolutely critical that there be a multifunctional team working in a consensual style. It is easy for the bias of the various corporate functions and individuals to creep in. If the relationship matrix were done by an individual, it would undoubtedly be very different from the results achieved by a multifunctional team. The multifunctional team must resolve differences and converge on a consensus for each cell that best represents the responsiveness of the corresponding product expectation to the specific customer need.

A variety of symbols and numerics are used in the relationship matrix. It is common practice simply to use symbols for all positive responses in completing the relationship matrix. The fact that some product expectations may be partially negative in their effect is then captured solely in the attic of the House of Quality (to be described shortly). It is common practice to use three symbols for positive relationships. One symbol, often two concentric circles (◎), represents a product expectation that strongly tends to satisfy the customer need; it is given a strong weight, most commonly 9. A second symbol, often a single circle (○), represents a product expectation that moderately tends to satisfy the particular customer need; it is given a moderate weight, most commonly 3. A third symbol, often a triangle (△), represents a product expectation that has a weak tendency to satisfy the customer need and is given a weak weight, often 1. Of course, a blank cell means that the product expectation is not responsive to the customer need—a weight of zero.

It is a common error to fill amost every cell in the relationship matrix with a symbol. This reflects the common misconception that nearly everything is related to nearly everything else. However, in preparing the relationship matrix it is best to maintain a somewhat higher hurdle for significance. Experience has shown that for the relationship matrix to be most useful, fewer than half of the cells should contain a symbol. Actually, many of the good relationship matrices are quite sparse. It may be that it is best to strive for having only one-quarter to one-third of the cells filled. Of course, the objective is not to fill a certain percentage of the cells, but simply to maintain a realistic hurdle of significance so that every slight relationship isn't being noted. Once this hurdle of significance has been raised high enough, then the resultant filling of the cells should simply be accepted as the result of sound consideration by the team.

The evaluation of the relationship matrix by the multifunctional team usually involves a considerable amount of discussion. The various corporate functions have different viewpoints, and consensus does not come quickly for some cells in the matrix. These differences can easily get out of hand; the matrix could take several person-years to be completed. Since this amount of effort is rarely warranted, the following approaches keep the time within reasonable limits:

(1) Do not allow the matrix to become too large. Impose strong priorities on rooms 1 and 2 so that the matrix is not larger than roughly 30×30.

(2) Rank-order the customer needs (room 1), and complete the relationship matrix in descending order of rank. Fix a time limit, and stop when the time has expired.

(3) Take a poll at the beginning of the consideration of each cell. If there is consensus, do not discuss; immediately move on to the next cell.

The team can evaluate the relationships on two primary considerations:

(1) Does it make sense in principle?
(2) Is it supported by field observations?

If the answers to both questions are yes, then the evaluation is probably correct. When the product expectation is a new feature, there will not be any historical field data, and some discrete market research will be helpful.

Step 12—Verify Fidelity of Expectations

After the initial completion of the relationship matrix, we check for completeness. Empty rows or columns are a sure sign of trouble. Basically, an empty row means that there is a customer attribute unpaired with a product expectation. This will obviously lead to failure to fulfill a customer need. Inversely, an empty column suggests that we are planning to satisfy some product expectation for which no customer need has been identified. If further consideration by the multifunctional team verifies this initial conclusion, then a change must be made. In the case of an empty row, an additional product expectation is needed; in the case of an empty column, it would appear that the product expectation can be deleted. However, it could also be that some customer needs do exist but have not yet been identified.

A column with too many relationship symbols in it has probably been defined too broadly.

The team iterates around the loop of rooms 1, 2, and 3 until consensus is reached that the three rooms are consistent. This is already a marked improvement over tradition. The corporate expectations are responsive to customers and are well understood by team members from all of the corporate functions. If we do a super job of achieving success in rooms 1, 2, and 3, we will already have traveled a long distance toward meeting the customer's needs.

Although the evaluation of the relationship matrix by the team can be hard work, it has great benefits. It is hard work because functional differences and other variations in perception are brought into the open and resolved. If they weren't, they would remain very strong after the product planning was completed and could cause great mischief during the remaining stages of development. Team members learn from each other; this pays off in both the current development project and future projects. The hard work pays off in team understanding, consensus, and commitment to the corporate product expectations, which have been made responsive to the customers.

Next, we turn to benchmarking to better understand the current best products.

CUSTOMER PERCEPTIONS (BENCHMARKING)—ROOM 4

Step 13—Complete Customer Competitive Survey

The team searches out and graphically displays the customers' perceptions of existing products. It is important to have the right market segments, the right products, the right customers, and the right questions.

Clearly, it is desirable to learn the customers' perceptions in the targeted market segment. Also, exploring the next higher market segment is thought-provoking, because features tend to migrate down market as costs decrease and expectations increase.

Typically, one of the products for the benchmarking in room 4 would be the corporation's own current product in the targeted market segment. The team would also want to examine the other leading products—leading in terms of sales, technology, or other traits—as a way of learning a lot about the marketplace.

Lead users (early adopters) are always very informative (von Hippel, 1988). They know the most about the use of the product, and will have valuable insights. Also, the team will want to obtain the perceptions of ordinary users, who may not have such developed instincts about the product but who represent the typical purchaser.

These customer perceptions are usually obtained by a questionnaire, which is designed around the customer attributes (room 1) that have been identified for this market segment. Focus groups are another good method for bringing in the perceptions of customers about existing products. Also, existing consumer literature can be useful in forming a complete perspective on customers' reactions to existing products.

It might become excessively laborious to interrogate customers about every need at the most detailed level in room 1. Two techniques are commonly employed to keep the task within bounds: (1) the questions are based on the second level, the summarized, broader statements of customer needs (note from the previous description that VOCALYST® integrates this step with the customers' formation of the affinity groups); and/or (2) further development of priorities is done to reduce the number of queries to an acceptable limit.

Commonly, customers' perceptions are obtained through written surveys. The most frequently used scale is a simple itemized scale, from very poor, which is scaled as 1, to very good or excellent, which is scaled as

5. Other scales, such as the Likert scale (Urban and Hauser, 1981), can also be used.

Some teams do the work of rooms 1 and 4 together, in one interaction with customers, or go through room 4 directly after room 1. Other teams prefer to obtain the greater understanding that comes from going through rooms 2 and 3 before searching out the customers' perceptions. Some teams show the emerging House of Quality to customers and solicit their reactions.

Interaction with customers to learn their perceptions is often a great eye-opener for the cloistered technical specialists. The successful completion of room 4 gives the team a good start toward quantifying the corporate expectations for the new product.

Next the team evaluates the same products from the corporate viewpoint.

CORPORATE MEASURES (BENCHMARKING)—ROOM 5

Names for the benchmarking of room 5 are *corporate measures*, *technical competitive evaluation*, and *technical competitive benchmarking (CBM)*. These are the results of technical tests on existing products.

Step 14—Perform Competitive Technical Tests

The corporate measures are obtained from the same technical tests that will be subsequently used to evaluate the new product. The technical tests were developed or reexamined by the team during the preparation of room 2. Technical tests provide the corporate technical perspective on the existing products. These evaluations can start at the same time that the customer perceptions are sought for room 4. Some tests for room 5 are already satisfactory and unlikely to be changed by the team's work on rooms 1, 2, and 3. These tests can start at the very beginning, simultaneously with the room 1 work to bring in the voice of the customer.

At the same time that the current products are being measured, it is often beneficial to assess technology trends. This provides another technical perspective on the marketplace.

Step 15—Check for Consistency

After room 5 is initially completed, we will have two evaluations of existing products. One evaluation has been done by customers. The other evaluation has been done by technical people, almost always within our corporation. Now we must compare the two evaluations for consistency. Often, there has been a serious problem: the in-house corporate test does not give similar results to the reactions of the customers. The technical specialists, who may feel very possessive about the test, often resist changing it. A very satisfactory technical test may just not relate well to customers' reactions.

We use the House of Quality as the basis for a comparison between corporate measures and customer perceptions. We check the customer perceptions, the technical competitive benchmarking, and the relationship matrix. The relationship matrix indicates which customer perceptions should be compared with specific technical evaluations. When a lack of consistency between the customer evaluation and our technical evaluation occurs, then we should suspect that there is something wrong with the customer perception evaluation, the technical evaluation, or the relationship matrix. Further work will be needed to resolve this inconsistency and make a correction so that the message is consistent.

Often the tests need further improvement to monitor more closely the technical factors that contribute to customer satisfaction. In evaluating a car, for example, the engineers see the suspension, while the customers feel the handling and ride. If our tests are so great, the engineers might say, why aren't we close to 100% customer satisfaction? This attitude can help lead to great improvement in corporate tests.

The relationship matrix (room 3) was first used by the team to help make corporate product expectations (room 2) consistent with customer needs (room 1). Now the relationship matrix has been used to help ensure that corporate measures are consistent with customer perceptions.

CORRELATION MATRIX: EVALUATE SPECS TOGETHER—ROOM 6

Step 16—Complete the Correlation Matrix

The correlation matrix is the triangular attic at the top of the House of

Quality. It shows the relationships between each pair of product expectations. Particularly important are negative relationships. A negative correlation means that satisfaction of both product requirements during the design activities will be challenging to the team. For example, the peak closing force for a car door is negatively correlated with the ability to seal out wind, rain, and dust. The sealing ability will be enhanced by increased "crush" on the seal, but this will increase the maximum closing force. The negative correlation of two product expectations signals that special attention will be required during the design activity to meet both of these product expectations.

The correlation matrix in the attic of the House of Quality signals an opportunity to overcome inherent conflicts between expectations. It is important not to rush into a premature trade-off. As an illustration of the traditional approach to product development, a product development engineer was once told that customers wanted a door that sealed out wind, rain, and dust. The engineer replied, "No problem—we will use our famous big-bulb weatherstripping; of course, it will take 35 pounds to close the door. Oh, you want 8 pounds; no problem, we will use our famous superslim weatherstripping. Of course, you realize that some wind and water will leak in." As a design engineer, he was pushing for a premature trade-off to make his design task easier. Such trade-offs are nothing more than allocation of failure.

Premature trade-offs are not the objective of the attic in the House of Quality. The objective is to identify conflicts in expectations early so that a major effort can be made to satisfy both expectations. Much later in the development schedule, if we have not been completely successful, we can allocate shortfalls between the expectations. The objective now during product planning is to plan the effort that will give us a good probability of being successful on both expectations. We want to give our customers a door that closes with 8 pounds of push and never leaks.

Conflicting requirements are common. Another example is size and expandability for a workstation computer. Small size is very important to customers. One of the advantages of bringing in the voice of the customer is that the engineers become much more sensitive to the customer's need. A few trips to work sites drive home the need for small size. The customer also wants expandability, the ability to add cards with more memory, and other expanded capabilities.

Although most attention in the attic is frequently on the negative correlations, the positive correlations can be used to help identify major marketing opportunities. For example, if two delighters have a positive correlation, they may make up one superdelighter that can be emphasized during development and, later, in marketing.

The attic also signals the expectations that should be measured especially well. If two expectations that are important to consumers are in conflict, we had better have accurate measurements that correlate very closely with customer feelings. An example is softness and strength for facial tissues. Good customer-oriented measurements enable us to improve both characteristics, and to find the best balance point between them.

New technology will often change the best balance point and enable better functionality for both expectations. An example is active suspensions for automobiles. In the past, there has been an inexorable trade-off between a luxurious ride and cornering ability. Active suspensions greatly improve the ability to achieve both. We must be careful not to become too comfortable with long-standing compromises. New technology creates breakthroughs that we want to provide to our customers.

The attic also provides insights into needed communications among various teams that make up the total product development team (PDT). People working on conflicting expectations must maintain close communications. It may be a signal that two teams should be merged into one to ensure a concentrated attack on the conflicting expectations.

Room 6, the attic of the House of Quality, helps us to optimize the entire product, avoiding suboptimization of the various bits. In combination with room 7 it directs attention to critical issues and opportunities.

PLANNING: CONCENTRATE ON THE CRUCIAL FEW PRODUCT EXPECTATIONS—ROOM 7

Aids in planning the subsequent design and development work that are displayed in the House of Quality are the relative importance of customer attributes; the technical difficulty of the product expectations; and the importance of each product expectation.

The importance ratings of the customer needs are used to calculate the importance values for the product expectations. (1) Importance, (2) difficulty, and (3) conflict (room 6) combined signal the need for concentrated development effort.

Step 17—Calculate Expectation Importance

It is common to use a scale of 1, 3, and 9 to describe the relative importance of the customer attributes. The three symbols for positive responses that were used in the relationship matrix (room 3) are given the weights 1, 3, and 9. Then the importance of each product expectation is found simply by multiplying the importance of each customer attribute by the relationship symbol for the specific product expectation that is being considered, and summing the products, as displayed in Figure 4.6.

The first product expectation in Figure 4.6 has a strong relationship (9, represented by concentric circles) relative to a customer need that has an importance of 3. Then the contribution of this customer need to the importance of the product expectation that is under consideration is 27. This multiplication is carried out for each customer need to which the product expectation is responsive. All of the multiplicative products are added up, and their sum is the importance of the product expectation.

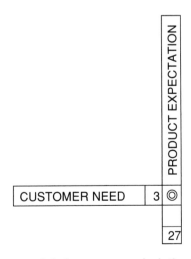

FIGURE 4.6. Importance calculation.

The straightforward calculation of the importance of each product expectation is often sufficient. However, sometimes it can lead to misleading attention to one area simply because that area has been broken down into more detailed (and thus more numerous) characteristics and thus receives a big score. Alertness to this problem will usually lead to easily overcoming it by good judgment and normalizing of the importance scores.

Step 18—Evaluate Technical Difficulty

The multifunctional team judges the difficulty of satisfying each product expectation. The team judgment is entered into each column in room 7, commonly on a simple scale of 1 to 5.

The importance and difficulty of each expectation, and the correlation between each two expectations as found in the attic of the House of Quality, are all used together as aids in planning the subsequent work. If two product expectations are high in importance and high in difficulty and have a strong negative correlation with one another, then it is important on all three counts to plan for special attention to them during the subsequent design activities. Special attention involves using all available design and development methodology, and going into great detail to simultaneously achieve these two important but conflicting characteristics.

Together, the importance and difficulty of expectations and the correlations between them provide strong guidance for planning resources and communications.

TARGETS: QUANTIFIED EXPECTATIONS—ROOM 8

Step 19—Determine Specification Values

The quantified product expectations specifications include both the target values (values that provide ideal customer satisfaction) and the customers' tolerances around the target values. More completely, the product expectations specifications can specify the values that will provide complete customer satisfaction, and also specify some measure of the degradation in customer satisfaction as the values actually achieved deviate from the target values. To be highly relevant, the measure of degradation of customer satisfaction should be monetary. This enables quality to be expressed in the same units as manufacturing cost. As we proceed to consider the entire design and development process, we will find that this ability to have manufacturing cost and quality lost expressed in dollars is overwhelmingly important to the achievement of good balance (trade-off) between cost and quality.

For strong guidance during the subsequent development work, we make a clear distinction among nominal-is-best, smaller-is-better, and bigger-is-better expectations. An example of nominal-is-best is a power supply that is intended to provide 5.2 volts. The customer satisfaction target is 5.2 volts, and we also specify a tolerance, such as ±0.1 volts. We can also implement the quality loss function by stating the quality loss that is expected at the tolerance limits.

For smaller-is-better expectations it is important clearly to recognize that the ideal (unachievable) customer satisfaction target is always zero. Therefore, it does not have to be specified. The specifications that have been traditionally stated are tolerances, or deviations from zero that are judged to be the acceptable limits. There has been some confusion about this, as these tolerance values have often been spoken of as targets. For example, the acceptable background density on a copy was specified to be 0.02, and this was referred to as the target. Of course, the customer really wants zero, a completely white background. Keeping in mind that smaller-is-better specifications are tolerances, not targets, encourages continuous improvement.

Room 8 completes the House of Quality with quantified expectations that are responsive to the customers. In setting the values, we are strongly guided by the competitive benchmarking. The basic starting point is to set the values at best in class for every characteristic, and then to extrapolate to the market entry date for the new product, allowing for continuous improvement.

It is important to set both numbers and definitions for the corporate expectations that will be responsive to customers' needs. In the traditional process the numbers were usually known. However, they were often unrealistic with respect to the competitive marketplace. Even worse, the characteristics themselves were often weakly defined relative to customer perspectives, and often there was a glaring lack of consensus within a corporation regarding the meaning of the expectations. These problems are overcome when the specifications are the result of completing the House of Quality. The specifications that result should be:

(1) Responsive to customers
(2) Competitive
(3) Commonly understood within the corporation (consensus)

Such clear specifications provide the strong foundation for the remainder of the development work.

An example of partially complete rooms 1, 2, 3, and 8 for a copier is shown in Figure 4.7.

VOICE OF CUSTOMER	MISFEED RATE A	MULTIFEED RATE B	JAM RATE C	COPY RATE D	JAM CLEARANCE RATE E	PAPER DAMAGE RATE F	UMC G		
1 ALWAYS GET A COPY	◎								
2 NO BLANK SHEETS		◎							
3 NO JAMS TO CLEAR		○	◎						
4 MEDIUM SPEED				◎					
5 COPIES ON CHEAP PAPER	◎	◎	◎						
6 COPIES ON HEAVY PAPER	◎		◎						
7 COPIES ON LIGHT PAPER		◎	◎						
8 EASY TO CLEAR JAMS					◎				
9 NO PAPER DAMAGE						◎			
10 LOW COST							◎		
	< 70 / 10^6	< 30 / 10^6	< 100 / 10^6	70 +/- 2 CPM	< 20 SEC	< 100 / 10^6	< $6000		

TOTAL SYSTEM EXPECTATIONS

FIGURE 4.7. Example of rooms 1, 2, 3, and 8.

MAKING THE HOUSE A WORKING PLAN

Step 20—Analyze and Select Areas for Concentrated Effort

Finally, after the House of Quality is completed, the team reviews and analyzes it to ensure that the most complete guidance is obtained in carrying out the design and development activities. Now is the time to plan the development tasks in detail. All of the following help the team to plan concentration of effort on the crucial few product expectations:

- Importance ratings
- Difficulty
- Conflicts (identified in the attic, room 6)
- Structure (affinity groups, both needs and images)
- Kano characterization

The House of Quality does not have to be redone for every project. The definitions of the characteristics (voice of customer and product expectations) remain quite stable in many industries and can often be reused for 10 years or more. The importance ratings are more dynamic, as technological advances make delighters more available. Customer satisfaction levels are the most dynamic. Thus, although the values in the House of Quality need frequent updating, the basic structure can often be carried over. Executives of leading QFD companies have called QFD a visible memory of the company.

ENHANCEMENTS: PARAMETRIC ANALYSIS AND MATRIX ANALYSIS; LITERATURE SEARCHES

Other important product planning activities that are not usually recorded in the House of Quality include

- Parametric analysis and matrix analysis
- Literature searches

Parametric analysis and matrix analysis are further ways of evaluating the competition, or, more generally, the status of products and technology in the marketplace. They supplement the competitive benchmarking that is embedded in the House of Quality.

Parametric Analysis

Parametric analysis consists of plotting two characteristics against one another. An example for aerial access platforms, or cherry pickers (Pugh, 1991), is shown in Figure 4.8. This was prepared in the early 1980s and shows the parameter payload multiplied by height plotted against gross vehicle weight. The data are plotted for very many products—as close as possible to 100% of available products. The data tend to fall close to two trend lines. Furthermore, the better performance—the higher line on the graph—tends to be associated with one concept, the articulated boom. The lower performance tends to be associated with an alternative concept, the telescopic boom. However, some articulated booms are on the lower line, which immediately reveals that they have failed to achieve the better performance of most articulated-boom products.

This example helps to illustrate the uses of parametric analysis:

(1) It helps us evaluate whether the concepts are more static or more dynamic.
(2) It helps in guiding concept selection.
(3) It guides major quantitative design decisions.

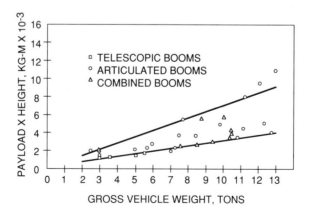

FIGURE 4.8. Example of parametric analysis.

If all products lie on one straight line, the product concept is static. There is a dominant design, which everyone is using. (There is more about static versus dynamic conceptual status in Chapter 8 and about concept selection later in this chapter.) Of great interest are products that lie above the conventional line, indicating some form of change from convention. This could be simply due to an increase in efficiency, or a conceptual breakout. The significance is that parametric analysis leads us to investigate further. In doing concept selection, a concept should be sought that will be superior on the parametric analysis graph. If a static concept is satisfactory, then the trend line can be used to guide the selection of critical parameter values. For example, if we select the articulated concept and require a payload multiplied by a height of 8 kg-m $\times 10^{-3}$, then we should plan on a vehicle weight of 12 tons.

When we do parametric analysis, it is important to make many plots. Raw data are plotted. Also, rational parameters are formed on the basis of dimensional analysis and simple applications of the engineering sciences. It is very beneficial to mount all of the plots on walls so that they can readily be viewed in relation to each other. Unsuspected patterns often emerge.

Matrix Analysis

Matrix analysis is essentially the application of the Pugh concept selection process (Chapter 3, and later in this chapter) to existing products. This helps in selection of the products that are evaluated in rooms 4 and 5 of the House of Quality. This reverse concept selection also provides the team with insights into the strengths of existing designs, which are very helpful in the subsequent concept generation and selection for the new product.

Literature Search

A thorough search of all types of literature provides the team with invaluable information. First, it provides the data for the parametric analysis and matrix analysis. Also, it provides a broad view of the marketplace and trends. Patents, legislation, reports, books, proceedings, product information, market data, and evaluations of products will give the team a more complete picture of the context for its new product.

The House of Quality and the enhancements provide guidance in all ensuing activities. The first application is to the selection of the product concept (total system architecture). The corporate expectation attributes (column headings, room 2 of the House of Quality) become the basis for concept selection in the Pugh matrix. Then the corporate expectations, including the quantified targets (room 8), are deployed to become the requirements for the subsystems. The relationship among these activities was displayed as the top three boxes in Figure 3.7. The application of the House of Quality improves concept selection by making it responsive to customers.

PROGRESS CHECK

This is the end of the House of Quality (HoQ) subphase. A small progress check helps to ensure that the product expectations specifications describe a world-class product and can guide the team to a winning concept.

Progressive Freeze

At the completion of the HoQ subphase, the elements of the business strategy and the product strategy that are relevant to the newly undertaken development are frozen. The product expectations specifications are complete. However, they will not at this time be absolutely frozen, in order that opportunities that are developed during the remainder of the concept phase and the design phase might be used to further tailor the specifications to achieve greater advantage in the marketplace.

Business strategy and product strategy (see Chapter 8) will be in a constant state of ongoing development. Out of their ongoing development, the need for the specific product development program has been identified and has led to the beginning of the work at the start of the concept phase. The complete business and product strategies will have generated initial definitions for all strategy elements affecting the incipient product and development program. During the HoQ subphase, the business and product strategy has been firmly defined by proceeding to the next level of detail, which is the product expectations specifications.

At the completion of the HoQ subphase, there will be a completed business plan that defines the financial requirements, such as revenues, profits, return on sales (ROS), return on investment (ROI), return on assets (ROA), and investment. Also, there will be a definition of the relationship of this part of the program to the sales and development activities of the remainder of the corporation. This will specifically consider the future positioning of the corporation in the international economy—its market share, and the likely effects of international economic trends for the next 10 years.

The product strategy defines a complete product family, specifying the market segments that are targeted for each product in the family, the competitive benchmark products, and the date of market introduction for each family member. These are formed into a family plan, which includes the product currently being developed.

The major activity of the HoQ subphase is the preparation of product expectations specifications for the complete product family. It includes the following steps:

- The customer needs are stated in the voice of the customer.
- These needs are systematically deployed into the product expectation characteristics.
- Competitive benchmarking is completed, relative to both the customer needs and the product expectation characteristics.
- A competitive evaluation is made, relative to product expectation characteristics. It forms the basis for the product expectations specifications for the new product.

This activity is done in a style that leads to consensus and commitment among all functions of the corporation. This includes consensus and commitment from the top manager of each corporate function, such as sales and service. The objective of this progress check is to identify opportunities for improved clarity and unity.

Criterion for Completion of the HoQ Subphase

The primary criterion for deciding whether the HoQ subphase is complete might be:

- Do the product specifications define winning expectations?

At the conclusion of the HoQ subphase, the completed work has enabled the product conceptual response to a clearly identified marketplace.

SELECTING A WINNING CONCEPT

The results from the House of Quality have a strong influence in selecting the winning product concept—the one that will provide customer satisfaction (see Figure 4.9). The development of the House of Quality and the selection of the total system concept should not be carried on independently and serially. Throughout the House of Quality preparation, the team keeps in mind that one of its primary purposes is to develop a superior concept. This provides good guidance in performing the detailed steps in the House of Quality preparation and is a reminder that the preparation of the specifications is the best time for generating new product concepts.

The generation of new concepts is primarily the work of individuals. There are two conditions for creative concept generation: (1) the individuals who generate the concepts are deeply involved in preparing the specifications (House of Quality), and (2) they are in a creative environment. A creative environment is one in which product people are not mired in bureaucratic busywork and fire fighting. In an environment that encourages creativity, the creative concept generators respond to the stimulus of customer needs by thinking up concepts. As the needs become more and more deeply understood during the development of the House of Quality, it is natural to respond spontaneously with concepts. It is a goal of the House of Quality activity to develop concepts. The House of Quality is not an end unto itself; it is a means to the end of getting a better concept and then guiding the development of that concept.

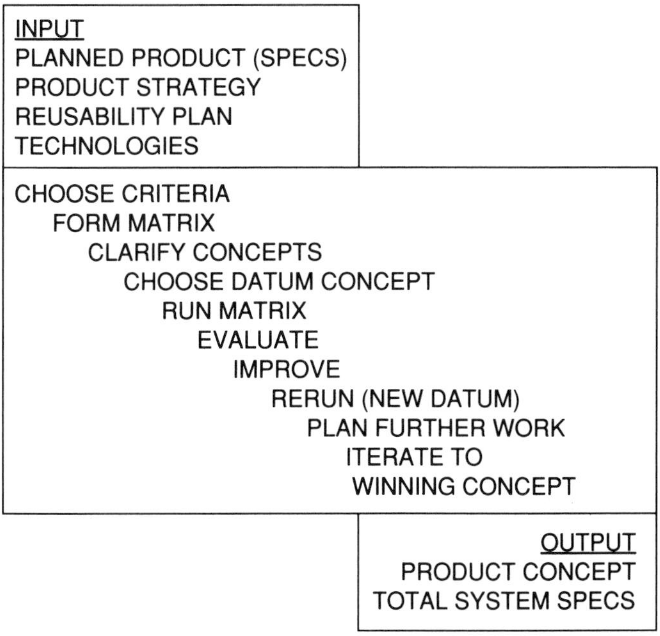

```
INPUT
PLANNED PRODUCT (SPECS)
PRODUCT STRATEGY
REUSABILITY PLAN
TECHNOLOGIES

CHOOSE CRITERIA
    FORM MATRIX
        CLARIFY CONCEPTS
            CHOOSE DATUM CONCEPT
                RUN MATRIX
                    EVALUATE
                        IMPROVE
                            RERUN (NEW DATUM)
                                PLAN FURTHER WORK
                                    ITERATE TO
                                        WINNING CONCEPT

                                            OUTPUT
                                        PRODUCT CONCEPT
                                        TOTAL SYSTEM SPECS
```

FIGURE 4.9. Total system concept selection subphase of the concept phase.

There can be a dedicated time for concept generation after the House of Quality is completed. The first step is for any new participants to become deeply familiar with the House of Quality, so that the requirements are fully understood. Then all members of the concept team review the concepts that emerged during the House of Quality preparation. New concepts are generated on the basis of the full set of information. Since concept generation is a synthesis that is affected by individual perceptions, each individual is encouraged to generate several concepts. This provides us with a sufficient variety of concepts so that we can then enter into a team activity. The concepts that are generated during the House of Quality preparation or shortly thereafter are the starting point for the application of the Pugh (1981) concept selection process.

EXAMPLE OF A WINNING ARCHITECTURE

An example of a winning product concept is the Xerox 1075 copier, which first appeared in 1981. It was the result of a major product concept activ-

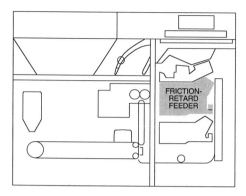

FIGURE 4.10. Total system concept (architecture).

ity that was known as the *third-generation activity*. As shown in Figure 4.10, the 1075 architecture exemplifies the types of decisions that are made during the concept selection for the total system architecture. The major decisions that are made during concept selection are:

(1) The basic technologies for the subsystems (e.g., friction retard feeder)[2]

(2) Their packaging into a complete product (represented by the outlines of the subsystems)

Also completed is enough system engineering to verify the feasibility of the subsystems' playing together in the configuration that is chosen. A prime example is the timing diagram to ensure that all events are coordinated and that there is sufficient time for each event.

---

[2]A semifictionalized account of the development of the friction retard feeder will be used as a case study to illustrate the principles that are the subject of Chapters 4 through 8. The particular feeder first went into production as a subsystem of the Xerox 1075 copier in 1981; it has since been used in several Xerox copiers and printers and is still in production today. Most of the *activities* described in the case study are fictitious. The methods described in this book, as well as various kinds of diagrams, were unknown at the time this subsystem was being developed, from 1976 to 1981. The case study is meant to show how the friction retard feeder might be developed if the Xerox 1075 were being developed today. The numerical data used in the case study are close enough to the data from real life to accurately illustrate all points.

PUGH CONCEPT SELECTION (AND GENERATION)

Concept selection is performed by the multifunctional team with the help of the matrix-based process that was developed by Stuart Pugh (1981). Although it is usually referred to as the Pugh concept *selection* process, one of its great strengths is that improved concepts are *developed* by the team as a result of the discipline and insights that this process provides. The Pugh concept selection process starts with the concepts that have been generated, usually by individuals in response to the stimulation of the development of needs in the House of Quality. During the selection process, further new concepts are generated, many of them hybrids or other variants of the starting concepts, and the concept that is finally selected is rarely exactly one of the starting concepts.

The Pugh concept selection process was developed over many years of successful practice by eliminating procedural dysfunctions as they became evident. In the absence of experience, many methods that have proved to be dysfunctions once seemed very appropriate, and care must be taken not to reintroduce them. A dysfunction that has appeal is to be highly quantitative. Numbers are manipulated, and the concept with the highest score wins. However, this easily becomes mind-numbing numerology. It is much more productive to minimize the role of numbers, and to encourage the team to develop insights that lead to better concepts.

The Pugh concept selection process has 10 steps that are carried out by the multifunctional team:

Step 1. Choose criteria.
Step 2. Form the matrix.
Step 3. Clarify the concepts.
Step 4. Choose the datum concept.
Step 5. Run the matrix.
Step 6. Evaluate the ratings.
Step 7. Attack the negatives and enhance the positives.
Step 8. Select new datum and rerun the matrix.
Step 9. Plan further work.
Step 10. Iterate to arrive at the winning concept.

Each step will now be described in operational detail. An example of a team performing these steps is available on videotape (Clausing, 1992), which is a dynamic way to learn the process.

Step 1—Choose Criteria

The criteria that we apply to the concepts are derived from the product expectations that are the column headings in the House of Quality. These in turn were deployed from the voice of the customer, so the concept that is selected is made responsive to the customer. In simple cases the column headings could be taken directly from the House of Quality and entered into the rows of the Pugh concept selection matrix (see Figure 4.11).

Almost always in actual practice the team will want to further refine the column headings to formulate the criteria for concept selection. The corporate product expectations that are the column headings in the House of Quality (HoQ) are test- or inspection-oriented. They are formulated to be applied at the end of product development to ascertain that the product has met expectations and should proceed into production and to the marketplace. For concept selection the criteria should be more oriented toward creativity. Therefore, the team refines the criteria, on the basis of the HoQ, to be most productive in the concept selection process.

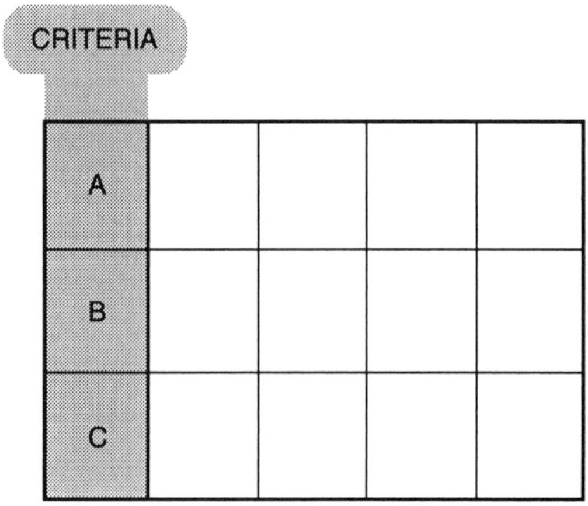

FIGURE 4.11. Concept selection criteria.

Another reason for the team refinement from the HoQ to the concept selection criteria is to avoid an excessive number of criteria. Concept selection works best with 15 to 20 criteria, while the HoQ often has many more columns. Many criteria that are important to check at the end of development may not make much difference in the concept selection and therefore can be ignored, or taken into account at a higher level of abstraction (a group heading that summarizes several more detailed requirements). On the other hand, it is sometimes important to include criteria that do not come from the HoQ. Patent coverage and technical risk are two examples that in some cases should be included in the criteria for concept selection but are not usually in the HoQ.

Another reason for the team to refine the information in the columns of the HoQ in order to formulate the criteria for concept selection is to strengthen the team consensus. To be successful it is very important for the team members to have a common understanding of the criteria that the winning concept must satisfy. Working together, the team comes to a common understanding of the requirements, clear enough to guide rapid further evolution of the concepts.

Usually the criteria are formed by a three-step activity:

(1) Individual team members form their lists of 15 or 20 criteria (based on the columns of the House of Quality and on functional analysis).

(2) In a team work session, the lists of criteria that have been prepared by individual members of the team are merged, discussed, and prioritized. An approximate ordering is all that is required.

(3) At the beginning of the first working session of the team in which the matrix will be formed and run, the criteria are discussed one by one to strengthen the common understanding. The choice of the final 15 to 20 criteria is verified. The criteria are listed in order of priority, first priority at the top.

Manufacturing cost should almost always be one criterion. Often it is difficult to estimate the cost at this early conceptual stage. In many cases cost can be replaced by a simple measure of complexity that needs only to be able to detect significant differences between the costs of different concepts.

In forming the final list of criteria, it is very helpful to consider the ability of each criterion to differentiate among concepts. A criterion may be very important, but if every concept satisfies it well, it will not help in selecting the final concept, and it should be left out of the concept selection matrix.

There is a natural tendency to want to determine a relative weight for each criterion. However, this should usually be avoided. The criteria are simply listed in order of priority, as the team decides in brief consideration. Valid relative weights are difficult to determine at this stage, and they are not generally needed. If the winning concept is superior with respect to every criterion, then there is no necessity for weights. That should be our initial goal. Even if we are not completely successful, the final decision will usually depend on only a very few criteria. Once they have been identified, a trade-off study can be conducted.

It is important that the refinement of the criteria not be allowed to bog down the working of the group. Debate may occur among the team members, and the quick conclusion will be that more information is needed. Make a note of the needed information, and the uncertainty will be resolved before the next concept selection team meeting.

Step 2—Form the Matrix

The criteria, which are usually initially written on a flip chart, are entered onto the matrix as the row headings. This is another opportunity to quickly firm up the common understanding and the commitment to the criteria. Then the concepts are attached to the matrix as the column headings (see Figure 4.12).

We prepare the matrix itself and hang it on the wall before the start of the team meeting. Typically it is roughly 5 feet high by 15 feet long and has been lined to define the rows and columns.

Step 3—Clarify the Concepts

We clarify the concepts one by one, to achieve common understanding (Figure 4.13). This is a crucial step. At the start of the team's first work

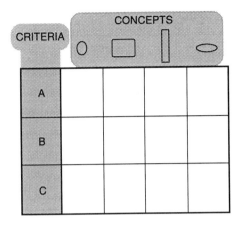

FIGURE **4.12.** Formation of the matrix.

session on concept selection the members of the team have a wide range of understanding of each concept. Here in step 3 the discussion brings everyone up to a high level of understanding. At its best this is a continuation of the invention process. The contributions from the varied experiences of the team improve the concepts, and often identify critical evaluations for the feasibility of each concept.

At its best this step is highly productive. This is creative work at its best, an exciting interaction among the varied experiences of the team members to further develop the concepts. It is critical for success that

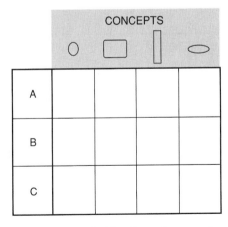

FIGURE **4.13.** Clarification of concepts.

this activity also develop team "ownership" of each concept. If each concept remains identified with an individual rather than with the team, then political negotiation may dominate the team interactions.

This step greatly improves the team's understanding of the concepts. In these visual, connective team methods, vigilance is required to avoid lapsing into mere form filling. Clarification of the concepts is a great opportunity for creative interaction that takes advantage of the wide range of experience of the team.

Step 4—Choose the Datum Concept

Next the team chooses one of the concepts to be the *datum* for the first running of the matrix (Figure 4.14). This is the reference concept with which all of the other concepts are compared. It is important to choose one of the better concepts; a poor datum causes all of the concepts to be evaluated as positive relative to it, causing delay and offering little to increase the insight of the team.

Each team member gives his or her guess as to the best concept. If there is a strong majority for one concept, then it becomes the datum. Frequently there is a wide divergence of opinion. Then a simple and quick process is to have each team member give three top choices in rank order, add up the votes, and choose the concept with the most votes as the datum. It is not important which concept is the initial datum as

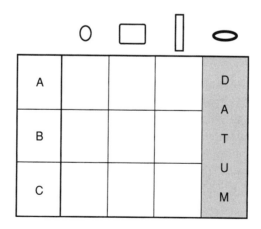

FIGURE 4.14. Choosing the datum.

long as it is a relatively good concept. (In subsequent iterations the next datum is usually selected as the best concept chosen in steps 5 through 8, which will be described next.)

The column under the datum is marked DATUM in big letters to identify it clearly.

Step 5—Run the Matrix

Now we do the comparative evaluation. Each concept is compared with the datum for each criterion—in other words, each cell of the Pugh concept selection matrix is evaluated. The first criterion is applied to each concept, then the second criterion, and so on. We start the evaluation with the first cell, the application of the first criterion to the first concept. Is the first concept better or worse than the datum in its ability to meet the first criterion?

The evaluations use a three-level rating scale: better (+), worse (-), or same (S); see Figure 4.15. Same (S) means that the concept is not clearly significantly better or worse than the datum. A natural desire to use more levels in the hope of achieving a more precise and differentiated comparison should be strongly resisted. Experience has shown that the consistent application of the three levels is a challenge. Occasionally one concept will seem to be exceptionally superior to the datum for a criterion,

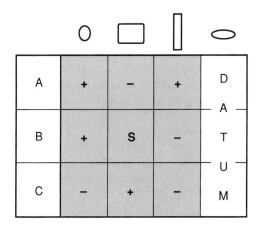

FIGURE **4.15.** Running the matrix.

and you may want to evaluate it as ++. Do not. The three-level ratings will lead to the best concept after the iterations are complete. In subsequent iterations the datum is changed, and there will be an opportunity for second-order differentiations. For example, a concept that seemed to deserve a ++ in the first iteration can be made the datum in a later iteration. Another concept that was + in the first run of the matrix will now be negative relative to the more superior datum. Thus, all important differences will have their effects; the three-level scale provides the greatest productivity for concept selection.

The primary benefit does not come from filling in the form with +, −, or S. The major advance is the new insight that is gained by the team members, for insight is the team's emphasis in evaluating each cell. A brief, sharply focused team discussion reveals divergent viewpoints and brings illuminating contributions from the varied experiences of the team members. This sharing of different perspectives greatly increases each team member's understanding. The facilitator keeps the running of the matrix moving along. An average of roughly one minute per cell is appropriate. Of course, the time invested varies greatly from cell to cell. The facilitator avoids long, drawn-out discussions, which usually result from a lack of information. Repetitious speculation is cut short with a note to find or develop the needed information.

As insights are aroused by the stimulation of running the matrix, a team member will exclaim, "If we combine this feature from concept 3 with that feature from concept 11, we will have a better concept." The facilitator encourages the perceptive participant to sketch the better concept and put it up as a new column heading on the matrix. One of the great advantages of the Pugh concept selection process is that it helps the team to develop better insights into the types of conceptual features that are strongly responsive to the requirements. This leads to more and better creativity, both in the team's work sessions and later in individual reflections about the conceptual response to the requirements that have been deployed from the needs of the customer.

The running of the matrix usually takes approximately half a day; rarely should it be allowed to take more than one day. Much more happens than the recording of +, −, and S. The criteria are refined; applying them to the concepts leads to new insights that are used to sharpen the criteria. Sometimes a criterion is dropped because it becomes apparent that it will not differentiate among the concepts. Hybrid concepts are created. Most important, creative insights grow in the minds of the team members as the relation between conceptual responses and requirements becomes better developed. This leads to outstanding performance during the remainder of the concept selection activity.

The evaluations are all done relative to the datum. This very specific comparison is much more effective than attempts to do abstract evaluations, such as the eventual likelihood of meeting the specification. Now the team is simply striving for the best concept it can come up with in the available time. If it is better than all of the alternatives, including benchmarks, then it is the desired one.

Step 6—Evaluate the Ratings

After the running of the matrix, the scores are added. The number of pluses and minuses is recorded at the bottom of the column for each concept. The team does not take the sum (minuses subtracted from pluses), since that might cause some important conceptual features to be overlooked. For example, a concept with 3 pluses and 10 minuses would be quickly dismissed as a −7. However, the three positives may have been provided by some conceptual elements that might be useful in creating a good hybrid concept. Do not allow quantitativeness to drive out insight.

Step 7—Attack the Negatives and Enhance the Positives

The team attacks the negatives, especially for the most promising concepts. Often a concept can be rather easily changed to overcome a negative evaluation with respect to a criterion. A short team discussion reveals the improvements that can be readily identified.

In a similar style, the team reinforces the positives. It seeks to apply strong positive features to other concepts. This leads to hybrid concepts. Any hybrid or other new concepts are added to the matrix before the next evaluation.

Step 8—Enter a New Datum and Rerun the Matrix

Next the team chooses a different concept as the second datum and runs the matrix again. Usually the second datum is the concept that has received the best rating in the first evaluation. However, the intent is not to verify that it is the best concept, but to gain additional insights that will inspire further creativity to enhance the best concepts. Often the second datum is a hybrid concept, or one that was formed by enhancing one of the original concepts. The team interaction that is fostered by the Pugh concept selection process often leads to major improvements in concepts during a short work session of the team.

The second running of the matrix helps the team to develop additional insights because the new datum gives a different perspective. Earlier, the example was given in which two concepts were both rated + in the first running of the matrix but one seemed as though it should be ++. The shifting of the datum will help reveal when such distinctions are accurate. Generally the new datum will help clarify relative strengths and weaknesses and further strengthen the team's base for further creative work.

Step 9—Plan Further Work

At the end of the first working session, usually no more than one day in duration, the team plans further work to do before the next concept selection working session. This work commonly includes gathering more information, conducting analyses, performing experiments, and recruiting help, especially from people who can provide support in areas that are critical to the emerging dominant concept. The next concept working session is scheduled, usually for one to three weeks later.

Step 10—Iterate to Arrive at the Winning Concept

The team returns armed with very relevant information that was not available in the first working session. Also, the team members have often conceived some new concepts, perhaps hybrids or other extensions of the concepts that were in the matrix at the end of the first working session. Of course, some of the worst concepts from the first matrix have been dropped (after they have been studied for positive features that might be incorporated to improve a hybrid). The matrix is run again, and the team continues to iterate until it has converged to the consensus dominant concept.

In some cases, customers can be involved in the selection of the final concept. Corning redesigned its measuring cup after watching how "real people" cook with it in the company's test kitchens in upstate New York. Corning designers watched as people cooked with seven different prototypes, each with different open-bottom handles designed for the normal grip of a person's hand (*New York Times*, April 6, 1988). The customers' involvement in concept selection can be via verbal description, drawings, or—for simple products such as the measuring cup—having customers try different models in actual use.

APPLICATIONS OF THE PUGH CONCEPT SELECTION PROCESS

Industrial applications have demonstrated that the Pugh concept selection process is a key component of successful product development. It overcomes cash drain 3, the eureka concept, the euphoric rushing off with the first concept that appears appealing after cursory consideration. Usually such concepts are found to be quite vulnerable and would not withstand the competitive gauntlet of the Pugh concept selection process.

The Pugh concept selection process is successful with all types of products, from automobiles and gyroscopes to integrated circuits and software. It has also been successfully applied to services such as banking and tourism, and to the selection of organizational structure. Actually, it can be applied to any selection where there are clear criteria and well-defined alternatives.

To be successful in the marketplace, products must have invulnerable concepts. The Pugh concept selection process helps the team to move forward with a strong concept that will stand the test of time and the competitive pressures. Equally important, the team has come to understand the strength of the concept—the reasons that it is superior to the alternatives—and is dedicated to its success. The team is ready to move forward with confidence to develop the concept into a commercial product.

After the Pugh concept selection process is used by the team to select the winning product concept, the team next moves toward subsystem design. The first action is to deploy the total system requirements to the subsystem level, in the context of the selected total system architecture.

This deployment of the requirements will depend on the architecture that is selected. Having selected a winning concept, the team is now ready to deploy the requirements to the subsystem level in preparation for subsystem design.

PROGRESS CHECK

A small progress check is held to verify that the product concept and the total system expectations are compatible and define a winning product.

Progressive Freeze

The total system architecture is frozen at this time. It is possible that during the design phase some small changes will have to be made in order to achieve subsystem interface compatibility. In the successful organizational culture, however, this will be an exception rather than the rule.

Criterion for Successful Concept Selection

The suggested primary criterion for success at this point is:

• The product concept is a winner.

The expectation is that the concept, once we have developed it into the finished product, will become the competitive benchmark against which all other products will be compared.

DEPLOYMENT TO THE SUBSYSTEMS (SS)

On the basis of selected total system architecture (TSA), a TS/SS design matrix is prepared, which helps the team to make decisions at the level of the total system (see Figure 4.16). The total system expectations from the House of Quality are deployed into subsystem (SS) expectations, as displayed in Figure 4.17. The input (rows) into the TS/SS design matrix are the House of Quality total system expectations (columns)

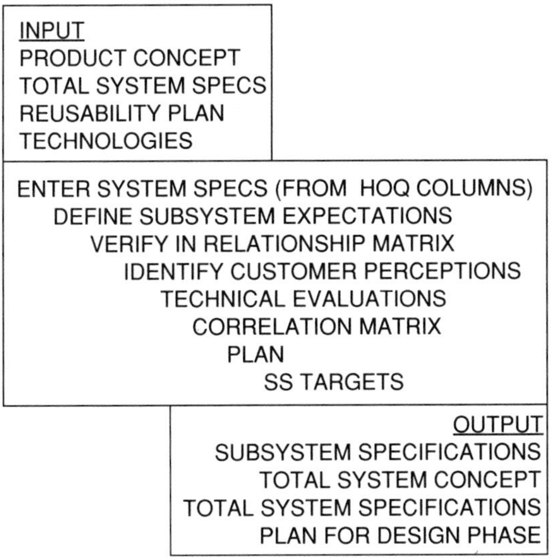

```
INPUT
PRODUCT CONCEPT
TOTAL SYSTEM SPECS
REUSABILITY PLAN
TECHNOLOGIES

ENTER SYSTEM SPECS (FROM  HOQ COLUMNS)
DEFINE SUBSYSTEM EXPECTATIONS
VERIFY IN RELATIONSHIP MATRIX
IDENTIFY CUSTOMER PERCEPTIONS
TECHNICAL EVALUATIONS
CORRELATION MATRIX
PLAN
SS TARGETS

OUTPUT
SUBSYSTEM SPECIFICATIONS
TOTAL SYSTEM CONCEPT
TOTAL SYSTEM SPECIFICATIONS
PLAN FOR DESIGN PHASE
```

FIGURE 4.16. Subsystem specs subphase of the concept phase.

that are relevant to the specific subsystem. The remaining fields (rooms) of the TS/SS design matrix are completed by the team with a style and actions that are essentially the same as those used for the House of Quality. However, the team often decides that some of rooms 4, 5, 6, and 7 are not needed for a specific subsystem. There is a TS/SS design matrix for each new subsystem that is being developed for the product. (Some subsystems will be carried over from previous products—see Chapter 8—and usually the TS/SS design matrix is not prepared for them.)

We will now take up our fictionalized case study of the friction retard feeder of the Xerox 1075.[3] There are three types of TS/SS deployment, and each is illustrated in Figure 4.17. An example of the first type involves the misfeed rate. Since misfeeds in a copier can occur only in the feeder, the total numerical requirement for the misfeed rate is simply in its entirety deployed to the expectations for the feeder. Thus the total system expectation that the misfeed rate will be less than $70/10^6$ becomes the numerical expectation for the feeder itself.

---

[3]See the section Example of a Winning Architecture, earlier in this chapter.

	TOTAL SYSTEM EXPECTATIONS		1 MISFEED RATE	2 MULTIFEED RATE	3 JAM RATE	4 COPY RATE	5 JAM CLEARANCE TIME	6 PAPER DAMAGE RATE	7 UMC	8 PAPER SPEED	9 DELIVERY TIME
A	MISFEED RATE	$< 70/10^6$	◎								
B	MULTIFEED RATE	$< 30/10^6$		◎							
C	JAM RATE	$< 100/10^6$			◎					◎	◎
D	COPY RATE	70 ± 2 CPM				◎				◎	
E	JAM CLEARANCE TIME	< 20 SEC					◎				
F	PAPER DAMAGE RATE	$< 100/10^6$						◎			◎
G	UMC	$< \$6000$							◎		
	SYSTEM DESIGN DECISIONS, SUBSYSTEM EXPECTATIONS		$< 70/10^6$	$< 30/10^6$	$< 30/10^6$	70 ± 2 CPM	< 20 SEC	$< 40/10^6$	$< \$250$	11.7 ± 0.3 ips	141 ± 10 msec

FIGURE **4.17.** Deployment of expectations from total system to subsystem.

An example of the second type of deployment is jam rate. Jams can occur throughout the paper path of a copier, and therefore the required jam rate for the feeder can be only a fraction of the total expectation for the copier. In Figure 4.17, by way of illustration, the jam rate for the feeder is shown to be 30% of that for the entire copier, a value based on experience. The important point is that not all of the total system expectation can be deployed to any one subsystem.

The third type of deployment is illustrated by paper speed and delivery time. These are system engineering decisions that are made by conducting system engineering at the level of the complete system. In this case, these decisions stem primarily from the analysis of the timing diagram for the copier. The decision is that the paper speed must be 11.7 inches per second in order for the copier to meet all of its expectations. Within the total cycle time to make one copy, the system analysis leads to the decision that the delivery time of the sheet from the feeder to the transport that carries it to the photoreceptor should be 141 milliseconds, to enable the sheet of paper to match up with the image on the photoreceptor.

There is no special technique required for the team to cope with the various types of deployment. With a little experience, the distinction is usually obvious, and the deployment proceeds without difficulty.

After the requirements are deployed to the subsystems, the *concept phase* (for the concept of the total product system) is almost complete, ready for the concept-phase review.

PROGRESS CHECK

The objective of the progress check at this point is to verify that the detailed product expectations specifications and the product concepts that have been selected for the product family are responsive to the ongoing business and product strategies, and have enabled success in the marketplace. This review usually includes participation by a corporate officer who has the authority to commit funding for the remainder of the development process. If the review shows that the specifications and selected concepts will not be winners in the marketplace, it is almost always preferable to go back and start again at the beginning of the concept phase. Usually, however, this check consolidates a successful start.

PROGRESSIVE FREEZE

The team reviews the specifications in the context of the selected concept to ensure that together they define a winning product. The specifications are deployed from the total system level to the subsystems.

The product concept layout is frozen at this time. This includes first-order packaging of all subsystems and major components. The macro styling is also frozen at this point. "Frozen" means that any subsequent changes to the layout are minor in the context of the total system. The concept for final assembly is complete.

Also frozen at this time is the selection of all technological concepts for each subsystem or major functional area. If any new technologies are major departures from the corporation's prior practice, it is important to ensure that they have matured sufficiently. In choosing the technological concepts, the team has implied that it believes it will meet all product expectation specifications, and that after completion of optimization the corporation will be the world leader in cost and performance. To give reasonable expectations of world-class potential, the technological concepts will now have been demonstrated to perform very well at near nominal conditions.

It is extremely important at this point to have made comparisons of the selected concept with alternative concepts. This comparison of many different concepts for their ability to meet the product expectation specifications will have been done in a thorough and systematic style; all alternatives will have been explored, to open the team's thinking to new and better synergies. The conclusion of this concept process will have created consensus and commitment on the part of the development team.

It is essential to success that at this time the feature set and the total product family be compatible with the business and product strategies, and that they be potential winners in the marketplace. It is also critical that there be a development plan that encompasses all members of the product family. This development plan is fine-tuned for the specific product under development at a given time. It includes resources for the entire remainder of the process, although there will be more reviews to confirm the wisdom of final commitment of these resources. The plan at this time must include staffing for at least the next phase, which is the design phase.

ALL THE STEPS FOR SUCCESS

In the traditional approach to product development the game has often been lost by the end of the concept phase. The concept is flawed, and the best development afterward can only produce a well-developed product that is unattractive to customers. By taking all of the steps that are described in this chapter, you can develop a concept that is inherently strong.

All of the steps are necessary. There may be a tendency to try shortcuts, but this should be resisted, because it will bring back the cash drains of the traditional process. All of the steps are needed for vigilant information processing. At the level of the most detailed steps, some variation may be successful. This is especially true for bringing in the voice of the customer, where there are competing approaches that bring good results. The team can tailor the process to its culture. Also, we do not want to become rigid, but continually to seek improvement. But this does not mean that we should not follow the steps that are outlined in this chapter. They should be replaced only when we have good reason to believe that a superior approach has been developed.

Attention to all of the steps may seem time-consuming. There is a natural tendency to "get on with it." However, time that is well spent here will pay off later by saving rework. This will greatly reduce the total development time. Therefore, the check at the end of the concept phase is very important to ensure that the product will be successful and the development time short.

CRITERIA FOR COMPLETION OF THE CONCEPT PHASE

The two primary additional criteria are:

- The program plan must enable success.
- The subsystem specifications must support a winning product.

These are in addition to the previous criteria at the completion of the total system concept selection subphase:

- The product specifications must define winning expectations.
- The product concept must be a winner.

The application of total quality development to the concept phase overcomes

- Cash drain 2: disregard for the voice of the customer
- Cash drain 3: the eureka concept

The strong product concept, responsive to customers, and the deployed subsystem specifications provide a successful completion to the *concept phase*. Next we are ready to develop the concept into a design during the *design phase*.

43 STEPS FOR THE SUCCESSFUL CONCEPT PHASE—A SUMMARY

CONCEPT PHASE INPUT

Product strategy (S1)
Reusability plan (S4)
Technologies (T8)

HOUSE OF QUALITY—PLANNING A SUCCESSFUL PRODUCT
(*TS HoQ Matrix, Figure 3.7*)

<table>
<tr><td></td><td>Step</td><td>Page</td></tr>
<tr><td>**Room 1—Voice of the Customer**</td><td></td><td></td></tr>
<tr><td>*Step 1—Plan*</td><td>C1</td><td>112</td></tr>
<tr><td>*Step 2—Interact with customers*</td><td>C2</td><td>114</td></tr>
<tr><td>*Step 3—Develop an image of the customers*</td><td>C3</td><td>117</td></tr>
<tr><td>*Step 4—Scrub the data to achieve clarity*</td><td>C4</td><td>118</td></tr>
<tr><td>*Step 5—Select significant voices*</td><td>C5</td><td>120</td></tr>
<tr><td>*Step 6—Structure the needs*</td><td>C6</td><td>120</td></tr>
<tr><td>*Step 7—Characterize the customer needs*</td><td>C7</td><td>121</td></tr>
<tr><td>**Room 2—Product Expectations**</td><td></td><td></td></tr>
<tr><td>*Step 8—Develop the product expectations*</td><td>C8</td><td>126</td></tr>
<tr><td>*Step 9—Organize the product expectations*</td><td>C9</td><td>129</td></tr>
<tr><td>*Step 10—Define tests for the product expectations*</td><td>C10</td><td>130</td></tr>
<tr><td>**Room 3—Relating the Corporation to the Customer**</td><td></td><td></td></tr>
<tr><td>*Step 11—Evaluate the relationship matrix*</td><td>C11</td><td>133</td></tr>
<tr><td>*Step 12—Verify fidelity of expectations*</td><td>C12</td><td>134</td></tr>
<tr><td>**Room 4—Customer Perceptions (Benchmarking)**</td><td></td><td></td></tr>
<tr><td>*Step 13—Complete customer competitive survey*</td><td>C13</td><td>136</td></tr>
</table>

CONCEPT PHASE OUTPUT

Total system specifications (House of Quality)
Total system concept (includes subsystem technologies)
Subsystem specifications (TS/SS design matrix)
Plan for design phase

CHAPTER

5

The Design

■ **Subsystem Design**

■ **Piece-Part Design**

■ **Progress Check for World-Class Design**

■ **38 Steps for the Successful Design Phase —
A Summary**

A t the start of the *design phase*, we already have in place the product concept (total system architecture), the basic technologies for the individual subsystems, and the specifications for the subsystems. We have developed these during the *concept phase* (Chapter 4) so that now we expect them to be responsive to the voice of the customer, to incorporate new technologies that enable market leadership, and to implement the corporate product strategy. In the design phase we develop the product concept into a complete and detailed production-intent design.

All of total quality development uses basic concurrent engineering. This is especially critical during the design phase. The concurrent process that is carried out by the multifunctional product development team (PDT) is used in designing the product (for functionality, producibility, and maintainability), the production capability, and the field-support capability. Our PDT must include development engineers with experience and training in all of these areas. The complete story of design includes basic concurrent engineering (Chapter 2), and also the partial design, partial production, and engineering sciences (Chapter 1) by which the unit design tasks are completed. In this chapter we concentrate on those design activities that go beyond basic concurrent engineering to achieve world-class concurrent engineering by better defining the unit design tasks.

It is good discipline to think of the design phase as further divided into two subphases as shown in Figure 5.1:

- Subsystem design
- Piece-part design

The subsystem design defines the values of the critical design parameters (dimensions, electrical characteristics, moduli of elasticity, friction coefficients, and viscosities, for example) that become the specifications for the piece parts. These values ensure that the piece parts will integrate together to form robust subsystems and a good total system.

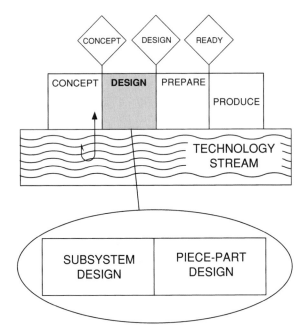

FIGURE 5.1. The two subphases of design.

Good piece-part design is very important. Even more important are the values of the critical design parameters that make the system robust and responsive to customers. These are determined during subsystem design. Then it is the objective of piece-part design to provide the values of the critical design parameters at low total cost (manufacturing cost and field cost). Therefore, it is a very important success factor that we have defined the values of the critical design parameters before the piece-part design progresses very far. During the *subsystem* design subphase we (1) define the values of the critical design parameters and (2) make the early major decisions on the most important piece parts. Together these two activities reveal the requirements for the second subphase of design, the detailed design of piece parts.

In the *piece-part* design subphase, the team completes the detailed design of all of the piece parts. Functionality and assembly requirements have essentially been satisfied during the subsystem design. The emphasis during piece-part design is producibility of the piece parts, including tolerance design.

The design phase of total quality development plays a major role in overcoming four of the cash drains:

Cash drain 4: Pretend designs
Cash drain 5: Pampered products
Cash drain 6: Hardware swamps
Cash drain 7: Here's the product. Where's the factory?

The emphasis is on designs that are superior to benchmarks, are producible, have robust functionality, and continue the responsiveness to customers that was started during the concept phase.

SUBSYSTEM DESIGN

At the beginning of subsystem design the total system concept (architecture) has already been defined. The locations of all of the subsystems (packaging) are known, the basic technology is known for each subsystem, and the initial values for the interface specifications have been defined. The subsystem expectations have been defined in the TS/SS QFD matrices. These were deployed from the House of Quality.

Subsystem design and all subsequent development activities concentrate primarily on the subsystems that are new in the product that is being developed. Many subsystems will be reused, that is, retained from a previous product. (See Chapter 8 for more about reusability.) These subsystems are to be changed very little. They should be changed only to ensure compatibility with the new subsystems, or to make cost or performance improvements that have been clearly identified and are within the scope of the development of the new product. The following description applies to the development of the new subsystems.

At the beginning of subsystem design we have the subsystem expectations that were deployed from the House of Quality for the total system. (It is also possible to prepare the House of Quality for just a few subsystems, or even one subsystem.) The subsystem expectations for the paper feeder (to continue our fictionalized case study, last seen in Figure 4.17, near the end of Chapter 4) are shown in Figure 5.2. The columns are

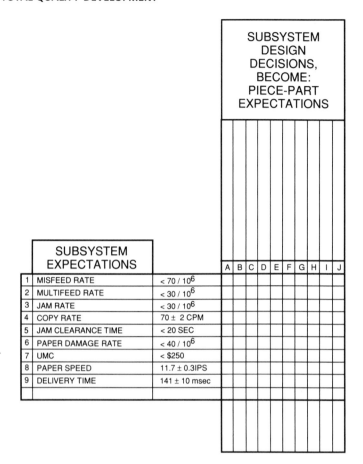

FIGURE 5.2. Subsystem expectations.

for the critical decisions that we will make during the subsystem design, which then become the expectations for the piece parts.

ACTIVITIES

Subsystem design has two activity tracks: (1) the skeletal design, and (2) the early critical decisions on filling in the skeletal design to form the complete, detailed, production-intent design. It is the objective of subsystem design to define all requirements down to a level of detail that will enable the subsequent design activities to focus on the detailed comple-

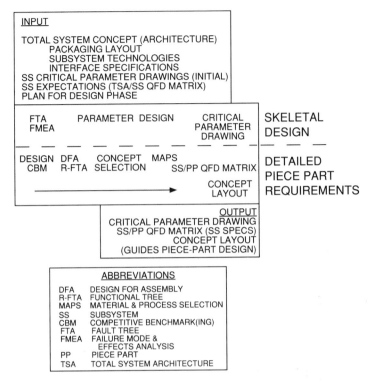

FIGURE 5.3. Subsystem design.

tion of the design of well-defined piece parts. The activities of subsystem design are outlined in Figure 5.3.

Skeletal Design

Our team uses fault tree analysis (FTA) and failure modes and effects analysis (FMEA) to identify the critical functional parameters, both control factors and noise factors, that are used during parameter design to optimize robust performance. Next the parameter design is completed to achieve a robust design. This overcomes cash drains 5 and 6. Robust design is the most important improvement for achieving faster time to market. At the completion of the skeletal design, we finalize the critical parameter drawing—sign it, frame it, store it in the computer for quick retrieval, or do anything else that's likely to get people to pay attention in the particular organizational culture. The critical parameter drawing must guide and constrain the subsequent detailed piece-part design.

Detailed Piece-Part Requirements

Concurrently with the skeletal design, other early critical decisions are made to complete the requirements for the detailed design of piece parts. The intention is to leave only very clearly defined piece-part design as the work to be completed during the next subphase.

We start this work with design competitive benchmarking (DCBM). This involves teardown of competitive products, functional and reliability analyses, and cost breakdown by part and function. This overcomes the pretend designs (cash drain 4) that are new and different but not better than existing products. DCBM gives the subsystem team an understanding of the best existing designs and is accompanied by the design principle *beat the benchmark design or use it*.

Then we begin the detailed design of the new subsystem by starting the design for assembly (DFA) and the preparation of the functional tree (R-FTA, which literally stands for "reverse fault tree analysis"). We go ahead with concept selection for any major functional areas that need to be resolved. Material and process selection (MAPS) is done for the most critical parts, usually by using the Pugh concept selection process, which has been described in Chapter 4. (The Pugh concept selection process can be applied at any level of the system, as is suggested by Figure 3.7.) These activities make a good start on developing a producible product, thus overcoming cash drain 7 (here's the product; where's the factory?).

We capture the emerging design in a conceptual layout drawing. This will have been developed into the production-intent design layout by the end of piece-part design. The layout drawing adheres absolutely to the critical parameter drawing and displays the emerging design decisions. As this work is progressing, we develop the subsystem/piece-part QFD matrix to guide and document the critical subsystem design decisions. This ensures that the design decisions are faithful to the total system expectations, which in turn were faithfully deployed from the voice of the customer in the House of Quality.

As we do the work, there is continuous communication and iteration between the skeletal design and the activities to flesh it out into a complete design, all carried out by the multifunctional product development team (PDT). The skeletal design provides the best functional values for the most critical design parameters, and the detailed piece-part requirements provide cost and space constraints to the skeletal design. Therefore, they are carefully coordinated; neither activity is allowed to advance too far ahead of the other. By keeping the two activities closely integrated, all of the decisions take into account functionality, producibility, and all aspects of the design. Here, for simplicity, the skeletal design will be described first, and then the activities to fill out the skeletal design into detailed piece-part requirements will be described.

SKELETAL DESIGN

The skeletal design consists of three steps, as displayed in Figure 5.3:

- Identification of the critical design parameters
- Parameter design, the optimization of the critical design values
- Recording the critical values in the critical parameter drawing

The critical parameter drawing is the skeletal design. It displays the critical values that ensure robust functionality. They become the targets for piece-part design. For example, the critical parameter drawing might show that between points *A* and *B* a spring is needed with a certain spring rate and compression, which have been determined during parameter design. Then the piece-part design task is to design (or select) a specific spring that will achieve the specified spring rate and compression.

Identification of the Critical Parameters

Our multifunctional PDT identifies the critical parameters by means of a team activity that effectively utilizes our experience. The possible choices include the use of analyses and simple experiments. However, widespread practice has revealed that it is best for the team to use a visual, connective method to bring out and integrate the members' collective experiences. This sometimes takes the form of simple brainstorming or similar approaches. More powerful are relational networks such as the fishbone cause-and-effect (Ishikawa) diagram (see, for example, Shiba,

Graham, and Walden, 1993). The methodology that has been found to be most powerful is the combination of the fault tree (FTA, for fault tree analysis) and the failure modes and effects analysis (FMEA) table.

Failure Analysis

Functional trees, fault trees, and failure modes and effects analysis (FMEA) all provide essentially the same analysis. However, experience has demonstrated that it is beneficial to do all three. Each induces a different psychological response, and the union of the three provides the most complete insights to guide the design.

The functional tree is used to help guide the design of the new product, with the emphasis on cost-effective functionality. The fault tree and the FMEA table are helpful in developing reliability. They are especially valuable in identifying the critical parameters that need to be optimized to achieve robust functionality.

The functional tree (Figure 5.4) is a top-down (T) analysis (decomposition) of good function; that is, it will be composed of positive statements (+). The fault tree (Figure 5.5) is a top-down (T) analysis of faults (failures of function); thus, it is made up of negative statements (−). FMEA (Figure 5.6) is a bottom-up (B) analysis of failure modes (faults); thus, an FMEA table contains negative statements (−). To summarize:

Functional trees	R-FTA	T+
Fault trees	FTA	T−
Failure modes and effects analysis	FMEA	B−

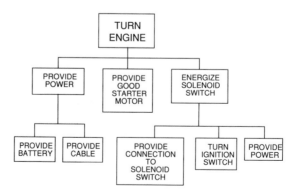

FIGURE 5.4. Simple functional tree (R-FTA) for a starter motor.

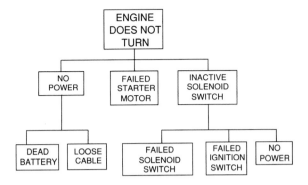

FIGURE **5.5.** Simple fault tree for a starter motor.

In Japan, the reverse nature of the functional tree and the fault tree is captured by the abbreviations FTA (fault tree analysis) and R-FTA (reverse fault tree analysis; i.e., functional tree). In the United States, the functional tree has been known as the FAST (functional analysis system technique) diagram. Functional relationships and fault relationships are always shown as trees, to best display the relationships. FMEA is always shown as a table, to display more information.

Functional trees are used to guide the creation of the design, as will be described in Figures 5.24–5.29. Fault trees and FMEA tables are used to guide the quantification and improvement of reliability and robustness. It is best to prepare both the fault tree and the FMEA table

FAILURE MODE	EFFECT	CAUSES
NO POWER	ENGINE DOES NOT TURN	1.DEAD BATTERY 2. LOOSE CABLE

TYPICALLY SEVERAL ADDITIONAL COLUMNS
COUNTERMEASURES
SECONDARY FAILURE MODES
PARTS
PROBABILITY, SEVERITY, ETC.

FIGURE **5.6.** Simple FMEA table for a starter motor.

and to use them as checks against each other. Still better insight into the functionality of the new design is obtained by iterating among the functional tree, fault tree, and FMEA table until all three are consistent with each other.

The fault tree can be filled out with logic symbols and Boolean algebra that can then be used to calculate system failure rates from component failure rates. This method is particularly used in industries where failure could be catastrophic, such as the missile and nuclear industries. However, in consumer industries it is unusual to have precise reliability data on components, particularly for a new design. Therefore, the Boolean algebra has been little used. Instead, where the use of fault trees is highly productive is in leading into the optimization of robust functionality.

Paper Feeder Fault Tree Example

The paper feeder of the Xerox 1075, shown in Figure 5.7, will be used as an example for many points in this book, as was noted in Chapter 4. A partial fault tree for the paper feeder is shown in Figure 5.8. The wrap angle (actually, the amount of arc with which the feed belt is in contact as it wraps around the retard roll), α, is identified by the PDT as a critical parameter. A small wrap angle contributes to excessive multifeeds. This suggests that the angle should be made as large as possible. Also, the PDT has noted from its experience that wear of the retard roll causes significant reduction of the wrap angle.

At the bottom of the fault tree are the critical parameters, both control factors and noise factors. In Figure 5.8 the initial value of the wrap angle, α_0, is a control factor. We can control it by selecting the best value. The amount of wear, α_0 minus α_t, is a noise factor, an undesirable variation that degrades functionality. The value of α_0 will vary from one unit of production to another by what we'll call $\Delta\alpha_0$, another type of noise factor. Also noted at the bottom of the fault tree as another critical parameter is the paper-to-paper friction difference, $\Delta\mu_{pp}$, between the first interface in the paper stack and the second interface. When this friction difference is positive, it creates a positive force that tends to drive the second sheet through the retard zone and thus create a multifeed. This is a noise factor that is imposed by the conditions of customer use. The customers choose their paper and impose it on the paper feeder.

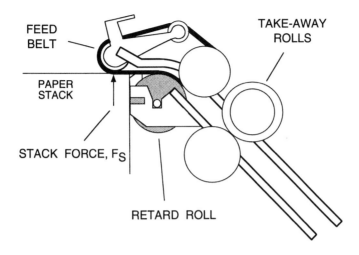

FIGURE 5.7. Paper feeder.

In summary, the fault tree displays four types of factors: control factors, and three types of noise factors. The values of control factors such as α_0 are used to optimize the functionality of our system. This makes

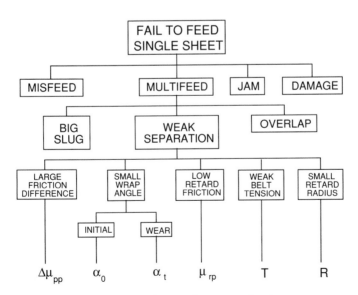

FIGURE 5.8. Fault tree for paper feeder.

the product system robust against the degradations of performance that are caused by the three types of noise factors:

- Variations in conditions of customer use, such as $\Delta\mu_{pp}$
- Production variations, such as $\Delta\alpha_0$
- Wear, and other deteriorations, such as $\alpha_0 - \alpha_t$

Our task is to optimize our system to make it stay close to ideal customer-satisfaction functionality, even in the presence of the three types of noises. This selection of the best values for the control factors, such as α_0, is called *parameter design*.

Paper Feeder Functional Tree Example

The functional tree for the paper feeder is shown in Figure 5.9. (The complete functional tree for the feeder has approximately 100 functions; in other words, there would be 100 boxes in Figure 5.9.) Comparison with Figure 5.8 makes it clear that the functional tree and the fault tree are very similar. However, as was noted earlier, it is usually beneficial for our team to prepare both, somewhat independently. The psychological responses are different, and added insights into the requirements for the subsystem are gained by preparing both. Note that the fault tree naturally has noise factors at the bottom of the tree. Noise factors will not normally appear at the bottom of the functional tree.

Functional Analysis and QFD

Functional analysis means the combination of the functional tree, the fault tree, and the FMEA table. Each of these provides its most useful guidance when all three are prepared and made consistent by iteration. They form a statement of the requirements for the subsystem design. The subsystem is required to perform the functions without failure.

The QFD matrices also state the requirements, as shown in Figure 5.2. It might at first seem that these two types of requirement statement are independent, or possibly even conflicting. However, they are completely consistent, and it is a strength of total quality development to emphasize and take advantage of the consistency.

For the paper feeder the top function is FEED SHEET. The functional tree is prepared by using a verb and a noun to describe each function.

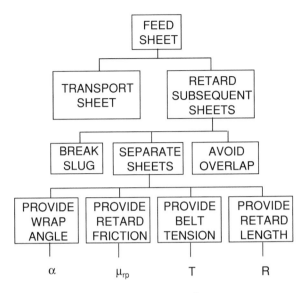

FIGURE 5.9. Functional tree.

Obviously, we have many specific expectations in mind when we describe the intended function as FEED SHEET. However, we cannot write these details on the functional tree, which in its totality is already quite complex, with approximately 100 functions. Instead, these detailed amplifications of our functional intent are the expectations in the QFD matrices. For example, the subsystem expectations that are the rows in Figure 5.2 are amplifications of the function of the feeder, FEED SHEET. When we write FEED SHEET in the functional tree, we mean, Feed one sheet with the misfeed rate less than $70/10^6$, with the unit manufacturing cost (UMC) less than \$250, and with all of the other caveats in the QFD matrix (see the rows of Figure 5.2). Thus, the functional analysis and the QFD matrices are completely consistent and reinforce each other to form a powerful statement of requirements that helps guide our team to a better design. Further detailed suggestions on the integration of functional analysis and QFD are in the MIT working paper by Sontow and Clausing (1993).

The subsystem requirements that are the rows in the subsystem/piece-part (SS/PP) QFD matrix (see Figure 5.2) can be viewed as having two sources:

- Requirements deployed from the total system expectations (House of Quality)
- Amplifications of the functional requirement—FEED SHEET, for example

The functional analysis is very technical in its nature, strongly based on the engineer's fundamental training. The functional tree and the fault tree provide the structures of equations. For example, the functional tree states that the separation tendency (actually, the separation force) is a function of α, μ_{rp}, T, and R. The functional analysis can be used to develop the best possible set of equations to help guide the optimization of robustness. The SS/PP QFD matrix is not so purely technical, but rather represents a technobusiness perspective. It amplifies the purely functional statement of the requirements with statements of business needs that are based on the customer's requirements. This duality between function and QFD matrices applies at all levels of the product system. By considering both paths to the subsystem expectations, the team develops the strongest possible insights into the requirements. This leads to a superior design.

Initial SS/PP Design QFD Matrix

The functional analysis makes a good start at identifying the critical subsystem decisions, which become the column headings in the SS/PP QFD matrix. The critical functional parameters that are identified in the fault tree, functional tree, and FMEA table are one type of column heading (piece-part expectation) in the SS/PP QFD matrix; for the feeder example, they are entered into the matrix shown in Figure 5.10. In addition, some types of subsystem decisions are generic, such as system engineering decisions (timing and speeds, for example), operability (jam clearance, for example), costs, and safety. As the functional analysis is developed, the most critical subsystem decisions start to become clear.

The team makes as many of the critical decisions as possible by utilizing the members' collective experience, aided by the visual connective methods of the QFD matrices and functional analysis. When the collective experience abetted by extended QFD is not enough, then the team branches into systematic optimization, which is called *parameter design*.

SUBSYSTEM EXPECTATIONS		RETARD FRICTION COEFFICIENT	RETARD BRAKE TORQUE	RETARD RADIUS	WRAP ANGLE, α	BELT TENSION, T	TRIGGER TIME	TAR ACTION TIME	TAR SURFACE SPEED	JAM CLEARANCE STRATEGY	UMC BREAKDOWN
		A	B	C	D	E	F	G	H	I	J
1	MISFEED RATE	$< 70 / 10^6$	◎						◎			
2	MULTIFEED RATE	$< 30 / 10^6$	◎	◎	◎	◎	◎	◎		○		
3	JAM RATE	$< 30 / 10^6$						◎				
4	COPY RATE	70 ± 2 CPM							◎			
5	JAM CLEARANCE TIME	< 20 SEC									◎	
6	PAPER DAMAGE RATE	$< 40 / 10^6$	◎									
7	UMC	< $250										◎
8	PAPER SPEED	11.7 ± 0.3 ips								◎		
9	DELIVERY TIME	141 ± 10 msec							◎			

SUBSYSTEM DESIGN DECISIONS, BECOME: PIECE-PART EXPECTATIONS

FIGURE 5.10. Some critical subsystem decisions.

The first step is to analyze the factors that have been identified with the help of functional analysis.

Analysis of Factors

When we optimize a design, there are five types of factors (also called *parameters* or *variables*) that we measure, and for some types we select the nominal values. We save much time when we learn to quickly sort each of the factors in a design into one of the five categories. The PDT identifies these factors with the help of fault trees.

We have already seen from the example of the feeder in Figure 5.8 that there are two types of factors at the bottom of the fault tree: control factors and noise factors. In addition, there is a type of factor to measure the functionality at the top of the tree, the feeding of a single sheet in Figure 5.8. Also, there are two special types of control factors: an adjustment factor that adjusts the output, and a signal factor that dynamically signals the need for a change in the output. In summary, the five types of factors are:

- Functional: Measures the output from the system.
- Control: Design parameters; we can control (select) the values.
- Noise: Undesirable variations; cause functionality to be degraded.
- Signal: Commands a dynamic system to produce a response.
- Adjustment: Shifts response. For a static system, the mean value of the response is shifted. (In this case, the adjustment factor is sometimes called a *passive signal*.) For a dynamic system, the slope of response versus signal is changed.

Now each type of factor will be described in more detail.

Functional Factors. Functional factors (metrics) are measures of the output from the system and characterize the system performance. For an electrical power supply, the functional metric is the voltage that is measured at the output terminals. Voltage is an example of a continuous functional variable.

Control Factors. Control factors are design parameters. We can control the values of these parameters by simply selecting early during development the values that give us the best performance. We change the values of the control factors to improve the performance. Examples are resistances and inductances in electrical circuits.

Noise Factors. Noise factors are unwanted variations that cause performance degradation. The production variance of the design parameters is one kind of noise. For an electrical power supply, examples of customer-use noises are the ambient temperature and variations in the line voltage that is providing power as an input to the power supply.

Signal Factor. A signal factor is used to change the response in a desired way. In dynamic cases, the desired response is not a constant value, but depends upon the magnitude of a signal that we put into the system. An example of a dynamic system is the steering system for a car. The response is the turning radius of the car, and the signal factor is the angle through which we turn the steering wheel. A high-quality dynamic system will provide a consistent correlation between the response and the signal.

Adjustment Factor. An adjustment factor changes the response in a simple and desirable way. The adjustment factor is just a special kind of control factor. For Sam the marksman (Chapter 3), the position of the sights on his rifle is the adjustment factor. In dynamic cases, the adjustment factor can be a multiplier between the response and the signal. For example, in a steering system, the steering gear ratio is an adjustment factor. The value of the steering ratio is to some extent a matter of driver preference rather than an important robustness factor. Robust steering performance gives the driver a consistent feel for the road. The adjustment factor adjusts to the driver preference for fast or slow turning, but does not change the fundamental robustness.

Parameter Design

Product parameter design is the most important activity in Taguchi's quality engineering (see Figure 3.11). The purpose of parameter design is to improve robustness. Robustness simply means achieving excellent functionality under the wide range of conditions that will actually be encountered. All products function moderately well under ideal conditions. Robust products continue to function well when the conditions are tough, a great attraction to customers.

In response to the findings of the failure analysis (see Figure 5.8), there are three approaches to improve the robustness of function:

- Improving the concept; changing to more robust physics
- Changing a critical parameter value to an obvious feasible limit
- Parameter design; systematic optimization

The last of these is powerful but should be used only after the first two approaches have been thoroughly explored. For the paper feeder, as an example of the first approach, a new concept for the retard roll was selected to minimize the wear; this will be described under the heading Concept Selection later in this chapter (p. 239). This is an example of the close coordination that must be maintained between the skeletal design and the production-intent design. It would have been a mistake to optimize the traditional design when a more robust design was emerging from the concept selection activity. As an example of the second approach, the wrap angle in the paper feeder should be as large as possible to avoid multifeeds. Unless this creates some other problem, the value of the wrap angle should be taken to its feasible upper limit. The PDT decided on 45°, three times the value for previous feeders. (This is a form of optimization. After careful analysis the decision is obvious, so systematic optimization methodology is not needed.)

After new concepts have been selected and some of the critical parameters have been taken to obvious feasible limits, there are usually many critical design parameters that remain to be optimized. The experience of the PDT, effectively marshaled with the help of QFD, reduces the range of values, but systematic optimization is needed to find the value that will provide the most robust function. Thus, it is natural to branch from QFD, and related activities such as fault trees, into parameter design when experience is insufficient to find the best value.

Optimization Process

After we identify and analyze the critical factors, with the help of the fault tree and FMEA, the optimization of functionality is done in seven steps:

(1) Define objective, in terms of the best functional metric.
(2) Define feasible alternative design values.
(3) Select some options for evaluation.
(4) Impose noises.
(5) Evaluate performance of selected options.
(6) Select best design values.
(7) Confirm robust performance.

The following example is unrealistically simple in order to clearly introduce the basic mechanics of the optimization of robustness.

Simple Optimization Example: Electrical Circuit

A very simple example will help to introduce the robustness process. Figure 5.11 shows a very simple electrical circuit. In this circuit, a voltage V is applied across a series connection of a resistor with resistance R and a coil with inductance L. The voltage is AC with frequency f, and it produces a current, y, in the circuit.

The factors in this design are:

y Output electrical current, 10 amperes (A)
V Input voltage, 100 V (AC)
f AC frequency, either 50 or 60 Hz
R Resistance; standard deviation is 16.33%
L Inductance; standard deviation is 16.33%

For the purpose intended, let us assume that this circuit has a target value of 10 A for the current. This example is taken from Japan, so the input voltage is 100 V. This is the nominal value. Of course, there will be some variation around 100 V. For historical reasons, part of Japan has electrical power at 50 Hz, and the rest of Japan has electrical power at 60 Hz. For economical production, it is advantageous to have electrical devices that work well at both 50 and 60 Hz.

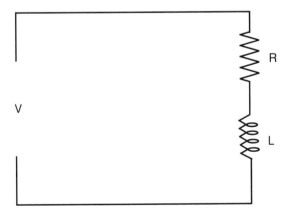

FIGURE 5.11. *RL* circuit.

First we identify the character of each of the factors.

y Functional factor; has a target value of 10 A.

V Noise factor; we have no control over the actual value, and there will be undesirable variations about the nominal value of 100 V.

f Noise factor; takes value of 50 or 60 Hz.

R Control factor; we are free to select the optimum value for R, or the value that will give the best system performance.

L At first, this may seem to be another control factor. However, once the nominal values for y, V, R, and f are specified, the nominal value of L can be determined. Therefore, we are not free to independently control the value of L. L is an *adjustment factor* that we use to keep the nominal value of the output equal to the target value of 10 A.

Now that we have analyzed the factors, we implement the seven-step optimization process.

1. Define Objective. The objective in this simple example is to keep the current at the nominal (target) value of 10 A. The failure modes to be avoided are excessive current and inadequate current. This will be achieved by minimizing the variance around the target value. However, we remember Sam the marksman (Chapter 3), who had small variance but was temporarily out of the bull's-eye. We want a metric that recognizes small variance, even when the mean value is temporarily off target. We want a metric that will identify the design that will have a small variance after the mean is adjusted to the target value, 10 A in this example.

We want the standard deviation of the current to be small, but small compared with what? Is 1.0 A a small standard deviation? If the mean value were 100 A, we probably would believe that 1.0 was a very small standard deviation. However, when the mean value is 10, we might judge that 1.0 is a fairly large standard deviation. Therefore, it is reasonable to compare the standard deviation with the mean by taking the ratio between the two.

The ratio between the mean and the standard deviation also provides the capability to recognize a small standard deviation even when the mean is temporarily off target. If in a specific evaluation the mean is 20 A and the standard deviation is 1.2 A, then by taking the ratio we are recognizing that when the mean is adjusted to 10 A, the standard deviation will also probably be reduced by the same ratio, i.e., to 0.6 A. If another condition gave a mean value of 10 and a standard deviation of 1.0, the ratio would alert us that a mean of 20 and a standard deviation of 1.2 is actually better, even though the standard deviation is temporarily larger. (See Appendix A for a detailed description.)

This concept of taking the ratio of the mean to the standard deviation is expressed in the figure of merit that is called the signal-to-noise (SN) ratio; see Equation (5.1), which follows. The SN ratio actually uses the square of the mean divided by the square of the standard deviation. This is because: (1) the quality loss depends upon the square of the standard deviation, and (2) the algebra of statistics utilizes quadratic forms. The numerator has a correction because the measured square of the mean ($\frac{1}{n}S_m$) will overestimate the actual value. (This is derived in any statistical text. For example, if the two values 3.1 and 2.9 are measured, the average of the squared values will be 9.01, which is greater than 9.00.)

$$\text{SN ratio} = 10 \log E \left[\frac{m^2}{\sigma^2} \right]$$

$$= 10 \log \frac{(1/n)(S_m - V)}{V} \tag{5.1}$$

where

$E =$ expectation
$m =$ mean
$\sigma =$ standard deviation
$n =$ number of measurements of y
$y =$ functional metric
$S_m = 1/n(\Sigma y_i)^2$
$V =$ variance $= \sigma^2 = 1/(n-1)(S_T - S_m)$
$S_T = \Sigma y_i^2$

There are a total of n measurements of the functional metric y_i. In many cases each value of y is measured under a different noise condition. This enables the SN ratio to more fully reflect the effect of noises. Equation (5.1) is the nominal-is-best SN ratio. It applies when the functional, customer-satisfaction goal is to maintain a single nominal value, 10 A in this example.

2. Three Feasible Values. When the values V, R, f, and L are all equal to their nominal values, then the value of the output will be equal to the target of 10 A. However, V, R, f, and L all have variations around their nominal values. These variations will cause the output to deviate from the target of 10 A. We want to choose a nominal value for the control factor R that will minimize the variation of the current, y, that is caused by the variations in V, f, R, and L. To search for the design (value of R) that is most robust against noises, we first choose three feasible alternative values for the nominal value of R. Assume that in the initial design of the circuit, a value of 5.0 ohms was selected for R. We will also try a larger value and a smaller value, seeking improvement. We take for the three feasible alternative values of R the values 2.78, 5.0, and 9.0 ohms (Ω), which are in equal ratios. The intent is to span the feasible space of design parameter values, usually with equal intervals on an arithmetic or a geometric scale.

Next, we calculate the value of L, for each value of R, that will keep the nominal output on the target of 10 A (for simplicity, the value of f is taken to be 55 Hz in making these calculations). This calculation is done by applying the circuit equation

$$y = \frac{V}{\sqrt{R^2 + (2\pi f L)^2}} \tag{5.2}$$

The nominal values of L (in henries) that correspond to the three feasible alternative nominal values of the control factor R are as follows:

Design Point	R	L (to keep nominal current of 10 A)
1	2.78 Ω	0.0278 H
2	5.0 Ω	0.0251 H
3	9.0 Ω	0.0126 H

These values of L adjust the nominal value of the current to the target of 10 A.

3. Select Alternatives for Evaluation. Since there are only three design alternatives, we can easily evaluate all three of them. In more realistic problems there are thousands or millions of alternatives and orthogonal arrays are used to select a balanced sample for evaluation, as will be described shortly.

4. Impose Noises. Now that three feasible alternative design points have been selected, we wish to evaluate the robustness against noises of each design point. The only significant circuit-level failure modes are the two kinds of excessive deviation of the current from its target value—in other words, excessive current and inadequate current. We need to select noise conditions that will excite both failure modes. For this simple device the evaluation of the deviation of the current can be done analytically, using the circuit equation, Equation (5.2). To evaluate the robustness against noises of each of the three design points, we need to calculate the variations in current, y, that are caused by the variations (noises) in V, R, f, and L. To do this, we use a simple numerical procedure. We select representative values for the variations of V, R, L, and f, as shown in the following table:

Value	V (V)	R (Ω)	L (H)	f (Hz)
Low	90	0.8 × nominal	0.8 × nominal	50
Nominal	100	Nominal	Nominal	55
High	110	1.2 × nominal	1.2 × nominal	60

The three values for each of the noises are obtained by taking the nominal value and adding and subtracting the standard deviation times $\sqrt{\frac{3}{2}}$. (The $\sqrt{\frac{3}{2}}$ is used to make the variance of the three points that represent the noise equal to the actual variance.) For f, of course, we have fixed high and low values, and we take a fictitious intermediate value of 55.

Now we have four noises (the variations of V, R, L, and f), each represented by three values. This gives a total of 81 (3^4) combinations. We see that things could easily become quite complicated. We could calculate the value of y for all 81 of the combinations. We would have to do that for each of the three design points, a total of 243 calculations. In this case, with a simple equation, we could easily use a computer to do the 243 calculations. However, we always want to seek simplifications in the process.

From Equation (5.2), we see that the large value of V and the small values of R, f, and L will give the largest value for y, tending to cause the failure mode of excessive current. Conversely, the small value for V and the large values for R, f, and L will give the smallest value for y, tending to cause the failure mode of inadequate current. Of course, when V, R, f, and L all have their nominal values, the value of y will be equal to the target value of 10 A. Thus, we need calculate only three values of y in order to characterize its variance in response to the four noises. When the noise values are combined in this way we get what is called a *compound noise factor*. In the following calculations the three combinations of the noises give values of y that are called y_{min}, y_{nom}, and y_{max}.

5. Evaluate Performance. We evaluate the performance at each of the design points—three, in this example. At each design point the performance is evaluated for each of the noise conditions—again three, in this example. This enables the robustness against the noises to be determined for each of the design options.

For design point 1 ($R = 2.78\,\Omega$, $L = 0.0278$ H),

$$y_{min} = \frac{90}{\sqrt{(2.78 \times 1.2)^2 + (2\pi \times 60 \times 0.0278 \times 1.2)^2}}$$
$$= 6.91\,\text{A}$$

$$y_{nom} = \frac{100}{\sqrt{(2.78)^2 + (2\pi \times 55 \times 0.0278)^2}}$$

$$= 10.00 \text{ A}$$

$$y_{max} = \frac{110}{\sqrt{(2.78 \times 0.8)^2 + (2\pi \times 50 \times 0.0278 \times 0.8)^2}}$$

$$= 15.03 \text{ A}$$

Three values of current have been calculated to evaluate the effect of noises on the performance of design point 1. The first calculation is with the noises in the direction that drives the output current low, the second calculation with nominal values (the magnitudes of the noises are zero), and the third calculation with the noises in the direction that drives the output current high. Next, the similar three calculations are repeated for the second and third design points.

For design point 2 ($R = 5\,\Omega$, $L = 0.0251$ H),

$$y_{min} = \frac{90}{\sqrt{(5 \times 1.2)^2 + (2\pi \times 60 \times 0.0251 \times 1.2)^2}}$$

$$= 7.03 \text{ A}$$

$$y_{nom} = \frac{100}{\sqrt{(5)^2 + (2\pi \times 55 \times 0.0251)^2}}$$

$$= 10.00 \text{ A}$$

$$y_{max} = \frac{110}{\sqrt{(5 \times 0.8)^2 + (2\pi \times 50 \times 0.0251 \times 0.8)^2}}$$

$$= 14.77 \text{ A}$$

For design point 3 ($R = 9\,\Omega$, $L = 0.0126$ H),

$$y_{min} = \frac{90}{\sqrt{(9 \times 1.2)^2 + (2\pi \times 60 \times 0.0126 \times 1.2)^2}}$$

$$= 7.37 \text{ A}$$

$$y_{nom} = \frac{100}{\sqrt{(9)^2 + (2\pi \times 55 \times 0.0126)^2}}$$

$$= 10.00 \text{ A}$$

$$y_{max} = \frac{110}{\sqrt{(9 \times 0.8)^2 + (2\pi \times 50 \times 0.0126 \times 0.8)^2}}$$

$$= 13.97 \text{ A}$$

6. Select Best Design Value. We can readily see that design point 3 is the best. The values for the current have less scatter; the standard deviation is the smallest. In this example, the nominal values of the output are the same for all three design points, because the value of L was used to adjust all of the nominal values to the target of 10 A. Therefore, there is no ambiguity in choosing design point 3 as the best. However, this is possible only because this example is so simple. Generally, we have to do a little more calculation to put the response in the best form for evaluation.

For the RL circuit, the data that are calculated from Equation (5.1) are:

Design Point	S_T	S_m	V	SN Ratio (dB)
1	373.65	340.05	16.80	8.07
2	367.57	337.08	15.25	8.47
3	349.48	327.40	11.04	9.80

The SN ratio is plotted in Figure 5.12.

We see that the SN ratio is still improving when R has the value of 9 Ω. Therefore, we project that we could achieve further improvement by increasing the value of R. However, R cannot be bigger than 10 Ω and still achieve the target value of 10 A for the output.

In this very simple example a confirmation is not needed. The selected design ($R = 9$) has already been evaluated. For more realistic optimizations, interpolation must be done. Then the design point that has been selected must be evaluated to confirm that it gives very robust performance.

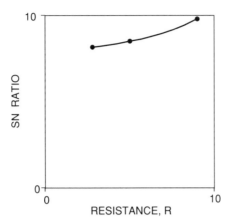

FIGURE 5.12. SN values for *RL* circuit.

In summary, this example of a very simple electrical circuit has demonstrated the change in the nominal value of a design parameter *R* (control factor) to improve functionality, in this case by reducing the variance of the output. This is the basic concept of product parameter design. The steps that were used in this example were:

Analyze problem. The system performance equation was written. (When an equation that accurately describes system performance is available, then it is very efficient to do the optimization analytically. Commonly, a system performance equation is not available and the optimization is done experimentally.) The factors were identified and classified as functional output, control, noise, and adjustment factors. Then the seven-step optimization process was implemented.

Step 1—define objective. The failure modes were analyzed, and the nominal-is-best signal-to-noise ratio was selected.

Step 2—select feasible alternative values. Three feasible alternative values were chosen for the control factor *R* (in this example, there was only one control factor). The nominal values of the adjustment factor *L* were selected to keep the output on target (10 A). (In this simple example, it was possible to adjust the value of the adjustment factor at the beginning of the process and keep the nominal value of the output on target for each of the trial design points. Commonly, the adjustment factor is selected and adjusted after most of the data analysis is complete.)

Step 3—select alternatives for evaluation. This example was so simple that all three design options could be evaluated.

Step 4—impose noises. The noises were represented by taking three values for each of the four noises. The three values were nominal and plus and minus $\sqrt{\frac{3}{2}}\sigma$ (where σ = standard deviation). The exception was for f, which had known high and low values. A compound noise factor was defined. This included all four noise factors in such a way that when the compound noise factor was moved in one direction, one type of failure mode occurred (the output became small) and when the compound noise factor was moved in the opposite direction, another type of failure mode occurred (the output became large). (In this simple example, the compound noise factor saved us only some simple calculations. However, when the performance evaluation must be done experimentally, the compound noise factor is extremely efficient in reducing the number of experiments and the time required.)

Step 5—evaluate performance of selected alternatives. Three values of output (corresponding to three values of the compound noise factor) were calculated for each of the trial design points.

Step 6—select the best design values. The three values of output were used to calculate the signal-to-noise (SN) ratio for each of the trial design points. The value of the control factor that gave the largest signal-to-noise ratio was selected as the best design value. This design value kept the functionality as close as possible to the ideal customer satisfaction value, 10 A in this example.

Step 7—confirmation of robust performance. This was not needed in this simple example.

Now that some of the mechanics of robustness optimization have been described in this very simple example, we turn to a more complete description of the optimization process.

Step 1—Define Objective (Functional Metrics)

The most important step in the optimization of robust functionality is to develop (or select) the best metric to use in evaluating the functionality. Once we have a good metric, it is relatively easy to find changes in the values of the critical design parameters that improve the metric. We seek a functional metric that has properties that enable us to quickly do the optimization:

- One number captures the essential physics of the function.
- The metric incorporates the effect of the noises.
- The ease of making an adjustment is recognized (as it was for Sam's shooting, in Chapter 3).
- Effects are additive; if changing control factor A causes 10% improvement and changing B causes 20% improvement, then the two combined should produce 30% improvement.
- The metric utilizes all information.
- The metric is based on the quality loss function.

We have a natural tendency to use metrics that have been found to be appropriate in the evaluation of field performance. This has been a major failure in the traditional development process, for field metrics are usually not well suited for the early development of functionality, since they lack some of the properties just listed. Failure (defect) rate is a good example. Although it is good for measuring the final performance, it fails badly as a developmental metric. It does not recognize the ease of making an adjustment. Sam would have been judged as having a 100% failure rate in hitting the bull's-eye, even though Sam can easily change his failure rate to zero by making a simple adjustment. Failure rate is also very poor for additivity, and it does not effectively utilize the available information. Failures occur because some parameter has exceeded a limiting value. For example, if two lines on a VLSI circuit are too wide, they will product a short-circuit failure. Rather than just measure the occasional failure, it is much better to measure the line width.

Taguchi has pioneered a better class of functional metrics that he named signal-to-noise ratios; he was the first to extend the use of this term beyond its older, more obvious applications. The signal is the functionality that we want, and the noise refers to the deviation or degradation of performance from the ideal. For a television picture, the signal is the picture that is sent out from the station. Noise is snow and other degradations in picture quality. Thus, we want a large value for the signal-to-noise ratio. There are a large variety of types of signal-to-noise ratios. One of the most important tasks is to develop (or select) the best signal-to-noise ratio for a particular device. Signal-to-noise ratios are described in more detail in Appendix A.

Although we would like to have a single metric to quantify the functionality, it is obvious that a single number can at best measure the results of a single set of physics. If a product has several sets of relatively independent physics, then several metrics will be required, one for each set of physics. For example, in a copier there are four sets of physics that have little to do with each other: copy handling, imaging, document handling, and finishing of the copy sets. It seems clear that optimizing the copy handling will not optimize the image quality, nor will it improve the functionality of document handling and stapling. Therefore, at a minimum, a metric will be needed for each of these modules of the total system.

It is also clear that one metric cannot capture every detailed quirk of performance. For example, image quality has many detailed components, such as hollow characters, ragged edges, and dark background. We seek one image quality metric that captures the essence of the physics. It characterizes the transfer of energy from the source (whether document, computer, or photographic subject) to the final image. Once it is maximized, the physics has been greatly improved. Then detailed experimentation can determine the best balance among the residual image-quality deviations from the ideal.

Paper Feeder Example. The simplest metric for the paper feeder is failure rate, the percentage of trials in which a single sheet is not delivered. However, as noted in the previous paragraphs, this is not a good metric. It is traditional to break this down into three components: misfeed rate, multifeed rate, and jam rate, as suggested in the fault tree (Figure 5.8). This is an improvement on a composite rate, but a continuous variable is much to be preferred. One good metric is the time of arrival of the sheet at the output from the feeder, the take-away rolls (TAR) in Figure 5.7. When the sheet is late, the feeder is tending toward a misfeed. When the sheet arrives early, it is tending toward a multifeed. This is an example of using the measurement of a continuous performance variable as the functional metric.

Another approach is to measure threshold values of a critical parameter at which a failure mode is excited. For the feeder, such a critical parameter is the stack force, the normal force between the feed belt and the paper stack. If the stack force is very small, a misfeed is certain to happen. If the stack force is very large, a multifeed is certain to happen. This provides a convenient metric for both failure modes, as is displayed in Figure 5.13.

When we make the misfeed threshold small and the multifeed threshold large, then there is a large operating window in between for successful operation. A stack force near the center of the operating window will provide good paper feeding. Another perspective is that even when bad papers reduce the width of the operating window, reliable feeding can still be achieved. The larger the width of the operating window, the more robust the feeding functionality.

To achieve a wide operating window, we want the misfeed force to be as close to zero as possible, and the multifeed force to be as large as possible. Typically, we measure the thresholds at some high failure rate, such as 10% or 50%, so that the experimentation time is greatly shortened. Of course, the desired rates are very much smaller, but we only want to make comparisons among different design options, so the actual rates are not important. By defining the threshold forces at high misfeeding and multifeeding rates, we save much time. We have to run only a few hundred sheets of paper to determine the threshold forces.

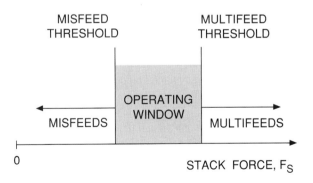

Figure 5.13. Force thresholds as functional metrics.

We make n measurements of the misfeed threshold force, F_{mi}, usually one measurement at each of n different noise conditions. However, to save time we often combine all of the noises that tend to cause misfeeds into one compound noise. Then the value of n is 1. The n measurements are repeated for each control condition. Then these n values are used in a smaller-is-better SN ratio for one control condition, with the calculation repeated for each control condition (design option):

$$\text{SN ratio} = -10 \log \frac{1}{n}(F^2_{mi,1} + F^2_{mi,2} + \cdots + F^2_{mi,n}) \qquad (5.3)$$

This is a standard SN ratio. Zero is the ideal customer satisfaction target, unattainable, but always to be strived for. The values of F are squared because of the quadratic quality loss function (Chapter 3). Thus, after dividing by n, this is proportional to the quality loss that is averaged over the different noise conditions that were used in the n tests. Taking the logarithm has been found usually to improve the additivity. Multiplying by 10 is simply a convention; it makes the units decibels. The negative sign is to make the value of the SN ratio become larger as the threshold force becomes smaller. As the values of force approach zero, the logarithm becomes negative, and the negative sign makes the SN ratio become positive. Background (black) density on a copy is another example of a smaller-is-better metric. The customers want the background to be white—in other words, zero density. The smaller-is-better SN ratio is used whenever the ideal customer satisfaction value is zero.

For multifeeds, the sample procedure is used, but now the threshold force should be as large as possible. Therefore, the values of force are put into the bigger-is-better SN ratio. A little reflection will confirm that if we take the reciprocal of the multifeed threshold force, it will again be the smaller-is-better case.

$$\text{SN ratio} = -10 \log \frac{1}{n}(F^{-2}_{mu,1} + F^{-2}_{mu,2} + \cdots + F^{-2}_{mu,n}) \qquad (5.4)$$

We see that this is the same as the smaller-is-better SN ratio except for the negative exponent on F, which indicates the reciprocal. As the force becomes larger, the logarithm becomes smaller, and the negative sign makes the SN ratio become larger. To obtain a single figure of merit, we can simply add the two SN ratios to obtain the overall SN ratio for misfeeding and multifeeding:

$$\text{SN ratio} = -10 \log \frac{1}{n}(F_{mi,1}^2 + F_{mi,2}^2 + \cdots + F_{mi,n}^2)$$
$$-10 \log \frac{1}{n}(F_{mu,1}^{-2} + F_{mu,2}^{-2} + \cdots + F_{mu,n}^{-2}) \qquad (5.5)$$

This example shows some important aspects of the development of functionality metrics. The PDT thinks carefully about the physics of the device to determine which of the continuous variables that could be measured best characterizes the functionality. Often there will be more than one approach; in this example, both time of arrival and threshold force could be used. The team chooses one measurement and identifies the ideal value—zero, in the smaller-is-better case. This then leads to the incorporation of the measurement into a standard type of SN ratio.

Common Types of SN Ratio. The most common types of SN ratio are:

- Smaller-is-better (introduced for the paper feeder)
- Bigger-is-better (introduced for the paper feeder)
- Nominal-is-best (introduced for the *RL* circuit)
- Proportional-is-best

A power supply is a commercial example of nominal-is-best; there is a target (nominal) output voltage that is ideal. Proportional-is-best is exemplified by imaging and by steering a car. On an image we want the gray scale to be equal to the gray-scale value on the original. In steering we want the turning radius of the car to be proportional to the angle of the steering wheel. In other words, we want the output to be proportional to a signal that is given to the product. In the case of the copier we give the signal in the form of the original document. In the case of the car we signal by turning the steering wheel. Appendix A describes SN ratios more completely.

The work of the PDT to define the best functionality metric is by far the most important step toward the optimization of robust function. Combined with the earlier failure analysis, which identified the critical control and noise factors, the appropriate SN ratio is almost all that is needed to quickly complete the robustness optimization.

Next we want to plan the experimentation to quickly find values for the critical control factors that are close to optimum, as close as we can get in a short time. Time to market is very important, so we generally want to follow an 80/20 rule: achieving 80% of the possible gain in 20% of the time that would be required to make the full improvement.

Step 2—Select Feasible Alternative Values

Our PDT picks feasible values for the critical control factors. Each factor has an initial value that we have selected as the best value based on our experience. When our experience indicates nothing more precise than a range of values, we usually select for our initial value a value in the middle of the range. It is usually prudent to select a smaller value and a larger value, seeking improvement. This then gives three alternative feasible values: the initial value, a larger value, and a smaller value. Usually we select these values to span most of the feasible range; staying too close to the initial values is guaranteed to minimize the improvement.

Two levels are often used instead of three, although with the disadvantage that trends could be missed when the graph of signal-to-noise values versus control-factor values is far from a straight line. It is everyone's nightmare to measure the same SN value at two endpoints, missing the superior value at the mid-range. More than three levels are sometimes used, especially when discrete options are included, such as six materials.

If the evaluations must be done experimentally, which is usually the case for electromechanical systems, then we take care to reduce the number of trials. The first step in doing this is to prioritize the critical design parameters, on the basis of our team members' experience. The priorities we establish rarely turn out to be exactly right, but this step does improve the efficiency of the optimization. It helps to experiment first with the control factors that most affect functionality. In a continuation of our paper feeder case, assume that we find and prioritize 20 critical design parameters that we might identify at the bottom of our fault tree.

We decide to include the 13 at the top of our list of 20 in the first round of experiments. In experimental evaluation it is uncommon to use more than 13 control factors (with three levels for each) in one set of experiments, although in rare instances as many as 40 are used.

Paper Feeder Example. For our paper feeder we have selected the 13 critical design parameters at the top of our priority list:

(1) Wrap angle (feed belt around retard roll)
(2) Belt tension (in feed belt; important for creating normal force against retard roll)
(3) Retard coefficient of friction (stops second sheet)
(4) Radius of retard roll
(5) Retard brake torque
(6) Entrance angle (on entrance guide; breaks up big slugs of paper)
(7) Friction coefficient on entrance guide
(8) Mouth opening at entrance
(9) Angle between feed belt and stack
(10) Contact point between feed belt and stack; distance from stack edge
(11) Width of feed belt
(12) Feed belt velocity
(13) Take-away roll velocity

We judge these to be the 13 most important design parameters, by starting with the experience of our PDT members, clarifying our first result by preparing the fault tree (Figure 5.8), and verifying the fault tree with an FMEA table. There are other important design parameters; we will have an opportunity to evaluate them during second and third iterations of the optimization process.

After the control factors have been prioritized, the PDT selects three feasible alternative values. For example, we select the following values for the first two critical design parameters:

Critical	Level		
Parameter	1	2	3
Wrap angle	35°	40°	45°
Belt tension	5 N	10 N	15 N

Now the PDT has 13 control factors with three levels of feasible alternative values for each. This seems to be fairly moderate, not biting off more than can be chewed. However, even this innocent-appearing problem has 3^{13}, or 1,594,323, discrete design points—that is, combinations of design values, each of which might be the best. Obviously, we can try only a few of these, so we need a good strategy. The primary approach is designed experiments that yield a large amount of information from a relatively few experiments.

Number of Control Factors. Roughly 20 critical design parameters are usually about the right number for the optimization process. The actual number that the team will identify depends on (1) the size and complexity of the system, and (2) the criticality threshold. If an entire complex product, such as a car, copier, or computer, is taken as the unit for optimization, the number of critical parameters can easily be 1000 or more. This is far too many for optimization in one activity. Likewise, if the criticality threshold is allowed to be too low, there will be an excess of design parameters, many of them not very important to the fundamental functionality of the system. Making the right judgment about the size and complexity of the system and the criticality threshold is essential to the success of the team.

For complex products the optimization is done at the subsystem level. However, this still leaves much to the judgment of the team. For a car, should the unit for one optimization activity be the engine, the entire power train, or the valve train within the engine? There is not a universal answer to this question. As our team becomes more experienced at doing optimization, we learn the best path. Sometimes it is best to do optimization at more than one level. For example, there could be activities to optimize both the engine and the entire power train. The engine optimization could optimize 20 engine design values. The power train optimization could optimize 20 power train values, of which 10 are engine parameters. In other words, work on the entire system optimizes the most criti-cal design values. Then work at the next level down—the engine, for example—optimizes the design parameters that were not quite critical enough to be considered in the optimization of the higher-level system.

Priorities are needed to maintain the right level of criticality. With the help of the fault tree, the team prepares a prioritized list of the critical design parameters. If we judge that the top 20 on the list control most of the functionality, then we proceed with the optimization. However, if we judge that many more than 20 design parameters are involved in the fundamental functionality of the system, then the system probably needs to be decomposed into smaller units for optimization.

Once the appropriate decomposition of the system and the appropri-ate criticality threshold have allowed us to identify roughly 20 critical design parameters, the optimization is ready to proceed. Three feasible alternative values for each of 20 parameters give 3.5×10^9 options, far too many. Typically, the top 8 or 13 parameters are included in one opti-mization. Even 13 parameters leave 1,594,323 options, so a small subset need to be selected for actual evaluation.

Step 3—Select Alternatives for Evaluation

Designed experiments enable us to efficiently sample the many design points. As described in Chapter 3, orthogonal arrays define balanced sets of values so that all levels of each factor appear an equal number of times and all combinations of levels for any two factors appear an equal num-ber of times. These are the simple, commonsense requirements for sys-tematic experimentation. Orthogonal arrays have been found to be very useful for optimizing robust functionality.

The L_{27} orthogonal array contains 13 columns and 27 rows (see Fig-ure 3.14). The 27 rows define 27 trials (experiments or calculations) out of the total of 1,594,323 design options (13 design parameters at 3 levels each). The other most-used array for robustness optimization is the L_{18}, which has eight columns, one with two levels and seven with three lev-els. Also, columns can be modified to better fit a particular optimization requirement. For example, in an early Xerox application, the first two columns of the L_{18} were combined to form one six-level column. This was used to evaluate six materials, along with six continuous-variable design parameters, which were assigned to the other six columns.

Paper Feeder Example. For the first round of optimization, we assign our 13 critical design parameters to the 13 columns of the L_{27} orthogonal array. The simple approach is to assign the first parameter, wrap angle, to the first column. Then the parameters are assigned in order until take-away roll velocity is assigned to the 13th column. However, sometimes we want to improve upon this simple approach. Some parameters will be easy to change during the experimental work, while others will be difficult. The most difficult parameter to change is best assigned to the first column. Then it has to be changed only twice during the experimentation. Completing the experimentation quickly is essential for success.

The assignment of the 13 critical design parameters for the feeder to the L_{27} defines 27 different combinations of design values—in other words, 27 different setups of our paper feeder that we will evaluate, seeking the best combination.

Randomization. In traditional experiment design, it has been common to randomize the order of performing the 27 experiments. This has been a response to the possible problem of systematic changes in the environment. For example, if we conduct the first nine experiments in the morning, the next nine in the afternoon, and the final nine the next morning, we could be confused by differences in the environment between morning and afternoon. This would make level 2 of the first column appear different from levels 1 and 3, even if each level inherently had the same performance. We must guard against this possibility. However, randomization of the experimental sequence will often greatly extend the time to complete the experimentation. The alternative is to ensure that systematic changes in the environment do not occur. In robustness optimization we are imposing a control on the environment by maintaining large values of noise, so randomization is usually neither required nor desirable.

Step 4—Impose Noises
An essential aspect of robustness optimization is reflected in challenging the design with rather severe values of noises. This early imposition of noises serves the purpose of problem prevention, to avoid extensive rework of the design later during development. We impose noises to

excite failure modes. Therefore, it is very important that we select noises that will cause all of the failure modes.

The basic principle is to excite each failure mode. Thus, if low humidity, low temperature, and high electrostatic charge combined together are known to cause one failure mode, and high humidity, high temperature, and low electrostatic charge cause an "opposite" failure mode, then this defines a good compound noise factor. In this way we commonly take only two noise values.

For a device with a simple, continuous-variable output, such as the output voltage from a power supply, this is straightforward. There are two primary failure modes, excessive voltage and inadequate voltage. First, combine all of the noise values that drive the voltage down and measure the output voltage. Then reverse the values of the noises, driving the output voltage to the high side, and measure the output voltage. The difference between the two output voltages is a simple measure of robustness. The design with the least spread between the two voltages is the robust design.

Of course, if the evaluation trials are easy, then we do not have to be so stringent in reducing the number of noise values. This is especially true if the evaluations can be done on a computer, rather than requiring experimentation. Then it is common practice to use an orthogonal array to select a sample of noise combinations.

Once the noise combinations have been selected, they are applied to each of the design combinations that were selected for evaluation in step 3.

Paper Feeder Example.   The paper feeder is not as simple as a power supply. We are primarily concerned about two failure modes, misfeeds and multifeeds. The most important noise factor is the paper that is being fed. Misfeeds will be excited by paper with strong forces that tend to hold back the first sheet, such as a large value of the friction coefficient in relation to the second sheet. Multifeeds will be excited by large differences in friction across the second sheet. When the friction at the 1-2 interface is large and the friction at the 2-3 interface is small, the net friction force on the second sheet tends to drive the second sheet through the retard zone and cause a multifeed. The two failure modes cannot be excited by simply reversing the deviations from nominal for the most important noise factors, as can be done for a power supply.

Instead, special "stress stacks" of paper have to be selected or prepared, one for misfeeds and the other for multifeeds. The only sure guideline we have for selecting the noises to use during robustness optimization is for our PDT to thoroughly consider the physics of the system function, using fault trees to help organize its thoughts.

The effect of noise (type of paper) on the thresholds is displayed in Figure 5.14. With good paper, the two thresholds are far apart, a very good SN ratio. However, this is because very little noise is being put into the system, so there is little noise in the performance. The real tests are the difficult papers, which can be simulated by stress stacks. They give a much narrower operating window. We use these to challenge the system, early in development, long before our customers will challenge our product. By optimizing with large noises (difficult papers), we select the best design values to withstand the rigors of the marketplace.

The paper feeder exhibits another complexity that is often encountered. In addition to the two primary failure modes, there are other failure modes. The feeder must be made robust against them also. An exam-

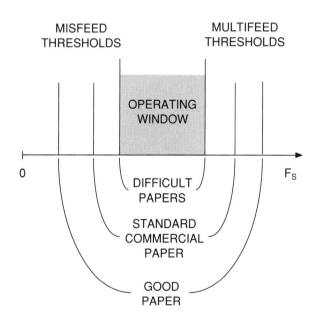

Figure 5.14. Effect of noise on functionality.

ple is paper damage. If the forces on the paper are excessive, then the paper will be damaged. This requires another test set of noises that will tend to cause paper damage. One set of noises is needed for each failure mode. We must make our product robust against the noises, not waiting for the problems to occur later during development or in the field.

Summary—Challenging the Design. We select noises to challenge the design by causing the major failure modes. This enables the design to be improved (made more robust), so that the failure modes are much less likely to occur in the field. If the performance evaluations can be done on a computer, or if the experimentation is very easy, then an orthogonal array is used to sample the many combinations of noises. However, for most experimental evaluations this would lead to an excessive number of trials. Usually, compound noise factors are used; one noise combination is used to excite each failure mode. For many systems this means that only one or two noise values are needed.

We apply the defined noise combinations to each design combination—in other words, to each row in the orthogonal array of the control (design) factors. This gives each design an equal opportunity to demonstrate its ability to cope with the noises.

Step 5—Evaluate Performance of Selected Alternatives

Next we evaluate the performance of the design and noise combinations that we have selected. Since all of the noise combinations are applied to each design combination (row of the control orthogonal array), the total number of evaluations is equal to the product of the number of design combinations and the number of noise combinations. We seek enough information to be able to pick the most robust combination of design values.

Paper Feeder Example. First we set up our paper feeder according to the first row of the L_{27} orthogonal array (see Figure 3.14), with all of the values at level 1. For example, the wrap angle is set at 35° and the belt tension at 5 newtons (N). All of the 13 critical design parameters are set at their level-1 value. Then we challenge the feeder with our misfeed stress stack and our multifeed stress stack. This is done for each of the 27 design points that are defined by the L_{27} orthogonal array.

We decide to use a 50% misfeed rate to define the threshold. For example, for the third design point we set the stack force to 0.5 pound and make 10 attempts to feed, with seven misfeeds. At 0.6 pound there are five misfeeds, and at 0.7 pound there are two misfeeds. We conclude that 0.6 pound is the threshold force for misfeeds for design combination 3, and we enter this on our data sheet. Then we place our multifeed stress stack in the feeder, repeat the procedure, and find that the multifeed threshold is 0.7 pound.

We repeat this for all 27 design combinations. This is usually done in a sequence that facilitates the changes in the fixture. If there is one design parameter that takes a long time to change, then we run the first nine experiments with it constant; thus we have to change it only twice. Of course, we must take care that there is not some systematic change occurring that would confound our results. For example, if the humidity were low for the first nine runs and high for the second nine runs, we might mistakenly attribute the effect of humidity to the design parameter that was changed after nine trials.

After we complete the experimentation with the feeder set up in each of 27 combinations of design values, we have data such as shown in the following table:

| | Threshold Force (lb) | |
Trial	Misfeed	Multifeed
3	0.6	0.7
24	0.3	1.1

These data are displayed in Figure 5.15.

Summary—Evaluating Design Combinations. We evaluate the performance for each noise condition, and we repeat the series of evaluations for each design combination. By doing so, we can evaluate the ability of each design to avoid the failure modes that are caused by the noise.

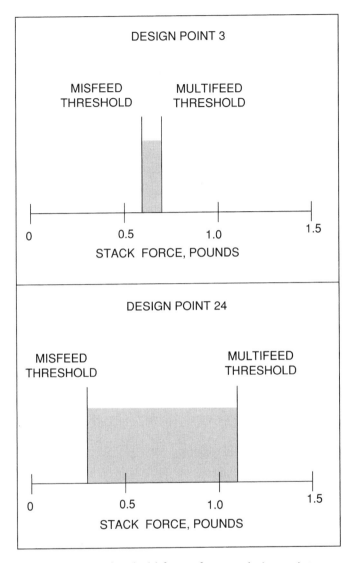

FIGURE 5.15. Threshold forces for two design points.

Step 6—Select the Best Design Values

After the data are obtained, they are used to calculate the value of the functional metric, the SN ratio that has been selected. This is then used to select the best design.

Paper Feeder Example. We can easily observe from the data which of the 27 design points have produced the biggest operating window. However, we actually want to select the design that is the best, or close to it, from among the complete 1,594,323 options. Since we have evaluated only 27 options, the probability that the best was among them is small. Therefore, we must interpolate among the 27 data points to find the design point that is the best on the basis of our data. The interpolation is more efficient when the SN ratio is used, so first we calculate the SN ratio from the raw data. To do this we use Equation (5.5). In this example, the value of n is 1 for both of the terms in Equation (5.5); we used only one stress stack and measured one value of the threshold force for both misfeeds and multifeeds. The calculated values for the SN ratio are as follows:

Threshold Force

Trial	Misfeed	Multifeed	SN Ratio (dB)
3	0.6	0.7	1.34
24	0.3	1.1	11.3

The absolute values of the SN ratio are meaningless, since they will change if the amount of input noise is changed. However, the relative value will be unchanged and clearly distinguishes the better design points. In this example the difference of 10 decibels is a large advantage for design point 24 over design point 3.

The SN values for all 27 design trials are given in the following table:

Trial	SN (dB)	Trial	SN (dB)	Trial	SN (dB)
1	−8.94	10	5.10	19	3.48
2	0.74	11	9.11	20	9.42
3	1.34	12	8.26	21	8.41
4	4.29	13	5.10	22	8.16
5	8.24	14	7.44	23	10.8
6	6.52	15	10.6	24	11.3
7	6.75	16	5.58	25	9.90
8	10.2	17	9.83	26	14.6
9	9.46	18	11.0	27	16.5

To estimate the effect of each control factor, we seek to match patterns in the SN data with patterns in the changes that we made in the control factors over the full set of 27 trials. For example, if the SN data show the pattern in Figure 5.16, then the changes in the value of the SN ratio are entirely due to the changes that we made in the first control factor, assigned to column 1 of the L_{27} orthogonal array. Column 1 changes only after trials 9 and 18, which is exactly the pattern in the SN data in Figure 5.16. This simple observation leads us to calculate the average pattern in the data corresponding to the pattern of changes for each control factor.

To find the average pattern in the data that matches the pattern by which we changed control factor 1, we first calculate the average of the first nine SN ratios, for which control factor 1 had its level-1 value. This gives an average value of 4.29 decibels (dB). We repeat this calculation for the second nine values and the third nine values:

Control Factor 1

Level	SN (average, dB)
1	4.29
2	8.00
3	10.3
Overall average	7.52

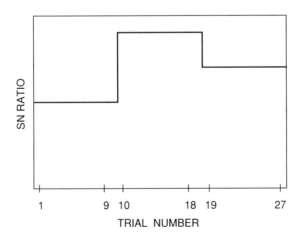

FIGURE 5.16. Pattern in SN data.

These data are plotted in Figure 5.17. Level 3 for control factor 1 is the best, giving 2.8 dB more robust functionality than the average value of 7.52.

We repeat this procedure for each control factor, finding the best level for each critical design parameter and calculating the improvement above the average. This gives our best estimate of the optimum design point, the best out of the 1,594,323 options, and the expected robustness when we will actually evaluate this best design. The best design point in this example is expressed as 3323322233333, where each digit is the best level for each of the 13 critical design parameters given in sequence. For example, as we have seen, level 3 is the best for control factor 1.

To calculate the expected robustness for our chosen design, we add the improvements to the overall average SN value. For example, we add the improvement of 2.8 dB from control factor 1 to the overall average of 7.5 to obtain 10.3. Since this was the average value when control factor 1 was at level 3 during the 27 evaluations, this seems to be a reasonable prediction. Control factor 2 gave the biggest improvement, 3.2 dB, so the expected robustness after changing both control factors 1 and 2 to their best values is 7.5 + 2.8 + 3.2 = 13.5 dB. We proceed to add the improvements from other control factors to determine the expected value

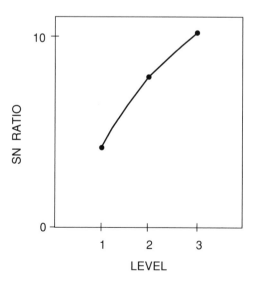

FIGURE 5.17. SN for control factor 1.

of robustness when we evaluate our chosen design. The complete list of improvements is as follows:

Design	Improvement	Design	Improvement
2	3.2	12	0.58
1	2.6	10	0.53
3	1.7	8	0.48
4	1.6	11	0.39
5	1.6	9	0.23
6	0.75	13	0.20
7	0.63		

However, it is prudent not to depend on all of the individual improvements from every control factor. There is inevitably some randomness in the data, and the additivity that we are striving for will never be perfect. A simple procedure is to rank-order all of the improvements from largest down to the smallest. In this example, we record the 13 values of improvement from 3.2 and 2.6 down to the smallest value. Then we discard the improvements from the bottom half of the list and calculate the expected robustness as the overall average plus the improvements from the top half of the list. (However, we change the values of all of the control factors to the optimum values, unless there is some reason not to, such as increased cost.) In this example the result is an expected robustness of 18.0 dB. We ignore the 2.4 dB of supposed improvement from the six factors at the bottom of the list.

After the robustness is optimized, we must often do an adjustment to achieve the best performance. The concept of adjustment was introduced with Sam the marksman in Chapter 3. He had excellent robustness, but his initial cluster was outside the bull's-eye. By adjusting his sights he moved the cluster into the bull's-eye.

For the paper feeder, the adjustment factor is obvious. We adjust the performance by adjusting the value for the stack force. Clearly, we want it to be somewhere near the middle of the operating window. Too far to either side would drastically favor one failure mode over another. For example, if we set the value of the stack force to be very small, near the left boundary of the operating window, the multifeed rate would be very small. However, the misfeed rate would be high. We use adjustment to achieve the best balance between the failure rates for different failure modes. For the feeder, misfeeds are slightly less objectionable than multifeeds. This is reflected in the subsystem expectations, Figures 5.2 and 5.10. The specified misfeed rate is approximately twice the multifeed rate. Therefore, we adjust the value of the stack force a little toward the left of the center of the operating window. The smaller value of the stack force slightly favors misfeeds. A little analysis and experimentation will determine the value of the stack force that gives approximately the 2:1 ratio of misfeeds greater than multifeeds.

For a nominal-is-best performance parameter, the adjustment is usually of the mean value of the output to the target. Thus, for a nine-volt power supply, the mean is adjusted to the target of nine volts. This favors both failure modes equally. If there were some reason to favor high voltage over low voltage, then the mean would be set a little over the target value.

For nominal-is-best performance we must find a control factor that is useful for adjusting the output. We look in our data for a control factor that has little effect on the SN ratio but does change the mean value. This factor is then used as the adjustment factor.

For smaller-is-better performance, the concept of adjustment does not apply during design. The target is zero, which cannot be achieved. We use all of the factors that reduce the output to improve the SN ratio. Because the target is unachievable, the concept of adjustment does not apply. This is also true for bigger-is-better performance.

We predict the final performance after the adjustment is made. This prediction is stated in the functional metric itself—misfeed rate, for example.

The prediction of the performance for the best design point can be improved by using analysis of variance (ANOVA), as described in many standard texts. However, the simple rule of thumb of dropping the SN improvements from the bottom half of the list is sufficient for product people who are not familiar with ANOVA.

Next we perform a confirmation evaluation to determine the actual value.

Summary—Using SN Values to Find the Best Design. The SN value is calculated for each design combination (each row of the control orthogonal array). The average SN value is then calculated for each level of each critical design parameter. The level that gives the best average SN value is tentatively chosen as the best for each of the critical design parameters. The SN value for the best design is predicted.

Step 7—Confirmation of Robust Performance

The product is set up to the combination of values that the data indicated was the best. Then we evaluate this design to confirm its robust functionality.

Paper Feeder Example   To continue our fictionalized case study, we test the feeder setup to our chosen design: 3323322233333. This gives an SN value of 17.1 dB—not as much as predicted, but much better than the value for our initial design. We are very happy, even though it is not as good as the prediction.

Summary—Confirming Robustness.   The performance predictions are inherently quite uncertain. We are sacrificing accuracy in order to shorten the development time. The predictions simply give us a rough feel for what to expect. If the confirmation result is too far away from the prediction, then we suspect that something is wrong and more effort is needed to improve our robustness procedure. However, a substantial improvement is usually achieved, which is critical to the successful development of our new product.[1]

Iteration

After the confirmation is completed, we typically carry out one or two more iterations of the optimization process. We drop the design parameters that produced little improvement and pick up some new parameters from our prioritized list that we developed from our fault tree. For example, we might drop the four design parameters that had the least effect and pick up the next four on our priority list. Also, we narrow the range

---

[1]This has been an introduction to the optimization process to achieve robust performance. An excellent book on this very important subject is *Quality Engineering Using Robust Design*, by Dr. Madhav Phadke (1989). The reader is strongly encouraged to further pursue the subject of robust design.

of values that we will try for the design parameters that produced good improvement during our first iteration. Thus, we seek to fine-tune the best value for the most important parameters.

Three iterations are usually all that is needed. In the feeder example, we repeat the application of the L_{27} orthogonal array three times, adding three confirmations for a total of 84 evaluations. In planning the robustness optimization, it is quite likely that we planned for 84 evaluations, and decided that it was within our schedule. We always seek the best balance between time and robustness improvement.

After making a substantial improvement in robustness, we want to ensure that it is captured in the subsequent piece-part design and maintained during production preparation and actual production. To accomplish this we prepare a critical parameter drawing.

Critical Parameter Drawing

The optimized values for the critical design parameters are displayed on the critical parameter drawing. The example for the paper feeder is shown in Figure 5.18.

This is the skeletal design. Experience has shown that this documentation is by far the best form for achieving commitment and follow-through during the subsequent design activities. The objective is to achieve a low-cost design that incorporates the critical parameter values to ensure robust functionality.

Benefits of Robustness

The benefits of achieving robustness early are enormous. The benefits to the customer are direct. The product functionality stays close to ideal customer satisfaction under the actual conditions of use. Also, the cost is reduced because the reduced sensitivity to production variations lessens the need for high precision, inspection, scrap, and rework. Most important of all the benefits, our schedule is shortened. The remainder of the product development program from this time on will go much more smoothly than in the traditional process, because much rework of the design has been eliminated.

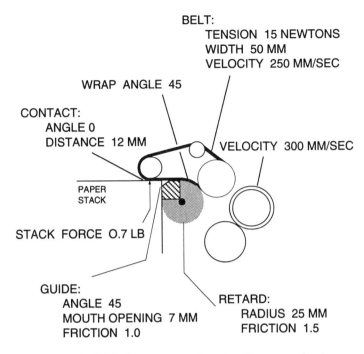

BELT:
TENSION 15 NEWTONS
WIDTH 50 MM
VELOCITY 250 MM/SEC

WRAP ANGLE 45

CONTACT:
ANGLE 0
DISTANCE 12 MM

VELOCITY 300 MM/SEC

PAPER
STACK

STACK FORCE 0.7 LB

GUIDE:
ANGLE 45
MOUTH OPENING 7 MM
FRICTION 1.0

RETARD:
RADIUS 25 MM
FRICTION 1.5

FIGURE **5.18.** Critical parameter drawing for paper feeder.

In the traditional process the subsystems were developed to some degree of feasibility before full systems were tested. Then when the full systems were tested, a large new crop of problems arose, causing great anguish and delay. These were often referred to as *system interactions*, because they occurred when the subsystems were integrated together into the total system. However, they were primarily manifestations of the lack of robustness. For example, subsystem A was developed to some degree of feasibility, but robustness was not emphasized, so it was still sensitive to noises. At the initial system integration, subsystem A was interfaced with subsystems B, C, and D for the first time. These provided a new set of large noises to A. Since A was still sensitive to noises, its performance became very erratic. Much rework of the design followed in build-test-fix cycles that greatly extended the development time.

Now, in *total quality development*, A is made robust before system integration. B, C, and D are also made robust. Benefit is gained in two ways.

Subsystem A is robust and so has less reaction to noises from B, C, and D. Also, B, C, and D are robust and so the magnitudes of the noises they put out are smaller. Combined, these two benefits greatly reduce the problems of erratic performance after system integration.

The early optimization of robustness greatly accelerates our schedule by eliminating much of the development rework that was inherent in the traditional process. This is problem prevention at its best.

DETAILED PIECE-PART REQUIREMENTS

Now that the branch into systematic optimization has been described, we return to the other design activities. In parallel with the skeletal design, other early critical decisions are made to complete the requirements for the detailed design of the piece parts. This is represented in the bottom half of the main box in Figure 5.3. Thus begins the filling-in around the skeletal design, going from the critical parameters to the complete production-intent design. It is done in parallel with the skeletal design, with very close communication and iteration between the two activities. The critical decisions are made by applying extended QFD, including functional analysis and Pugh concept selection. For example, in the paper feeder (see Figure 5.7), it is clear to the PDT very early during the subsystem design that the wrap angle of the feed belt around the retard roll is a critical parameter. Its precise value during production will be strongly determined by the bridge across the paper path that supports the feed mechanisms. The PDT can immediately start to work on the basic design of the beam (bridge), not waiting for a complete determination from the skeletal design activity of the exact best value for the wrap angle. The challenge in designing the beam is to achieve precise relative positions between the feed belt and the retard roll, while keeping the manufacturing cost to a minimum.

This activity is best done by carrying out the tasks that are outlined in the piece-part section of Figure 5.3. The end objective is to complete the material and process selection (MAPS), and to define the piece-part requirements in the subsystem/piece-part (SS/PP) QFD matrix. This is done primarily for the parts that are most critical for the strong impact they have on costs, or for which there may be difficulty in controlling the critical design parameter values with the required precision.

As an example for the feeder, the result of MAPS is aluminum die castings. The SS/PP QFD matrix captures important values from both the skeletal design and the detailed piece-part requirements design. Examples of the former are wrap angle (feed belt around the retard roll) and the coefficient of friction between feed belt and paper. An example of the second type of design characteristic is the decision to use dowel pins to locate the two parts of the beam with respect to each other. This type of decision is easily within the ability of the PDT to make on the basis of the members' collective experience, and it forms an important starting point for the second subphase, piece-part design.

Design Competitive Benchmarking

Design competitive benchmarking (DCBM) is a very important step in achieving a low-cost, producible, competitive product. The objective of our PDT is to become aware of the best producibility practice around the world, and to beat the benchmark cost for every subsystem. The engineers on the multifunctional team take apart the competitive benchmark products, prepare cost estimates for each part, and judge the functional roles of each part. The functional roles are used to allocate cost to function. The guidance provided by the complete information has proven powerful in achieving cost reduction, and in leading to better designs. This is a primary step in overcoming cash drain 4, pretend designs that are new and different but not better.

The combination of QFD matrices and functional analysis to provide the most productive statement of the requirements was described much earlier in this chapter (under the heading Functional Analysis and QFD). The second major step of QFD, the design matrices, deploys functional requirements into part characteristics. In one of the primary roots of QFD, value analysis and value engineering (VA/VE), it has been a common practice to use a functional tree and a hardware tree (or an indented bill of materials, a complete hardware list in outline form) to provide strong guidance to the design. The functional tree (R-FTA, or FAST) was introduced earlier along with the fault tree (FTA) and the failure modes and effects analysis (FMEA) table. When the functional tree is arranged as rows and the hardware tree is arranged as columns, with a relationship matrix between them, the format (shown in Fig-

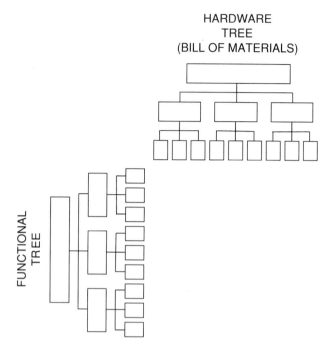

FIGURE 5.19. Function and hardware together.

ure 5.19) is appropriate for the second step of QFD. (For convenience, the product is referred to as hardware. Nearly everything that is being described can also be applied to software and services.) Hardware trees have often been displayed as indented bills of materials (BOMs). Hardware trees and indented BOMs are two alternative displays to communicate the same structure.

In DCBM the cost of the product is then estimated down to the part level (Figure 5.20). It is important that all manufacturing and assembly costs be allocated to the parts. The resulting cost for each part is sometimes called the *fully burdened* part cost. Failure to allocate manufacturing and assembly costs to parts may result in distorted comparisons in which some part costs are low but the manufacturing costs are high.

Next the team estimates the functional purpose of each part, as shown in Figure 5.21. For example, the first part is judged to contribute to three functions. The part is considered to be more essential to one of the functions. Half of the functional rationale for the part is assigned to that

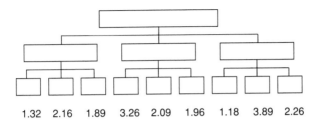

FIGURE **5.20.** Cost allocated to piece parts.

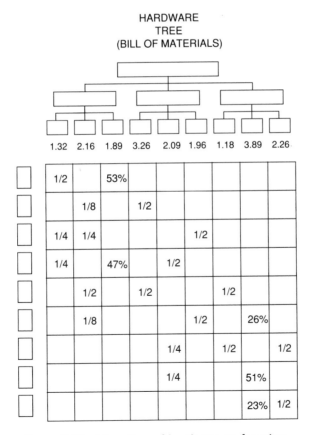

FIGURE **5.21.** Allocation of hardware to function.

function. Simple fractions are usually used in this functional allocation, although percentages may be employed if there is some basis for doing so. Be careful not to be misled by fictitious numerical precision.

When all the parts have been allocated to functions, we multiply the part cost by the fraction and replace the fraction with the cost. At this point all part costs have been expressed as functional costs; see Figure 5.22. The functional costs are then summed horizontally to determine the total cost of each function (Figure 5.23). The function costs may be summed to the higher-level product functions. If the bill of materials, functional tree, and allocation have been done properly, *the total functional cost should equal the total part cost.*

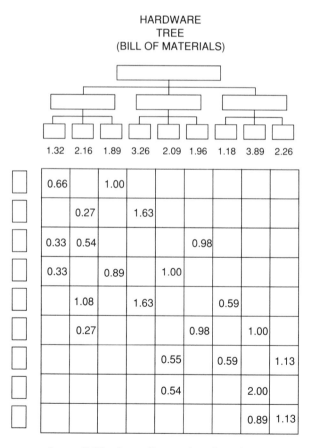

HARDWARE
TREE
(BILL OF MATERIALS)

	1.32	2.16	1.89	3.26	2.09	1.96	1.18	3.89	2.26
	0.66		1.00						
		0.27		1.63					
	0.33	0.54				0.98			
	0.33		0.89		1.00				
		1.08		1.63			0.59		
		0.27				0.98		1.00	
					0.55		0.59		1.13
					0.54			2.00	
								0.89	1.13

Figure 5.22. Cost allocated to function.

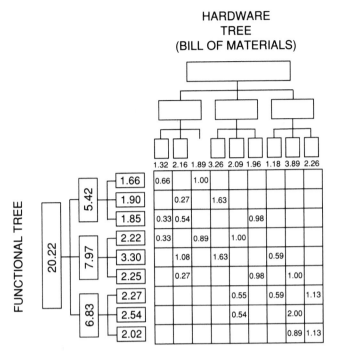

FIGURE 5.23. Cost allocated by hardware and function.

The resulting functional costs provide guidance to the team in developing new concepts. We can compare *functions* between competitive products more readily than we can compare *parts*, because not all competitive products use the same types of parts.

As we compare products, we seek opportunities to provide the *same or better functions at lower costs*. We usually cannot reduce the cost of all functions, but through careful comparison and trade-off we can determine a subsystem concept with a lower *total* cost. This process may appear to be painfully meticulous, but the rewards are well worth the effort.

As an example, Xerox Corporation used design competitive benchmarking in developing a new copier. We evaluated four competitive products and found that the Canon design for one of the subsystems was functionally superior and cost 25% of the existing Xerox design.

The Xerox engineers were challenged to *beat the competitive benchmark design or use it*. While it is unpalatable for most engineers to use a competitor's design, the Xerox PDT carried the Canon design for about a month. During that month the engineers worked with new insight and motivation and created a superior design at half of the Canon cost.

Without design competitive benchmarking, the PDT might have achieved a 10 to 20% improvement and been quite content with the progress. Through the competitive benchmark process, Xerox achieved more than an 85% cost reduction! *Don't compare yourself with yourself.* Look at the best in the world.

The process that is outlined in Figures 5.20 through 5.23 for cost can also be used for reliability and other specifications. This will help deploy specifications to lower levels of the system.

Design—Detailed Piece-Part Requirements

After the design competitive benchmarking, the PDT starts to make the critical early design decisions for our subsystem. We proceed through a combination of:

- Design for assembly (DFA)
- Development of the functional tree for our new design
- Concept selection
- Material and process selection (MAPS)

Along with the last of these (MAPS), we undertake a basic (partial) machine design. Underlying and supporting these activities are the basic design activities, which were referred to in Chapter 1 as "partial design." It is our objective here to make the decisions leading to a low-cost, easily maintainable and operable design that will provide the critical parameter values that ensure robust functionality.

Good reliability is achieved by products that are both robust and mistake-free. Robustness is developed by the critical parameter optimization. Our best approach to being free of simple mistakes is to avoid them as we create the design. Mistakes range from simple human error, such as a reversed diode, to partial design tasks that are improperly done. An example of the latter is a gear train in which shafts are cantilevered excessively so that there is undesirable noise and gear wear. The design of a gear train is easily within the competence of most mechanical design engineers, so this failure is a mistake. In a complex product there are very many decisions, so it is easy for hundreds of mistakes to occur. The best hope for greatly reducing the number of mistakes that occur is knowledge-based engineering, which takes the form of computer software that captures the knowledge of product people who are very good at some aspect of basic design and makes it readily available. In its best form, the software also automates the design so that once the requirements are stated the design is automatically produced by the computer. Although this approach has seen considerable progress in the design of electronic products, it still needs much development before it can be widely used for the more complex and varied geometries of electromechanical design.

Design for Assembly

We carry out DFA early to help us decide the number of parts, and to guide the design so that it will be easy to assemble. After several critical part features have been identified, a decision must be made: incorporate the features in one part, or in several parts. DFA helps us make that decision. Maintainability and operability are considered at the same time. Some designs that are very easy to assemble are hard to maintain because parts that must be serviced are buried deep within the assembly. Also, the cost of fabricating the piece parts is taken into account before a final decision is made about the number of parts. Sometimes a decision based solely on DFA would lead to parts that are difficult and expensive to make. The final decision about the number of parts is based on achieving the least total cost. A widely used approach has been developed by Professors Geoffrey Boothroyd and Peter Dewhurst (Boothroyd, 1992).

The Functional Tree Guides the Design

The functional tree is developed as the design progresses. This is the same type of functional tree that was developed during design competitive benchmarking, but now it is for the emerging new design. This helps to ensure that the design of each functional area is kept simple, consistent with the function that it is required to perform. It provides a constant reference to the benchmark designs. Our goal is to keep our costs lower than the design competitive benchmark cost for each function. Sometimes we trade off a higher cost in one area because it enables us to achieve a lower cost in another area for a net reduction.

When doing design competitive benchmarking, we complete the functional tree during one short activity. This is possible because the products already exist. In doing a new design, we do not have a complete product as yet, so we alternate between the functional tree and the hardware tree as the design progresses.

Consider the example where the functional requirement (FR) is MAKE IMAGE. Now we must go to the hardware tree. What is the design parameter that corresponds to MAKE IMAGE? The corresponding box at the top of the hardware tree is CAMERA; see Figure 5.24. However, this contains no new information. CAMERA is simply a name for the device that is being designed to make the image and is essentially tautological. The next key box on the hardware tree is LIGHT-SENSITIVE SHEET, which is on the second level of the hardware tree; see Figure 5.25. This decision is critical because it selects the basic physics that will be utilized. The corresponding function is SENSITIZE SHEET; see Figure 5.26.

Once the physics has been selected, the remaining functional requirements on the second level (for a very simple camera) can be determined by considering the physics of light:

FR_22—Light from the object must be focused on the sheet.
FR_23—The amount of light must be controlled to match the sensitivity of the sheet.
FR_24—Unfocused (stray) light must be blocked from the light-sensitive sheet.

FUNCTIONAL TREE   HARDWARE TREE

$FR_1 1$ $DP_1 1$

MAKE IMAGE   CAMERA

FIGURE 5.24. Hardware responsive to function.

FUNCTIONAL TREE   HARDWARE TREE

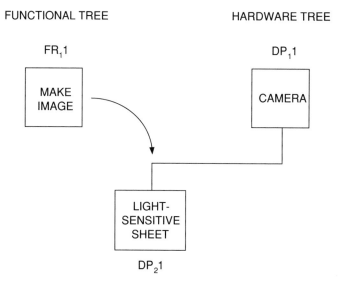

FIGURE 5.25. Critical hardware decision.

FUNCTIONAL TREE   HARDWARE TREE

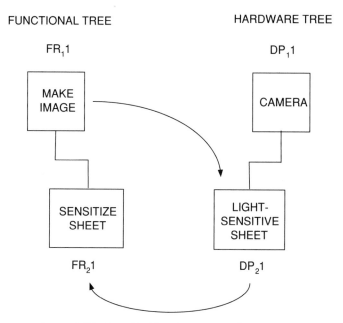

FIGURE 5.26. Detailed hardware and function pair.

(The subscript 2 refers to the level in the tree.) The remaining functional requirement is to hold in place the elements (components) that perform the four basic functions. The complete functional tree at the second level is displayed in Figure 5.27.

The hardware components to perform FR_22 through FR_25 can now be easily defined; see Figure 5.28, which also shows the following sequence of decision making:

(1) FR_11
(2) DP_21
(3) FR_21
(4) FR_22 FR_23 FR_24 FR_25
(5) DP_22 DP_23 DP_24

The decision-making sequence does not strictly alternate between functional requirements (FR) and design parameters (DP), for FR_21 has led directly to FR_22 through FR_25. [Professor Nam Suh, in his book *Principles of Design* (1990), has emphasized that design work alternates

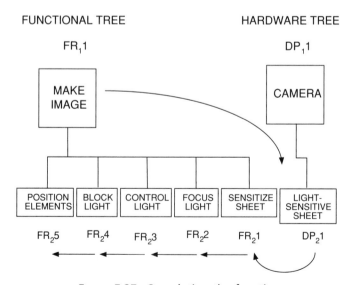

FIGURE 5.27. Completing the functions.

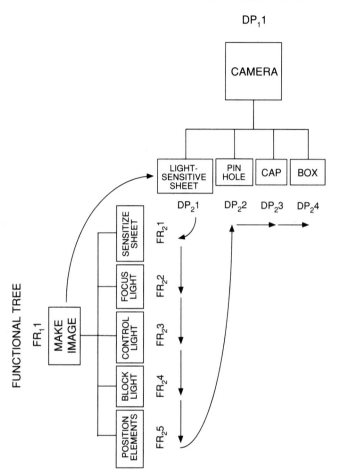

Figure 5.28. Complete example of alternation between function and hardware during design.

between requirements and hardware.] Alternatively, we might conclude that DP_21 has led directly to FR_21 through FR_25; thus:

(1) FR_11
(2) DP_21
(3) FR_21 FR_22 FR_23 FR_24 FR_25
(4) DP_22 DP_23 DP_24

Roughly speaking, it is certainly true that the design process alternates between the functional tree and the hardware tree.

The final result, in the format of Figure 5.19, is shown in Figure 5.29.

Note that there is a one-to-one pairing between $FR_2 1$ and $DP_2 1$, between $FR_2 2$ and $DP_2 2$, and between $FR_2 3$ and $DP_2 3$. However, $FR_2 4$ and $FR_2 5$ are both achieved by $DP_2 4$, the box that both blocks out stray light and positions the elements of the camera. Another concept would

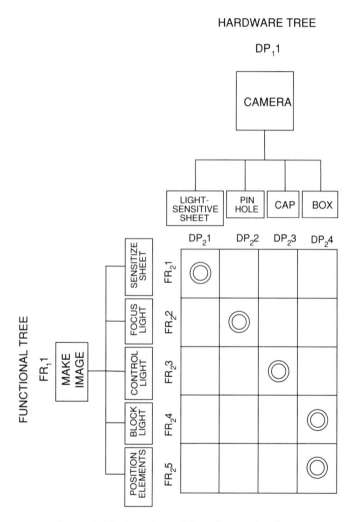

Figure 5.29. Relation of function to hardware.

be to have a bellows (or simple cloth) to block out the stray light, and a skeletal frame to position the elements. This maintains the one-to-one pairing between FR_2X and DP_2X. Professor Suh has emphasized the advantages of such a simple relationship between the requirements and the hardware. However, even the solid box will satisfy this relationship if different features of the box control the two requirements. Then each feature can be designed to satisfy its requirement.

The combination of the functional tree and the hardware tree helps guide the PDT to a cost-effective design.

Concept Selection

In alternating between the functional requirements and the hardware decisions, we have the opportunity to select superior concepts. Sometimes we can improve the robustness of our subsystem by selecting a superior concept for some functional area of our subsystem. An example for the paper feeder of the Xerox 1075 is the retard roll. To continue our fictionalized case study, in our previous design the roll was driven so that it rotated very slowly, roughly once per hour, to distribute the wear over the entire surface of the roll. However, the life of the roll was still only 5% of the copier life. Therefore, we are seeking new concepts that will provide longer life.

We observe from experience that the retard roll is actually seldom required during the operation of the feeder. Because of inertial separation there is usually only one sheet fed from the stack of paper. The sudden engagement of the clutch accelerates the top sheet very quickly, so that the second sheet cannot follow. This is equivalent to the proverbial pulling the rug out from under something without disturbing it. Therefore, one conceptual approach to increasing the life of the retard roll is to arrange for it to be active only when more than one sheet is fed from the stack.

One concept is to incorporate a brake inside the retard roll. The torque of the brake is chosen to be at an intermediate value so that the roll turns when there is only one sheet in the nip between the retard roll and the feed belt but stops turning when two sheets are present. The relatively high coefficient of friction (more than 1.0) between paper and the retard elastomer allows a single sheet to overcome the brake torque; but the much smaller value of the coefficient of friction (less than 0.5) between two sheets of paper is not sufficient to overcome the brake torque, and the roll stops turning and retards (holds back) the second sheet.

We create many candidate concepts to increase the life of the retard roll:

- Friction brake
- Magnetic brake
- Feedback control (two-sheet sensor and electrical brake)

At the same time, we look into a variety of concepts using composite materials for the retard surface, one hard material to minimize wear, and another material with a higher friction coefficient to hold back the second sheet.

The reader can think of other concepts. We put these concepts into the Pugh concept selection matrix. We develop the criteria from the functional tree (Figure 5.9), the fault tree (Figure 5.8), and the SS/PP QFD matrix (Figure 5.10). The criteria are dominated by:

- Long wear life
- Minimizing misfeeds
- Minimizing multifeeds

We run the matrix and select the friction brake.

This is an example of concept selection at the subsystem level—actually, at a somewhat lower level, which we can call the functional-area level. The Pugh concept selection process can be applied at all levels. It can also be applied to production processes. Actually, it is very successful in making any decision in which there are well-defined concepts and criteria.

Subsystem/Piece-Part QFD Matrix

Throughout the subsystem design, the PDT uses the subsystem/piece-part (SS/PP) QFD matrix, which was introduced in Figures 5.2 and 5.10. The subsystem expectations are deployed to subsystem decisions, which become the piece-part expectations; see Figure 5.30. The decisions from the parameter design are entered here, as well as the decisions that were primarily guided by EQFD. An example of the latter is jam clearance,

SUBSYSTEM EXPECTATIONS		RETARD FRICTION COEFFICIENT	RETARD BRAKE TORQUE	RETARD RADIUS	WRAP ANGLE, α	BELT TENSION, T	TRIGGER TIME	TAR ACTION TIME	TAR SURFACE SPEED	OPENING NIP	UMC BREAKDOWN
		A	B	C	D	E	F	G	H	I	J
1	MISFEED RATE	< 70 / 10⁶	◎						◎			
2	MULTIFEED RATE	< 30 / 10⁶	◎	◎	◎	◎	◎	◎		○		
3	JAM RATE	< 30 / 10⁶						◎				
4	COPY RATE	70 ± 2 CPM							◎			
5	JAM CLEARANCE TIME	< 20 SEC								◎		
6	PAPER DAMAGE RATE	< 40 / 10⁶	◎									
7	UMC	< $250										◎
8	PAPER SPEED	11.7 ± 0.3 ips							◎			
9	DELIVERY TIME	141 ± 10 msec						◎				
			1.50 ± 0.25	40 ± 4 in-oz	0.880 ± 0.005 in	45	15 N	100 msec	120 msec	11.7 ± 0.3ips	REF. Y	REF. Z

Header note: **SUBSYSTEM DESIGN DECISIONS, BECOME: PIECE-PART EXPECTATIONS**

FIGURE 5.30. Subsystem/piece-part QFD matrix.

which was simply listed as a strategy in Figure 5.10. Now the team has defined the specifics; for example, the operator should be able to open the nip between the feed belt and the retard roll to make jam clearance easy.

As the subsystem decisions become more developed, the team also prepares the next QFD matrix (see Figure 3.7 for the relationships among the matrices). An example for the paper feeder is shown in Figure 5.31. We see that the beam that spans across the paper path has a critical role in controlling the wrap angle, α. The feed belt is mounted on the top part of this beam, and the retard roll is mounted on the bottom part.

	PIECE-PART DESIGN DECISIONS, BECOME: PRODUCTION PROCESS REQUIREMENTS									
	RETARD			BEAM						
PIECE-PART EXPECTATIONS	1	2	3	4	5	6	7			
A RETARD FRICTION COEFFICIENT	1.50 ± 0.25	◎								
B RETARD BRAKE TORQUE	40 ± 4 in-oz									
C RETARD RADIUS	0.880 ± 0.005 in									
D WRAP ANGLE, α	45				◎					

FIGURE 5.31. Piece-part design matrix.

Therefore, the spacing between the top and bottom parts of the beam determines the wrap angle of the feed belt around the retard roll. Also, the beam is a rather large and complex part, with a large manufacturing cost. The piece-part design for parts that are critical to function and cost is started as soon as the requirements are sufficiently clear, usually near the end of subsystem design.

Figure 5.31 is just a hint at the complete requirements for the beam. An entire piece-part design matrix might be prepared just for the beam. The appropriate portion of the functional tree and the fault tree are again combined with the QFD matrix (as was seen previously at the subsystem level) to form the full set of requirements. This prepares the team to work on the design decisions for the beam, or bridge—geometry, material, and production process. The macro geometry is determined by the function; the beam must span across the paper path. The major decisions to be made are the number of parts (one, two, or several) and the material and process.

Material and Process Selection (MAPS)

Success in product development is greatly helped by early selection of the material and the production process for part formation. An example for the feeder is the beam, shown in Figure 5.32, that bridges across the paper path and supports the mechanisms. We know from the robustness optimization and the work on the retard roll that wear of one millimeter from the radius of the retard roll renders it dysfunctional. Therefore, the bridge must be able to position the feed belt relative to the retard roll with an uncertainty that is small compared with one millimeter. Otherwise, the wear life of the retard roll could turn out to be very small in units with large production variation. Thus, the bridge must hold the spacing within

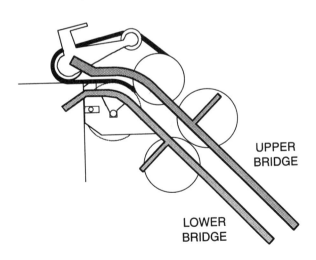

FIGURE 5.32. Example of material and process selection (MAPS).

approximately 0.1 mm. This is sufficient guidance to enable us to select the process and material for the bridges. Some alternatives are:

- Aluminum die casting
- Aluminum extrusion
- Sheet metal
- Composite polymer

Although some work has been done on developing a specific selection process for MAPS, it appears that for most purposes the Pugh concept selection process is currently the most general approach. The Boothroyd-Dewhurst methodology (Boothroyd, 1992) can provide information and in some cases is sufficient to make the decision. Our PDT chooses aluminum die casting. We decide to make the beam in two parts, top and bottom, joined together by fasteners. This is a major decision, because two parts will increase the variability of the wrap angle. However, the decision reduces the manufacturing cost, because if the bridge were made as one part, the geometry would be difficult to cast. This is an example of part cost dominating assembly. DFA would lead to making the bridge as one part. However, the reduced part cost with two simpler parts outweighs the added cost of assembling them into one bridge.

This early selection leaves time for the detailed design work to drive down the costs, and to make functional improvements. The time can be used to develop the best tolerance that can economically be achieved between the two parts, and thus the most economical control over the wrap angle of the feed belt around the retard roll.

We also do a finite-element analysis (FEA) of the bridges to ensure that the operating deflection is not excessive. More challenging, we apply FEA to improve the design so that warp due to the relief of residual stresses during machining does not produce excessive variation of the opening between the two bridge parts. This prevents a large variation in wrap angle that would lead to multifeeds and other problems.

PROGRESS CHECK

Now we have a firm expectation of what the manufacturing costs of the product will be. The features and quality expectations are well defined.

Approval to proceed here is almost a final commitment. We have essentially defined the product as it will be when it goes into production, and it is possible to now anticipate the product's marketplace viability.

Outputs

The completion of the subsystem design leads to three primary outputs:

(1) Critical parameter drawing
(2) SS/PP QFD matrix
(3) Concept layout (which includes early decisions on critical parts)

These provide the guidance that is needed to design piece parts during *piece-part design*. The primary outputs from subsystem design specify the requirements for the piece parts.

Other Activities

For conciseness, we have mainly emphasized only the design of the product subsystem in this description of the first part of the design phase. There will, of course, be some additional total system engineering, although most of this was completed in the concept phase. And, in the spirit of concurrent engineering, other activities are carried out at the same time by the multifunctional PDT. These extend the product subsystem design activities into the related functions.

Along with design for assembly (DFA), there is design for maintainability, design for operability, and the design of the operational systems themselves: the conceptual design of the assembly system and process, and the conceptual design of the field-support system. Along with material and process selection (MAPS) for the major piece parts, we design the concepts for the production tooling. Material is ordered for long-lead tools, and make/buy decisions are made on many critical parts. Of course, many of these decisions will be constrained by strategies that extend beyond the specific product program. They can include, for example, strategies to make all injection-molded parts, buy all sheet metal parts, and have all assembly of small electromechanical subsystems done in Singapore.

In addition to these more technical activities, the business plan is fine-tuned, and there is long-range planning of the marketing activities. It is imperative that the technical community and the business and marketing community be in consensus about the plans and expectations for the emerging new product.

Criterion for Success of the Subsystem Design Phase

There is one suggested primary criterion at the end of subsystem design: the design is sufficiently better than benchmarks (and is expected to be better than competitors' design at shipping approval).

The primary outputs from *subsystem design* should give high confidence of superior

Robustness
Unit manufacturing cost (UMC)
Features
Operability
Field support

These superiorities are compatible with the expectations of the business plan. In addition, the subsystem design yields a clear total quality development plan for the completion of the development, backed by the consensus and commitment of the team.

Progressive Freeze

At the end of subsystem design, the critical piece-part concepts are completed and frozen. The concept of each part is complete to a point where a cost estimate has been prepared. The concepts for the production tools are complete. If the product is to have its own microprocessor control system, the control requirements that the software must be responsive to are frozen. Final styling is complete and frozen. Any further changes in styling would be injurious to the cost and quality of the product and cannot be allowed.

The business plan is complete and frozen. The product expectation specifications are finalized. Production volumes by year and geographic region have been determined in full, as have production sites and volume of production at each site. The detailed financial plan has been completed; this outlines expected pricing and sales by major region. Freezing the business plan means that changes in it will not subsequently impact the product development process. Of course, as the start of production is approached and as distribution and sales and service begin, there may have to be adjustments in the business plan to reflect conditions in the marketplace. These adjustments may be to distribution, sales, and service operations, and possibly to production volumes, but they are only the tailoring of these operations to the then-existing market environment *and to the product that has been developed.* They cannot be allowed to alter the development activity. Such perturbations to the development process have a fatal fascination. There is always some temptation to change the product in response to quarterly changes in perception of the marketplace; however, the only real effect of such attempts is to raise the cost, lower the quality, and delay the final product. After this progress check, the business plan cannot be allowed to affect the product that is being developed.

A rigorous manufacturing cost estimate that has credibility throughout all functions of the corporation has been prepared and is a key basis for this progress check. The designs of all subsystems or functional areas equal or exceed competitive benchmark designs. The FMEA and FTA and the status of the critical parameter optimization lead to the expectation that the functional robustness of the product will meet or exceed the business plan goal. Concepts for assembly tooling and the assembly process, and concepts for any dedicated machine tools that are required, are frozen at this time. It is clear that the designs of all subsystems and functional areas are production-intent designs. Suppliers have contributed to the design of most purchased parts.

At this critical progress check, the design is well developed and should, in all ways, lead to the expectation that the product will be a world leader.

PIECE-PART DESIGN

At the beginning of *piece-part design* (see Figure 5.33), the subsystem critical parameter drawing has been essentially completed, the SS/PP QFD matrix is complete, and the concept layout has documented the subsystem concept in considerable detail, including the most critical design for assembly (DFA), functional-area concept selection, and material and process selection (MAPS) decisions.

In summary, there is high confidence about the robustness of the subsystem as defined in the critical parameter drawing, and a strong start has been made in adding to the skeletal design to form the complete design. The requirements for all critical piece parts are well defined.

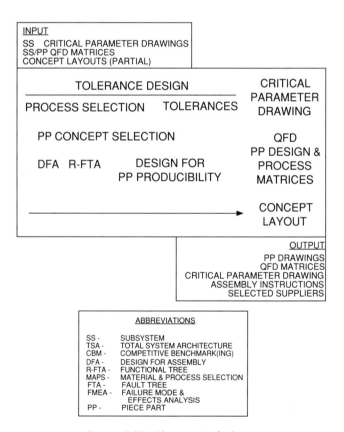

FIGURE 5.33. Piece-part design.

ACTIVITIES

In subsystem design, the parameter design was essentially completed. The nominal values of the critical design parameters were optimized to achieve robust functionality. These optimized nominal values are the targets for production.

Now, in piece-part design, we carry out tolerance design to select the economical precision level around the nominal (target) values for the critical design parameters. For each critical part feature (critical design parameter), we select the specific material removal processes, machine tools, operational tools (e.g., cutting tools), and critical process parameter values. These define the unit manufacturing cost (UMC) and standard deviation (σ). In many cases traditional good practice provides sufficient guidance. For critical and unique features, a trade-off (balance) analysis is needed. The σ for a critical part feature is deployed up the functional tree (R-FTA) to the level of a customer-observable quality characteristic. This is used to establish the quality loss function. The decisions in the process tree are then made to minimize the total cost (UMC + quality loss). Then a tolerance is calculated and documented on the production drawing.

Piece-part concept selection is completed; some of the most critical decisions have been made in subsystem design, such as the decision to use aluminum die castings for the two bridge parts for the paper feeder. Detailed DFA and piece-part producibility are worked out, the functional tree (R-FTA) is completed, and the QFD piece-part design and process matrices are prepared, all in close coordination. All of these are used to guide the creation and completion of the piece-part drawings. This is the design; the only changes hereafter are to correct mistakes (human errors in the details). The subsystem concept layout is continuously evolved and used as the basis for assembly drawings. At the total system level, a "big picture" is maintained to ensure compatibility among the subsystems. Critical life tests are started; some may have been initiated earlier in subsystem design.

TOLERANCE DESIGN

In parameter design, the best nominal (target) values are selected for the critical design parameters. In tolerance design, we select the economical precision around the nominal values in two steps: (1) selecting the right production precision, and (2) putting tolerance values on drawings.

Selecting the Economical Production Precision

The intrinsically more important part of tolerance design is the selection of the best production precision. Strictly speaking, this has nothing to do with tolerances at all. Tolerances are the numbers that go on the drawing. This section describes the selection of the production process with the best combination of UMC and standard deviation. This is the important activity in tolerance design, and it was introduced in Chapter 3, Figure 3.15.

Simple Example: Electrical Circuit

Now we return to the specific example of the simple RL electrical circuit (Figure 5.11). Parameter design was completed on this circuit. The resulting optimum nominal values are:

$$R = 9.0 \, \text{ohms} \, (\Omega)$$
$$L = 0.0126 \, \text{henries} \, (\text{H})$$

The target (nominal) value for the current is 10.0 amperes (A). Let us suppose that evaluation of customer needs and the circuit functionality, and of the field logistical costs, gives the customer tolerance (Δ_C) as 4 A and the cost of the countermeasure (L_C) when the customer tolerance is exceeded as $100:

$$\Delta_C = 4 \, \text{A}$$
$$L_C = \$100$$

Using the quadratic quality loss function from Chapter 3, the average quality loss is:

$$L_A = \frac{L_C}{\Delta_C^2} V_{\text{cur}} = \frac{100}{(4)^2} V_{\text{cur}}$$

where V_{cur} is the variance of current, averaged over many units of production. We cannot directly select the precision (variance) of the current, but we can select the precision of the lower-level parameters, the resistance and inductance. We need a generic method to determine the variance of the system performance parameter once we know the variances of the lower-level parameters.

The relationship between the system performance parameter and the lower-level parameters is given by Equation (5.6), which is the Taylor series for the system performance parameter. Since we are considering tolerances, which are normally relatively small, it is sufficient to take only the linear terms in the Taylor series and ignore the higher-order terms.

$$y = m + b_1(x_1 - m_1) + b_2(x_2 - m_2) + \cdots$$

$$y - m = \sum_{i=1}^{K} b_i(x_i - m_i) \tag{5.6}$$

where

$y =$ system-level functional parameter
$m =$ mean value of y
$x_i =$ lower-level (design) parameter i
$m_i =$ mean value for x_i
$b_i =$ (sensitivity) coefficient for term i in the Taylor series

A bar above an expression denotes the average value of the expression. The variance of the system performance parameter can be written in terms of the variances of the lower-level parameters as follows:

$$\overline{(y - m)^2} = \sum_{i=1}^{K} b_i^2 \overline{(x_i - m_i)^2} \tag{5.7}$$

Equation (5.7) comes from Equation (5.6) as a result of squaring both sides and averaging over many units of production; it expresses the fact that the variance of a sum is equal to the sum of the variances (for independent variables).

Now, returning to the circuit example, we must determine the sensitivity coefficients, b, of the resistor and the inductor on the current. This is most easily done by determining the value of current for three combinations of resistance R and inductance L:

$$(\Delta R, \Delta L) = (0,0), (1.8, 0), (0, 0.00252)$$

These three combinations represent the nominal values, a small change in R, and a small change in L.

For only nominal values ($\Delta R = \Delta L = 0$),

$$y = 10.00 \text{ A}$$

For a small change in resistance R ($\Delta R = 1.8$, $\Delta L = 0$),

$$y = \frac{100}{\sqrt{(10.8)^2 + (2\pi 55 \times 0.0126)^2}}$$
$$= 8.59 \text{ A}$$

and

$$b_R = \left| \frac{\Delta y}{\Delta R} \right| = \frac{1.41}{1.8} = 0.78 \text{ A/}\Omega$$

where b_R is the sensitivity coefficient for the resistor. This calculation is displayed graphically in Figure 5.34.

For a small change in inductance L ($\Delta R = 0$, $\Delta L = 0.00252$),

$$y = \frac{100}{\sqrt{(9.0)^2 + (2\pi 55 \times 0.01512)^2}}$$
$$= 9.61 \text{ A}$$
$$b_L = \frac{0.39}{0.00252} = 155 \text{ A/H}$$

where b_L is the sensitivity coefficient for the inductor (coil).

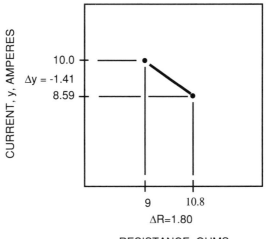

FIGURE 5.34. Numerical calculation of sensitivity.

Next, we talk to our vendors for resistors and inductors and learn the values of the low-cost standard deviations:

$$\sigma_{R,\mathrm{lc}} = 0.30\,\Omega$$
$$\sigma_{L,\mathrm{lc}} = 0.0020\,\mathrm{H}$$

Now, using Equation (5.7), we calculate the variance of the current:

$$V_{\mathrm{cur}} = (0.3 \times 0.78)^2 + (0.002 \times 155)^2$$
$$= 0.15$$

The quadratic quality loss function gives

$$L = \frac{100}{(4)^2}(0.15)$$
$$= \$0.94$$

where L is the quality loss. Thus, the average quality loss, averaged over all of the units in the field, is expected to be $0.94.

Now let us consider the effect of selecting grade 1 resistors and inductors, with standard deviations that are only half those for low-cost components. This will, of course, increase the UMC of the components:

Resistor: Δ(UMC) = \$0.10 $\sigma = 0.15$
Inductor: Δ(UMC) = \$0.40 $\sigma = 0.0010$

Next we evaluate these options. Using a grade 1 resistor:

$$V_{cur} = (0.15 \times 0.78)^2 + (0.002 \times 155)^2$$
$$= 0.109$$
$$L = \frac{100}{(4)^2}(0.109) = \$0.68$$

The expected quality loss is reduced by \$0.26 (0.94 − 0.68) by using the grade 1 resistor. It costs only \$0.10 extra, for a net saving of \$0.16.
Now using a grade 1 inductor:

$$V_{cur} = (0.3 \times 0.78)^2 + (0.001 \times 155)^2$$
$$= 0.0787$$
$$L = \frac{100}{(4)^2}(0.0787) = \$0.49$$

The expected quality loss is reduced by \$0.45 (0.94 − 0.49) by using the grade 1 inductor. It costs \$0.40 extra, for a net saving of \$0.05.
If we use a grade 1 resistor and a grade 1 inductor:

$$V_{cur} = (0.15 \times 0.78)^2 + (0.001 \times 155)^2$$
$$= 0.0376$$
$$L = \frac{100}{(4)^2}(0.0376) = \$0.23$$

The expected quality loss is reduced by \$0.71 (0.94 − 0.23) by using grade 1 for both components. This verifies that the total saving is the sum of the individual savings (0.26 + 0.45). The savings are summarized as follows:

	Quality Loss	UMC	Net
Grade 1	Savings	Increase	Savings
Resistor	$0.26	$0.10	$0.16
Inductor	$0.45	$0.40	$0.05

We see that for both components, selecting grade 1 will give a savings in cost (factory cost plus field cost). However, for the inductor we might decide to select the low-cost grade, with a reduction in UMC of $0.40, rather than wait for the longer-term benefit of quality loss reduction.

Careful attention should be devoted to the fact that in choosing the best production precision, we did not have any need to use manufacturing tolerances. The reader is encouraged to review the foregoing analysis to ensure a clear understanding of the almost superfluous role of manufacturing tolerances (numbers on the production drawing). Manufacturing tolerances have become traditional for two reasons:

• Design and manufacturing are separate; tolerances are a communication tool.
• Inspection with go/no go gauges was the traditional practice.

Both of these traditions are self-defeating in most modern enterprises. Manufacturing tolerances are needed only when process control temporarily goes awry and inspection must temporarily be used. Then the manufacturing tolerance is used as the sorting criterion. The calculation of economical manufacturing tolerances will be described shortly. However, go/no go gauges are usually not adequate. They must be replaced by measurements that enable implementation of the concept of adherence to the customer satisfaction target.

Summary—Selecting The Right Production Precision
The production process (or precision grade of a purchased component) is selected to minimize the total cost—the sum of the expected quality loss in the field plus the unit manufacturing cost (UMC). The variation of components is used to determine the variation in the customer-observable functional parameter. This is then used to calculate the quality loss that is produced by the component. The quality loss is combined with

the manufacturing (or purchase) cost to select the option (production process or vendor) with the least cost. This is the important activity in low-cost tolerance design.

Calculating the Manufacturing Tolerance

Although the selection of the right process (or grade) is usually the most important step, it is also necessary to determine the best manufacturing tolerance value—the value that will go on the production drawing. This can be used to sort the good from the bad when all else fails.

Taguchi's *quality engineering* uses a system of three-tiered tolerances (Figure 5.35). We start with the customer tolerance (Δ_C), the value at which the average customer (sometimes thought of as the 50th-percentile customer) will be sufficiently dissatisfied that he or she will call for corrective action. Associated with the customer tolerance is a quality loss in dollars (L_C) that is the cost of the countermeasure in response to the

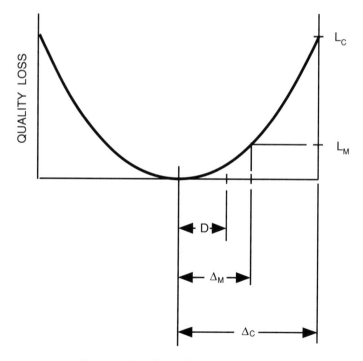

FIGURE 5.35. Three-tiered tolerances.

customer's dissatisfaction. This cost will be relatively large because of the field logistics that will be involved.

The same countermeasure can be applied much more cheaply in the factory. The much smaller quality loss in manufacturing (L_M) has associated with it a manufacturing tolerance (Δ_M). The manufacturing tolerance will be much smaller than the customer tolerance because it costs must less to implement the countermeasure in the factory. This is the tolerance that goes on the drawing.

We can save still more money by using the adjustment limit D (to be described in Chapter 6) to limit variation during production. The customer tolerance and the quality loss that would be incurred at the customer's site establish the quality loss function. In factory operations we limit the usual variation to the range of $\pm D$, the adjustment limit. As is indicated in Figure 5.35, we save a great deal of money in quality loss avoidance by limiting the range to $\pm D$ instead of $\pm\Delta_C$.

This concept of three-tiered tolerances based on the quality loss function clearly leads to production operations with the units of production bunched tightly around the customer satisfaction target value.

The manufacturing tolerance is calculated to minimize the total cost. The quality loss is given by the quadratic relationship

$$L = \frac{L_C}{\Delta_C^2}\Delta^2 \qquad (5.8)$$

where L is the expected quality loss, L_C is the loss at the customer's tolerance (in other words, the cost of the countermeasure in the field), Δ_C is the customer's tolerance, and Δ is the actual deviation from the customer satisfaction target for a specific unit of production.

The cost of the countermeasure when performed in the factory, L_M, is used in defining the manufacturing tolerance. Putting the cost of the countermeasure in the manufacturing site and the unknown value of manufacturing tolerance into Equation (5.8) and slightly rearranging gives the next equation:

$$\Delta_M = \sqrt{\frac{L_M}{L_C}}\Delta_C \qquad (5.9)$$

Equation (5.9) establishes the value of the manufacturing tolerance. If a specific unit of production has a measured value of Δ that is greater than Δ_M, then it should not be shipped. It is cheaper to fix it in the factory at a cost of L_M than to incur the greater value of the quality loss in the field. Conversely, if the value of Δ is less than Δ_M, then the product should be shipped. The quality loss in the field will be less than the cost of the countermeasure in the factory, L_M. Thus, the value of Δ_M is the boundary between products that should be shipped and products that should be reworked.

Because the cost of the countermeasure in the manufacturing site will usually be much less than the cost of the countermeasure at the customer's site, the manufacturing tolerance is significantly less than the customer tolerance. If the repair work (countermeasure) in the factory is very cheap, it pays to "repair," or adjust, nearly all of the units. Then the manufacturing tolerance becomes very small, so that only the units that are already very good do not receive the inexpensive adjustment that improves customer satisfaction. (Recall that the manufacturing tolerance is the tolerance that is put on the drawing.) If, on the other hand, the product has to be inspected (as will be explained), no product outside of the manufacturing tolerance should be shipped.

In actual practice, the value of the performance parameter is usually held to the tighter range of the adjustment limit, $\pm D$, during on-line QC. Therefore, there should never be any products outside of the manufacturing tolerance, and inspection (after production is complete) should not be needed. The only operational use for the manufacturing tolerance is in the unusual case in which the on-line adjustment process has failed. Then the products that have been made while the adjustment process is not operational will have to be inspected, and the manufacturing tolerance will then be used to determine whether they should be shipped or reworked. The adjustment limit will be described in Chapter 6 during the consideration of on-line QC.

When the performance parameter that is observed by the customer is directly controlled by the manufacturing process, then Figure 5.35 and the description just completed are all that is needed. In many cases, however, the customer-observable system performance parameter is not directly controlled in manufacturing. In these cases, we must determine the customer tolerance for the lower-level parameters that are *actually* controlled in manufacturing. Examples are the resistance and the inductance in the simple circuit case.

The customer tolerance for a lower-level parameter is simply

$$\Delta_{C,LL} = \frac{\Delta_C}{b} \tag{5.10}$$

where b is the sensitivity coefficient; see Equation (5.6). When the lower-level parameter has the value $\Delta_{C,LL}$, the customers become unhappy because the customer-observable functional parameter is at the customer tolerance, Δ_C. In many cases, we may be able to reasonably estimate the customer tolerance for the lower-level parameter directly, on the basis of our experience or a simple experiment or calculation.

As an example of the calculation of lower-level customer tolerances, Equation (5.10) is applied to the simple RL circuit:

$$\Delta_{C,R} = \frac{4}{0.78}$$
$$= 5.13\,\Omega$$
$$\Delta_{C,L} = \frac{4}{155}$$
$$= 0.0258\,H$$

These are the customers' tolerances for the components. Of course, the customers do not know that they have these tolerances. However, we know that if the components are this far off target, then the customers will be dissatisfied with the deviation of the current from their target.

We consider the case in which the evaluation of the costs of the countermeasures in manufacturing, for both the resistor and the inductor when they go outside the manufacturing tolerance, equals $4 for both of them:

$$\text{Loss}_{M,R} = \text{Loss}_{M,L} = \$4.00$$

Now, by using Equation (5.9), we find the manufacturing tolerances:

$$\Delta_{M,R} = \sqrt{\frac{4}{100}} \, (5.13)$$

$$= 1.03 \, \Omega$$

$$\Delta_{M,L} = \sqrt{\frac{4}{100}} \, (0.0258)$$

$$= 0.00517 \, \text{H}$$

These values are used when inspection is appropriate.

Paper Feeder Example

We made a rough application of tolerance design during *subsystem design* when we chose aluminum die casting as the material and process for the two bridge parts that control the critical dimensional relationship between the feed belt on the upper bridge and the retard roll and entrance guide on the lower bridge. We established on the basis of simple approximate calculations that a tolerance of approximately 0.1 mm was in order, and our PDT judged that aluminum die casting was appropriate.

Selecting the Production Process

Now we are doing more detailed and precise tolerance design. For example, we have three choices for the surface on the top bridge where the feed belt subassembly is mounted: no machining, milling, or milling followed by grinding. We follow the procedure that was introduced in Chapter 3; see especially Figure 3.15. This is essentially the same process as for the *RL* circuit that was just described. There, we chose from among commercial options for components. Here we are choosing from among production-process options. The type of choice and the analysis are exactly the same. We calculate the incremental unit manufacturing cost (UMC) and the expected quality loss for each option and choose the option with the least total cost. We do this and find that the intermediate option, milling, has the least total cost. Then we calculate the production tolerance to be put on the drawing.

Calculating the Tolerance

In this case we have a ready reference for the customers' tolerance: the amount of wear that can be tolerated on the retard roll, which is 1 mm (note that this is a one-sided tolerance). Replacing the roll in the field has a cost of $100. Replacement of the roll before the copier leaves the factory costs $20. Therefore, the total factory tolerance for the parts that position the feed belt and the retard roll is:

$$\Delta_M = \sqrt{\frac{L_M}{L_C}} \Delta_C$$

$$= \sqrt{\frac{20}{100} \times 1}$$

$$= 0.45 \, \text{mm}$$

We split this between the top and bottom bridges and convert it from a one-sided tolerance to a two-sided tolerance ±0.11 mm for each bridge. We still must allocate this among all of the parts that position the feed belt: the bracket, shafts, and pulleys. We conclude that ±0.05 mm is the correct tolerance for the machined surface (land) on the die casting. We add this to the critical parameter drawing; see Figure 5.36. Actually, the total tolerance of 0.45 mm goes on the critical parameter drawing, and the more detailed tolerance calculations and values go on attached sheets. Also, the tolerance of ±0.05 mm is put on the piece-part drawings for the upper and lower bridges.

We should keep in mind once again that in most cases when things are going as we like, we do not need to use the tolerances. If the process capability is good enough, then the nominal (target) value, the capability of the process that we have selected, and on-line quality control combined will keep the dimension within an acceptable range. We would use the tolerance only under exceptional conditions; suppose, for example, the die casting source has a problem in one batch and warp is greater than usual. Then we have to inspect every part and use the tolerance as the rejection or rework criterion.

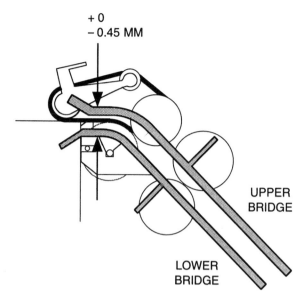

+ 0
− 0.45 MM

UPPER
BRIDGE

LOWER
BRIDGE

FIGURE 5.36. Tolerance on critical parameter drawing.

100% Inspection

Although on-line QC usually eliminates the need for inspection, there are exceptions. In some important cases, the process capability is always pushed to the ragged edge and 100% inspection must be the rule. VLSI chips are a good example. The process capability has improved at a tremendous rate. If 4K chips were still standard, yields would be very near to 100%, and inspection would not be needed. However, as the industry pushes on toward 64M chips, inspection is still required. All of the improved process capability has been used to pack more elements into a fixed space. The reduced cost and space per function more than justify the costs of the inspection and the scrap chips.

DETAILED PIECE-PART DESIGN

In parallel with the tolerance design, we complete the detailed, production-intent design of all of the piece parts. Actually, the two parallel paths in Figure 5.33 are primarily for diagrammatic convenience; they are really one integrated activity.

DFA and Functional Tree

Design for assembly and the functional tree, which were started during the subsystem design, are continued down to a more detailed level. Both continue to provide strong guidance.

Piece-Part Concept Selection

During piece-part design, we continue to use the Pugh concept selection process to make major decisions. We already used it on piece parts to select the aluminum die castings for the two bridge parts. Another example is the retard roll.

The piece-part expectations that are in the columns of the subsystem/ piece-part QFD design matrix are used to perform concept selection for the piece part. An example from Figure 5.30 is the coefficient of friction of the retard roll, which has a target value of 1.5. The piece-part expectations are used as criteria (row headings) in the Pugh concept selection process. An example of a selected piece-part concept is the choice of microcellular polyurethane material for the retard roll (see Figure 5.37).

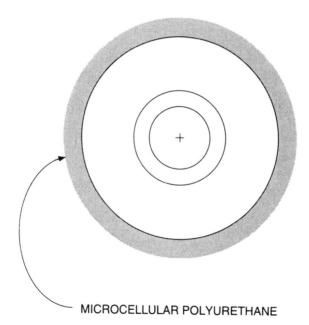

MICROCELLULAR POLYURETHANE

FIGURE 5.37. Example of piece-part concept selection.

The decision is made in this example that microcellular polyurethane material will best meet all of the piece-part expectations that have been defined in the subsystem design matrix. The selected piece-part concepts are then designed in detail.

Design for Production

Much design for production has already been done: robustness optimization, tolerance design, DFA, MAPS, and piece-part concept selection all improve the producibility of the design. The total subject of design for production has three elements:

Design for producibility
Process engineering
Factory capability

Design for Producibility

Many of the tasks in this stage have already been done. Now we apply design rules for very detailed producibility—for example, do not tap to the bottom of a blind hole, do not punch a hole too close to the edge of the sheet metal, and myriad lessons learned about production. This knowledge is brought to bear directly by PDT members with production experience, and indirectly by knowledge-based engineering. The latter captures the best production knowledge (and all other knowledge that can be codified) and makes it readily available in computer software, or other documentation.

Process Engineering

Process engineering is carried out as the product is designed. The piece-part design matrix, which was introduced in Figure 5.31, provides the requirements for process engineering. It is completed as shown in Figure 5.38. Then we use the piece-part process matrix to help us make the critical process engineering decisions, as shown in Figure 5.39.

The design matrix shows that our team decided to make the beam of two aluminum die castings, and that we are concerned about warp that might affect its ability to hold the wrap angle to a value near its target

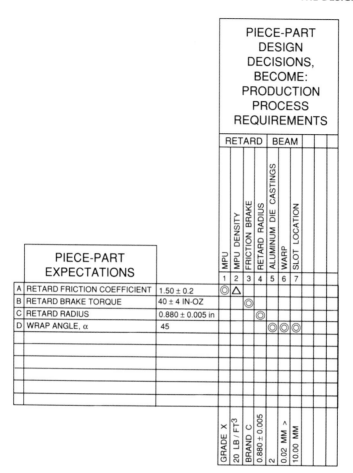

FIGURE 5.38. Piece-part design matrix.

of 45°. There are two types of warp that must be guarded against: (1) distortion during machining due to residual stresses that were locked in during the casting, and (2) elastic spring-back after machining if a casting is distorted by the clamp that holds it during machining. The latter is addressed in the process engineering matrix by the design of a clamping fixture that will avoid distortion. Also addressed are key process values, such as the cutter speed to machine the slot that locates the position of the retard roll.

Although the design and process engineering matrices are shown separately in Figures 5.38 and 5.39, the decisions must be made together.

		PROCESS ENGINEERING DECISIONS, BECOME: PRODUCTION OPERATIONS REQUIREMENTS									
PRODUCTION PROCESS REQUIREMENTS		VULCANIZING TEMPERATURE	RAW MATERIALS	VENDOR C	GRINDING SPEED	PURCHASE	SLOW COOL	CLAMP GENTLY	CUTTER SPEED		
		A	B	C	D	E	F	G	H		
1 MPU	GRADE X	◎	◎								
2 MPU DENSITY	20 LB / FT³	◎	O								
3 FRICTION BRAKE	BRAND C			◎							
4 RETARD RADIUS	0.880 ± 0.005				◎						
5 ALUMINUM DIE CASTINGS						◎					
6 WARPAGE							◎				
7 SLOT LOCATION								◎	◎		
								FIXTURE CF-147	2000 RPM		

FIGURE 5.39. Piece-part process matrix.

The ingenious team can combine the two matrices into one matrix to emphasize the concurrent nature of the decisions about geometry, material, and production process.

Factory Capability

By factory capability, we mean the design of the production tools, such as the clamping fixture to hold the aluminum die casting without distortion during machining. In traditional product development, the start of tooling design is usually much delayed. It is a key principle of *total quality development* that the tooling design is started early and is to be almost complete at the end of the design phase.

The design of the factory capability can involve much more than tooling design, including the design of a new factory. The greater the scope of the activity, the earlier it must start. For design purposes, production equipment—even a new factory—can be treated as a new product. It can be best developed by the complete application of total quality development.

PROGRESS CHECK FOR WORLD-CLASS DESIGN

The design is now complete. The cost, quality, and features are now clear.

OUTPUTS

The primary outputs from the design phase are the piece-part drawings, the critical parameter drawing, the QFD matrices, the functional analyses, the process descriptions, and the selected suppliers. These are then used during system verification (beginning of production preparation) to build total system models, which then verify the system's integrity and robustness. Before the model is built, the piece-part drawings are audited against the critical parameter drawing. This ensures that the piece-part drawings (which will be used in production) correctly incorporate the functionality that has been developed and have then been recorded in the critical parameter drawing. After the system verification is completed, the simple mistakes are corrected. The product design is then complete.

OTHER ACTIVITIES

For conciseness, the design of the product has been the main emphasis in the description of the design phase in this chapter. In the spirit of concurrent engineering, all other required activities are also carried out by the multifunctional PDT. The selection of the production processes has already been described.

Along with design for assembly (DFA), design for maintainability and design for operability are completed. These are then verified during system verification and perfected during the remainder of production preparation.

The design for the assembly system and process and the design of the field-support system are complete. They too are "products" and are also developed by the PDT as part of the process that has been described. They are then initially verified and further developed during system verification, refined, and finally verified during pilot production (the last phase of production preparation).

SUMMARY OF MAJOR ELEMENTS OF THE DESIGN PHASE

Great benefit is obtained from the structure of the design phase in total quality development, as summarized in Figure 5.40. This ensures that the subsystem decisions, especially the optimization of the critical design parameters, are completed before the design of the piece parts is very far along. In the practice of the traditional process within some companies, the emphasis during design is on piece parts. There is inadequate attention to subsystem design. The design phase structure by itself when combined with basic concurrent engineering provides a big improvement relative to traditional product development.

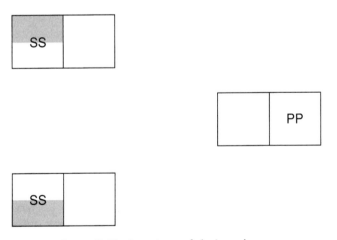

FIGURE 5.40. Structure of design phase.

In addition to the *design phase* structure and basic concurrent engineering, great improvement is also provided by the following better decision-making practices:

- Optimization of robustness
    Failure analysis (FTA and FMEA)
    Parameter design
    Critical parameter drawing
- Design competitive benchmarking
- QFD matrices
- MAPS
- Concept selection
- Functional trees
- Tolerance design
- Design for production

The structure and better practices of the design phase in total quality development produce much-improved definitions of the unit design tasks. The requirements for the unit design tasks are strongly developed by EQFD and Taguchi's quality engineering. The traditional success with the unit design tasks now leads to successful products.

The design phase of total quality development plays a major role in overcoming:

- Cash drain 4: Pretend design
- Cash drain 5: Pampered products
- Cash drain 6: Hardware swamps
- Cash drain 7: Here's the product. Where's the factory?

CRITERION FOR SUCCESS OF THE PIECE-PART PHASE

The overwhelming criterion at the end of piece-part design is essentially the same as the one at the end of subsystem design: the design is sufficiently superior to the expected competition.

Now, however, there is a much firmer estimate of unit manufacturing cost (UMC). The detailed drawings and processes are used to estimate the UMC. Also, the operability and field supportability will now be much firmer, and a more clear evaluation can be made. Features and robustness were largely defined at the completion of subsystem design, and they will be verified in the system verification test.

PROGRESSIVE FREEZE

At the completion of the design phase, the product design is frozen. The only subsequent changes will be the correction of simple mistakes. Attempts to make significant changes later have plagued traditional product development. Late changes cause confusion and greatly delay the completion of product development. A key element of total quality development is disciplined, progressive freezing of the decisions.

The tooling design is almost complete, both piece-part tooling and assembly tooling. The tooling design is then completed during system verification, on the basis of our experiences during the model build. Tool-building activities for tools having a long lead time have already been undertaken during piece-part design (and the ordering of these materials may have been done during subsystem design). The tools are built during production preparation and are verified in pilot production at the end of production preparation.

All suppliers have been selected. The production processes have been selected. Detailed drawings have been completed so that the full-system prototypes can be built.

It is critical to schedule well the making of decisions and then not to readdress them. In total quality development the emphasis is on delivering the product to the market quickly, before the business environment changes.

BENEFITS

At the completion of the design phase, we have accomplished large benefits, compared with those of the traditional approach to product development:

- Design is responsive to customer needs.
- Concept is dominant, carefully selected over strong alternatives.

- Design is fully production-intent:
    Design for assembly
    Design for piece-part producibility
    Design for maintainability
    Design for operability
    Choice of production processes and design of tools
- Design is superior to benchmarks.
- Design is robust against noises; its functionality stays close to ideal customer satisfaction under actual conditions of production and use.

In summary, at this stage in the development program, the application of total quality development has overcome cash drains 2 through 7. Perhaps most important of all, our PDT knows that we have a winner and knows why it is a winner. The technical community and the business and marketing community are in consensus that the expected superiorities of the new product, including schedule, are compatible with the expectations of the business plans. *The entire organization is committed to the success of the product in which we take pride.*

38 STEPS FOR THE SUCCESSFUL DESIGN PHASE—)
A SUMMARY

DESIGN PHASE INPUT

    Total System Specifications (House of Quality)
    Total System Concept (includes subsystem technologies)
    Subsystem Specifications (TS/SS Design Matrix)

SUBSYSTEM DESIGN

	Step	Page
Identification of Critical Parameters		
Conduct Fault Tree Analysis (FTA)	D1	183
Conduct Failure Modes and Effects Analysis (FMEA)	D2	183

[2]Done in parallel with identification of critical parameters.
[3]Done in parallel with parameter design.

PIECE-PART DESIGN

Tolerance Design (Figure 3.11)

Detailed Piece-Part Design

DESIGN PHASE OUTPUT

Detailed Drawings
Critical Parameter Drawings
Concept Layout
Complete Set of QFD Matrices
Assembly Instructions
Selected Suppliers

CHAPTER

6

Getting Ready For Production

- **System Verification — Demonstrating Robustness**

- **Getting Ready**

- **Pilot Production**

- **World-Class Product**

- **23 Steps for the Successful Production Preparation Phase — A Summary**

N ow that the design is complete, our attention turns to production. Of course, during the design phase we already emphasized production. The design that has been completed consists of:

The product (geometry and material to achieve function)
The production capability (including process engineering)
The field-support capability

During the *design phase*, the product has been designed for producibility, the production processes have been chosen (at least for critical part features), and the production tooling design has been almost completed, lagging the product design only slightly. This is a huge advance over the obsolete serial style of development, which would only start considerations relative to production during this *production preparation phase*, after the product design was supposedly complete. This led to the major problems of cash drain 7 (here's the product; where's the factory?). One of our main objectives is to overcome these obsolete dysfunctions. Now we have tremendous improvements: a robust product design, responsive to the customers, with economical tolerances embedded in the selected production processes. In this production preparation phase we put our new design into production while overcoming cash drains 8 and 9:

- Cash drain 8: We've always made it this way
- Cash drain 9: Inspection

Cash drain 8 is overcome by QFD for production and by process parameter design, the optimization of the robustness of the most critical production processes. Cash drain 9 is overcome by on-line quality control.

The production preparation phase has three subphases, as displayed in Figure 6.1. In *system verification*, we build prototypes and verify the robustness. This then leaves us free to concentrate on correcting simple design mistakes during the *getting ready* subphase. At the same time, the production tooling is built. Then, in *pilot production*, everything comes together and is validated, and we put our new product into production.

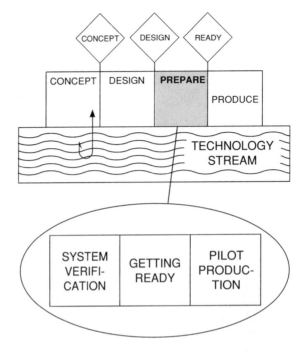

FIGURE 6.1. Production preparation subphases.

In doing production preparation we continue to use the multifunctional PDT. The PDT resolves all problems by finding the root causes and changing them to eliminate the problems. All decisions are made after careful consideration of functionality, producibility, and field supportability.

SYSTEM VERIFICATION—DEMONSTRATING ROBUSTNESS

As shown in Figure 6.2, we build the first prototypes, finalizing the production tooling design as we do so. Then we debug the prototypes to eliminate the most debilitating mistakes, and in the culmination of our skeletal design activities we verify the robustness (in the system verification test, or SVT). This subphase is the transition from design to concentration on production, and it could easily be included as the final subphase in the design phase.

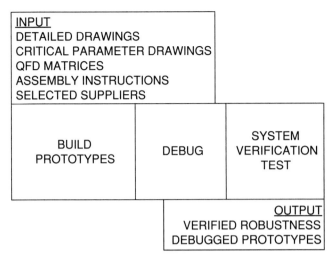

INPUT
DETAILED DRAWINGS
CRITICAL PARAMETER DRAWINGS
QFD MATRICES
ASSEMBLY INSTRUCTIONS
SELECTED SUPPLIERS

BUILD PROTOTYPES

DEBUG

SYSTEM VERIFICATION TEST

OUTPUT
VERIFIED ROBUSTNESS
DEBUGGED PROTOTYPES

FIGURE 6.2. System verification subphase.

BUILDING PROTOTYPES—DESIGN INTO HARDWARE

The prototypes are built from the completely production-intent drawings, using the production processes insofar as is feasible. This helps to verify the design decisions. Since production tooling is not yet available, many processes used in building the prototypes cannot yet approximate the actual production method. However, we make every attempt to stay as close as possible to the production environment.

Forming Parts by Machining

Some parts that are to be formed in production by forging, casting, or molding may have to be machined from commercially available shapes. Even here we make the dimensions completely realistic. For example, draft angles that are required in the production molds are machined into the parts, so that the prototype part is dimensionally the same as it will be in production. The material is also the production material. Then the only difference is in the material microstructure, which will have better flow lines in the production process. Any tests that depend on the microstructure, such as fatigue tests, are postponed until production parts are available. Most functionality does not depend on microstructure and can therefore be completely tested in the prototype systems.

Soft Tooling

Although some parts will have to be machined from commercial shapes, many times soft tooling can be used to produce parts that are almost the same as production parts. We make the parts in the most realistic way that is feasible, as this will uncover problems that otherwise will be delayed until pilot production or later. Rapid prototyping (see Ashley, 1991), the quick production of molds for parts by innovative methods such as three-dimensional printing (this method in particular is covered in Sachs et al., 1992), is greatly increasing our ability to make the building of prototypes more realistic relative to actual production.

Assembly

The assembly of the prototypes is made as realistic as possible. We make every effort to use production workers and processes. We begin to develop the assembly processes that were designed during the design phase. They will be further developed during pilot production.

Verification of Production Tooling Design

During the building of the prototypes, the design of the production tooling is verified on paper (or in the CAD activity). Appropriate teams review the design of each tool in light of their experience with building the prototypes. This activity goes on throughout the building of the prototypes. Many potential problems are identified and corrected, avoiding much rework during pilot production. All tool designs are completed by the end of system verification.

Solving Production Problems

During the building of the prototypes, many problems inevitably occur. There is a natural tendency to feel that each problem is peculiar and unique, and unlikely to occur again. However, experience has shown that every problem encountered during the building of the prototypes should be taken very seriously, documented, and corrected. The root causes are identified and eliminated so that the problem does not occur again. This is a great opportunity to avoid future problems.

DEBUG PROTOTYPES

Despite our best care, some mistakes become incorporated into the prototypes. Therefore, we first debug the completed prototypes to eliminate the mistakes which can be quickly identified and which most affect the operation of our product. Our intention is to make the prototypes function as intended, eliminating simple mistakes that were made in design or during the building of the prototypes.

There are several approaches to effective debugging:

- Part audit
- Functionality audit
- Robustness check

We can use all of them in series.

Part Audit

We audit the parts to ensure that they correctly meet our intention. In actual production, later on, the parts will already have gone through the quality checks that we designed into the production processes; thus, we will be relying primarily upon on-line quality control during full-scale production. Most of our on-line QC is not yet operational for the building of the prototypes, however. We could use 100% inspection of the prototype parts as a substitute, but during the debugging of the prototypes we want to avoid the cost and time of 100% inspection.

A much more efficient approach is to measure the values of the critical parameters that are on our critical parameter drawings. These are the characteristics that we have identified as being most important to the functionality of our product. Many of these are composite characteristics, contributed to by several parts. For example, the wrap angle in our paper feeder is determined by the spacing between the two aluminum die-cast bridges, and by the details of the shafts and pulleys that locate the feed belt and the retard roll. Thus, if the composite critical functional parameter checks out correctly, it verifies that several parts are satisfactory without the necessity of measuring each part. The audit of the critical parameters in the prototypes has been proven by experience to be highly effective as a method of auditing the parts.

Functionality Audit

In the functionality audit, we operate the prototypes and audit the functions. In its simplest form, we push the button and see if anything happens. Often direct observation will reveal some serious problem. Actually, if our product has moving parts, it is not a good idea to push the button first, but rather the system should be turned over by hand to ensure that there is not some major interference.

However, the more extensive functional audit is done with instrumentation that can detect and measure the major operational events. For example (to continue with our case study of the paper feeder), our feedhead has two clutches. We measure their time of operation and check them against our timing diagram. If they are incorrect, then we search for the root cause in the sensors, clutches, relays, power supplies, and—most suspect of all—software. The functional audit is effective in quickly finding problems.

Robustness Check

The purpose of the present debugging phase is to enable us to start running the system verification test (SVT), the verification of robustness. A highly effective debugging procedure is to simply perform a preliminary SVT on our prototypes, comparing the robustness of the prototypes with the robustness that was achieved during the design phase. We want to ensure that we still have the robustness that we developed. This is a very significant test that quickly tells us if the functionality is as intended. For example, for our paper feeder we use the same stress stacks that we used in optimizing the robustness and again determine the threshold stack forces for misfeeds and multifeeds. If they are the same as the optimized values that we achieved during the design phase, then we can be confident that the detailed design and the prototypes built have captured our functional intent.

The preliminary SVT may be the most efficient approach to debugging. With more experience we may develop more confidence in relying primarily upon it, and the need for the audits may wither away.

System Verification Test (SVT)—Beat the Benchmark

With completion of the debugging comes the proof of the pudding: do we have the robustness that we thought we had at the conclusion of the design phase? This test is critical to the remainder of our product program and is one of the major events of total quality development. If we have captured robust functionality, then the product is nearly ready. Otherwise we would be doomed to a schedule-breaking sequence of build-test-fix rework, which has plagued the traditional process. If we have been successful in the earlier phases, then the SVT should be an almost routine success.

In the SVT we measure the robustness of our new prototypes, and compare it with two important standards:

- Competitive benchmark robustness
- Robustness achieved during the design phase

In the SVT, some of our prototypes are tested side by side with the benchmark products. We apply the same noises to both, and measure the same signal-to-noise ratios. Our product should have superior SN values. Who wants a product that is not as functional as the best product already in the marketplace? Also, we compare the signal-to-noise ratios from our prototypes with the values that we achieved earlier during the design phase. They should be the same; otherwise, some mistake has been made during the detailed design or during the building of the prototypes.

Noises and Measurements

Applying the same noises and measuring the same SN ratios is straightforward if the competitive benchmark product has the same technologies as our new product. In our example of the paper feeder, if the competitive product also has a friction retard feeder, then we can use the same stress stacks and again determine the SN ratio by measuring the threshold stack forces.

However, if the competitive product has different technology—a vacuum feeder, for example—then the same stresses and measurements will not be feasible. The vacuum feeder does not have a stack force, and stacks that put stress on the friction retard feeder will not put stress on the vacuum feeder. This is a great challenge—to find a robustness test that is valid for more than one technology. In Chapter 5, it was mentioned that the robustness could be measured by observing the time of arrival of the sheet at some appropriate point. This is the more "global" requirement for a copy-handling system; it has to deliver a sheet of paper to an image transfer point. The copy sheet must arrive at a fixed point on the imaging medium (photoreceptor) at a certain time so that it is properly matched with the image. Therefore, time is a more relevant system-level metric than stack force, and it is independent of technology.

Applying the same stresses to two different technologies is difficult to do. In principle we want some severe condition that presents roughly a 3σ position with respect to all of the conditions that will be found in the marketplace. The actual value is not so important, but it must be approximately the same number of standard deviations for both technologies. Stresses on the friction feeder are represented by friction values; on the vacuum feeder, stresses are represented by ranges of sheet porosity. We must select stress stacks for both that are about 3σ with respect to conditions in the marketplace. This is not something that can be done with great accuracy, but our best effort will still leave us with much less risk than if the comparison with the benchmark product were not made.

Calibrate Robustness

Often we can also test another product currently in the marketplace that has the same technology as our new product, in order to obtain a better perspective. By testing the robustness of two products whose market performance is known, we can obtain a more certain determination of the functionality of our new product. In our *current* product, we have a friction retard feeder (FRF), and it is our perception that it undergoes about twice as many shutdowns in the field as the vacuum feeder in our competitor's product. Now, by measuring the robustness of both, using different stress stacks as described in the previous argument, we obtain a field calibration of the difference in SN values. This overcomes the uncertainty that is introduced by the need to use different stress stacks for different technologies. The result is shown in the following table.

	Field Shutdown Rate	SN Ratio
Current (FRF)	$100/10^6$	10.3
Competition (vacuum)	$50/10^6$	11.4
First prototype (FRF)	NA	17.1

We see that under the test conditions we used, the competition's 1.1-dB (11.4 – 10.3) laboratory advantage for its vacuum feeder is equivalent to a 2× advantage in field performance. Therefore, we need an improvement from our current FRF to our new first prototype FRF of enough gain in SN ratio to be more than a 2× improvement in the field. To translate SN gain to the improvement in rate, we use the ω transform (also known as the *logit* transform; Phadke, 1989). For the small rates that we have, cutting the rate by half requires an SN ratio increase of about 3 dB. Thus, if we improved the SN ratio of our current feeder to 13.3 dB (10.3 + 3), it would be about equal in shutdown rate to the competition's.

The difference between 13.3 dB and 11.4 dB represents the inconsistency in our present test procedure. We can use this information to improve our test procedure so that the SN values for the different technologies will be the same for the same performance. For now we observe that 13.3 would give us parity, and the gain from 13.3 to 17.1 gives us a superiority of 3.8 dB, more than a factor of 2 in expected field performance, over the best current competitive product.

DEMONSTRATE SUPERIOR ROBUSTNESS

At the completion of the SVT we have verified that the robustness that we developed during the design phase has been captured in the first full-system hardware, the first prototypes, and is superior to the competition. This places us in an excellent position to rapidly complete the product program, without the long delays doing the build-test-fix rework of the traditional approach.

PROGRESS CHECK

The purpose of a progress review at this point is to judge whether or not the expected quality of the product in the marketplace will be sufficient for commercial success. If the total development process has been well executed, the probability of passing this review will be at least 95%. For those unusual development programs that are found lacking at this point, it would generally be wise to return to the start of the *concept phase*, redefine the market entrance date, and start a new development process. This is a hard decision to make at this time, but it usually would be preferable to limping along with an inadequate product.

Progressive Freeze

At this time, the system verification is complete, and the product has won its head-to-head comparison test by showing better signal-to-noise ratios than the competitive benchmark product. Also, the problem set that has been found on the first prototypes, when plotted on a reliability growth curve, leads to the expectation that problem-identification tests, the problem-solving process, and the reliability growth methodology will achieve the quality and reliability goals that are in the business plan.

With both the critical parameters and the mundane-many parameters meeting all expectations, we can confidently expect to capture the success that has been enabled, and to have a world-leading product. Therefore, we should now see final commitment of funding, resources, and all other requirements to complete the product program. There will not be any further consideration of canceling or altering this product program.

The tool design for production is now completed and frozen. The experience gained during the building of the full-system prototypes has provided final information that is necessary for the completion of the tool design. The prototypes have been completed. All problems associated with the building of the prototypes have been indentified, and the corrective actions have been defined. It is very important not to ignore any of these problems, for they would then occur again during the building of the next prototypes.

Criteria for Concluding the Prototype Phase

The suggested primary criteria are:

- The product demonstrates superior robustness to the benchmark product(s).
- A corporate consensus on success has been achieved.

Superior robustness is a key element of total quality development. This verifies that robustness has been successfully achieved, and completes the overcoming of cash drains 5 (pampered products) and 6 (hardware swamps).

The second criterion is critically important. If the product people feel that they have a winner but the sales and service people have doubts, the product is not likely to succeed. Consensus that the new product will be a winner is essential to success.

GETTING READY

The second subphase of production preparation has two tracks, as shown in Figure 6.3. The top track is correcting the mistakes in the product design. The second track is developing the production capability. This includes building the production tooling, planning production operations, doing process parameter design, and developing on-line QC.

CORRECTING DESIGN MISTAKES

Major mistakes (the 10 cash drains) are avoided by the total quality development that is the subject of this book. Inevitably, many simple mistakes will creep into our design. In a large, complex product there are on the order of 10 million decisions. Even an error rate of only 0.01% will result in 1000 mistakes. Experience has shown that on the order of 1000 mistakes is not uncommon. Fortunately it is relatively easy to find and correct these simple mistakes once robustness is achieved, so that erratic performance does not mask the simple mistakes.

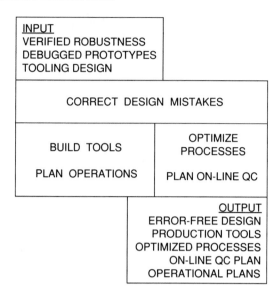

FIGURE 6.3. Getting-ready subphase.

These mistakes range from reversed diodes to partial design tasks that have been incorrectly done. An example of the latter is a gear mounted on a cantilever shaft that has excessive overhang. The result is noisy gears and rapid wear. It was certainly within the normal competence of partial design to size the shaft properly. Therefore, the failure to do so is a simple mistake that must now be corrected.

Avoid Mistakes

The first line of defense against simple mistakes is to avoid them in the first place. Knowledge-based engineering is moving to computer systems that capture all of the knowledge and automate the simple partial design tasks. It can be hoped that this will soon greatly reduce the number of mistakes.

Solve Problems

We eliminate mistakes once they have occurred by a straightforward application of:

- Design verification testing
- TQM methods to find the root causes
- Correction of the drawings

Reliability growth curves help us to be realistic about the time that is required. With robustness ensured before the mistake correction activity is emphasized, the mistakes are not masked by the symptoms of lack of robustness. Also, knowledge-based engineering reduces the number of mistakes that flow through to this correction activity. This unglamorous work requires discipline to root out every mistake, but it consists of straightforward engineering that can now be completed in a relatively short time because of (1) the early success in achieving robustness, and (2) the fewer mistakes that occur.

Complete the Design

In addition to correcting the design mistakes, other activities during this time period help us to get the product ready for production. Some of the prototypes are devoted to developing procedures for field maintenance and the preparation of service manuals. Some are devoted to testing operability and to the development of operator training. Testing is done that will lead to the required regulatory approvals, although actual regulatory approval may require production machines, not prototypes. The prototypes are used to ensure that all regulatory standards are within our grasp and will be satisfied in routine fashion.

At the conclusion of "getting ready," and before the start of pilot production, the design of the product is complete. There will not be any more changes, unless they are required to overcome a production problem. But of course, the early emphasis on production during the design phase greatly reduces the number of production problems. Also, the early emphasis on low-cost design makes manufacturing cost reduction activities unnecessary. The early emphasis on robustness makes reliability improvements unnecessary. The great improvements in the development process during the concept and design phases are now paying off.

For most products we will need only the one round of engineering prototypes. This should be our goal. In the past the extensive dependence on build-test-fix led to many rounds of prototypes, as many as 10. This only led to hardware swamps (cash drain 6), with great expenditure of time and money. In total quality development we now save time and money because of the front-end work that we have done.

DEVELOPING PRODUCTION CAPABILITY

While the design is being perfected, we also develop the production capability. Production tools are built, the processes are optimized for robustness so that part variation is minimized, and production operations are planned in concert with the production-process engineering that was done during the design phase.

Production Tooling

The design of the production tooling is completed during the building of the first prototypes, and the tools are built while the mistakes are being rooted out of the product design. In the past the long times to complete the build-test-fix iterations of the product design provided a time cushion for building the tools. In total quality development the time to complete the product design is greatly reduced, so the time to build the tools must also be greatly reduced.

Start Early

Although the concentrated effort on tool building begins after the building of first prototypes, much time is saved by starting long–lead-time items much earlier, during the design phase. For example, if we are going to forge a connecting rod, we need a block of air-hardening tool steel to make the forging dies. The size of this is sufficiently well known to be ordered at the beginning of the design phase. The delivery time for such material can be three months. In the traditional way, this tool steel would not be ordered until the start of the getting-ready stage, or later. By ordering it early we have saved three months. This is indicative of the approach to reducing the tooling time.

Progressive Freezes of Decisions

Machining of tools that are on the critical schedule path is started before the detailed design of the part is completely finished. A cavity is roughed out, and then finished when the part design is complete in every detail. This is another important aspect of concurrent engineering. This is enabled by progressive freezing of the design. Major decisions are frozen first, and the design is progressively frozen until the final details are almost frozen at the end of the design phase. A few changes are made during system verification as a result of improvements that are identified during the building of the prototypes, and then the product design is completely frozen. The critical parameter values are frozen at the completion of subsystem design, along with the material and process selection (MAPS) for the most important parts.

This enables an early start on tooling. The tooling is often still designed by specialists, who are part of the multifunctional team. The product parts and the tooling to make and assemble them are designed by one team in one activity to design one system, all integrated together.

Continuous Improvement

The shortening of the tooling time needs to be continuously improved. This is largely a matter of taking out all slack time, much in the way that Mr. Shigeo Shingo (1985) did for single-minute exchange of dies. As the time for correcting product design mistakes is greatly reduced, it is a challenge to the tool design and building activity to keep pace.

Process Parameter Design

As the product was made robust during the design phase, now we make the production processes robust so that the parts are inherently more uniform. Factories have noises that make the parts vary from one unit of production to the next. By optimizing the robustness of the production processes, we minimize the effect of these noises, and the parts have less variation.

Tolerance design (Chapter 5) is a trade-off between cost and precision. Process parameter design is an improvement that creates a better set of trade-off options. In tolerance design we move along the existing trade-off curve (A in Figure 6.4). We pay extra money to purchase more precision, and seek the balance point that minimizes the total cost. Process parameter design moves us to a better trade-off curve (B in Figure 6.4).

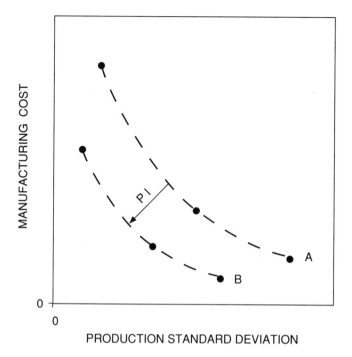

FIGURE 6.4. Process Improvement (PI).

The procedure for process parameter design is exactly the same as for product parameter design (Chapter 5), with one exception. For products, we have to introduce explicit values of the most important noises, since normal laboratory conditions do not well represent the actual conditions of use in the hands of customers. However, the production processes are optimized under the actual conditions of production. Therefore, we do not have to introduce values of noises that represent realistic conditions. (But sometimes we use an analytical model; then we do have to explicitly introduce the noises into the calculation.) For experimental optimization we simply use the actual conditions of production, which introduce the real noises. Care is taken to keep the noises representative. We avoid any special care or precision in making the parts during process parameter design, so that the variations that occur will be representative of actual production. Then we optimize the critical process parameters to minimize production variation.

Usually, we wait for the production tooling, so that the process parameter optimization is done under the most realistic conditions. This means that the process parameter design is usually completed during pilot production, since some of the tools will arrive just in time to start pilot production.

An example of process parameter design is the improvement of the aluminum die casting process for casting the aluminum bridges that support the mechanisms of the paper feeder (Figure 5.32). The multifunctional PDT identifies six critical process parameters: accumulator pressure, plunger velocity, plunger area, flow coefficient, gate area, and cavity pressure. Three levels are chosen for each process parameter, and the six control factors are assigned to columns in the L_{36} orthogonal array.

In this case an analytical model is available for performing an initial parameter design. Since an analytical model is being used, we must introduce the noises—also by using an L_{36} noise array. The numerical values in the noise array are based on the standard deviations of the process values during normal production. The calculations are completed and the SN values analyzed to find the best value of each control factor, just as for product parameter design. In our continuing hypothetical case study, the confirmation calculation reveals that the standard deviation of the critical dimensions that control the wrap angle and the belt-to-guide angle has been reduced by 50%. This is then confirmed in actual production, which enables us to machine the finished dimension in one pass instead of two, thus saving unit manufacturing cost (UMC). Process parameter design improves quality (standard deviation) and/or UMC.

Starting in 1980, Taguchi's process parameter design has been increasingly applied in the United States, with great benefits. Usually it is done experimentally. Savings of millions of dollars have been reported for just one process improvement.

Production Operations Planning

By using QFD, we plan that operations on the factory floor will be in concert with the voice of the customer. The process engineering that was done during the design phase, and initially verified during prototype building, is now extended to the many details of factory operation.

In many cases the teams are now expanded to include production workers and others who are most familiar with the factory floor.

The planning for production operations includes determining the settings of controls on machine tools, providing for the maintenance of the equipment and the training of the operators, determining the flow of the material, and setting up quality checkpoints. The decisions for factory operation are triaged. The most critical process values are optimized in process parameter design. The decisions that are important but do not require systematic optimization are made by the multifunctional team with the help of QFD. At the lowest level, many decisions are made without the assistance of the processes of QFD and quality engineering, depending primarily on successful experience. These are increasingly being made by knowledge-based engineering software, which in its most powerful form can automate much of the production planning.

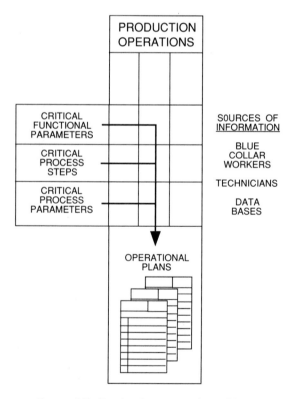

Figure 6.5. Production operations QFD.

During the design phase, we considered product function, hardware, and production processes together to select the best processes and process values. In process parameter design the most critical process values are optimized. Now in production operations planning we deploy from the process parameters to actual operations on the factory floor. This is displayed generically in Figure 6.5.

A specific example for milling the slot that positions the retard roll into the aluminum die casting that is the bottom part of the bridge for the paper feeder is shown in Figure 6.6. The processes are on the left (diagonal cross-hatching), and the production operations are on the right (grey shading). The critical functional parameters that are affected are displayed in the upper left corner. (The wrap angle α has already been introduced; γ is the contact angle between the feed belt and the entrance guide.) The critical operation (the only example that

F_{CR} : $\gamma = 0$ $\alpha = 45$		OPERATIONS		
	SLOT DIMENSION	MACHINE SETTING	*	
P	CLAMPING FIXTURE CF147	CLAMP TO "D" M4 FASTENER 1.8+/-0.18 NM		
R	CUTTER SPEED 2000 RPM			
O				
C	CUTTER MC295			
E	CUTTING FLUID TYPE F5			
S				
S	CUTTING FLUID FLOW 50 ML/S			

FIGURE 6.6. Operations planning matrix for the paper feeder (partially completed as an example).

is shown) is to clamp the aluminum die casting into the holding fixture without distortion. If the bridge were held in a deformed position while the slot was milled, then the elastic spring-back when the casting was released from the holding fixture would change the value of the critical dimension. The experienced team notes the clamping surface, the type of fastener, and the clamping torque.

The remaining operations for the slot are conventional and pose no unique problems. Therefore, they are defined by knowledge-based engineering, computerized or human. QFD is not needed for them. The PDT could choose to record the data in the QFD matrix, but here that is not shown in Figure 6.6. The complete record shows all of the production operations that contribute to the critical functional parameter of the angle between the feed belt and the entrance guide. This is a key feature of total quality development; production is related to functionality, which is related to customer needs and satisfaction.

For simplicity, only one column is shown in Figure 6.6. The rest of the complete matrix (as represented by the asterisk) includes columns for state of maintenance, operator training, and quality control point. Other activities are often included, as decided by the team. Often a separate QFD matrix is prepared for each type of factory activity. These QFD matrices for production operations planning complete the deployment from the voice of the customer to the factory floor (see Figure 3.6).

On-Line QC

An activity that warrants special emphasis is on-line quality control (QC) for factory operations. Even the most optimized processes will eventually stray far from the target unless the operator intervenes. How often does the operator intervene, and what action is taken? These are basic issues for ensuring good production quality.

QFD for production, tolerance design, and process parameter design creates the production capability that enables low-cost, high-quality production. However, if the production is done open-loop (without on-line QC), excessive production variance will occur. On-line QC consists of intervention into the process to reduce the production variance, and thus to reduce the quality loss.

Optimum Intervention

If there were zero intervention on the factory floor, the quality loss would be very large, as displayed in Figure 6.7. Increasing intervention is able to greatly reduce the production variance, and thus reduce the quality loss. However, the intervention increases the unit manufacturing cost (UMC), as shown in Figure 6.8. The intervention takes time, which increases the manufacturing cost. The total cost is the sum of (1) the incremental UMC to pay for the intervention and (2) the quality loss, as shown in Figure 6.9. This simple qualitative reasoning reveals that there is an optimum amount of intervention that minimizes the total cost, visible in Figure 6.9.

Three Types of On-Line QC

There are three types of on-line QC: feedback, feed-forward, and inspection. In feedback control the production results are measured and fed back to the previous process, where corrective action is taken. The corrective actions are usually of three types: adjust process to target, repair process, or revise the process. We will return to feedback QC, after first describing the other two types.

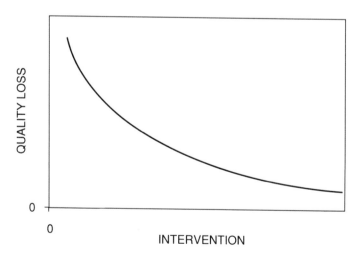

FIGURE 6.7. Quality loss reduced by intervention.

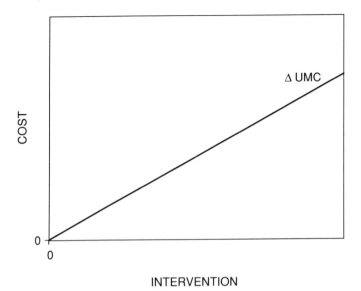

FIGURE **6.8.** UMC increased by intervention.

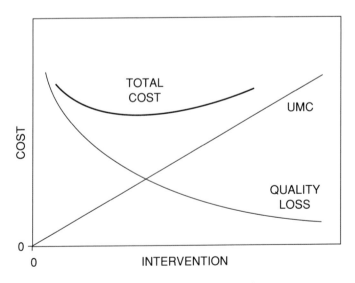

FIGURE **6.9.** Optimum Intervention.

Feed-Forward Control. In feed-forward control the results are measured and fed forward to a subsequent process, where corrective action is taken before that process is performed. Examples of feed-forward methods are selective assembly and process parameter adjustment.

The classic example of selective assembly is the fitting of automobile engine pistons to cylinders. To minimize combustion gas blow by (leakage) and reduce noise and wear, it is critical to achieve small clearances between the piston and the cylinder. To achieve the small clearances, it has long been the practice to measure the diameters of pistons and cylinders (production results from previous processes) and selectively assemble big pistons to big cylinders. The entire spectra of piston and cylinder sizes are matched to achieve good fits. (Continuous improvement has greatly reduced the number of size categories that are needed, but selective assembly is still widely used to ensure a good fit between piston and cylinder.)

An example of process parameter adjustment is the molding temperature for polymers. If the glass transition temperature of the batch of polymer is measured as $10°$ higher than nominal, then the molding temperature is increased by $10°$.

Inspection. Inspection consists of sorting the good parts from the defective parts after production. Historically, this approach played a major role in the development of manufacturing industry. The rigorous use of go/no go gauging to separate the good parts from the bad made the principle of interchangeable parts feasible. This separation was first done in a limited way at the federal armories at Springfield, Massachusetts, and Harpers Ferry, Virginia (now West Virginia), in approximately 1850. It first had a crucial economic role in civilian industry when it made possible Henry Ford's assembly line in 1913. Although go/no go separation is still widely used, it is to a considerable extent obsolete. Dr. W. Edwards Deming has written powerfully against it. There are two major problems: (1) it makes improvement difficult; and (2) it is expensive, because a bad batch often has to be scrapped. Improvement is difficult because numerical measurements are not made. A part that barely meets the tolerance requirement is not distinguished from one that is very close to the target. It is better to measure the value and then work to continuously reduce the variation, thus improving customer satisfaction.

However, if improvements in process capability are continuously utilized to design smaller features, then inspection will still be necessary. This is the case with integrated circuits. It is economical to scrap some chips in order to package more elements on one chip.

Today, go/no go gauges are often used at the actual workstation to inspect parts immediately after they are produced. This has the advantage that production problems are quickly identified, thus avoiding the scrapping of an entire batch. However, it still cannot distinguish a part that is close to the target from one that barely meets the tolerance. Measuring actual values enables continuous improvement.

Note that in feedback and feed-forward control, we act upon the process, while in inspection we act upon the product. Acting upon the process has the advantage that troubles are detected before many bad parts are made and the process is adjusted so that good parts are again made.

Next, the feedback adjustment of processes to the target is described in more detail.

Shewhart Feedback Control. After 1913, when go/no go gauging enabled Henry Ford's continuous-flow assembly line, it quickly spread throughout manufacturing industries. A short time later, however, during the 1920s, Dr. Walter Shewhart at the Bell Laboratories of AT&T developed a very different approach to on-line QC. His approach emphasizes the natural variation of production processes. Actual measurements are made at frequent intervals to ensure that unnatural variations due to special causes are not affecting the process. The measurements are plotted on a control chart to help assess the degree to which the variations are only the natural ones, and the extent to which the natural variations lie within the desired production tolerance. If six standard deviations of the natural variation of the process lie within the total tolerance range, the process is said to be *capable*, with a process capability index, C_p, of 1.0.

The Shewhart process is very different from the go/no go gauging approach that Henry Ford had just made popular. Not surprisingly, it was resisted. AT&T production during the 1920s was done at the Western Electric factory in Hawthorne (near Chicago), which had 35,000 employees, 5000 of whom were inspectors. The 5000 inspectors saw the Shewhart approach as a threat to their job security, and saw it to the door in short order.

During World War II a group that included Deming led the implementation of Shewhart control charts in the defense industry, where it was quite successful. The extreme pressures of wartime production reduced the cultural resistance. However, when the war ended, there was great pent-up demand after 16 years of economic depression and war. Anything could be quickly sold. There seemed to be little need for careful quality control. The use of the Shewhart control charts quickly faded from American industry.

Deming included the Shewhart method in the lessons he communicated to leading Japanese industrialists starting in 1950. Shewhart control charts became a major element of Japanese success during the 1960s and 1970s. When American factory managers sent study missions to Japan starting approximately in 1980, they returned extolling the virtues of Shewhart process control. Thus, Shewhart control was reimported into the United States 35 years after its use had been discontinued, and more than 50 years after it had been developed by Shewhart. During the 1980s its use became significant in the United States, although go/no go gauging was still relied on extensively.

Modern Feedback Adjustment. In the meantime, Taguchi's on-line QC was developed and started to replace Shewhart control in the most progressive Japanese companies. Taguchi's method of on-line QC has the objective of economically keeping production values for dimensions and other specifications near their target values, which have been determined during product parameter design. The inherently small values for production standard deviations that have been achieved during process parameter design are maintained and further reduced during actual production operations.

In traditional industrial practice, machinists used a process of checking and adjusting. They performed a machining or fabrication action and then measured (checked) the dimension and adjusted the process. For example, a lathe operator made a cut, measured the diameter, compared the measurement with the target on the drawing, and—if the difference was excessive—adjusted the position of the cross-slide to compensate for the discrepancy. This is basically a sound approach.

However, the frequency of checking, and the amount of deviation from the target that would trigger an adjustment (the adjustment limit), were left to the individual preference of each machinist. The checking interval often varied from more than one measurement per part to one measurement every several parts. The adjustment limit that triggered the adjustment of the process (turning the cross-slide leadscrew micrometer dial, for example) was most often the tolerance on the drawing. However, many machinists, especially those who operated precision machine tools such as cylindrical grinders, prided themselves on holding the dimension to a smaller range of variation than the tolerance on the print.

The modern approach returns to the traditional procedure of checking and adjusting. The new improvement is that the checking interval and the adjustment limit are set at the values that minimize the total cost (manufacturing cost plus expected quality loss). The operational procedure is shown in Figure 6.10. D is the adjustment limit, and Δ_M is the manufacturing tolerance that is on the drawing.

An initial checking interval, n_0, and adjustment limit, D_0, are chosen on the basis of experience. Then a few parts are made to determine the required frequency of adjustment, u_0. On the basis of these data, new values, n_1 and D_1, are calculated that will reduce the total cost. These are then used in production to determine u_1, and then n_2 and D_2 are cal-

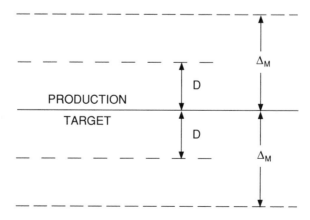

FIGURE 6.10. Checking and adjusting.

culated, which further reduce the total cost. Usually a few iterations bring us close to the best values for n and D, which minimize the total cost.

This process is based on the trade-off that is displayed in Figure 6.9. The cost of intervention, checking, and adjusting increases as intervention becomes more frequent (n and D become smaller), as shown in Figure 6.8. However, the quality loss becomes smaller (see Figure 6.7) as the average deviation from the target value becomes smaller, because of the more active checking and adjusting. We operate at the values of n and D that minimize the total cost (Figure 6.9).

For example, if n is 3, then parts 1, 4, 7, 10, and so on, are measured. If the measurement is within the adjustment limit D, no corrective action is taken. When the measurement is outside the adjustment limit, the process is adjusted back to the target.

In many production processes the adjustment action is simple. On a lathe, the cross-slide leadscrew micrometer dial is turned. In other processes—for example, injection molding—the adjustment is not so readily identified. The molding machine does not have a dial to change the dimensions. In such cases we determine the best adjustment factor(s) during process parameter design. For injection molding we use some combination of temperature and pressure.

Finding the best values for n and D is essentially a trial-and-error iterative process. If the incremental UMC (unit manufacturing cost) to pay for the checking and adjustment is less than the expected quality loss, then we increase the amount of intervention (to make the values of n and D smaller). If the expected quality loss is less than the cost of intervention, then we make the values of n and D bigger. To estimate the expected quality loss, we make a rough assumption about the variation of the measurement that we are controlling. The expected quality loss, L_A, is:

$$L_A = k\sigma_M^2 \tag{6.1}$$

where

L_A = expected quality loss averaged over all of the production
$k = L/\Delta^2$
σ_M = standard deviation of the measured values

Since we do not measure every part, we cannot directly calculate the standard deviation. Therefore, we make some rough assumptions so that we can calculate an approximate value for σ_M without depending on measurements. To do this we assume that the values of the quality characteristic are uniformly distributed between $+D$ and $-D$ for most of the production interval between adjustments. The variance (σ^2) of a uniform distribution is $D^2/3$, so we assume this as the variance for most of the parts. However, the last few parts before adjustment clearly cannot be uniformly distributed, but instead will lie close to $+D$ (or $-D$). These parts have a variance of D^2.

How many parts will have values that lie close to D? We assume that the last half of the parts during the last checking interval have values near D. Half of the checking interval is $(n + 1)/2$, so the fraction of parts with variance D^2 is $(n + 1)/2u$. Thus, the variance for all of the parts that are made during one adjustment interval is roughly estimated as

$$\sigma_M^2 = \left(1 - \frac{n+1}{2u}\right)\frac{D^2}{3} + \frac{n+1}{2u}D^2 \tag{6.2}$$

Each term in Equation (6.2) is the variance multiplied by the fraction of parts with that variance. Often the value of $(n + 1)/2u$ is small compared with 1, giving

$$\sigma_M^2 = \frac{D^2}{3} + \frac{(n+1)}{2u}D^2 \tag{6.3}$$

This is used to calculate the expected value of the quality loss, and the values of n and D are iteratively optimized, as described previously.

To speed up the iteration, we can use some mathematics to calculate the next values for n and D, instead of simply relying on judgment. We want to minimize the total cost, given by

$$C_t = \frac{B}{n} + \frac{C}{u} + k\sigma_M^2 + \text{UMC}_0 \tag{6.4}$$

where

B = cost of checking one part
C = cost of making one adjustment
UMC_0 = (constant) cost without on-line QC

Rewriting,

$$C_t = \frac{B}{n} + \frac{C}{u} + k\left(\frac{D^2}{3} + \frac{n+1}{2u}D^2\right) + \text{UMC}_0 \tag{6.5}$$

Now we would like to use the standard calculus approach of taking the partial derivatives with respect to n and D, setting each equal to zero, and solving to find the values of n and D that give the minimum value of total cost. However, the equation still contains the adjustment interval, u, which depends on D. In order to differentiate, we need the relationship between D and u. To obtain this we assume that the values for the parts follow a random-walk process, which gives

$$\frac{u}{u_0} = \frac{D^2}{D_0^2} \tag{6.6}$$

Substituting this, doing the differentiation, and solving gives

$$n_1 = \left(\frac{2Bu_0}{kD_0^2}\right)^{1/2} \tag{6.7}$$

$$D_1 = \left(\frac{3CD_0^2}{ku_0}\right)^{1/4} \tag{6.8}$$

We use these to calculate the values for the next iteration. (For subsequent iterations, the subscripts are advanced to 2 and 1, and so on.) This speeds up the convergence relative to simply using our judgment to decide the next values.

The assumptions that were used in deriving these equations are very rough. However, they are used only to improve somewhat on our judgment in determining the next values for n and D, so precisely correct models are not required.

Usually, we determine the best values for n and D during pilot production and then use them during full-scale production. This optimized checking and adjusting form of on-line QC has two advantages over the much older Shewhart approach:

(1) There are no control charts, so that this method is easier for operators.
(2) The standard deviation usually becomes smaller.

Both approaches are usually superior to reliance on go/no go gauges, which were the new control technology in 1850. Optimized checking and adjusting has the greater potential, and gaining its benefits is a major opportunity in total quality development.

Progress Check

At the completion of the getting-ready subphase, we have the equipment and processes to manufacture the product. The progress check at this point is meant to identify any areas that need concentrated activity to ensure a smooth entrance into production.

Progressive Freeze

At the completion of the getting-ready subphase, it is imperative that, for all identified problems, corrective actions be defined and implemented. The correction of mistakes is essentially complete, except for a few more mistakes that should be found during pilot production.

Tool building is complete, as is, essentially, the validation of tools. The tools are needed to start pilot production.

Service documentation is complete, ready for final production. Other aspects of service, such as service training, are also ready.

Tolerance design should be essentially complete. However, there will be some fine tuning of the tolerance design during process parameter design just prior to the start of production.

Also at this time, most of the operating systems should be loaded with the design data for the new product, and they should be activated so that they can be used during the building of the production prototypes during pilot production.

Criterion for Completeness of the Getting-Ready Subphase

One suggested criterion is indicative of the criteria that are helpful at this time: Tooling validated.

There are many other elements that are also now ready. *Tooling validated* is a surrogate for all of them. We could use as a broader criterion *operational capabilities validated*.

PILOT PRODUCTION

After the design corrections are complete, the production tools are available, the critical processes have been made robust, the production operation planning has been completed, and the on-line QC has been made ready, everything comes together in pilot production (see Figure 6.11). A limited number of units of the new product are produced as they will be in steady production. The objective is to train the production people, make necessary improvements in the processes, validate the tools, balance the workloads, and eliminate all problems before ramping up to full-scale production.

ORGANIZATION

The biggest innovation in total quality development for pilot production is organizational. The multifunctional PDT is responsible for pilot production. It is expanded by bringing in the factory people who build the products. The PDT now eliminates essentially all of the problems, before

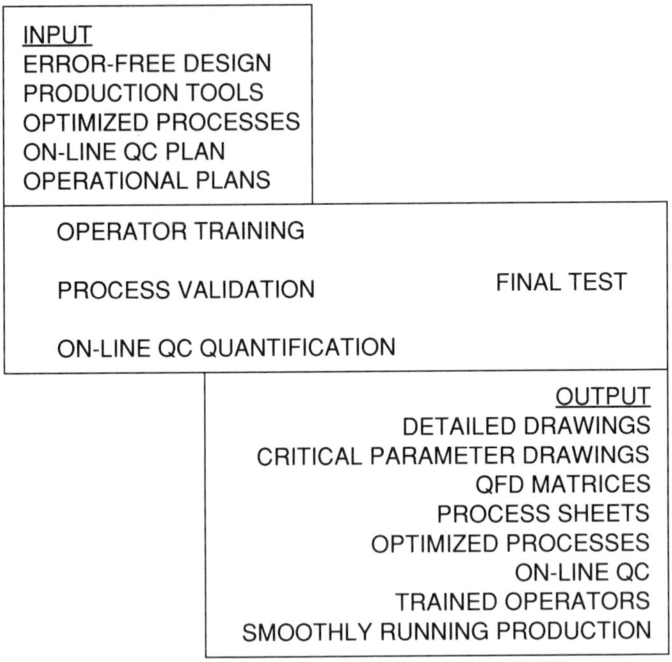

```
INPUT
ERROR-FREE DESIGN
PRODUCTION TOOLS
OPTIMIZED PROCESSES
ON-LINE QC PLAN
OPERATIONAL PLANS

   OPERATOR TRAINING

   PROCESS VALIDATION                    FINAL TEST

   ON-LINE QC QUANTIFICATION

                                     OUTPUT
                          DETAILED DRAWINGS
                  CRITICAL PARAMETER DRAWINGS
                                QFD MATRICES
                             PROCESS SHEETS
                        OPTIMIZED PROCESSES
                                 ON-LINE QC
                           TRAINED OPERATORS
                 SMOOTHLY RUNNING PRODUCTION
```

FIGURE 6.11. Pilot production subphase of the production preparation phase.

the product is transferred to production operations. When the product *is* transferred, the factory people who have been on the PDT during pilot production return to production operations. Some of the development engineers on the PDT—including some who have been on the PDT since well before pilot production—may also transfer into production operations for a short time. (A few may stay for an extended time as a developmental assignment to learn more about production.)

The PDT responsibility for pilot production makes clear that the PDT is responsible for solving all developmental problems—from the voice of the customer through pilot production. This clear assignment of responsibility overcomes very serious problems in the traditional process in which the manager of development and the manager of production spent endless time in nonproductive arguments about who was responsible for each problem. Now, the energies can be concentrated on solving problems.

Making the Factory Floor Responsive to Customers

A main objective of pilot production is to train the operators. Initially, this is the responsibility of the PDT members who have been on the team since before pilot production. In the past, the factory operators could only strive to achieve the numbers on the drawings, with little or no understanding of the need for holding the tolerances that were given to them "over the wall." A prime objective of total quality development is to enable the operators to understand product functionality so that they can relate their work to customer satisfaction. This has been helped by the participation of some factory people in the QFD for production operations planning. Now, in pilot production, this understanding is transferred to all of the factory operators. The intent is to realize the vision of Figure 3.6 (Chapter 3). QFD helps everyone to relate the factory floor activities to customer satisfaction.

Once the factory operators have been allowed to learn how their work is ultimately connected with customer satisfaction—by way of all the decisions that have been made in between by the PDT, as suggested in Figure 3.6—the emphasis is then on quality circles and self-managed work teams to make continuous improvements around the basic decisions that have been made during development. After sufficient time has been allowed for the production operations to get running smoothly, the responsibility is transferred to the production operations management.

Process Validation

A primary activity of pilot production is to validate the effectiveness of the production processes. During the design phase, we made process engineering decisions. Then, in the getting-ready subphase, we extended these decisions into operational planning. Now, we confirm that the actual production results are as we have planned.

The effective method of process validation is to monitor the standard deviations of the critical functional parameters. If their process capability indexes are as planned, then we can be confident that the individual processes that contribute to the variability of each critical functional parameter are behaving as expected. This ensures that production is meeting customer satisfaction goals.

Monitoring the process capability of the critical functional parameters is much more effective than attempting to manage every detail of production. By validating production at this higher level of scope, total quality development achieves great effectiveness.

FINAL TEST

Before the responsibility is shifted away from the PDT, a major test is performed on the units that have been produced. It has a name such as *field-readiness demonstration test* or *shipping approval test*. It is a large test modeled on the full spectrum of customer use conditions. It attempts to duplicate the complete population of customer conditions so that the results will be representative of actual field performance.

In the past, such tests were the prime mode of activity during the entire getting-ready subphase. However, they are very inefficient, as most of the time is spent running unchallenging conditions during which no problems are found. Therefore, such a test should now be reserved as only a final step.

This test should not be regarded as a significant event in the development process. It comes at the end of development, when it is too late to have a beneficial effect on the development. By following the total quality development process we are now completely confident of the outcome of the test. The test is now conducted primarily for the benefit of the sales and field-support organizations, to help them share the PDT's confidence in the new product and to give them results to use in fine-tuning their sales and support plans.

PROGRESS CHECK

In traditional product development, the progress check following pilot production is regarded as the most important check. In total quality development it is in many respects the least important check. The problem-prevention approach makes this an anticlimactic check at the end of development. It is too late to help the development activity. However, it does have the important purpose of assuring the people in operations (manufacturing, sales, service, etc.) that they have a strong new product.

Everything is complete now, and nearly everything is frozen. A few things, such as on-line QC and the balance among different segments of the assembly process, can still be fine-tuned, but even they should be essentially complete.

The two suggested primary criteria for judging pilot production completeness are:

- Production has competitive capability.
- All corporate functions concur on shipping approval.

The production preparation phase has overcome cash drains 8 and 9.

WORLD-CLASS PRODUCT

Having eliminated all problems and passed the field-readiness demonstration test, we place the product into production. The development time, UMC, quality, and customer satisfaction features are all much better than in the traditional process.

Cash drains 2 through 9 have been explicitly addressed in Chapters 4 to 6. Cash drain 1 will be addressed in Chapters 7 and 8, on technology and strategy. Cash drain 10, about lack of teamwork, has been addressed throughout the book. It will be further emphasized in Chapter 9, which is about the management of product development. In summary, total quality development overcomes all of the cash drains.

The world-class product is achieved by emphasizing improved requirements for the unit design tasks. Functional analysis is amplified in QFD matrices, starting with the voice of the customer. They are used to develop the criteria in the Pugh concept selection process, through which the product concepts are selected. The functional parameters, hardware parameters, and costs are combined to select the production processes. Taguchi's system of quality engineering is used to optimize the values of the critical parameters, and to provide cost-effective precision. All of this defines the requirements for the unit design tasks, which are then carried out with the traditional proficiency. The difference is that in total quality development, success with the unit design tasks brings success with the product.

The entire organization takes great pride in its world-class product: first to market, lowest in cost, and number one in customer satisfaction.

23 STEPS FOR THE SUCCESSFUL PRODUCTION PREPARATION PHASE—A SUMMARY

PRODUCTION PREPARATION PHASE INPUT

Detailed Drawings
Critical Parameter Drawings
Complete Set of QFD Matrices
Assembly Instructions
Selected Suppliers

PRODUCTION PREPARATION PHASE OUTPUT

Detailed Drawings (mistakes eliminated)
Critical Parameter Drawings
Complete Set of QFD Matrices
Process Sheets (validated processes)
Optimized Processes
On-Line QC
Trained Operators
Smoothly Running Production

CHAPTER

7

Technology Development

- **Advantages of a Technology Stream**
- **Development Process for Winning Technologies**
- **Successful Roles**
- **Benefits**
- **Nine Steps for Successful Technology Development — A Summary**

New technologies are the foundation for new products. The development of new products has been described in Chapters 4, 5, and 6 on the assumption that everything was developed within a product program. Many products are developed this way. However, a better approach once a corporation is established in an industry is to develop new technologies outside of any specific product program. When the new technology is sufficiently mature, it is fished out of the *technology stream* and brought into a program to develop a specific product. This is displayed in Figure 7.1.

This chapter describes the application of the principles of total quality development to the development of the new technologies that are the lifeblood of manufacturing companies.

ADVANTAGES OF A TECHNOLOGY STREAM

There are three reasons to pursue a dedicated technology development program:

(1) To enable time for creativity (without holding a product program hostage)
(2) To provide a creative environment
(3) To develop flexible (robust) technologies that can be used in several products

Now each of these will be described to provide the clear basis for a dedicated technology organization and activity.

SHORT AND CERTAIN PRODUCT SCHEDULES

A distinct technology development activity greatly reduces schedule uncertainty in the product programs. If we consider only mature technologies eligible for selection into a product program, we eliminate the traditional large schedule uncertainties that are caused by immature

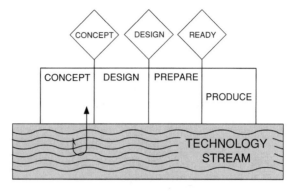

FIGURE 7.1. Fishing out winning technologies.

technologies, and by attempts to invent during the product program. The two major schedule uncertainties that are caused by the absence of a parallel technology stream are displayed in Figure 7.2:

- Invention uncertainty during the *concept phase*
- Robustness uncertainty during the *production preparation phase*

Invention Uncertainty

The time constant for creativity is incompatible with the short schedule that is required for new products. The time to invent a significant new technology is highly uncertain, but is typically a year or more. In contrast, the time for concept selection in a market-driven product develop-

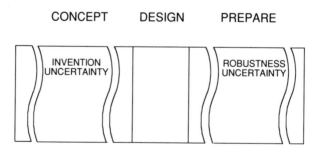

FIGURE 7.2. Schedule uncertainty without a technology stream.

ment program is a matter of a few months. The certainty of a short product development schedule is critical to success. When technologies are developed within a product program, the duration of the concept phase becomes highly uncertain. In effect, the program becomes technology-driven rather than market-driven. Usually, it is much better for the concept phase to be limited in duration, using only those technologies that are currently available. Then the product can be introduced into the marketplace in a timely and certain fashion.

During the concept phase, it is easy for us to develop the anxious concern that the product may not have the performance-to-cost ratio that would make it highly superior in the marketplace. Our anxiety is further fed by the design engineers' culture, which emphasizes creativity even when it is not appropriate. This frequently leads to very wishful thinking that some major inventions will occur during an unrealistically short time span, such as the next three months. Usually, we should go ahead with the technologies that we have in hand, get a good product into the marketplace, and meanwhile proceed in technology development to invent and develop to maturity the next round of basic technological improvements.

Robustness Uncertainty

The traditional lack of emphasis on robustness creates great schedule uncertainty during *production preparation*. The erratic performance that is caused by lack of robustness leads to many rounds of build-test-fix rework of the product design. The effect of the lack of robustness is particularly severe during production preparation, as the subsystems are then integrated and provide large new noises to each other. The resulting chaos and confusion greatly delays progress and causes havoc with the schedule.

It might seem that the development of new technologies directly on the product program would speed the new technologies to market, even though it delays the product program. However, even this is not true when considered over several product programs. The chaos that is created when technologies are developed directly on programs causes delays that *slow* the technologies' introduction to the marketplace. The short and certain product development schedules that are enabled by the *prior* development of mature technologies in the technology stream do speed the new technologies to market.

CREATIVE ENVIRONMENT

In addition to providing the necessary *time* for invention, the dedicated technology development organization can provide the *environment* for creativity. It can be isolated from the fire drills of product development and carried out with somewhat less bureaucracy. The type of engineer in technology development differs from the product engineer. Technology development emphasizes creativity and robustness development, whereas product engineering emphasizes having a great deal of knowledge at one's fingertips and being able to apply it quickly with very few mistakes. Few people are very good at both. Therefore, it improves productivity to have technology development distinct from product development.

We must take care that our organization is not characterized by cloistered groups of technical specialists looking inward within their own specialty, but the advantages of separate technology and product organizations are too large to be ignored. The product development environment emphasizes many decisions promptly made with very few errors. The technology development organization creates an environment where creative work can flourish.

FLEXIBLE TECHNOLOGIES — A KEY TO TOTAL CORPORATE FLEXIBILITY

We gain great benefit by emphasizing flexible technologies, or technologies that we can readily apply to more than one product. They provide a great improvement in market presence for the amount of development activity spent on them. Although much has been written about flexible manufacturing, it is just the tip of the iceberg. The winning corporations will achieve total corporate flexibility in order to achieve short time to market and responsiveness to customers. It is the objective of the technology organization to provide flexible technologies that are mature and ready for reliable and quick integration into a variety of products. Also, we develop flexible production-process technologies with which we are able to make a wide variety of parts with little dedicated development effort.

DEVELOPMENT PROCESS FOR WINNING TECHNOLOGIES

We develop new technologies by going through the following sequence, which is displayed in Figure 7.3:

- Technology strategy
- Creative work
- Robustness development
- Selection and transfer

The last step, selection and transfer, is carried out in conjunction with total system concept selection during the *concept phase* of the development of a specific product. This integrates robust, superior new technologies into the new product.

TECHNOLOGY STRATEGY

Technology strategy guides the technology development effort to the technologies that are most needed, to technology sets for specific products, and to reusable and flexible technologies. This first step in the technology development process is described in Chapter 8, Successful Strategy.

CREATIVE WORK

All of development is dependent upon having some good new ideas. Otherwise, our products will become stale. Creative work, the second step in the technology development process, is done in three steps:

- Definition of needs
- Invention
- Concept selection

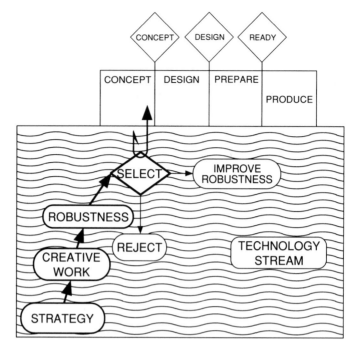

FIGURE 7.3. Technology development process.

This is essentially the same as during the concept phase as described in Chapter 4, except that now there is time for invention.

Often, the new technology is developed at the subsystem level. Sometimes the development is for specific functions. An example for cars is noise, vibration, and harshness (NVH). NVH is not restricted to one subsystem. Rather, it is a subfunction of the car. In the language of robustness, it is all part of the performance *noise*. Ford had great success as a result of performing QFD for NVH. Here the term *subsystem* will be used with the understanding that technology development is also applied to subfunctions and to collections of subsystems.

In technology development, the House of Quality and the Pugh concept selection process are usually applied to a subsystem rather than to a total system. The rich understanding of the customers and the aid to creative work that are described in Chapter 4 are now applied to technology development. Here they have their greatest impact, as our engineers have the time and environment to focus creatively on the needs of customers. In technology development, we typically address a broader range of customers, so that we can develop flexible technologies.

Definition of Needs

Definition of the customers' needs is done in the most general terms as part of the technology strategy (see Chapter 8). Then, at the level of creative work, a House of Quality is prepared for a *particular* technological area, often a subsystem. This incorporates information from relevant recent-product Houses of Quality; feedback from customers, the sales channels, and the field-support organization; and new market research focused on the technological area.

The emphasis on *customer needs* focuses the invention activity on the real requirements, steering technology development away from the notorious "sandbox" mentality. Mere creativity is channeled into creative work. As the needs are defined, concepts are developed in the minds of the technologists, with the help of paper and computer tube. Usually, this is the most productive use of the House of Quality—to guide creative work in the creative environment of the technology organization.

Invention

Successful invention is enabled by three elements:

(1) Deep immersion in the definition of needs
(2) A creative environment, not burdened with emergencies and bureaucracy
(3) Deep knowledge of engineering sciences and prior technology (see Figure 1.1)

Invention involves rearranging the physics for application to meeting a socioeconomic need. This requires good insight into the engineering sciences. Deep immersion in the definition of needs motivates invention to meet the needs. A creative environment provides time and space for concentrated thinking about matching the engineering sciences to the needs. Gradually, the physics and the related hardware start emerging on paper in response to the needs.

In the initial "paper" studies, we formulate a mental model of the hardware and the functional relationships. Functional trees and hardware trees help to further develop the embryonic concept, as outlined in Chapter 5. After the mental development has gone about as far as it can go, we shift the invention process to the laboratory. A breadboard (broadly defined as the simplest hardware that incorporates the basic concept) is built, and the invention process continues. The initial operation of the breadboard quickly reveals that the mental model is not exactly correct. "Oh, look, the airflow is attaching to this wall, not to that one." We revise the mental model to correspond to the observations of the physics, and change the hardware accordingly.

It is important to realize that this initial work in the laboratory is still invention, not to be confused with subsequent laboratory work to develop robustness. The styles of the two types of work are very different. Superficially they appear very similar; both are experimental work in the laboratory (supplemented by analysis) to examine new technological concepts. However, an attempt to impose the same style on both types of activities would cause major problems. The inventor has the freedom to make topological changes to the concept to rearrange the physics into the right regime to meet the needs.

Concept Selection

As the invention work progresses, the technologists have sessions in which they work with the Pugh concept selection matrix (described in Chapter 4). This helps them clarify their thinking and leads to refinements of the concepts, and in some cases to entirely new concepts. In product development, the team quickly converges to a consensus concept. In technology development there is less time pressure, and the technologists can take the time that is needed to enable more creative work before they converge to a selected concept for further development. Sometimes two concepts may be carried forward for further technological development. Of course, it still sometimes happens that only one feasible concept is thought of, and it is carried forward without concept selection. Although this has the danger of being a "eureka" concept (cash drain 3), it may still provide an occasional winner.

There is a tendency for the invention activity to drag on beyond the point where it is still productive. When the selected concept has been refined to the point where it appears to be feasible, and when the mental model is satisfactory and no longer changing significantly, we advance the new concept to robustness optimization. Often, this means that the concept moves from the inventor to a technologist who is experienced and proficient at the optimization of robustness. The psychologies of the two activities are very different. During invention, the embryonic concept needs nurturing and protection. During robustness optimization, however, the concept must be attacked and made to fail so that it can be improved. Although some technologists are good at doing both, the change in required psychology is usually helped by a change in personnel. Unless this is done promptly, the invention activity will tend to be prolonged beyond the point of diminishing returns.

Robustness Optimization

The third step of the technology development process, optimizing the robustness of new concepts, is a powerful boost to development efficiency. It provides two major advantages:

(1) Flexible technologies that can be used in many products
(2) Efficient *production preparation*; little rework of the design

The new concept is made robust before it is eligible to be considered for selection into a new product. This is critical to overall success. The process for robustness optimization is as described previously for subsystem design (Chapter 5). Now it is done during technology development. Subsequently, during the subsystem design subphase of product development, robustness is at most refined slightly to accommodate system constraints, or to make some final improvements that were not quite completed during the technology development.

In developing robustness, there are two cardinal rules: (1) use hardware that is convenient, and (2) subject the hardware to realistic noises, including noises coming from other subsystems. Often, the subsystem is a convenient unit to work on for robustness optimization. Other times, a combination of subsystems is appropriate.

Robustness Hardware

Getting the hardware right is a key to the quick optimization of robustness. The hardware used now is very different from earlier invention hardware. Two types of hardware are commonly used for the optimization of robustness:

- Dedicated robustness fixture
- Mule

It is very important that the hardware be capable of imposing the important noises on the system that is to be optimized for robustness. Also, there is always the possibility that the "hardware" can be a computer—in other words, that the optimization is done analytically. The following discusses each of these four ideas in sequence: the two types of hardware, and the two ways of optimizing robustness.

Dedicated Robustness Fixture

We design the dedicated robustness fixture to facilitate the robustness experimentation. We make the critical parameters easy to change. Many are controlled by precision knobs, so that they can be quickly set to any value. For example, a dimension is controlled by a micrometer dial, or has a dial indicator to read the position. Also, the fixture is instrumented to make it easy to measure the important functionality metrics, such as the time of critical functional events. The dedicated robustness fixture is used when improvement is apt to extend over a considerable time and the capital investment is warranted.

Mule

A mule is a system that has been in production but is later modified for robustness development. The production "subsystem" (which could be any part of the system) is removed and replaced with the new technology. As an example, consider a finisher (stapler, binder, etc.) for a copier. Important noises will be paper curl, skew, oil on copy, and electrostatic charge. Therefore, the "pump" that supplies paper to the finisher for robustness development must be capable of controlling the values of the noises over the expected range of customer operation. We can do this with a paper feeder, a fuser, a curler/decurler, a corotron, and a skew adjuster, which we assemble from existing production hardware. This will enable the focus to be on the robustness of the finisher, not on the reliability of the supporting hardware. In fact, the paper pump can be a stripped-down production copier. This will be much cheaper, more reliable, and more quickly available than new experimental hardware.

Noises

The supporting production hardware is modified slightly to enable the noises to be more easily controlled. In a copier, for example, the production fuser will have an optimized flow rate for the silicone oil that is a release agent to help the paper separate from the fusing roll. The quantity of this oil is a significant noise factor to the finisher. In a robustness fixture we want to control the amount of oil so that we can vary it over the full range that is expected in the field. Therefore, we modify the production hardware slightly so that we can easily vary and measure the amount of oil. This is done for all of the important noises that the paper pump provides to the finisher.

Analytical Optimization

Of course, we should analyze the functionality of the device with the best math model that is appropriate to the importance and longevity of the concept. If the technology is likely to be an important one for a considerable period of time, then we will improve our productivity by investing in a thorough mathematical analysis. If this mathematical model is close enough to reality, then it can be put to use in the robustness optimization. This obviates the need for robustness hardware and saves much time. Even a simple math model will help in identifying the critical parameters and can be used for an initial round of optimization that narrows the ranges of values for the critical parameters, which are then finally optimized in hardware.

Robustness Process

The process by which we develop the robustness of new technologies is the same as that used during the design phase and has been described in Chapter 5. After the critical factors are identified with the help of the fault tree and the FMEA table, the optimization of functionality is done in seven steps:

(1) Define objective, in terms of the best metric.
(2) Define feasible alternative design values.
(3) Select some alternatives for evaluation.
(4) Impose noises.
(5) Evaluate performance of selected alternatives.
(6) Select best design values.
(7) Confirm robust performance.

The critical parameter drawing for the new technology goes with it into the product program. This helps to ensure that those involved in the subsequent design activities do not unknowingly compromise the robust functionality of the new concept.

The complete process of the optimization of robustness is carried out in three phases, as shown in Figure 7.4. Most of the optimization is done during technology development, to ensure that the technology is robust before it is selected as part of a product program. Then the robustness optimization is finalized during the design phase and verified in the total system during the system verification test (SVT).

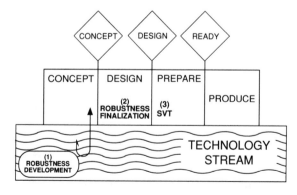

FIGURE 7.4. Three-phase robustness development.

Usually, little optimization will be left to do during the design phase. However, the system constraints may have forced some of the critical parameters away from their best values. Also, sometimes there will be some final improvement that was not quite finished during the technology development. The complete three-phase process ensures very good robustness within a short product development schedule. It eliminates the robustness uncertainty in the schedule during the production preparation phase.

Benefits of Early Robustness

The early optimization of robustness during technology development has four major benefits:

- Enabling of quick time to market
- Flexibility
- Customer satisfaction
- Low costs

Robustness is essential for the reduction of rework of the design, because one of the principal causes of rework is chaotic chasing of the symptoms of lack of robustness. The great reduction in rework enables quick time to market.

Robust performance enables a product technology to be flexibly applied to a variety of products. This is also true of production technology: robust production processes can easily be adjusted to make parts for a variety of products. Robust technologies can be easily and quickly adapted to new applications because the new noises will not bother them.

Quickness and flexibility are key advantages for international competitiveness.

Quick Integration

When new technologies are not robust, they are difficult to integrate together. The problem is indicated graphically in Figure 7.5. When a new technology is integrated with other new technologies in its first product application (A_1 through G_1 in Figure 7.5), it has been common experience to encounter many major problems. This is primarily due to lack

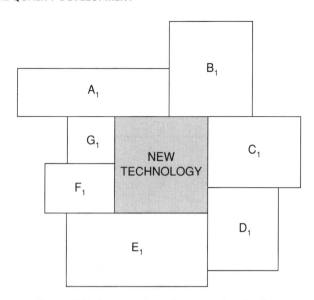

FIGURE 7.5. Integration of new technologies.

of robustness. Our new technology is not robust. The variations in the inputs from A through G present many new noises to our new technology. The magnitudes of these noises are large because technologies A through G are not robust either (the subscript 1 refers to the first product to which the technology is applied.) The interactions of the nonrobust technologies cause very erratic performance variations, leading to endless iterations of build-test-fix rework during production preparation.

In contrast, when robustness is emphasized, our new technology is little affected by the noises from technologies A through G. Also, A through G put out much smaller magnitudes of noise, because they too are robust. Therefore, the new technologies are quickly integrated, with little need for rework of the design. Robust technologies get products to the market while the market window is open.

Flexible Technology

Robust technologies are also easily integrated into more than one new product. When new technologies were not robust, they could not be easily integrated. Therefore, each production application required new dedicated development work, as indicated in Figure 7.6. As noted previously,

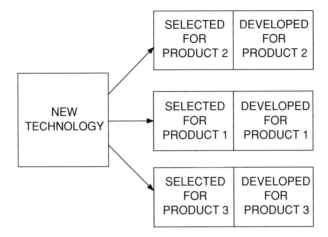

FIGURE 7.6. Application of nonrobust technology.

the integration of the new technology with new noise sources A through G in the first product is slow and unsure. This time-consuming process then has to be repeated in products 2 and 3, and in any other applications.

In contrast, we can quickly integrate robust technologies into several products, as indicated in Figure 7.7. Once the new technology is robust, then it is easily and quickly integrated into all applications. All that is

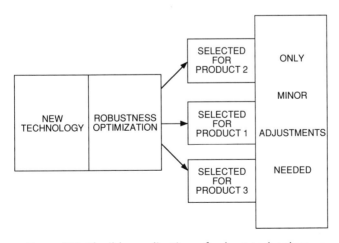

FIGURE 7.7. Flexible application of robust technology.

needed is adjustments to ensure that the nominal values at the interfaces are compatible. Adjustments are very easy to do. Robustness is the challenging task. By optimizing the robustness of new technology in advanced development, we create flexible technology. Our robust, flexible technology is easily adapted into a variety of products. This provides us with short product development times, responsiveness to the marketplace, and less consumption of precious development resources.

Exactly the same considerations apply to production technology. When new production technology is made robust, it can easily make any part with little additional specific development. During the robustness optimization, we treat the type and features of a part as a noise, in recognition of the wide variety of parts that we will want to make. By making the production technology robust with respect to the specific details of the part, we can use the technology to place any reasonable part straightforwardly into production with little delay.

For example, to develop the robustness of injection molding, we design one, or a few, complex parts that contain all of the major challenges to good part quality. Our robustness-challenging part or parts contain all of the strange shapes, thin flow regions, and sudden changes of cross section that tend to cause problems with injection molding. Then we optimize the robustness to achieve good reproducibility (small standard deviation) throughout all of the challenging regions of the complex part. Robust production technology saves much time in getting new products into production.

Robust technology is easily adapted into a variety of new products with little additional development. The paper feeder cited in the continuing example in this book was first selected for use in the Xerox 1075 copier, which went into production in 1981. Since then it has been used in many other Xerox copiers and printers, with essentially no additional development. This flexible technology is a critical efficiency in total quality development.

SELECTION AND TRANSFER

After a new technology is mature, it is eligible for selection and transfer into the system concept of a new product. This is the fourth and last step in the technology development process.

Technology Selection for Product Success

When we consider a new technology for selection into a product program, there are three possible outcomes, as displayed in Figure 7.3:

(1) The technology is selected for transfer into the product program.
(2) The robustness development is judged to be insufficiently advanced. Further improvement of robustness is planned.
(3) The technology is rejected. It offers too little improvement.

Selection into Product Program

To be selected into the product program, the technology must be:

- Mature
- Superior

Maturity. The most important component of technological maturity is robustness. Other characteristics are verified also: producibility, and anything else that might threaten the product schedule. Patents are investigated to ensure that we have the legal right to use the concept. Inherent safety problems and toxicity are other factors that could threaten a new concept. If producibility provides new challenges, then we develop the production processes as new technologies along with the new product technology.

Superiority. Of course, the new technology must offer significant improvement in customer-satisfaction-to-cost ratio. Otherwise, there is no point in selecting it to replace the existing technology. This concept is displayed graphically in Figure 7.8. Each technology eventually nears its asymptote, and then we switch to a superior technology. The objective for the development of new technologies in the technology stream is to have a superior technology ready when a previous technology has grown to its full potential and its further development would not keep it competitive.

Selection Process. Normally, a new technology is selected for a new product as soon as it is mature. Putting technologies "on the shelf,"

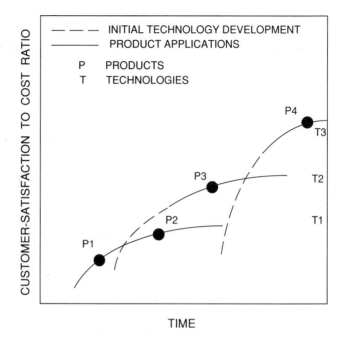

FIGURE 7.8. Evolution of new technologies.

to wait for some product-program shoppers to come along and "buy" them, is enticing but is unlikely to happen. If the new technology is any good, the more likely problem is that there will be attempts to put the technology into a new product before it is mature. This we strongly resist, to avoid chaos and confusion, and schedule delays and uncertainty on the product program. An integrated technology and product strategy (see Chapter 8) avoids these types of problems.

The selection of a new technology into a product program occurs as part of the total system concept selection using the Pugh process during the concept phase (Chapter 4). After its first product application, the new technology is eligible for selection into other new products.

There is an essential difference between concept selection in the concept phase and concept selection during invention of technology. In technology development, any idea is fair for consideration. However, during concept selection in the product concept phase, the concepts that are eligible for consideration are strongly constrained. The eligible concepts are from current products, competitive products, analogous products, or mature new technologies. These enable the market-driven schedule to be achieved.

More Robustness Needed

A second possible outcome is that more robustness development is needed. The technology will undergo more robustness optimization to be ready for the next product program.

Rejection

The desired potential superiority should have been clearly evident when the concept was selected for technology development and then entered into robustness optimization. Occasionally, however, the robustness development reveals that the performance of the new concept is not as attractive as was initially anticipated. Then it is rejected, and no further development is carried out.

Technology Transfer

Technology transfer can be very difficult. In the past, there has been an unfortunate tendency toward rivalry between the product engineering division and the technology organization (often called advanced development). This is indicated in Figure 7.9. The cultural barrier has traditionally caused very serious problems. "Not invented here" (NIH) becomes rampant, and other dysfunctions greatly lower the probability of success. In the worst form of NIH, product engineering wants to invent its own technologies and advanced development wants to develop its own products. This is another example of competitive instincts turned inward within the organization. They must be redirected against the competition.

The most powerful approach to successful technology transfer is to transfer people: product engineering people come into advanced development and work with the technologists to complete the technology development, especially to develop robustness; this is indicated in Figure 7.10. Then the technologists and the product engineers go into the product program after the new technology has been selected. After an appropriate time, often roughly six months, the technologists return to advanced development. The technologists and product engineers can be thought of as a technology transfer team.

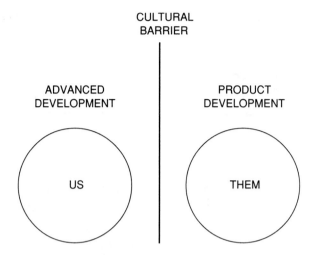

FIGURE 7.9. Cultural barriers hinder technology transfer.

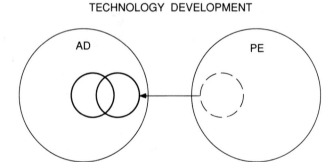

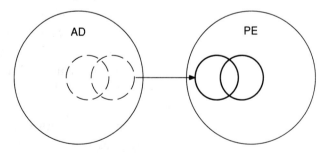

FIGURE 7.10. Transfer people to transfer technology.

Of course, there are many variations. People can exchange organizations for a period of roughly two years as a developmental assignment. Also, if a product engineer invents something significant, then he or she can transfer into advanced development to develop the invention.

Another problem that often arises in technology transfer is premature integration of hardware. Sometimes a certain amount of integration is beneficial. For complex products, the new technology is commonly at the subsystem level. An example is a new engine technology. Before technology transfer, it is sometimes beneficial to integrate some new technologies—an engine and a transmission, for example. This demonstrates the compatibility of the new technologies and enables clear evaluation of their potential improvement of customer satisfaction and cost.

Sometimes it is helpful to the optimization process to integrate some subsystems together. For example, it usually will not be worthwhile to spend much time optimizing the valve train by itself. Rather, the optimization is more efficient after the valve train is in the engine. This is integration that is beneficial to successful technology development.

On the other hand, some traditional activities to integrate new technologies before product development are largely dysfunctional. They stem from two unwarranted concerns:

(1) Subsystem interactions will later cause problems.
(2) Advanced development must impress product development.

The first is eliminated by robustness. The second is eliminated by the greater organizational integration of total quality development. Continued premature integration of technology for these dysfunctional reasons would be like an anchor on the organization. Usually, we can wait until the system verification subphase to build the first integrated hardware. This saves much time and money.

The transfer of people enables the effective transfer of new technology into products. The transferred people break down NIH and the other dysfunctions of the cultural barrier. They are especially helpful in ensuring that the critical parameter drawing is adhered to during design. Otherwise, there is a tendency for the robust functionality to wither away in the heat of the daily design decisions. The transferred people maintain the robust functionality during the design and production preparation phases.

SUCCESSFUL ROLES

Development work on the conceptually dynamic aspects of new products is done primarily in advanced development, and conceptually static work is done primarily in product engineering. It is the purpose of an advanced development organization to develop the dynamic new concepts that cannot be readily done on the schedule and in the environment of product engineering. The objective of product engineering is to develop a specific product that is aimed at a specific market segment at a fixed date of introduction. In advanced development, the work on the dynamic concepts is efficiently carried out until the new concepts are sufficiently mature, so that it is judged not hazardous to the schedule to include them in a specific development program for a new product.

Advanced Development

Dynamic improvements typically take longer than is prudent or necessary for the development of a specific product. Also, they have to be done in a somewhat different style, with more uncertainty and ambiguity and therefore more iterative trial and error. It is this distinction that has led to the formation of advanced development groups. These groups operate in a mode of invention and iterative improvements, with sufficient time to achieve maturity for the new concept, so that it can now be treated as essentially static. Then the new technology is incorporated into the short schedule of the product engineering group.

Product Engineering

In product engineering, a specific product is designed and developed to be introduced to a previously chosen market segment, with a fixed date of introduction. The date of introduction is selected to coincide with a large, open market window for the market segment. A six-month delay in reaching the marketplace tends to reduce the total profit by a large amount, typically roughly one-third. To avoid missing the open market window, and to achieve the best possible improvement in cost and performance, the product development activity must be carried out in a very disciplined style with emphasis upon holding a very short schedule. This usually precludes the complete development of major dynamic improvements within product engineering.

DIFFERENT STYLES

When this distinction is successfully made, the primary activity of the product engineering group is to very quickly develop the new product, with its accompanying production capability and field-support capability. It is the primary focus in such product engineering activity to maintain a very short schedule with a minimum of mistakes. It is not the purpose of such activity to invent dynamic new concepts, which would inevitably increase time and mistakes.

The incorporation into the new product of some dynamic improvements that have been developed to maturity in advanced development requires changes in the surrounding static subsytems. Also, additional engineering is required at the next level of detail. For example, if a subsystem was developed dynamically in advanced development, then many piece parts need to be finally defined during product engineering.

Product engineering must be able to design and develop such accommodating changes and new piece parts in a very short time with zero mistakes. There has been considerable confusion about this in traditional product development. Most product engineering has suffered from a desire to be too dynamic. This has caused significant shortfalls in quality of response to the tremendous challenge of developing static concepts in a very short time with hardly any mistakes, and with a low cost.

GENERIC IMPROVEMENT

The work of advanced development is actually broader than producing inventions. It is the objective of the work in advanced development to produce generic improvements. The improvements are generic in the sense that, after being developed to maturity in advanced development, they can then subsequently be applied to more than one product program. In the past, we have typically thought of the improvements in advanced development as being entirely new inventions. However, it is possible to make very important generic improvements that do not include new inventions.

It is important to have an open mind about the nature of generic improvements, and to use an effective process to sort out those improvements that are most desirable at any given point in time. Enhanced quality function deployment, applied during advanced development, can be very helpful in identifying the generic improvements that will be most beneficial. A famous example is the improvement of rust prevention at the Toyota Autobody Company in the late 1970s. This major generic improvement involved little, if any, invention but made a very large improvement in the marketplace.

BENEFITS

A successful technology stream is essential for international competitiveness. It brings major benefits:

(1) It greatly reduces schedule uncertainty in the product:

- Invention uncertainty is removed from the *concept phase.*
- The early optimization of robustness greatly reduces schedule uncertainty in the *production preparation phase.*

(2) It provides a creative environment, leading to more and better new technologies.
(3) Reusable, flexible technologies provide faster, less expensive development and the greater product variety that is increasingly at the heart of global competition. This is a major success factor for achieving corporate agility.

The technology stream enables our products to be both technology-rich and market-driven.

NINE STEPS FOR SUCCESSFUL TECHNOLOGY DEVELOPMENT—A SUMMARY

TECHNOLOGY DEVELOPMENT INPUT

Technology Strategy
Basic Strengths
Current Technological Environment

	Step	Page
Creative Work		
Definition of Needs	T1	323
Invention	T2	323
Concept Selection	T3	324
Robustness Optimization		
Robustness Hardware	T4	326
Robustness Process	T5	327
Selection for Product		
Check Maturity (primarily robustness)	T6	333
Check Superiority	T7	333
Select	T8	333
Technology Transfer	T9	335

TECHNOLOGY DEVELOPMENT OUTPUT

Selected Technologies

CHAPTER

8

Successful Strategy

S trategy is what integrates our success with specific development projects into the foundation for continued business success. Strategy is planning to make change work to our benefit. Successful application of total quality development leverages the success of our unit engineering tasks into the development of specific winning products and technologies. However, to achieve the fullest business success, we cannot develop a specific product in isolation. We strategically plan all development projects to ensure that we have the right amount of development to coordinate the various projects, to achieve efficiency in our development work, and to ensure that we have the right kind of development—neither too conceptually static nor chaotically dynamic.

Successful strategy enables us to achieve the maximum possible market presence that our successfully completed development of specific products and technologies will allow. If we develop each product in isolation, then we are expending a lot of development effort relative to our products' market presence. Successful strategy intertwines the development of various products to reduce our total development effort and to increase our market presence by creating a public perception of related products.

Thus, successful strategy maximizes the ratio of market presence to development effort. It is also our guide for making changes that negate our competitors' strengths, so that they will have difficulty in quickly following our lead. This sustains our competitive technical advantage, which then also gives us the opportunity to rearrange the market so that we achieve further competitive advantage.

The starting point for building on our success with a specific development activity is to reuse that success in more than one product. This enables us to offer an attractive product variety within the constraints of affordable development activities. By keeping much of a product conceptually static—reusing previous successes—while introducing some key improvements in subsystems or features to create attractiveness to customers, we provide great market presence with our affordable development activities. This is the objective of integrated product and technology strategies.

PRODUCT STRATEGY

The starting point for technical strategy is product strategy. We plan our products in relation to each other, not in isolation. An example is given in Figure 8.1, which shows a company's 10-year plan to introduce all the products in one of its lines of business, positioned by market segment. Each box represents one new product, showing its market segment and year of market introduction.

There are several elaborations that can be usefully added to Figure 8.1. The products might range from "clean-sheet" products to variant products (the categories of products are described in detail later in this chapter, under the heading Static/Dynamic Spectrum of Products), and an appropriate indicator can be added to each box. For example, F93 and D94 might be upgraded and downgraded variants of E92, in which case it is typical to draw lines connecting them to E92. Also, we include the product strategy for associated products as an overlay on the product strategy for the base product. For example, the product strategy for laser printers is an overlay on the product strategy for xerographic copiers. The laser printers reuse many of the subsystems in the copier. Strategy includes the planning of product families (Meyer and Utterback, 1993). For example, one family can be E92, F93, D94, and their associated products, such as laser printers. Careful integration of their strategies achieves a larger market presence for an affordable amount of development.

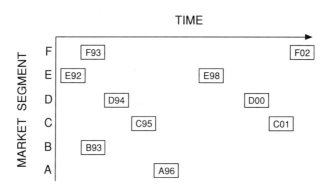

FIGURE **8.1.** Product strategy.

The product strategy is primarily market-driven. We need the products in Figure 8.1 to maintain our market presence. For each product, of course, we define the planned improvement in performance (quality) and cost that we expect will maintain or improve our market share and profit (ROI, ROA, etc.). This is based upon competitive benchmarking and observed rates of annual improvement. The product strategy is an opportunity to use QFD for strategic purposes, to make the strategy responsive to the needs of the customers. A key decision is the market segments in which we choose to compete. We achieve the most market presence by competing in all market segments, but we may decide that some offer too little financial return, or do not provide enough synergy with our total business. If we choose not to develop and produce a full line of products, then we may want a strategic alliance with other producers so that we can market a full line.

In planning our product strategy, we pay attention to the relative importance of the various market segments. This can change rather quickly, especially in industries that are not yet mature. An example from the 1980s is the computer industry. Initially, mainframe computers were dominant. Then, during the 1980s, first minicomputers and then personal computers became increasingly important. The marketplace wanted a considerable emphasis on decentralized computing. The technology evolved along a path that brought feasibility first to large computers. Thus, the marketplace and the technology were not in equilibrium. Conditions were ripe for large changes over the period of a decade. We need to be very aware of such lack of equilibrium. It offers opportunities to lead into segments of unmet customer needs. Also, we use total quality development to be fast followers, never falling too far behind new emphases in the marketplace. Experience teaches that it can be disastrous to be too dependent on some temporary relationship between technology and the marketplace. Several computer companies learned this to their sorrow during the 1980s and early 1990s.

The product strategy enables us to plan each specific development activity in advance, so that our programs start in a smooth and timely manner. The strategy helps us set appropriate goals for each product program. Most important, it integrates specific product programs so that each is not developed in isolation, thus enabling the total market presence that is implied by Figure 8.1 to be accomplished with a minimum of development effort. Development activities from one product are reused in subsequent products, as will be emphasized later in this chapter.

The product strategy sets goals from a market perspective. They are integrated with the technology strategy, from which we draw our plans for the basic product improvements that will support the product strategy.

TECHNOLOGY STRATEGY

The technology strategy can be laid out as is the product strategy in Figure 8.1, with the boxes now representing technologies rather than products. For all but the simplest products, the new technologies are usually incorporated at a subsystem level. For automobiles, for example, the new technology is often for the engine—or, even lower in the hardware hierarchy, for the valve train. Electronically controlled valves would be an example of a new technology. Thus, the technology strategies are not simply one diagram similar to Figure 8.1, but a technology map for each subsystem, or each functional area that might become more competitive with new technology.

PRODUCT AND TECHNOLOGY INTEGRATION

Maps similar to Figure 8.1 make good displays of the technology strategy, but even more insight for planning is provided by showing the relationships between the planned technologies and the planned products, as in Figure 8.2. This graph reveals the plan for the *initial* introduction of each new technology on a specific product. Thus, the first four new technologies are targeted for the first new product. These new technologies combined with the anticipated incremental improvements are expected to provide the required cost/performance improvement that is called for in the product strategy (Figure 8.1) on the basis of market pull. Of course, the new technologies in Figure 8.2 are for different subsystems. Figure 8.2 can be enriched by using codes or symbols for the different subsystems.

Figure 8.2 represents the plan for the introduction of new technologies with each new product. However, technology creation is uncertain,

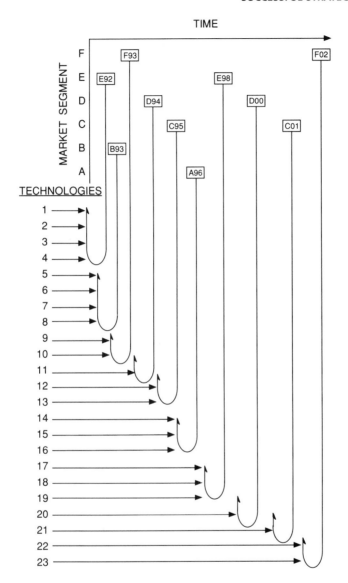

FIGURE 8.2. Product and technology strategy.

so each planned new technology may not be ready exactly as scheduled. New technologies cannot be forced into products according to the schedule of Figure 8.2. When the time comes for total system concept selection for a product, the technologies that are under development are evaluated as described in Chapter 7. We fish only the mature technologies out of the technology stream for inclusion in the new product. In Figure 8.2, four new technologies have been planned for the next new product. When the time actually arrives, four new technologies will most likely be ready. However, it is also quite likely that three or five will be ready. (If the number that are mature is consistently fewer than planned, then perhaps we should review the planning to reduce our bias toward excessive optimism.) The product should rarely if ever be held up because one new technology is not available as planned. It is usually better to proceed, in order to maintain market presence and gain additional experience and insight. The laggard new technology can be introduced in the near future in a variant or associated product.

This approach divorces technology delivery uncertainty from product schedule. The risk is shifted from the product schedule to the number of new technologies that will actually be included in a specific product. Usually this is a very positive trade-off. Maintaining the product schedule is paramount for market presence. This approach does not reduce the total number of new technologies that are available over a period of time; actually, it will usually increase technological productivity because time will not be wasted to fire-drill some immature technology into a product.

SUCCESSFUL TECHNOLOGIES

The technology strategy is prepared by matching market needs with the emerging technical capability. Market needs consist of new features that will delight customers, and the need for continuous improvement of the cost/performance ratio. When an existing technology is reaching the "mature" asymptote (see Figure 7.8), it is time to have an intrinsically better technology available. The market needs are compared with technological capabilities. It should go without saying that the term *technology* here includes technology for the product, production processes, and field-support operations.

The technologies that should be included in the strategy are common, competitive, analogous, and emerging technologies (Adler and Shenbar, 1990). Common technologies allow a company to be in the game. Competitive technologies provide advantage. Analogous technologies come from other industries. (For example, Swiss watchmakers in the 1960s should have been devoting more attention to electronic and display technologies.) Emerging technologies are those that are potentially important but too new for us to evaluate their role with much certainty.

In many industries there are competing technologies. An example is steam engines and internal combustion engines in the early days of the automobile. Today the dominant technology for copiers is the xerographic technology that was invented in 1938 by Chester Carlson. However, competitive technologies, such as the ink jet, exist as well. If it is uncertain which technology will win, then it is prudent to allocate some of the technology investment to the alternative technology.

SUBSYSTEM TECHNOLOGY MAPS

In addition to planning the initial application of the new technology, we also plan subsequent applications. These could be displayed on Figure 8.2 with enhanced graphics. Also, the total planned applications of each technology can be displayed in a subsystem technology map, as shown in Figure 8.3. (Each subsystem has its own technology map.) The map typically shows the technologies for the past 10 years (vaguely represented in the shaded area of Figure 8.3) to provide perspective, and the technologies that are planned for the next 10 years. Usually, the successful approach is to plan two or three technologies that span the entire range of market segments. A basic technology can usually be both enhanced and stripped down to span several market segments. Also, associated products should be included

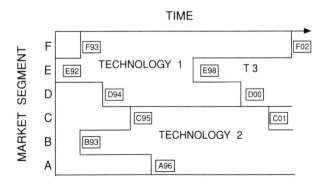

FIGURE 8.3. Technology map for one subsystem.

in the technology planning. For example, the laser printer technology application map is an overlay on the copier map.

Technology maps such as Figures 8.2 and 8.3 help us achieve a balanced approach, with neither too many nor too few new technologies and with all important areas covered. If technologies are introduced too frequently, product development will become bogged down and the manufacturing costs are likely to be too high. If new technologies are introduced too infrequently, the products will become stale and inferior. The actual density of new technologies with respect to time and market segments depends greatly on the industry. We want to plan new technologies to achieve dynamic variety that is appropriate to our own industry. Maps such as Figures 8.2 and 8.3 focus the technology development activities on critical areas.

DYNAMIC TECHNOLOGY STRATEGY

The technology strategy should always be complete, and should be updated frequently—at least once a year. Of course, not all planned technologies will materialize. Also, there will be some spontaneous invention. When an unplanned invention appears promising, it should be immediately incorporated into the technology strategy. The technology strategy greatly increases the likelihood that new technologies will be available when they are needed. It also provides for reusability of the technologies.

BASIC STRENGTHS

In addition to planning our products and technologies, we can further enhance our long-term success by planning our investments in basic technical strengths. Examples of basic technical strengths (in various industries) are:

- Electronic imaging
- Semiconductors
- Substrates

- Coatings
- Digital circuits
- Optics
- Imaging
- Video recording
- Mechatronics
- Bioengineering
- Precision mechanisms
- Optoelectronics
- Electronic packaging
- Fiber optics

These are not technologies in the sense of being subsystems that could be sold as independent products or incorporated into larger total systems. Rather, these are the basic strengths that support the technologies. For example, the basic strengths of optics, digital circuits, and precision mechanisms support optical scanner technology. Optical scanners can be sold as independent products, or they can be integrated as critical subsystems in printers or multipurpose products that can also transmit, as in facsimile (fax) machines.

Other basic strengths besides the technical ones are included in the formation of complete strategies. A complete set of basic strengths, according to Meyer and Utterback (1993), includes:

Technical
Customer needs understanding
Distribution channels (including field support)
Manufacturing

PLANNING FOR BASIC STRENGTHS

To maintain success, it is critical to nurture basic strengths and technologies. A great danger to long-term success is the hollowing out of an organization. After a period of success, it may become a temptation to continue to sell products that have become well known, and to reduce investment in basic strengths and technologies. For a while, the negative effect will be small; in the short run, profits may increase. The reputation of the products and continued incremental development of new products will maintain market share for a while. But inevitably, the static technologies and basic strengths will sink into decay, and the products will come to be perceived as old hat. Market share will plunge, and then it will usually be too late to rebuild capabilities in technologies and basic strengths in time for a company to remain a viable player in the marketplace.

Strong investments in basic strengths are the underpinnings for successful technologies. Without our nurturing basic strengths, the investments in technologies will soon be found to bring few results. Technologies, in turn, are the foundation for products. Our strategic planning and investment plan is three tiered; see Figure 8.4. Three-tiered strategic planning enables the maximum market presence for our investment, ensures that we have the necessary elements for success, provides opportunities for diversification (e.g., printers into fax machines), and alerts us to potential inroads from strengths that are foreign to our industry (such as when electronics and displays moved in on Swiss watch movements).

THREATS AND OPPORTUNITIES ANALYSIS

The three-tiered strategy is extended into a threats-and-opportunities analysis; see Figure 8.5. We must be on guard for strengths initially nur-

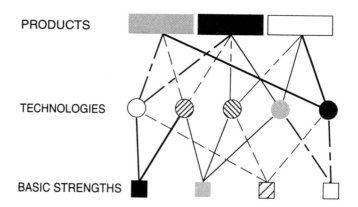

FIGURE 8.4. Three-tiered strategic planning.

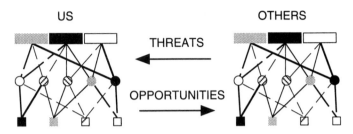

US   OTHERS

THREATS

OPPORTUNITIES

FIGURE **8.5.** Threats and opportunities.

tured in another industry that may expand to provide customer attraction in our industry. As a common example, a simple change of scale can provide the mediums for such an expansion. Electronics and displays that were initially applied to clocks and radios were soon scaled down to watches, and are now being scaled up to television sets; the companies that are quick to recognize and exploit the scaling opportunity reap the benefits, while others (Swiss watchmakers, for example) are caught off guard. Likewise, we have the opportunity to play the game to our benefit, expanding into markets that are new to us. We can achieve maximum business benefit by constantly looking for opportunities to further leverage our basic strengths and technologies by diversification and alliances, while guarding against unexpected competition from basic strengths that are new to us.

STATIC/DYNAMIC STATUS

For us to be successful, our product activities and organization must be matched to the static/dynamic status of our industry. If our strategic perspective is attuned to small changes in the geometry and material of turbine blades—typical of a relatively static industry—then we may have trouble with the frequent conceptual changes of a dynamic industry, such as microprocessors. Culture and practices that are good for static industries will not work well in dynamic industries, and vice versa. Vigilance is needed to ensure that our organization and processes are well suited for our industry and products, and particularly that they are appropriately located in the static/dynamic spectrum.

STATIC/DYNAMIC STATUS EVALUATION

The evaluation of the conceptual static/dynamic (S/D) status of a product (Pugh and Smith, 1976; Pugh, 1977; Pugh, 1983; Pugh, 1984; Hollins and Pugh, 1990) is closely related to the use of the Pugh concept selection process. If the conceptual status is static (also known as a *dominant design*), then the concept is known from existing products. Dynamic conceptual breakout can only be achieved through the application of the concept selection process or be left to chance. In the case of the Marathon dump truck (Pugh and Smith, 1974), it was not found possible to break out at the total system architecture level; at this level the overall concept was static. Breakout was possible at the subsystem level, however, for the four-wheel drive transmission.

In the case of the Giraffe (Pugh, 1979)—a rough-terrain forklift truck with telescopic boom—breakout with a new concept occurred at the total system architecture (TSA) level, as well as at the subsystem (SS) level, setting a new static concept for many others to follow.

Buggy whips are the classic example of an excessively static outlook. At the opposite extreme, random, unstructured attempts to be dysfunctionally dynamic usually lead to chaos and confusion, which greatly extend the development schedule, with accompanying failures in cost and quality. Concept selection is used to check out S/D status in a sensible, controlled manner; this is critical to success.

STATIC/DYNAMIC CASE STUDY

Now the static/dynamic (S/D) status will be described in more detail. The example is the Xerox 1075 copier, which included the paper feeder that was used as the example in previous chapters.

The Xerox 1075 copier was developed during the late 1970s and early 1980s and was put into production in 1981. The system architecture was a significant departure from previous copiers and was the outgrowth of a major advanced development activity that was known at Xerox as the *third-generation activity*. It is reasonable to think of this copier as having had at the time a rather dynamic system architecture. It has since been incorporated, with relatively small changes, into other Xerox copiers and printers, such as the 1090, 4050, and 5090. It is still today given serious consideration for new copiers and printers. Therefore, we can describe this TSA as having been dynamic in the late 1970s and early 1980s, and having remained relatively static since then.

In the TSA decisions for the 1075, it was decided to use a friction retard feeder. At this level of decision, the feeder could not have been thought of as dynamic. Friction retard feeders had long been used, probably having first originated in the late nineteenth century. At the time of the development of the 1075, the most recent and comparable friction retard feeder was found in the Xerox 9400 copier/duplicator, which had been put into production in 1976.

From 1973 until 1980, there was much advanced development work incorporated into the friction retard feeder. At the time that the product engineering work was started on the 1075, three functional areas had emerged as dynamic as a result of successful activities in advanced development: the feed area, the separation area, and the drives area. The improvements were:

FUNCTIONAL AREA	IMPROVEMENT
Separation area	Rotating retard roll
Feed area	Stack-force enhancement
Drives area	Independent drives

The improvements are noted in Figure 8.6. The feed area is where the feed belt rests upon the paper stack. The separation area is between the feed belt and the retard roll, where the second and any ensuing sheets that attempt to come along with the first sheet are retarded and prevented from going into the copier prematurely. The drive system drives both the feed belt and the take-away rolls, which are used to pull paper away from the separation region and feed it into the downstream part of the copy-handling module. The dynamic improvements in the three functional areas will now be described in more detail.

Rotating Retard Roll

The first dynamic concept was for the separation functional area. It consisted of the retard roll mounted on a slip brake, which was described in Chapter 5. This conceptual enhancement intrinsically increases the

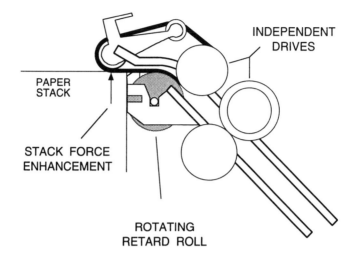

FIGURE 8.6. Paper feeder: an example of dynamic concepts.

robustness of the system. In this case, the reduction in retard roll wear greatly increased the robustness with respect to the noise of time and use.

Stack-Force Enhancement

Detailed studies in advanced development had led to the conclusion that the feed force is a very critical parameter and is often either too large or too small. When the feed force is too large, it tends to cause multifeeds; when the feed force is too small, it tends to cause misfeeds. It might seem simple to find an optimum feed force that will avoid both. However, this is tremendously complicated by the noises presented by paper and environmental conditions. With some kinds of paper and environmental conditions, the paper feeds very easily and there is no danger of misfeeds, but multifeeds are a significant danger. For such paper one would prefer to have a small stack force. However, other papers and conditions tend to have the opposite effect. They require a strong force to avoid misfeeds but have little tendency to cause multifeeds. For the first type of paper and environmental condition, we want the stack force set at a small value—for example, 0.3 lb. For the condition that tends to cause misfeeds, we might like to have the stack force set at a significantly higher value, approximately 0.7 lb. For customers to like the machine, they must not have to determine the conditions each time they make a copy and set the feed force accordingly.

These factors led to the second dynamic concept, U.S. patent number 4,561,644. The essence of this invention is that there is a sensor at the separation zone. The stack force is normally at a low value, approximately 0.3 lb. If the sensor in the separation zone does not see the lead edge of the sheet by the critical time in the cycle of the copier, a solenoid is activated to increase the stack force to approximately 0.7 lb. This then corrects the incipient misfeed. Thus, this invention keeps the stack force low, minimizing multifeeds, except in those critical situations when the requirement for larger stack force to avoid misfeeds has been proven by the actual operation. The system, in essence, makes its decision on a sheet-by-sheet basis. This conceptual enhancement made the basic subsystem concept inherently much more robust.

Independent Drives

The third dynamic concept was in the area of the drives. The conventional system had the take-away roll and the feed belt driven together. When the trail edge of the first sheet pulled out from the contact area between the feed belt and the stack, the belt was exposed to the second sheet and moved it forward. This aggravated the tendency for the second sheet to be fed into the downstream portion of the copy-handling module during the same cycle with sheet one—in other words, a multifeed. Evaluation of this problem led to the conclusion that separate drives should be designed for the feed belt and the take-away roll so that during the operation of the take-away roll, the feed belt is not driven. This improvement creates a bigger potential gap between the trail edge of the first sheet and the lead edge of the second sheet. This, too, provides conceptual enhancement of the robustness of the paper feeder.

Piece-Part Static/Dynamic Status

Going from the subsystem level down to the component or piece-part level, an example is the material for the surface of the retard roll. For such a critical element, concept selection is certainly warranted. In this case, however, the selected material was microcellular polyurethane. Concept selection verified the reuse of this static concept from the previous product.

Summary of Paper Feeder Static/Dynamic Status

The S/D statuses that have been described are summarized in Figure 8.7. Was the paper feeder appropriately dynamic? Its basic concept—friction retard feeder—was static. However, it had three highly dynamic areas. Therefore, the engineers felt that they were being very dynamic. The feeder was certainly very dynamic with respect to previous friction retard feeders. The three improvements were integrated together and made robust.

What about alternative concepts, such as vacuum feeders? The only safe approach is to take the viewpoint of the customers, who care little for the engineers' technical brilliance in creating the three dynamic concepts. In the final analysis we need dynamic cost/performance improvements. Otherwise, innovation may lead to differences, not improvements.

In this example, the friction retard feeder has continued to be used in other Xerox copiers and printers, so it was clearly quite dynamic in 1980. The concept has been held static since then, and has vied for applications with a slightly newer concept that is fundamentally very different, the top-vacuum-corrugation feeder (TVCF). We conclude that the three improvements and the robustness made the feeder superior. Its more than 12 years of production in several products is a great benefit of robust, flexible technology.

WINNING DYNAMISM

The example of the Xerox 1075 copier illustrates the principle of static/dynamic status evaluation. It is a serious danger to be too static or too dynamic. The United States has been seduced by the siren call of the home run product. The home run syndrome tends to regard every development program as comparable in magnitude to Moses descending from the mountain. To use a more direct comparison, every development is modeled, in this way of thinking, after the first xerographic copier. However, radical products such as the Xerox 914 (the first xerographic copier)

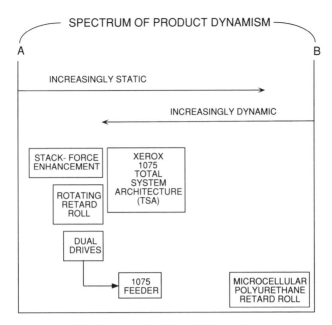

FIGURE 8.7. Case study of static/dynamic statuses.

are rare. Treating every product as radical simply wastes a lot of previous development effort. Product family planning—or planning to reuse much of the development effort—greatly reduces development time and investment, while maintaining dynamic product variety.

STATIC/DYNAMIC SPECTRUM OF PRODUCTS

The Xerox 914 has already been mentioned as a radical product, certainly near the dynamic extremum in characterizing products. At the other extreme are products that are slightly customized—for example, by attaching a different brand name. Further thought suggests several types of products, ranging from dynamic to static. Such a series of products (discussed below) is inevitably somewhat arbitrary; the important requirement is that it be able to make the distinctions that are relevant for strategic planning to achieve reusability and variety:

(1) *Genesis.* An example of a genesis product is the original camera by Daguerre (1839). There had not previously been any closely related product, and it has led to diverse families of products.

(2) *Radical.* The Xerox 914 copier (1960) has already been cited as an example of a radical product. It is generically a camera, and thus is a descendant of Daguerre's camera. At a high level of abstraction, both products had a lens, a recording medium, and a developer system. However, the recording medium and the developer system were very different for the two products. Eastman's Kodak camera (1888) was another radical product, also descended from Daguerre's camera.

(3) *New (to a corporation).* An example of a new product is the Kodak Ektaprint copier (1975). It was less than a radical product; Xerox had been making copiers for 15 years. Over 100 companies, including Kodak, had turned down the opportunity to bring the first xerographic (electrophotographic) copier to market. Although the Ektaprint was not radical, it was the first electrophotographic copier to be developed by Kodak. Getting into a new business is a major undertaking, even when the product is not radical. The Ektaprint was an excellent copier and left Xerox struggling to respond.

(4) *Clean-sheet (generational).* A clean-sheet generational product is a major step forward. An example is the Xerox 1075 copier (1981), the first of the third-generation Xerox products. The genesis, radical, and new products are by definition clean-sheet products—i.e., started by a clean sheet of drawing paper, with little design relationship to prior relatives (although a new product could be helped by a strategic alliance; then, some piece of the product may not be "clean sheet" from the ally's perspective). Do subsequent products ever have to be clean-sheet products, or is this practice simply a rather dysfunctional result of the home run, Moses-down-from-the-mountain ideology? You can answer this question for your industry. In the United States the tendency has been to depend excessively on clean-sheet products.

(5) *Market-segment entry (new).* A market-segment entry (new) product moves the corporation into a new market segment, following an earlier new (or radical) product. An example is the Xerox 2400, which initially moved Xerox into, and thus created, the mid-volume copier market segment (higher in copy volume than the 914 copier).

(6) *Market-segment entry (generational).* A market-segment entry (generational) product is a new product in a market segment following after a previous product in the same market segment. An example is the

Xerox 5090, which followed earlier high-volume copiers going back to the Xerox 9200 (1974).

(7) *Associated.* An associated product changes some technologies to provide a different capability. Thus, it is in a somewhat different market. An example is laser printers, which are based on xerographic copiers. The light optics are replaced by a laser ROS (raster output scanner). One trend is for products that were distinct (or whose antecedents were distinct) to merge into one big market and industry. The prime example is integrated information technology (Ferguson, 1990), where the trend is toward merging copiers, printers, desktop publishing, fax, VCRs, CD players, CD-ROM data-retrieval systems, multimedia personal computers, telephone networks, cameras, voice mail, and television. This is an example from which we can easily see basic strengths and technologies from a different industry move into our product segment. We have to be alert that the product variety from another traditional market does not unexpectedly intrude into our own product strategy. Put another way, the product variety stakes are rapidly increasing.

(8) *Variant.* Variant products are relatively small changes on a base product. They include feature enrichment or removal, and cost/performance upgrades. Often these changes move the product up or down market, sometimes into a neighboring market segment. An example is the Xerox 1090 copier, which increased the speed of the Xerox 1075 from 70 to 90 copies per minute and added some small improvements.

(9) *Customized.* Customizing of products extends over a range from adding brand names to fairly major changes for specific customers.

Genesis, radical, new, and market-segment entry (new) products are all by definition one-shot events; any follow-on products are of a different type. Customized products have a limited role in the general subject of product development. Although genesis, radical, and new products receive a lot of attention, they have been superseded when a corporation becomes a full-market competitor in an industry. Then the name of the game is clean-sheet (generational), market-segment entry (generational), associated, and variant products. In a mature industry, the market-segment entry (generational) products are either clean-sheet (generational) products or variant products. Therefore, most of the products that we plan for are clean-sheet, variant, or associated products. Traditional product development emphasizes 100% clean-sheet products, or variant products with 10% change. There is available to us a continuous spectrum of change between minimally variant products and 100% clean-sheet products. Planned reusability guides us to the economical amount of change from product to product.

DYNAMISM AT DIFFERENT LEVELS OF THE PRODUCT

As has been noted, concept selection, and therefore conceptual dynamism, can occur at any level from total system architecture (TSA) down to piece parts. The friction retard feeder exemplified dynamism at an intermediate level. Therefore, we must go beyond the characterization of the static/dynamic status of the entire product.

There is a tendency as an industry matures for the TSA to become static. Then the dynamic competition moves to lower levels of the system. The friction retard feeder is an example. In automobiles, the competition is primarily at the level of engines, suspensions, brakes, doors, and styling. In developing our strategy, we concentrate on the levels that will pay off.

Strategic planners have long made the distinction between radical products and incremental products (a generic name for the last three categories in the previous section). Henderson and Clark (1990) have documented that there are two other types of products—architectural and modular—and have emphasized the strategic competitive importance of architectural innovations. Architectural products emphasize changes at the TSA level, while modular products are primarily changed at the lower levels. This will be clarified by the introduction of the reusability matrix.

REUSABILITY

Family planning to enable reusability achieves much greater product variety. Reusability and product variety must be planned. The basic concept is well known: plan families that combine leveraged products with clean-sheet products to provide product variety and greater market presence relative to the development effort. Reusability in its simplest form is reusability of parts in more than one product. Of course, manufacturing has always loved this commonality. Flexibility requires a more subtle characterization of commonality and types of products.

The ultimate in commonality is keeping the piece-part design the same, i.e., using the same part in more than one product. However, if all parts and connections are the same, then the two products are the same. Less rigid commonality enables flexibility, while still greatly reducing the development work.

USEFUL DEGREES OF COMMONALITY

If the piece-part concept is the same as in a current product, but the detailed design is somewhat changed, then the development effort is still greatly reduced in relation to the development of a completely new part. For example, the material and process selection will not have to be redone. Since this is often a difficult and uncertain step, a great savings in development effort is achieved by reusing the concept of the piece part. Extending this logic gives the reusability matrix; see Figure 8.8 (Clausing, 1991). The lower left cell represents conventional commonality. The

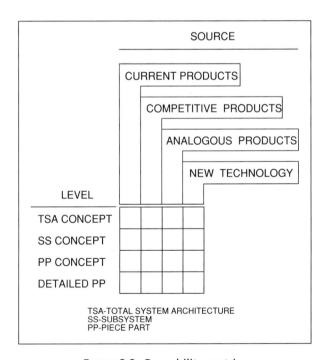

FIGURE 8.8. Reusability matrix.

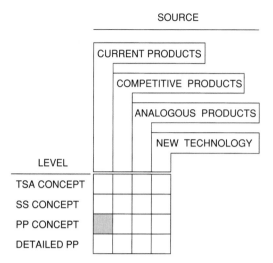

FIGURE 8.9. Piece-part concept commonality.

piece-part concept commonality that is described in this paragraph is represented in Figure 8.9.

The reusability matrix displays the commonalities that provide great product variety while reducing development effort, exactly our flexible goal. Only the four boxes in the right-hand column (see Figure 8.10)

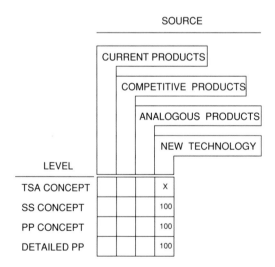

FIGURE 8.10. Home run product.

represent a total lack of commonality, i.e., a "home run" attempt. If the total system architecture is new, all subsystem concepts are new, and all piece-part concepts are new (which automatically makes all piece-part designs new), then there is zero commonality. Between 100% commonality (lower left cell) and zero commonality (right-hand column) there are degrees and types of commonality available to provide product variety while reducing the development effort.

In the previous section the static/dynamic spectrum from incremental (I) products to radical (R) products was described, and the extension by Henderson and Clark to include architectural (A) and modular (M) products was introduced. All four types of products are readily defined with the help of the reusability matrix; see Figure 8.11. Anything within the shaded region of Figure 8.12 is usually considered an incremental product, and Figure 8.13 similarly defines radical products. Often, an intermediate level of innovation will be most successful in the marketplace.

As a specific example, if 20 to 30% of the subsystem concepts are new technologies, consumers can find the product exciting even though the remaining subsystem concepts are carried over from a current product. This approach can reduce the development effort by an amount approaching the 75% reduction in new subsystems. Even new subsys-

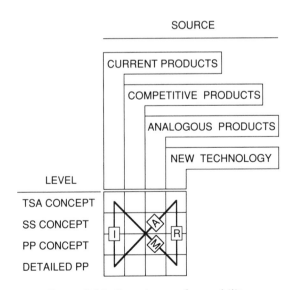

FIGURE 8.11. Four types of reusability.

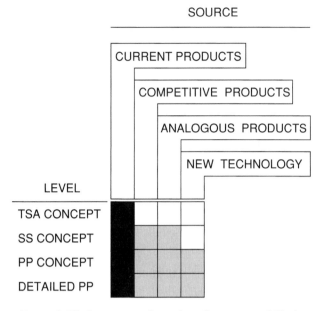

FIGURE 8.12. Incremental product (large reusability).

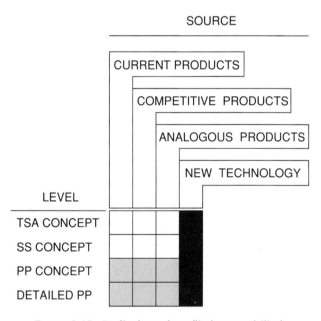

FIGURE 8.13. Radical product (little reusability).

tems can use many existing parts. At one extreme, simple hardware (fasteners, for example) can certainly be common. This potential commonality can be captured by a design strategy (policy) of using only a very restricted set of hardware. This can also be applied, usually to a lesser extent, to components such as bearings, gears, solenoids, clutches, and power supplies. You can apply the reusability matrix as a powerful tool for strategic planning.

REUSABILITY MATRIX CASE STUDY

An example of the reusability matrix (Figure 8.14) is for the Xerox 4850 highlight-color printer, which was introduced in 1991. This is considered to be an innovative product, since it does highlight color at full productivity (same throughput as black and white) by using a more

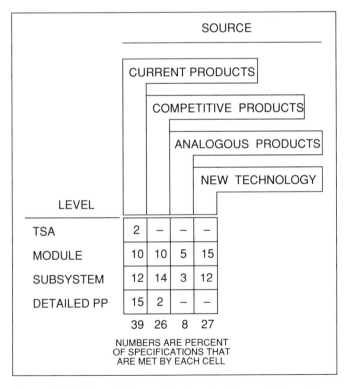

FIGURE **8.14.** Reusability matrix for the Xerox 4850 printer.

robust new enhancement to the xerographic process. Nevertheless, Figure 8.14 reveals that the product is only 27% new technology. (The 4850 team arrived at the numbers by attributing the achievement of each column in the House of Quality to one of the cells in the reusability matrix.) This is a good example of the principle that a product does not have to be 100% new (clean-sheet) in order to achieve dynamic market presence.

REUSABILITY IN PRODUCT STRATEGY

Product strategy can be formulated and evaluated by combining the type of product with the reusability matrix. A concise criticism of many product families in the United States is that they excessively emphasize clean-sheet products and do not achieve sufficient leverage with associated and variant products. This seems to be largely a matter of ideology, a fascination with the aura of radical products.

Is there ever a need for a clean-sheet (generational) product? For relatively simple products with rapidly changing technology, the clean-sheet (generational) product may be the best way to introduce new technology. An example was the change from mechanical watches to electronic watches. For complex products, however, the clean-sheet (generational) approach is highly dubious. It seems to have a technology-driven, home run psychological thrust with more problems than benefits.

A complex product may have 20 subsystems. If all of them are new concepts (technologies), the development task becomes very complicated. The coordination difficulties and the interacting problems make the magnitude of the task explode more than linearly in the traditional development approach. The task with 20 new technologies is more than 4 times as challenging as the new product with only 5 new technologies and 15 leveraged subsystems.

Does the clean-sheet approach buy enough market presence to warrant the great difficulty? Usually not. Engineers are very attracted by the mystique of the big bang product, but customers want only performance for price. Usually, a series of four products, each with one-quarter of its subsystems featuring new technologies, will buy more market presence than one big bang product, and the total development effort will be less. Even more important, the series of four will provide much greater responsiveness to changing conditions. The ratio of 4 is only illustrative;

the ratio might vary from 2 to 10 when this logic is applied to specific situations. The point is that less emphasis on clean-sheet (generational) products, and a richer menu of variant and associated products, will provide much greater product variety and flexibility. Even the prime rationale for clean-sheet (generational) products—getting new technologies into the market—is usually not valid. Too many technologies are kept waiting for the complete set, and the long development time actually slows the average time for technologies to reach the market.

The exact amount of reusability that is best will clearly be related to the degree of customer satisfaction. If customers are generally satisfied with our products, then we can emphasize reusability. However, if our products are not achieving high marks for customer satisfaction, then too much reusability would not be responsive to the marketplace. Thus, in planning reusability, a combination of the reusability matrix and QFD will be best. Figure 8.14 is a start at this integration.

The position of every product can be located in a three-dimensional space that has the reusability matrix as its base and the type of product as the third axis. The evolution of this 3-D space through time then defines the product strategy. However, 3-D spaces are somewhat difficult to visualize. It is simpler to display the type of product (and the specific actual products) versus time, using the traditional product map, and then to evaluate pairs of products by using the reusability matrix.

The fundamentals of this approach are displayed in Figures 8.15 and 8.16, which also compare the clean-sheet (generational) approach with the evolutionary approach. Although the best amount of new technology for a specific situation can vary from a few percent to 100%, the attitude that 25% is often roughly correct should be given strong consideration in preparing your strategy. Usually, four products with 25% new technology (Figure 8.16) will bring more business success than one 100% clean-sheet product (Figure 8.15).

FLEXIBILITY

A prime objective of strategy is flexibility. Much is written about flexible manufacturing, but the forward-looking successful company is improving toward total corporate flexibility. Flexible product development utilizes

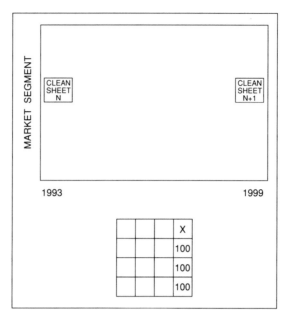

FIGURE 8.15. Clean sheet—no reusability.

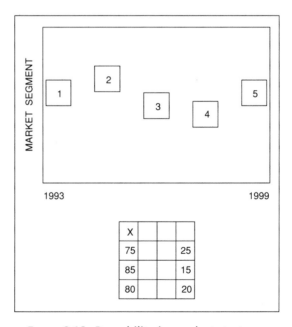

FIGURE 8.16. Reusability in product strategy.

product strategy, technology strategy, investment in basic strengths, and the reusability matrix to achieve market responsiveness and product variety.

Ideal flexibility would provide each consumer with exactly what he or she wants as soon as it is wanted. It would also make each new technology available as soon as it is invented. This would be done at a price that was immediately in line with other need/price ratios.

Reality has been quite different. In the case of the xerographic copier, for example, it took 22 years to bring the technology (1938) to market (1960). Product development times have often been 5 to 10 years. Consumers are frustrated because the exact product characteristics that they desire are not available. New technologies are often expensive luxuries, taking years or decades to come down a learning curve to widespread availability.

Flexible product development, coupled with flexible manufacturing and marketing, aims to overcome these limitations. Tremendous improvement is possible through a high-expectation attack on obvious barriers to flexibility.

HISTORICAL PERSPECTIVE

Before the beginning of the Industrial Revolution, a little more than two centuries ago, products were custom-made to satisfy the specific desires of individual customers. This satisfied the customers' functional needs, but the cost was very high because of the low power and precision of handcraftsmanship. Victor S. Clark (*History of Manufactures in the United States*, 1916; quoted in Hounshell, 1984) noted:

> Handicrafts and methods of production that follow the precedent of handicrafts, serve best an aristocracy of consumers, while factories serve best the consumption of a democracy.

With the advent of the industrial revolution, technology provided production capability of greatly increased power and precision. This technological production capability required huge increases in capital investment, with resulting great pressure for uninterrupted production. Long production runs meant that large numbers of customers had to take the same product, not usually exactly what they wanted. To maximize ROI, new products were introduced as seldom as possible. The cost reductions greatly increased the number of consumers, but consumers had to accept the sameness of the products.

A prime example is the Model T Ford, in production from 1908 until 1927, with a minimum price of $360. Total production of Model T's was 15,000,000. It has long been accepted that customers must accept a product that is not exactly what each individual wishes, in order to achieve a low cost. This trend reached its apogee in 1914 with Henry Ford's famous dictum that the customers could have any color that they wished—as long as it was black. According to an article in the *New York Times* of March 31, 1929 (quoted in Hounshell, 1984):

> When mass production started, individuality stopped. In order to reduce manufacturing costs and turn out automobiles in sufficient quantity to supply popular demand, producers had to evolve factory methods that permitted economical, high-speed operation. They had to concentrate the forces of men and machinery on the production of standard, stockstamped motor cars. Instead of making different cars, each manufacturer simply made the same car over and over again. Automobiles that came from the same plant had less individuality among themselves than a nest full of eggs from the same hen.

Since the 1920s, flexibility has slowly increased. Chevrolet's introduction of slightly increased flexibility beginning in 1923 reduced the Model T's market share from 55% in 1921 to 30% in 1926. Ford introduced colors in addition to black in 1926, but it was too late. Ford was forced into a very poorly planned changeover from the Model T to the Model A in 1927. Chevrolet's production went from 280,000 in 1924 to 1.5 million in 1929.

In summary, the Industrial Revolution greatly reduced flexibility during the period 1760–1920. Since 1920, flexibility has gradually increased. The great power that was released by the Industrial Revolution is only now being fully aimed at achieving flexibility. Flexibility is now the arena of international economic competition. The organizations that achieve short development times, product variety, and low-cost functional precision (adherence to customer satisfaction performance) will be successful in the rapidly changing economy of the twenty-first century.

CORPORATE LEARNING

Short development time and product variety are keys to flexibility and also enable great corporate learning. Not only is there the immediate benefit of products that customers like, but the cumulative effect is to create corporate competence that leaves less nimble competition far behind. The following case study (Stalk, 1988) illustrates the point:

> A classic example of a variety war was the battle that erupted between Honda and Yamaha for supremacy in the motorcycle market, a struggle popularly known in Japanese business circles as the H-Y War. Yamaha ignited the H-Y War in 1981 when it announced the opening of a new factory which would make it the world's largest motorcycle manufacturer, a prestigious position held by Honda. But Honda had been concentrating its corporate resources on the automobile business and away from the motorcycle operation. Now, faced with Yamaha's overt and public challenge, Honda chose to counterattack.
>
> Honda launched its response with the war cry, "Yamaha wo tsubusu!" ("We will crush, squash, slaughter Yamaha!"). In the no-holds-barred battle that ensued, Honda cut prices, flooded distribution channels, and boosted advertising expenditures. Most important—and most impressive to consumers—Honda also rapidly increased the rate of change in its product line, using variety to bury Yamaha. At the start of the war, Honda had 60 models of motorcycles. Over the next 18 months, Honda introduced or replaced 113 models, effectively turning over its entire product line twice. Yamaha also began the war with 60 models; it was able to manage only 37 changes in its product line during those 18 months.
>
> Honda's new product introduction devastated Yamaha. First, Honda succeeded in making motorcycle design a matter of fashion, where newness and freshness were important attributes for consumers. Second, Honda raised the technological sophistication of its products, introducing four-valve engines, composites, direct drive, and other new features. Next to a Honda, Yamaha products looked old, unattractive, and out of date. Demand for Yamaha products dried up; in a desperate effort to move them, dealers were forced to price them below cost. But even that didn't work. At the most intense point in the H-Y War, Yamaha had more than 12 months of inventory in its dealers' showrooms. Finally, Yamaha surrendered.

In the future, it will be flexibility or surrender.

Product variety and quick responsiveness to the marketplace are achieved by the *total quality development*, including successful strategy, that is the subject of this book. The successful strategy emphasizes reusability to minimize the total development that is required, and the total quality development process and teamwork reduce rework during product development, thus shortening development time. Strategic variety reuses basic strengths, technologies, and subsystem designs many times, introducing just enough innovation in each product to make it a winner in its market segment. The product variety itself becomes a great organizational asset, as the corporation's brand is perceived to be the source of product freshness and new ideas.

BARRIERS TO FOLLOWING

Product variety provides great market strength in itself. Even greater advantage is gained when the changes are difficult for competitors to quickly follow. Radical changes such as the Xerox 914 copier (1960) are certainly difficult to follow, and everyone would be delighted to find another such breakthrough; however, they are too rare to be a part of strategic planning. Henderson and Clark (1990) have observed that much less radical change can still be very difficult to follow. Architectural changes can sufficiently disrupt the organization, communication paths, and implicit assumptions of the previous market leader so that it cannot readily make the shift to the new dominant architecture.

Henderson and Clark describe in detail the case of photolithographic aligners that are used in the production of integrated circuits. During the period 1962–1986, the industry had in succession five major architectures: contact, proximity, scanners, step and repeat (first generation), and step and repeat (second generation). Each architecture brought a different market leader: Cobilt, Canon, Perkin-Elmer, GCA, and Nikon. In each of the four changes a new market leader emerged; the old leader was unable to follow the new architecture quickly and completely enough to maintain leadership. In all cases the previous market leader fell far behind.

In the aligner industry, architectural knowledge has been a basic strength. Each major change brought significant differences in the relationships among critical system parameters. The previous leader had difficulty in recognizing the dominant new relationships and kept viewing the new aligners as minor variants of the previous design in which it was the leader. This tendency was aggravated by corporate organization, which revolved around the major components—lens, for example—making it difficult for previous leaders to recognize new architectural relationships among the components. The failure was compounded by weak competitive benchmarking, which tended to dismiss the new innovations as mere copies.

In the aligner industry, systems engineering was a basic strength. However, none of the leaders developed this basic strength sufficiently to survive the transition to a new dominant architecture. Each dominant architecture was a unique creation of one organization. Focus on the product made it difficult for the leader to develop the basic strength that would have enabled it to quickly follow, perhaps even lead, to the next dominant architecture.

PLANNING FOR FLEXIBILITY

Conscious planning provides corporate flexibility. Study the aligner history, and learn to avoid the rigidity that plagued the former leaders. Use product strategy, technology strategy, investment in basic strengths, the reusability matrix, and short development time to be a leader in product variety and flexibility. The total quality development process and teamwork shorten the development time. This enables responsiveness to the market. Use the elements of strategy that are described in this chapter to ensure that the products that are developed bring business leadership.

TIME TO MARKET

A primary objective of total quality development is to shorten the time to develop new products. This is achieved by the more efficient development process, especially the reduction in rework, and the smaller amount of development that is planned for each product. Planned reusability provides new products with relatively little development effort, enabling each product to be quickly brought to market.

Quick time to market brings three important benefits: (1) responsiveness to changed market conditions is quick, (2) product variety is enabled, and (3) the product planning for each specific product remains valid (the product is brought to market before customers' expectations have changed).

STRATEGIC ACTIONS FOR SUCCESS

(1) Prepare a product strategy map.
(2) Prepare reusability matrices for each sequence of products.
(3) Prepare technology maps and technology/product integration maps.
(4) Prepare three-tiered maps (products, technology, basic strengths).
(5) Evaluate the static/dynamic status of your major product lines.
(6) Estimate all of the preceding for your competitors and potential allies.

Use the previous six actions to:

(A) Obtain the maximum market presence from a constrained amount of development.
(B) Plan product variety.
(C) Reuse designs, technologies, and basic strengths.
(D) Match organization and work style to the static/dynamic status of your products.
(E) Evaluate threats and opportunities posed by other organizations.
(F) Shorten development time (greater reusability and more certain starts).

The total quality development process and teamwork (Chapters 4 through 7) make individual product development programs successful. Good strategy integrates product success into business success.

STRATEGY SUMMARY

STRATEGY INPUT

Business Strategy (beyond scope of this book)
Current Environment

	Step	Page
Prepare Product Strategy	S1	346
Prepare Technology Strategy	S2	348
Maintain Basic Strengths	S3	352
Plan Reusability	S4	364

STRATEGY OUTPUT

Product Strategy
Technology Strategy
Reusability Plan

CHAPTER

9

Managing for Success

- **Product Development — Core Corporate Competency**
- **Management Style**
- **Improvement**

Product success requires that managers:

- Provide clarity, unity, and resources.
- Lead improvement.

Resources enable action; unity focuses the action; and clarity keeps the focus on the right objectives and activities (process) to achieve the objectives. Improvement ensures that this is done in the best possible (world-class) way.

PRODUCT DEVELOPMENT—CORE CORPORATE COMPETENCY

In order for total quality development to succeed, product development must be a core corporate competency. The CEO and the people who report directly to him or her must devote attention to nurturing product development as a key corporate competitive advantage.

If the top management of the corporation believes that success will come primarily from strong sales efforts, then product development is unlikely to flourish. "We can sell anything that you turkeys give to us," they might say. "And if you don't give it to us, we will get it from other places." To those having such an attitude, this book will provide little help. The same goes for a dependence on financial manipulation, or a strong service network.

There is clear evidence that corporations with strong products win. The top corporate management must make product development a core corporate competency. The total quality development process and the kind of management that is described in this chapter will then succeed.

MANAGEMENT STYLE

Management's role is to provide clarity, unity, and resources, and to lead improvement. To do this, the winning management style is to teach and coach, and to provide leadership that helps all members of the PDT to have a better perspective on their work.

A great challenge to managers is to adjust their role and style as they are promoted to higher levels. Most of the work is done at the lowest (entry) organizational level (level 1), or certainly at the two lowest levels (levels 1 and 2). Here the unit product development tasks, including all of the partial design activities (see Chapter 1), and much of the total quality development work are done. For example, the design of an electromechanical subsystem is done at the two lowest levels. The PDT engineers in the two lowest levels know enough about circuits and mechanisms, and the partial design tasks, to carry out the work. After mastering the ideas of this book they will be able to follow much of the improved approach, including EQFD and robustness optimization. Once it is understood that design includes product, production process, and field-support capability, PDT engineers at the first two levels can practice this approach as well. It is a prime role of management to reinforce this concurrent approach.

Product development engineers at level 2, which may be thought of as the first level of management, lead in doing the unit tasks. Their greater experience enables them to lead in doing the unit tasks well. Above the product development second level, the managers are not primarily doing the unit tasks. Rather, they are providing the right environment and style for the unit tasks. If the unit tasks are defined so that they are consistent with the overall goals of the development program and the corporation, then the first two levels can do the rest. It is a great challenge to the second level of management (level 3 of the organization) to let go of the execution of the unit tasks and help to provide the right definition and style.

Product people at the third level (second level of management) have gotten there because they were good at the first two levels. There is a great temptation for them to keep repeating their old successes, but this will become mere meddling and must be resisted. Instead, product people at level 3 and higher must concentrate on providing the environment and style so that the people on the first two levels can be successful in a way that will lead to program and corporate success.

A related problem in management is a failure to expand scope as we move to the third and higher levels. We reach the third level by being very good, for example, at electromechanical devices to handle paper in the copier. Now, at the third level, we are responsible for a broader scope of activities. There is a natural tendency to hover close to our original strength. This can easily lead to abdication of responsibility: "I don't know about software; please take care of it." It is all too easy for the manager to become a message center with inadequate value added. Instead of abdication, the manager arriving at the third level must broaden his or her scope by learning about the new responsibilities so that value can be added. This is another example of overcoming segmentalism. The third-level person does not have to become proficient at the unit tasks covered by the new responsibilities; this is for the first two levels of people. The third-level product person does have to become proficient in the new subjects at a higher, more integrative level of abstraction, so that value can be added in providing the right environment for all of the unit tasks—both the ones that he or she was proficient in doing, and the ones that have come with the increased scope of responsibility. Obviously, this point of learning the broadened scope in order to add value extends all the way up to the CEO.

Managers must make prompt decisions on issues. Otherwise the people doing the work will be left in limbo. Even the most complex issues can usually be resolved within two weeks. Most issues should be resolved within 24 hours.

The manager of a major product development program—say, a few hundred people—needs an assistant, the process and planning manager. There is a tendency to avoid this because of a fear of creating too many staff jobs. However, if the program manager of the independent PDT (see Chapter 2) is to put sufficient emphasis on clarity, unity, resources, and improvement, then help is needed to carry out these responsibilities. Otherwise they will not receive sufficient attention, and the product people on the first two levels will be left adrift.

Now we turn to the specifics of the management of product development: clarity, unity, resources, and improvement.

CLARITY

The TQM practice of *hoshin kanri* (policy deployment, strategy deployment) and the various areas of strategy (business, product, technology, manufacturing, field support, and marketing; see Chapter 8) ensure that the product development project is a high priority for corporate success in the current environment. Here we concentrate on the internal clarity of a specific product development program.

Overview of Program On-Line QC—PDCA

As do production operations, product development programs require on-line quality control (QC). That is, if the team never checks performance (progress) against the target (plan), then divergences tend to grow unchecked. The development control is a specific application of PDCA, the general management control approach that has been advocated by Dr. W. Edwards Deming.

PDCA stands for plan, do, check, and act and is frequently depicted as a wheel (Figure 9.1). This can best be understood as a combination of feedback and feed-forward control, diagramed for product development activities in Figure 9.2. The team plans program N initially (plan N1). Then the product development team (PDT) goes on to *do*, i.e., to carry out the initial (concept) phase of activities. Then the team compares the status (progress) with plan N1 in the first check. Discrepancies (problems) are fed forward and backward to guide acts that correct the discrepancies.

Feed-Forward

In feed forward, the team prepares a second iteration of the plan for product N, plan N2. This refines the original plan for the subsystem design subphase to achieve correction of the discrepancies.

Feed-Backward

In feeding backward, there are three actions: (1) improve the plan for the next product, product N +1; (2) improve the plans for advanced (technology) development; and (3) improve the generic corporate (or divisional) product development process. This is a form of organizational learning.

Xerox 4850 Program Management Process

A specific example is displayed in Figure 9.3. This is the program management process that was used to develop the Xerox 4850 highlight-color

FIGURE 9.1. PDCA wheel.

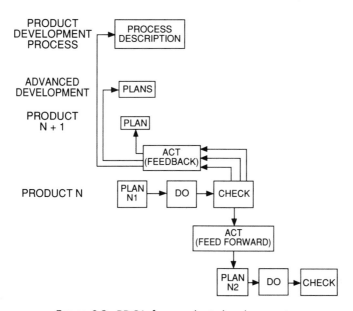

FIGURE 9.2. PDCA for product development.

printer, an innovative product that was developed in 70% of the bench-mark development time. Although the 4850 plan was not explicitly for-matted in the PDCA format, the shaded background is added to make clear that Figure 9.3 is the feed-forward form of PDCA for managing the internal program.

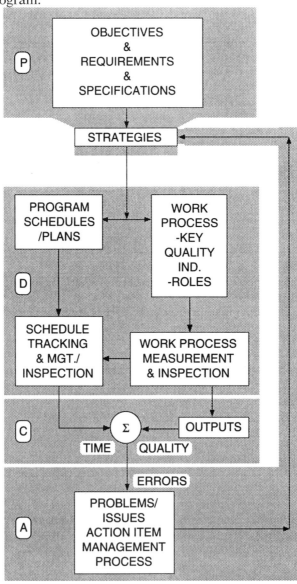

FIGURE 9.3. 4850 management process.

The four stages of PDCA are described next. Since *checks* have been problematic, they are described first.

Checks

The total quality management (TQM, TQC) literature describes the application of PDCA. This includes, for example, a sample agenda for a one-day, high-level check (president's QC audit) in the context of total corporate management (which uses *hoshin kanri*). Here we will concentrate on the checks for product development.

The checks in product development are commonly called *design reviews*, *phase-gate reviews*, or some similar name. The complete development activity is decomposed into phases, as described in Chapters 4, 5, 6, and 7 and displayed in Figure 9.4 (a repeat of the core of Figure 1.7). At the end of each subphase, we hold a progress check, as symbolized by the "flag" in Figure 9.4 at the end of each phase. As described in Chapters 4, 5, and 6, the concept phase is divided into three subphases; the design phase is divided into two subphases; and the production preparation phase is divided into three subphases. Thus, as shown in Figure 9.5, there are a total of eight subphases. In this description it is assumed that new technologies are developed to maturity in the technology stream and then selected during concept development. The exact number and the names of the phases can be tailored to the organization and product.

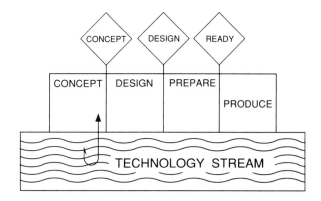

FIGURE 9.4. Total quality development phases (top level).

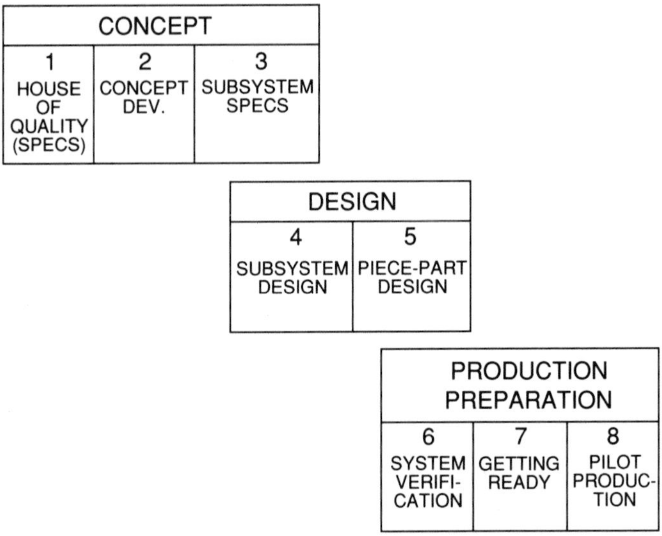

CONCEPT		
1	2	3
HOUSE OF QUALITY (SPECS)	CONCEPT DEV.	SUBSYSTEM SPECS

DESIGN	
4	5
SUBSYSTEM DESIGN	PIECE-PART DESIGN

PRODUCTION PREPARATION		
6	7	8
SYSTEM VERIFI-CATION	GETTING READY	PILOT PRODUC-TION

FIGURE 9.5. Total quality development phases (second level).

The check at the end of each subphase is primarily to further improve clarity and unity. The essential objectives are:

(1) Identify goals of unit design tasks that need to be clarified.
(2) Identify areas where teamwork needs to be strengthened.

The checks help in achieving the progressive freezing of decisions that was introduced in Chapter 3. The basic contents of these reviews have been described in Chapters 4 through 7. (The progress check for technologies is the selection activity, conducted when the technology is considered for selection into a product; see Chapter 7.)

Usually, product programs place more emphasis on some of the reviews than on others. The reviews at the completion of the three phases are considered to be major reviews. Since the decision as to whether a review is major or minor will usually benefit from being tailored to the specific development program and organization, no distinction will be made here.

Dysfunctional Checks

The checks in product development have traditionally suffered from two dysfunctions:

(1) Criteria are weak; often, the checks are little more than completion statements, unable to distinguish good progress from the mediocre.

(2) The style has often tended to be somewhat inquisitional—high-level "others" used it as an opportunity to kick the tires, or to demand that the trim line be lowered 10 mm—and in general, it reinforced a hierarchical authority with little value added.

Another problem with the checks has been their "laundry list" nature. A list of 276 criteria creates a "whiteout" syndrome: nothing is very important, and thematic guidance is lacking. A good style is to structure the criteria in a tree (or in an indented structure). There may be 276 detailed criteria at the lowest level of the structure, but at the top there are only 8 to 10 criteria (one or two for each subphase). This provides thematic guidance for each subphase.

Criteria as Motivators

Although the check criteria have been introduced here in the context of the checks in PDCA, their best role is to motivate and guide the right activities during each phase so that discrepancies do not develop (problem prevention). Managers should help the PDT to focus on the criteria at the beginning of the phase. This enables everyone to follow a good process; in effect, the check criteria become deployed (decentralized) into micro criteria that the team uses throughout the phase to prevent the development of discrepancies.

Good Criteria

We must word the criteria so that they enable us to distinguish between good results and mediocre progress. For example, at the completion of system verification, the criterion *system verified* (or *functionally demonstrated*) could mean almost anything; it is certainly not sufficient to prevent chaos and confusion during the subsequent subphases. An appropriately critical criterion is *superior robustness demonstrated in direct comparison with benchmark product*. Too often, the criteria are mere completion statements—*drawings completed*, for example. This tends to make the checks superficial and contributes to a perception that they are merely bureaucratic trappings.

The criteria have been described in Chapters 4 through 6. Table 9.1 is a summary of suggested effective criteria:

TABLE 9.1

Subphase and Criteria	
1. House of Quality (specifications development)	1. Product specifications define winning expectations.
2. Total system concept development	2. Product concept is a winner.
3. Subsystem specs	3. Program plan (including subsystem specs) enables success.
4. Subsystem design	4. Product design is superior to benchmarks.
5. Piece-part design	5. Product design is sufficiently superior to the expected competition.
6. System verification	6. Product demonstrates superior robustness to benchmark product(s).
	7. Corporate consensus on success.
7. Production preparation	8. Tooling validated.
8. Pilot production	9. Production has competitive capability.
	10. All corporate functions concur on shipping approval.

Total quality development emphasizes problem prevention. As the work progresses, we freeze the decisions. This discipline was introduced in Chapter 3. At the end of each subphase, we freeze the decisions that are appropriate for that time in the development process. Then we use the frozen decisions as the basis for the next subphase, not reconsidering the frozen decisions. The progressive freezes are a key enabler for short time to market. Table 9.2 lists suggested freezes.

The criteria of Table 9.1 and the freeze schedule of Table 9.2 are merely suggestive. In actual application, the team deploys them into detailed trees (or into indented structures). The detailed structures reflect

TABLE 9.2

Element	Specs	Concept Development	SS specs	SS design	PP design	System verification	Getting ready	Pilot production
	1	2	3	4	5	6	7	8
Business strategy	F							
Products strategy	F							
Product family plan	C	F						
Business plan	C			F				
Product expectation specifications	C			F				
Technologies selected		F						
Product concept		F						
Subsystem specifications			C	F				
Subsystem concepts		A		C	F			
Robustness optimization		A		C		F		
Final assembly concepts		C		F				
Styling		C		F				
Detailed design				C	F			
Tool design				A	C	F		
Final commitment to program						F		
Mistakes corrected							C	F
Tool building						C	F	
Service documentation							C	F
Tolerance design					A		C	F
Process optimized								C
On-line QC made operational								C
Line balance								C

The headings refer to the eight subphases; see Figure 9.5.

Legend: A—almost complete; C—complete; F—frozen.

the contents of total quality development. For example, the first three criteria can be developed as follows:

(1) Product specifications define winning expectations.

- Systematic deployment from the voice of the customer
- Customer options defined
- Product variants enabled per corporate strategy
- Business plan, based on concept and specifications, satisfies corporate strategy

(2) Product concept is a winner.

- Wins over alternative concepts in systematic comparison
- Expected to meet specifications
- Superior to competitive benchmark product(s)
- Static/dynamic status has been evaluated; concept and the development plans are compatible with status
- Product styling is superior
- Technologies selected
  —Compatible with corporate strategy
  —Maturity demonstrated, including robustness
  —Technology transfer nominally complete; remaining tasks defined

(3) Program plan enables success.

- Product parameter design (robustness optimization) plan enables success; critical design parameters are identified and performance metrics are selected (ideally, the robustness optimization is nearly complete)
- Detailed development plan meets all benchmarks
- All functions of the corporation have reached consensus on concept, specifications, and plans

An example of a criterion at the next level of the tree (or indented structure), under voice of customer, is the criterion for the image KJ diagram. During the check at the end of the specs subphase, we primarily look for gaps—lack of consistent clarity and unity. For example, we want all those on the various subteams to have the same images internalized in their perspective, and guiding their work. It is easy for divergence to creep in. The check is a major opportunity to reaffirm and strengthen the consistency (to achieve unity with clarity).

Further development and tailoring to the specific activity achieves the needed guidance. The detailed criteria and freeze schedule are developed to avoid the traditional problems, including the 10 cash drains. They reinforce the basic principles of total quality development.

Style

The style of the phase-gate reviews should be largely a self-assessment by the PDT. The reviews are an opportunity for the team to refocus, get their heads above the trees, and see what the forest looks like. Are all of the individual activities combining to achieve the desired results? Traditional concerns that the team will be strongly biased toward a positive assessment can be overcome by (1) ensuring that the messengers will not be shot, and (2) having a senior executive as a corporate facilitator of reviews, to help the team achieve objectivity. In the most positive style, the reviews become a natural and valued part of the work process, rather than a crisis that produces a fear psychology.

To make the phase-gate reviews a natural part of the work, the team does additional micro checks to facilitate the work process. These are often called *operations reviews*, and they are held much more often than the phase-gate reviews. When they are done well, little in the way of new data will be required for the phase-gate reviews. In this style, the phase-gate reviews are simply a natural part of the work process. They reinforce the operations reviews, which in turn reinforce the daily work.

Not only are the criteria often superficial, but the style has often reinforced the notion that the checks are an activity that serious product people would prefer to avoid. For example:

PDT manager: "Have you done your optimization?"
PDT engineer: "Yes."
PDT manager: "That's good."

This provides absolutely no added value. Instead, the needed style is captured in the Xerox 4850 program management process book:

Maurice (PDT manager) asked a totally different level of question! He asked "What are the results of your design optimization work, and when can we sit down and review it?" Wow, a totally different question! And everyone knew he would actually take the time (whatever was required) to actually review the work until he was satisfied.

In this style, the PDT manager reviews the work at a higher level of abstraction than the working level, and thus helps the team to develop new insights that are valuable in improving the total work. This is a key role in which the PDT manager provides added value.

Success requires that the style emphasize management by facts. Hierarchical position and other implications of power should play little or no role. Data, not hand waving, must rule. Ideally, the product development checks should be as similar as possible to production on-line QC. What are the standard deviations in relation to variations that will be seriously hurt (tolerances)? The checks are based on monitoring the process capability of the product development activities. Precise definitions of standard deviation and tolerance are often not easy, but this is the type of thinking that pays off in continuous improvement. For maximum benefit it is applied to the product, the production processes, the schedule, the resources, and every other metric that indicates the progress of the development program. Management by facts is a key to success.

Plan

The team makes the checks relative to the plan, as indicated in Figure 9.2. The plan starts with the relevant strategies (see Chapter 8), and describes the activities from bringing in the voice of the customer to starting production. The plan for the development of a specific product includes:

- Overall objectives
- Activities and schedule (Gantt chart and/or other project management schedule tools)
- Phase-gate review schedule and criteria
- Key-indicator management (tracking) process
- Work process; basically, the process described in this book
- Resource profile

The total quality development plan is more front-end–loaded than traditional plans, in order to prevent problems and the endless cycles of rework of the design. This does not necessarily mean that more time and resources will be devoted to the front end than in the traditional approach, but the percentage devoted to the front end will certainly be greater.

Managing key indicators is the institutionalization of management by facts. The product program management selects roughly 30 key indicators of development progress and focuses attention on them at all checks. This emphasizes the progress with time, with two very important features:

(1) The progress with time is planned so that each key indicator will reach the program target at approximately the start of production.

(2) The planned rate of change is compared with historical accomplishments; if the planned rate is much better, then there must be a planned change in the approach, along with a rationale that leads to the expectation that the new rate can be achieved.

The latter feature stems from the TQM aphorism "Insanity is believing that different results will be achieved from the same old process."

An example of an improved target is what has been achieved with reliability. As shown in Figure 9.6, reliability has traditionally grown at a certain rate. Despite many efforts, it has been very difficult to improve that rate. To reach the reliability goal in three years instead of five, there are two possible approaches, both displayed in Figure 9.6:

(1) Achieve a much faster growth rate (dashed line).
(2) Start at a much lower (better) unreliability level.

The first option has proved to be very difficult. The team fulfills the second option by achieving robustness early, coupled with use of a good knowledge-based engineering approach to minimizing the simple mistakes. QFD helps also by much better integrating the former serial activities. This is an outstanding example of the better results that come with the new way.

By managing the key indicators, the team makes good results almost routine. Examples of key indicators are:

• Reliability
• Defects per hundred machines (DPHM)

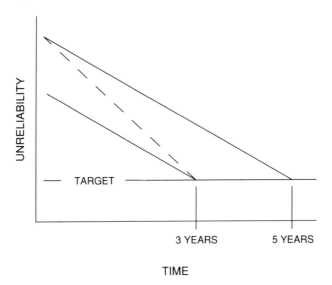

FIGURE 9.6. Example of growth to reach a product goal.

- UMC
- Feature/function content (software)
- Design change rate
- Software change rate
- Critical parameter certification
- Process certification
- Test volume
- Top customer quality metric (print quality for a printer, for example)

A total of about 30 key indicators (out of hundreds or thousands that could be identified) are managed for a fairly complex product. The team plots the planned values versus time. Then, during the checks, the team plots the actual data. The graphs are displayed on the walls of the product program "war room." Problems quickly become obvious, and the team takes corrective action. This is a great incentive to teamwork. When it becomes obvious that one subteam is having trouble, then others will come to help. They want the overall program to succeed, and they move vigorously to protect their bonus that is based on overall progress. Visible management by facts keeps everyone focused on the critical decisions.

Success requires that each type of output have a quality plan. Examples are:

- Design quality plan
- Manufacturing quality plan
- Software quality plan
- Testing quality plan

The management of each development program decides the exact structure of the set of quality plans. The important policy is that all those on the program be working in accordance with a quality plan. Otherwise, their activity can almost be guaranteed to be significantly lacking in quality. The quality plans focus on the key themes of this book—voice of the customer, robustness, concept selection, integration, multifunctional teams, and preventing mistakes—as well as on good partial design, including good engineering analysis.

A serious defect in most traditional plans is the phantom option. It has the appearance of prudent contingency planning, but is not actually available, as becomes painfully clear when attempts are made to implement it. An example of a phantom option is *evaluate cost/performance ratio; if not satisfactory, cycle back to concept selection.* Does this mean that we expect to do the concept selection badly the first time? Realistically, after a few additional months of work, we do not have any options that we did not have when we made the concept selection. Therefore, the cycle-back option is a phantom one. It primarily reflects a nervous lack of confidence on the part of the planners. Instead, we must do the work the best way we know how, and then forge ahead with the result. Otherwise, we will constantly miss the open market windows. When we do our best, the result is the best that we can achieve in the time frame. Phantom options will not change that for the better but simply present a confusing delusion of choice. The plan must focus the team on the realistic success factors.

It is critical to success to ramp up the staffing at the beginning with the right set of multifunctional product people. This is based on the strategies described in Chapter 8. A clear start is very important. This too often fell victim in the traditional process to a type of phantom option. Uncertainty about the corproate commitment to the embryonic product often kills it in the egg. The product should almost always be vigorously started in accordance with the product strategy. Of course, at the end of the concept phase, when only a small fraction of the total resources has been spent, the product should be carefully reviewed, and stopped if it is not a key element of the corporate strategy. However, this should rarely occur. If there is debilitating uncertainty surrounding the start of many product programs, it probably indicates that product development is not a key corporate competency. In such an environment the product people are discouraged, and good results cannot be expected.

The team prepares a good plan and shares it with everyone up and down the organization. There has been an unfortunate tendency to hold plans close to the vest. Then the team becomes confused about its activities, with a great loss of clarity. All should understand the plan and be committed to it. For this to be true, they must be involved in creating the plan. The plan is based on Chapters 4 through 7 of this book. The timing is determined by benchmarking that is relevant to the specific industry. Everyone must understand the rationale and be emotionally committed to the plan as a key success factor.

Do

Management's role in providing clarity in doing the work is accomplished through its leadership in the total quality development process, including the three major components: (1) basic concurrent engineering, (2) EQFD, and (3) quality engineering using robust design. Management gives strong emphasis to achieving a problem-prevention culture. The sociology of problem reaction is deeply ingrained. Management must ask about SN ratios at least as often as it asks about sunrise-meeting problem resolutions.

Also, management must follow a clear process, based on this chapter, and make it very visible and adhere to it. Keep in mind that management's role is not to do any development work, but to provide clarity so that the first two levels of the organization can concentrate on doing the right tasks in the right way.

All participants from the entry-level engineer to the product VP must understand that they are following the total quality development process and be clear that it is superior to traditional processes. If this consistency is lacking, confusion and chaos will result. Clear objectives and clear process provide the clarity that is needed for success. Managers must provide an environment where the best process flourishes.

Act

Having done the checks, it is very important to follow through with actions. There are four types of actions, as displayed in Figure 9.2:

(1) Feed-forward to fine-tune the plan for the current program
(2) Feedback to plan the next program
(3) Feedback to plan advanced development
(4) Feedback to improve the development process

Here we concentrate on the actions within the product program, the first type of action.

Although total quality development is very problem-prevention–oriented, some problems will still occur. The team must take prompt action. The actions can be beneficially divided into two groups:

(1) Issues—can be resolved by management decision
(2) Problems—cannot be resolved by management decision; require technical work

In both cases, it is important to assign responsibility and then track to ensure positive resolution. The approach emphasizes finding the root causes of the error and correcting them. Serious dysfunctions occur if there is wishful thinking that the error will disappear, or if the emphasis is on making the symptoms appear to disappear (temporarily).

Problems are managed in a problem management committee to ensure coordination and follow-through. The committee usually meets in sunrise meetings. As noted earlier, this develops a strong positive sociology. Although we do not want to become too enamored with sunrise meetings to the detriment of problem-prevention emphasis, they do provide strong attention to the errors that have been allowed to occur.

Managerial Focus for Clarity

Activities that are important to management become important to the organization. In addition to clearly focusing on the goals of the product program, management emphasizes the following:

- Total quality development (subject of this book)
- PDCA applied to product development
- Phase-gate criteria and style
- House of Quality
- Four phases of QFD
- Pugh concept selection
- Taguchi crucial eight (Figure 3.11)
- Critical parameter drawing
- Progressive freezing of decisions
- Management of key indicators

With these emphases, management helps to provide clarity. The other major element is teamwork.

UNITY

Managerial leadership plays a major role in helping to achieve unity, overcoming failures of cooperation (a major weakness cited in the book *Made in America*; Dertouzos et al., 1989)—cloistered groups of specialists looking inward within their own specialty, producing elegant solutions to questions that have become increasingly obsolete. TQM can help, as symbolized in Figure 9.7. More specifically, managers have opportunities with respect to organization, communications, and rewards.

Organization

Important organizational decisions are made at two levels:

(1) The multifunctional product development team (PDT)
(2) The higher-level executives

It is important for success to emphasize the principles of total quality development at both levels.

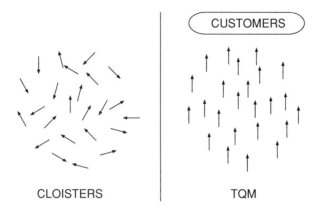

FIGURE 9.7. TQM as promoter of common goals.

Product Development Team

Concurrent engineering is best carried out when the multifunctional PDT is led by a strong manager (chief engineer) who is responsible for all aspects of product delivery, and all functions of the corporation participate. People who are doing significant work for the development program are part of the PDT while they are doing this work. There is a vast psychological difference between doing a task within a support group and doing it as part of the PDT. As part of the PDT, the contributor will (1) understand the specific requirements, (2) have the necessary close communications with other members of the PDT, and (3) be dedicated to the utilization of the task results to make design decisions. All three of these have a much lower probability of happening if the contributor remains within a support group.

To the fullest extent that is feasible, suppliers are made part of the PDT. This requires strategic alliances with suppliers, and having at most a few hundred suppliers, instead of the traditional several thousand. The entire performance of a supplier is taken into account; the business for the next order is not simply given to the lowest bidder on an over-the-wall request for quotation. There are long-term umbrella contracts for several years. As long as the supplier continues to improve, the orders keep flowing. The benefits are large for both parties.

It is important that the people from each function be able to (1) represent the knowledge of their function, and (2) gain the commitment of their function to the decisions that are made. Thus, the manufacturing people on the PDT must represent production operations. Dysfunctions will occur if the information is not provided or is wrong, or if the function subsequently disowns the decisions and wants major changes. For example, if production operations wants many major changes when the product enters into production, then the manufacturing people on the PDT have failed in one or both of these points.

Some people will stay with the PDT throughout the development program, while others will be on the team only during the phase that requires their expertise. The important criterion is that there should not be any sudden changes in the composition or size of the PDT, since that would both reduce teamwork and cause lack of continuity.

Collocation of all people on a PDT is a key success factor. Informal communications are essential to teamwork. If collocation is impossible, then much carefully planned travel is needed to overcome the handicap. Electronic media are as yet inadequate, because they do not provide the emotional interaction of directly working together. Investment in collocation has a high return.

These essential aspects of teamwork on a product development program have been described in more detail in Chapter 2, Basic Concurrent Engineering. Next we turn to a more global aspect of product-work organization.

Corporate Product Work

Multifunctional teams do total quality development. This leads to the consideration of an important organizational decision. There are three product activities within a manufacturing company, as displayed in Figure 9.8A. In the traditional organization, product development was an organization unto itself and process development and production operations were organized together and usually called "manufacturing."

This traditional organizational structure has two major problems. First, it tends to reinforce the serial approach to product development. Second, nearly all of the production emphasis is on production operations: shipping the product out the door. Often, the product design engineers are not even aware that the process development engineering organization exists somewhere deep within manufacturing.

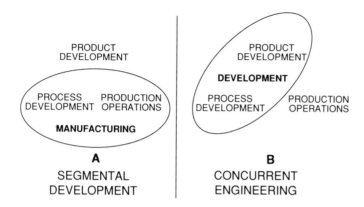

FIGURE 9.8. Major product organizations.

An improvement is shown in Figure 9.8B; process development is integrated with the product development organization. The result is two organizations: development, and production operations. This brings the process development people into a development organization in which their development of new processes is looked upon as a key element of developing new products. Their information is easily and directly integrated into the design activities.

As noted previously, the pilot production for the new product is done as part of the product development process under the direction of the chief engineer who manages the multifunctional PDT. Of course, during pilot production, the appropriate production operations people are temporarily assigned to the chief engineer's organization so that the required number of people and skills are available. This approach makes pilot production a key element of product development. It centralizes responsibility with the chief engineer for managing the completion of product development. The PDT eliminates all development problems before production operations takes responsibility.

It is critical to the organization of teamwork that no important development activity be left outside a team. Various interfaces, such as the interfaces between subsystems, are danger points. They can easily be outside any team, with reversion to the dysfunctional modes of negotiation and contracts. In the successful approach, we organize an interface team.

This can simply consist of one person from each of the interfacing teams, but it keeps this work within a team. The interface team then develops the functionality and design at the interface between the two subsystems. It should never be said that failure occurred because a needed activity fell between two teams.

Communications

Closely related to organization are the actual communications during product development. Organizations have tended to be very vertically oriented, with narrow trees (chimneys, or silos) of specialists. This has facilitated vertical communications and congruence of objectives, but the horizontal and diagonal ties have been weak.

During the 1980s, there was a trend in the United States to reduce the number of layers of management and broaden the span of control. Whereas in the past a manager typically had only a few direct reports, now each manager may supervise 10 to 20 managers (direct reports). This has been a good trend, but more is needed.

The objective is to facilitate all communications that are needed to carry out the product development activities. The activities may require a clear communication with a manager up one level and several branches away on the organizational chart. Traditional corporate cultures have strong biases against such communications, to the point where they often do not occur, or are awkward and ineffective.

To facilitate the communications that the product development activities require, a layered organization (communication pattern) is attractive. In a layered organization, our horizontal and diagonal communications are facilitated, not hindered by vertical biases. Also, each layer solves the entire problem, each at its level of abstraction. The chief engineer and the subsystem leaders span the entire product. Their decisions are complete at a high level of abstraction. Lower in the organization, the complete problems are solved at a more detailed level of abstraction. Within each layer there is more teamwork and interchangeability of players than in a typical tree-structured organization. Joel Moses' writings on ideology and organization (Moses, 1990) are recommended for thought provocation in this area (see also The Law According to Moses section of this chapter).

Rewards

Rewards emphasize the reinforcement of total quality development. They emphasize teamwork, and meeting the team's objectives. A key type of reward that has been too little used in engineering is the bonus. Much used in the remainder of corporate America, and even more so in Japan, the bonus is a powerful enticement to achieve two major enablers for success:

- Cultural change when implementing total quality development
- Team unity at the start of a new product program (or any other major activity)

Team bonuses are the reward for meeting objectives at the checkpoints as the product program progresses.

Bonuses, and all rewards, are based on results, not on process. Total quality development emphasizes excellent process as the way to meet objectives, not as an end in itself. The objectives are set very aggressively relative to competition. Realistic evaluation makes it obvious to everyone that the high expectations cannot be achieved by adhering to the old way. This promotes the full use of total quality development.

It might seem logical to reward people directly for using the process, but that runs the danger of creating "process groupies." Total quality development must be combined with a strong focus on the ultimate goals of the development program. Otherwise, great damage is done by the natural human tendency to focus on more local goals without adequately connecting them to the ultimate goal. The reward system plays a major role in overcoming this tendency and helping everyone to stay concentrated on goals that are meaningful to the corporation and its customers.

A promoter of unity is a high degree of egalitarianism in the reward system. The United States is not a leader, with a CEO/production-worker salary ratio of roughly 100 : 1, compared with 9 : 1 in Japan. The reward system for product development must reflect the fact that product development is a key corporate competency. Bonuses can help make the rewards for product people more egalitarian relative to the CEO and to other corporate activities.

QUESTIONS FOR MANAGEMENT TO FOCUS ON

To provide the new clarity and unity, managers will become adept at asking new questions that encourage the new way. Examples follow:

What is the robustness plan?
  What mules?
  What noises?
  What critical parameters?
  What training?
  Who is the adviser?
Are the technologies robust?
What is the SN ratio value? How much better is it than the competition's?
Where is the critical parameter drawing?
What is the reusability percentage?
What are the key competitive advantages revealed in the House of Quality?
Is the team small enough?
What percentage of the team is collocated?
Are the suppliers on the team?
Is the concept selection process as Pugh intended?
How is the voice of the customer deployed to the factory floor?
Has the design been progressively frozen in accordance with total quality development?
How can we better practice total quality development?

Managers are encouraged to tailor and enhance this list.

RESOURCES

Managers allocate corporate resources. The amount allocated to product development varies greatly from company to company, and especially from industry to industry. The resources assigned to a specific product development program should be appropriate, neither too large nor too small. Although this principle is obvious, it is often violated.

At the rich end of the spectrum, more resources can always be justified by a micro, bottom-up budgeting process. Everyone is sure that his or her task deserves more resources. However, the contribution of many of the cloistered tasks to the quality, cost, and delivery (QCD) of the new product is often nebulous. Too frequently, wrong questions are answered elegantly.

The lean end of the spectrum has been marvelously evoked by Tim Costello of General Motors: "Build it, and they will come." In the movie *Field of Dreams*, the hero hears voices whispering a similar sentiment from a cornfield, and builds a baseball diamond, and—sure enough—long-dead baseball stars appear to play. Some product development executives announce that the schedule has been cut in half and then wait for a similar miracle to occur: schedule it, and the sun will stand still.

The only certain guide is competitive benchmarking. If "they" are developing similar products in half the time with half the people, then it becomes difficult to justify our extra resources.

Despite the *Field of Dreams* evocation, there is merit in setting aggressive goals for reduced resources. Often, it jars people out of a rut, and creates greater receptivity to the implementation of the improvements of total quality development. Also, reduced teams tend to be more efficient than oversized teams. However, product development executives must couple aggressive goals with leadership of total quality development, not wait for *Field of Dreams* miracles.

It is very important to have the resources in place at the right time. In total quality development, there are critical activities at the beginning of each specific product program. The right number of product people with the right inventory of competencies must be there early.

IMPROVEMENT

The preceding descriptions of clarity, unity, and resources have covered the internal operations of total quality development. Managers must also lead in improvements, both the implementation of total quality development and continuous improvement. Implementation of total quality development allows the corporation to catch up, overcoming major problems, in the relatively short term, three to five years. Continuous improvement prevents falling behind again.

IMPLEMENTATION

Implementation of total quality development, or any other major improvement, is not easy; people naturally resist change. It will not just happen. Hard, conscientious work is required. All of the product people must share the conviction that the major change is necessary and will be successful. Two key enablers are usually required:

(1) Significant emotional event. For most American civilian companies, this has been the arrival of Japanese competition. For defense industries, it may be budget cuts (for example, those of the early 1990s).

(2) Top-level leadership. Without top-level leadership, the implementation will eventually go astray, displaced by the actual priorities of the executives.

Although top-level leadership is necessary, it is not sufficient. Success requires a thorough implementation process.

Four-Step Implementation Process

Successful implementation tends to follow a four-step process: (1) awareness, (2) education, (3) pilot projects, and (4) integration and institutionalization. It has been observed that this is very similar to the generic sales process: (1) awareness, (2) interest, (3) trial, and (4) purchase repeat. The implementation process is displayed in Figure 9.9.

There are many variants of this. The work on the total quality development process is sometimes concurrent with the pilot projects, and may start before the pilot projects. The generic improved process, as described in this book, must be brought into a corporation (or major division), tailored, and internalized.

Four-Quadrant Implementation Process

Another perspective on implementation comes from two familiar questions about the style of the implementation:

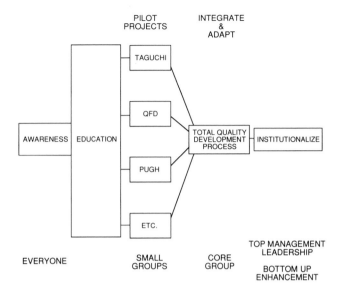

FIGURE 9.9. Implementation process for total quality development.

- Top down, or bottom up?
- Focus on content, or organizational development?

The questions are diagramed as a four-quadrant plot in Figure 9.10. The four emphases can be further characterized by examples:

Content focus—favored by engineers
Top down—Deming's lecture to executives
Organizational focus—Rosabeth Kantor's writings
Bottom up—quality circles

Experience with the four quadrants indicates that, if adhered to statically, none of them will bring success. The following observed problems are displayed in Figure 9.11:

(1) Isolated excellence. A core group of gatekeepers learns it; the rest of the organization remains outside and suspicious, not very willing to listen. Without top management leadership, organizational learning does not occur.

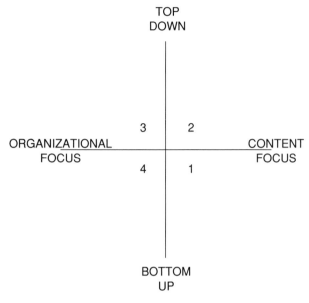

FIGURE 9.10. Four quadrants of implementation.

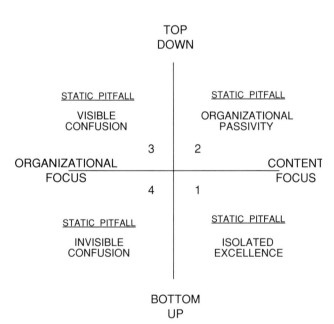

FIGURE 9.11. Pitfalls of static implementation styles.

(2) Organizational passivity. The vice president of design and production issues a memo: "Reduce supplier base by 80%." Nothing is likely to happen, because most of the people do not understand the intent, rationale, and required processes.

(3) Visible confusion. The top-down approach to organizational development can lead to great excitement, an enthusiastic desire to get on with the project. The CEO says, "Let's all do Deming." Lower in the organization, people are energized, but no one knows how to translate Deming's philosophy into action, and confusion ensues, which is very visible because it was initiated by the CEO. Content is missing.

(4) Invisible confusion. The people are energized by 29 interlocking committees and problem-solving activities. They become very eager to do *it*, but have no idea what it is—no content focus. (This approach works on very local issues where the local group is the expert on the content.) An attempt to rely solely on this employee-involvement approach will fail in the absence of the major new principles. Study and hard work will be required.

Successful Path for Implementation

We must avoid the four pitfalls. We can do so by not remaining statically in any one quadrant. Success requires a dynamic path through the four quadrants, as indicated in Figure 9.12.

Core Group

It appears from experience that the successful path is to start in the lower right quadrant with a core group (Figure 9.13). This can be initiated by top management, but is usually led by middle management. The core group learns, brings in, and tailors total quality development to the organization. Pilot projects are conducted, which start organizational learning on key elements, such as House of Quality and robustness optimization. The first three steps of Figure 9.9 are primarily in this phase.

Upper Management Learning

After the core group activities to tailor total quality development to the organization and the pilot projects have generated enough confidence,

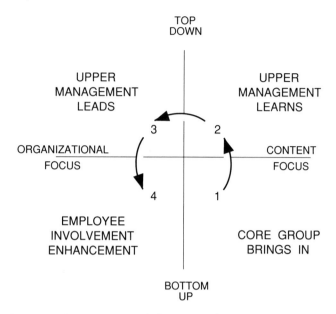

FIGURE 9.12. Dynamic path for successful implementation.

we move to the upper right quadrant (Figure 9.14). The core group helps upper management to learn and to develop an implementation plan that addresses organizational development. The hope that style 1 will be sufficient, and that the new way will spread widely by emulation alone, is doomed to failure. Top management must prepare for leadership.

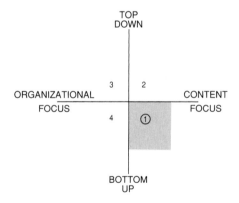

FIGURE 9.13. Core group bringing in total quality development.

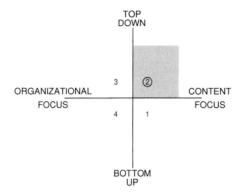

FIGURE 9.14 Upper management learning.

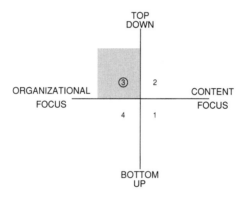

FIGURE 9.15. Upper management leadership.

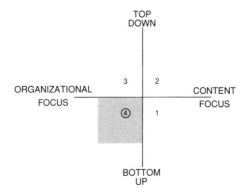

FIGURE 9.16. Employee involvement.

Upper Management Leadership

Next, we move to the upper left quadrant, organizational development, led by top management with clear understanding of the principles of the content (Figure 9.15). The implementation plan is put into effect with leadership from top management. Total quality development is now applied to major product development programs. Implementation is visibly one of the top three priorities of top management.

Employee Involvement

Next, the implementation process moves to the lower left quadrant (Figure 9.16). Now implementation is deployed with the energizing benefits of organizational development and employee involvement, and the clear content is further tailored to the context of the local work situation. Guided by the powerful basic principles of total quality development, each team adapts and enhances the details in the context of their work content.

Phases 2 through 4 comprise the fourth step (institutionalization) of Figure 9.9.

Leadership and Implementation Plan

Top management leadership is crucial. Attention must be focused on total quality development, the implementation plan for its introduction, and starting to manage as described in the first part of this chapter. The new way is organizationally very fragile until major successes have been completed. During this important interval, top management leadership is critical to overcome uncertainty and achieve the initial successes.

Implementation Plan. By the time the third quadrant is reached, we need to have prepared an implementation plan. This addresses in detail:

- Spreading of awareness and education to the entire organization
- Detailed description, tailoring, and internalization of total quality development, including phase-gate criteria
- Promotion of total quality development

- Operational training
- Arrangements with external consultants
- Development of internal advisers
- Development of users' groups
- Pilot projects
- Transition plan to achieve a feasible path from the old way to the new way, usually through triage of all product development programs:

  (a) Full implementation
  (b) Partial implementation
  (c) No implementation

Fine tuning and enhancement may require another loop around the four quadrants. Top management leadership of the organizational breakout is critical for success. The implementation plan must have a very high priority and be strongly integrated into the operating plan for the corporation (or division). Order-of-magnitude estimates of the value of implementing total quality development help to give perspective on realistic spending to ensure rapid and solid implementation. The value ranges from staying in business (long range) to major improvements in profit (3 to 5 years). Money does need to be invested for the future. *Made in America* (Dertouzos et al., 1989) reported that one of the six weaknesses that plague American manufacturing industries is short time horizons. Implementation will probably fail if it is funded by skimming a little contingency money out of the current operating plan. For implementation to succeed it must have a very high priority and be funded accordingly. The funds that are required are not large, but they must be budgeted in the operating plan. Money talks.

Training.   During the activities in quadrants 3 and 4, much training is required. The successful approach has two elements:

(1) Just-in-time training
(2) Learn, use, teach, inspect (LUTI)

The training is most effective in small bites, just when the team is ready to implement the new learning. The House of Quality training, for example, is one and a half days just before the team is ready to start building its House of Quality. The training includes actual practice in preparing a House of Quality for something simple, such as a rechargeable flashlight. Widely dispersed training programs are a waste of resources. The material will be forgotten before there is opportunity to practice it. Just-in-time training of teams is the winning way.

Management teaches the more integrative topics, starting at the top of the organization. This includes for, example, ratios, but not orthogonal arrays. The entire organization will come to share the new metric of functionality, the SN ratio. Orthogonal arrays are operational, and practicing familiarity with them is emphasized for the levels of the organization that perform the unit design tasks. The integrative topics, such as SN ratio, are disseminated throughout the organization via LUTI. First, the top management learns the content from the core team. Next, the top managers use it in some small, appropriate project. Then they teach it to their direct reports, and then inspect the first use by their direct reports. This training structure has many advantages, which are obvious upon reflection.

The dynamic path through the four quadrants is a road map that avoids the static pitfalls. It provides the opportunity for success. To achieve success, constancy of purpose is required.

CONTINUOUS IMPROVEMENT

After catching up, it is critical to have continuous improvement to avoid again falling behind. This is done primarily by TQM, the learning organization, and competitive benchmarking. The TQM literature is full of descriptions of the quality improvement process (QIP). The learning organization, as written about by Argyris (1991 and 1993) and by Senge (1990), for example, is important to continuous improvement. Competitive benchmarking is critically important. Our organization is a small fraction of one percent of the world's industrial activity. It is obvious that most improvements will occur elsewhere. We need to quickly find them and bring them into our organization.

TOTAL QUALITY MANAGEMENT

Total quality development can be thought of as two in-depth elements of total quality management (TQM) combined with technology readiness and basic concurrent engineering, as portrayed in Figure 9.17. Basic TQM consists of Deming's 14 points, the seven QC tools, the seven management tools, *hoshin kanri*, employee involvement, and other principles.

If the TQM movement is already strong within a company, then there may be merit in incorporating total quality development into TQM: the more developed institutionalization of TQM may speed the implementation of total quality development. Although it would seem too conservative to wait for TQM before implementing total quality development, it appears plausible that the culture change that accompanies TQM will facilitate the adoption of total quality development. Cultural change must occur for the adoption of total quality development to be successful.

CULTURAL CHANGE

Total quality development as described in this book may seem easy to learn and apply. In terms of cognitive learning, this is certainly true. The principles that are outlined here are not difficult to comprehend. After the principles are learned, the four-phase implementation process

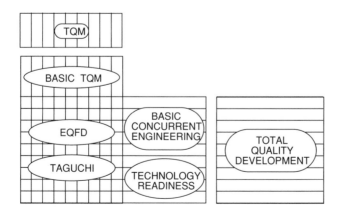

FIGURE 9.17. Total quality development in relation to TQM.

that is outlined in Figures 9.13 through 9.16 will start the practice of total quality development. However, the implementation of total quality development involves major change in the culture of the workplace. Culture does not change readily. David Kearns, then the CEO of Xerox, reflected on the tough changes that turned Xerox around (Alster, 1987):

> To make the changes that are required has been much tougher than I would have guessed. It's not just that the competition continues to improve and that your standards keep going up because I think that we understand that very well. But taking a large organization and then having to change measurement systems and change attitudes . . . The up-front investment and the training required to get people to change is huge.

Unless we recognize the need to effectively foster cultural change, our improvement efforts are apt to lead to disappointment.

Traditional Product-Development Attitudes

One perspective on the change in attitude and values is that total quality development emphasizes process, empowerment, problem prevention, and overcoming the 10 cash drains. The following typical quotations reveal the magnitude of the cultural change in switching from traditional product development to total quality development. The quotations are organized into 13 groups, the first three indicative of resistance to process, empowerment, and problem prevention, and the remaining 10 indicative of the ingrained nature of the 10 cash drains. These quotations evoke the mood of cultural resistance. Then the subject is presented in a more developed discourse.

Process
"We don't need a process; we'll figure it out as we go along."
"A defined process inhibits creativity."
"They've never been here and tried to make this process work."
"I'll do it because you told me to, but I know that it won't work."

Empowerment
"That drive train team actually wanted to choose a gear without my approval!"

"Of course, I couldn't give the budget to the team; who knows what they would do?"

"Just tell me what to do, and I'll do it."

"We know that we have the budget, but do you think that we should buy this oscilloscope?"

"Here, let me show you how to do that; I use to be the world's best electromechanical design engineer. Did I ever tell you about...?"

Problem Prevention

"We can't anticipate all of the problems, so let's forge ahead and solve them when they occur."

"Problem prevention? Sorry, I've got to get to the sunrise meeting!"

"If it ain't broke, don't fix it."

"Those guys with the magic hands will make it work."

Cash Drain 1—Technology Push, but Where's the Pull?

"The customers don't understand our exciting technology."

Cash Drain 2—Disregard for Voice of the Customer

"The customers don't know what they want."

"We rarely get any complaints."

"Our salespeople talk to customers."

"Customers are number 1 with us."

"Our engineers don't need to know about customers; we'll explain it to them."

"We use focus teams and prepare a really good report for our engineers."

Cash Drain 3—The Eureka Concept

"Once we get a good idea, we run with it."

Cash Drain 4—Pretend Design

"Of course, we wouldn't do it this way in production, but we'll fix that up later."

"We want to be creative, so we ignore the competition."

Cash Drain 5—Pampered Products (Lack of Robustness)

"Robustness?"

"Oh yeah, the guy down the hall is interested in that."

"We're already doing designed experiments."

"As long as the customers use our products in reasonable conditions, we have no trouble."

"If the factory just held tighter tolerances, everything would be fine."

Cash Drain 6—Hardware Swamps

"We build lots of prototypes so that we can react to all of the problems."

"We have a really slick way of doing build-test-fix."

Cash Drain 7—Here's the Product. Where's the Factory?

"Poke those guys in manufacturing and they'll start gobbling."

"Those guys in design don't understand the real world."

"I designed the product; production is their job."

Cash Drain 8—We've Always Made It This Way

"Our products already have very few factory defects."

Cash Drain 9—Inspection

"We have the world's best inspectors."

"We ship zero defects."

Cash Drain 10—Give Me My Targets, Let Me Do My Thing (Lack of Teamwork)

"Those guys in design just can't understand this new technology."

"Those bean counters cause incredible problems."

"Get those managers out of the way, and I'll show how it should be done."

"Those first-level engineers just never see the big picture."

"Those product people just don't understand about marketing and finance."

"I'm the most creative guy here; why would I want a team?"

"I don't know about software; you take care of it."

Summary of Traditional Product-Development Attitudes

The previous 13 categories contain many deeply held attitudes that must be changed if a corporation is to be successful by practicing total quality development. Learning the new way is fairly simple. Unlearning the old way takes time and may require significant intervention if it is to happen at all.

The successful practice of product development requires that we overcome the 10 cash drains. The emphases on process, empowerment, and problem prevention are the broad elements to overcome the 10 cash drains. Why are there deeply held attitudes that tend to perpetuate the 10 cash drains, and to cause managers to resist the emphasis on process, empowerment, and problem prevention? The answer may require an entire book, but some suggestions are:

- Individualism.
- Creativity is considered to be an overwhelming value.
- Taylorism is deeply rooted in the United States.
- Problem solving (rather than problem prevention) is prized.
- Learning that challenges assumptions is weak (Argyris, 1991).

The foregoing apply in the United States, and to a considerable extent in much of western Europe. In the United States these tendencies were aggravated by the easy economic success after World War II. When I started working in industry in 1952, the widespread use of relatively poor practices surprised me. However, the financial success was great, so it seemed that good practices were not that important. Old attitudes die slowly. Change to a more successful culture does not happen naturally. Strong, planned interventions lead to a culture that enables successful product development.

Cultural Barriers to the Improvement of Product Development

The previous section described the cultural changes within a company that are involved in the practice of total quality development. In addition, there are four types of cultural resistance to change itself, regardless of the specific details of the change, including the beliefs that:

(1) Product development is not important.
(2) Improvement is not needed.
(3) Of course we're for improvement!
(4) I'm out in front on this.

The last of these emphasizes public relations, rather than the needed level of substantive improvement.

A description of the four cultural resistances to the improvement of product development follows. Each description includes attitudes and analysis.

Product Development Is Not Important

Attitudes. "If we don't succeed in manufactured products, we can always go into the financial business."

"We'll never be as good as the Japanese (Germans/Americans)."

"We market managers do the real product design; the engineers just get the nuts and bolts right (sometimes)."

"Those product guys just don't understand the commercial aspects."

"We don't have to be good at products, we have such a great sales and service organization."

"We can always buy our products from Japan."

Analysis. If product development is considered to be of relatively little importance, then obviously there will be neither much energy nor constancy of purpose for its improvement. As was noted earlier in this chapter, product development is a core corporate competency in successful manufacturing companies. In many companies, however, there are typically some problems in achieving the degree of nurturing that will foster the needed improvements.

Even in companies that depend on product development, its low level in the organization often gives it a relatively low priority, so that major improvement is difficult. In American industry, few product development people have become CEOs. The decentralized corporate organization that has become favored usually keeps product people several levels from the top. Typically, there is the CEO, then group general managers, and then division general managers. Finally, the divisions may have product development executives. Even here, many divisions of famous manufacturing companies sell only services, or products that are purchased from other companies. Even if a division product development executive takes strong leadership for improvement, there are significant potential problems. The division general manager, group general manager, or CEO is likely to emphasize other initiatives and priorities. The thrust to improve product development is likely to be overwhelmed by other thrusts that seem more relevant to executives who have no experience in product development.

An example of a disruptive thrust from top management is reorganization. Even where effective product development leadership for improvement exists, time is of the essence. Otherwise, corporate reorganization will disrupt the major improvement effort. The time constant for improvement in the United States is longer than the time constant for major reorganization. Unless the improvement has taken hold at very high levels, the reorganization is almost guaranteed to be highly disruptive to the improvement activity. Therefore, it is important to have the CEO (at least the divisional general manager) involved sufficiently to make the improvement activity robust against the noise of corporate reorganization.

Often an attempt to improve product development will be inundated by other improvement activities that are broader in scope, and thus are appealing to high-level executives. One example is the current interest in reengineering the corporation. This is process improvement, usually rooted in activities such as order processing that are relatively simple compared with product development. Such improvement is good in itself. However, its apparent breadth of scope and relative simplicity can easily dominate the top executives' interest in improvement and drive out the more complex activity of improving product development. The best solution to this problem is to recognize that the implementation of total quality development is reengineering of product development. Thus, the implementation of total quality development can become part of the group thrust for reengineering, rather than be driven out by it.

If the top executives of the corporation explicitly believe that product development is not very important, then its improvement is unlikely to succeed. If it is only implicitly held to be unimportant, by being relatively low in the organization, then success requires that the top executives become involved in the thrust to improve product development. Otherwise it will be displaced by other priorities. Even if improvement is successful in one division, there is little natural tendency for it to become diffused into other divisions. One way to involve the top executives is to make the implementation of total quality development an element of a higher-level improvement activity, such as the reengineering that was mentioned in the previous paragraph.

The attempt to integrate product development improvement into the priorities of the group general manager is often up against great odds because of cultural barriers. In the simplest form of these cultural barriers, the executive thinks that product development people are not interested in improvement, and the product development people complain that the executive is not interested in product development. If neither of these attributions is tested, then they provide a certain roadblock.

Let us focus on the latter attribution. The product development people complain about their disempowerment: the executive just does not care enough about product development and is bound to disrupt the improvement effort with some competing priority. This expression degenerates into endless ineffectual negative commentary, not even conceptually related to any potential action. This provides sufficient catharsis to dissipate the energy for improvement. The situation seems to achieve static equilibrium, able to go on and on while the fortunes of the corporation deteriorate.

The blockage to improvement that is formed by untested attributions is effectively addressed in the work of Chris Argyris, which will be described in a subsequent section (Teachings of Chris Argyris) of this chapter. Untested attributions seal each group comfortably within its own environment. Therefore, the dysfunctional equilibrium tends to be perpetuated. We will return to this in the section on the work of Chris Argyris.

The untested attributions that are the foundation for the ineffective equilibrium are reinforced by many well-established managerial metaphors. These are recognized by everyone as *the said thing* in the organization. They make it difficult to get to the root of the problem and overcome it. These organizational defenses are aggravated by the tendency of product development people to *defer* to higher-level general managers.

At some time during the implementation of total quality development, the product people have to overcome their tendency toward excessive deference, masked behind commentary about disempowerment, and engage the top executives. This may start at the transition from phase 1 to phase 2 (Figure 9.14) of the implementation process, but certainly they must have the top executives' involvement before entering phase 3 (Figure 9.15). This is usually difficult within the culture. However, if it is not done, then product development is de facto not important enough for effective improvement to succeed. Atypical cultural intervention is needed to achieve sufficient leadership for the improvement to move forward.

Improvement Is Not Needed

Attitudes.   "Our congressman and senators have promised to protect our jobs; there's no need to take risks."

"It worked there, but it won't work here; we're different."

"We don't call it that, but we're doing the same thing."

"We tried it ten years ago; it didn't work."

"We're OK. This worked just fine in the 50s."

"My peers aren't doing it, so I can get promoted without it."

"Let's measure 29 metrics [all almost impossible to measure], and then decide if it's any good or not."

"I got to where I am by doing it the old way; why change?"

"We're already doing TQM; this would be too much."

Analysis.   Even in organizations that hold product development to be important, improvement is often thwarted by the cultural bias that it is not needed. This is observed to persist in the face of considerable evidence to the contrary. Therefore, it appears to be strongly supported by fear of change. As noted earlier, the practice of total quality development does involve major changes in attitudes. To take one example, managers are now expected to be good listeners and to support empowered teams. To an authoritarian manager whose self-perceived strength is espousing a brilliant strategy, this change can seem quite threatening. Multiply the threat by all of the changes, and the desire to advocate sticking with the good old corporate traditions is all too natural. The fear of change has to be addressed effectively. Simply bringing the fear out into the open, where it can be subjected to rational analysis of the need for improvement, may be very beneficial. The fear of change must be confronted.

The ability of everyone to rationalize should not be underestimated. The author once had the opportunity to witness a half-day simulation of product development that was enacted by 50 experienced product people as a training activity. There was a startling display of clear dysfunctions. Yet, afterward, the participants rationalized them away and declared success. We protect our cherished behavior by rationalizing away any data that reveal our ineffectiveness. Therefore, the approach to cultural change cannot be solely a cognitive one.

Everyone needs encouragement to focus on competitiveness in the international economy, and help to overcome his or her fears of the new way. An outstanding example was the leadership Frank Pipp provided in implementing basic concurrent engineering at the Xerox Corporation in 1981 and 1982. Pipp tremendously opened communications and patiently listened to the many lamentations, which essentially said that change is tough and frightening, so let us limit it. (Of course, no one actually said that change is tough and frightening. We all resorted to managerial metaphors, such as "let's not throw out the baby with the bathwater" and "we don't want things to get out of hand." Such bypassing metaphors would have filled a notebook that would have made any ethnologist happy.) In the face of this, Frank Pipp maintained amazing patience and constancy of purpose. He puffed on his pipe, tapped his fingers on the table, and said, "All that you say may be true, but we must make these changes in order to survive."

After a year everyone was saying the same thing. Initially, most people waited for the new thrust to pass. The group had just gone through a three-year effort at improvement, called somewhat ironically in retrospect The New Culture. It had eventually disappeared in a cloud of fancy footwork and attention diverted to the crisis of the day. When Frank Pipp took charge and started implementing basic concurrent engineering, most people assumed that it would go the way of The New Culture. Pipp's constancy of purpose eventually persuaded nearly everyone that this thrust was different. It did not ignore the bad news. Instead it focused on major problems to motivate improvement.

Also, Pipp took a dim view of fancy footwork, a term that is used by Chris Argyris (1990) to describe our behavior of striving to shift blame to others and credit to ourselves. Often we become so skilled at this that we do not realize that we are doing it. I still have a vivid memory of a senior executive demonstrating his best fancy footwork in front of a meeting of a large group. Frank Pipp immediately drew attention to the fancy footwork in a way that made it clear that it was no longer the norm. The realization that basic concurrent engineering was here to stay and that fancy footwork would not glean its previous rewards was a key element that enabled the culture to change. Of course, it greatly helped that basic concurrent engineering was seen to work.

Perhaps the Frank Pipp model was too unique to him to be generally applicable. However, it is true that strong leadership for change is essential. For bad things to happen, it is only necessary that good people do nothing. Leadership can come from all levels of the organization. At the end of the Design Productivity International Conference (Honolulu, February 1991), there was a discussion about implementation, with much wailing and lamenting about powerlessness. Finally, Mr. Tsuchiya, a high-level executive of the Fuji Xerox Corporation, gave an impromptu, highly dynamic speech. He started by asking how many of the audience members were managers. About two-thirds put up their hands. Go back and do something, Mr. Tsuchiya challenged them. All need to provide as much leadership as they can. If the product development people who recognize that improvement is essential attribute ineffective attitudes to higher management, and if they use the attributions as a basis for doing nothing, then the implementation of improvement becomes very difficult.

It is absolutely true that at some point the top product executives must exert leadership, or total quality development will fall by the wayside. They start in the second implementation quadrant (Figure 9.14), or earlier, by learning the process, with obvious emphasis on the aspects that are essential to product executives. They lead in the preparation of the comprehensive implementation plan, and its incorporation into the budgeting process. Then they lead in the execution of the implementation plan. After an appropriate success, the executives start softly giving voice to the clarity that "this is the way we do it here at the Y corporation [division]."

As emphasized elsewhere in this book, especially Chapter 2, a major problem in the United States, perhaps the root problem, is cloistered groups of technical specialists, looking inward within their specialty, producing elegant solutions to questions that have become increasingly obsolete.

This is a mountainous hurdle to cultural change. The "cloisters" can point with pride to the elegance of their solutions. "We don't need to improve. Our solutions are elegant." Because the cloistered culture already emphasizes excellence, it is difficult for it to learn improvements. They need help to understand that too often they address the wrong questions. Also, even when there is potentially useful output, the effective application to actual business problems is the exception.

There are four activities that help to focus cloistered specialists on better questions, and the effective use of results:

- Teams. When specialists become members of teams that extend beyond their cloister, their performance ofter becomes beneficially integrated.
- TQM. Specialists tend to resist the implementation of TQM. However, there is one bit that everyone finds tempting. TQM contains a quality improvement process, which usually starts out as follows:
  - What is my output?
  - Who are my (internal) customers?
  - What are my customers' requirements?
  These three questions have been effective eye-openers in the past.
- Broader perspective. Reading books such as *Made in America* (Dertouzos et al., 1989) eventually help some to the self-realization "If I'm so good, why are we in so much trouble?"
- Focus on action. Chris Argyris (1993) has said it well: "Learning should be in the service of action, not simply discovery or insight."

Overcoming dysfunctional specialization is a major challenge.

Cloistered groups of specialists, often referred to as *functional silos*, generate an us/them attitude. A similar problem is the relation between top management and the functions. The promotion of managers broadens their intended scope far beyond their original specialty. Too often, however, the executives abdicate their responsibility. Their actual role with respect to unfamiliar functions becomes merely bureaucratic, with little value added. This readily leads to an us/them attitude between the executives and the unfamiliar functions. An example is the attitudes mentioned earlier between the top executives and product development. This easily degenerates into a self-sealing us/them relationship, reinforced by untested attributions. As managers are promoted to the executive ranks, they have to become effectively broadened, not merely broadened on the organization chart.

Some may think that this problem of cultural blinders is primarily a problem among technical people. It is certainly rampant there, but it also occurs among executives and nontechnical people. It has become almost fashionable to observe that American business schools have been teaching the wrong stuff, or at least not exactly the right stuff. The problem of cloistered groups reinforcing their dysfunctional culture is epidemic in the United States. Everyone needs help in focusing on the broader economic goals of the division, the corporation, the country, the continent, and the world.

Of Course We're for Improvement!

Attitudes. "All we have to do is find the best practices in our company."

"Of course! We're already doing Design For X!"

"Total quality development? We're going to do that next week."

"Total quality development? It's on our list of 82 things to implement."

"We'll introduce the House of Quality on the mini project. It will spread from there."

Analysis. Even in organizations that acknowledge the need for improvement of product development, there is usually trouble based on the assumption that it can be implemented quickly and straightforwardly. This has two main sources: (1) only a small segment of total quality development is considered, and (2) the cultural barriers are ignored. Since readers of this book will want to implement all of total quality development, we will concentrate on the second problem.

Usually the need for an implementation plan is overlooked. There is a hope that successful application on one project will lead to spontaneous diffusion. All of the evidence is to the contrary. An accompanying hope is that top management involvement will not be needed. Experience has taught that phase 3 (Figure 9.15) requires an implementation plan that is led by top management. The fundamental aberration is the expectation that management as usual will bring about an unusual change in culture. The implementation of total quality development requires strong management attention. It certainly must be one of the top-three priorities of the product development executive. It probably also needs to be on the top-three list of the higher-level executives.

I'm Out in Front on This

Attitudes. "I just love to practice total quality development."
"We want to show you how well we are doing."

Analysis. One path that limits the cultural change is to talk the new language while adopting a stance of being out in front. However, the design of the interactions with the core team who have brought in total quality development strives to create a positive impression, rather than to facilitate learning. A clear indicator is meetings with presentations of accomplishments in which no questions are asked and no help is solicited from the people who are most knowledgeable about the new way.

Usually, these meetings are marked by the giving of approval and praise. This bypasses the ineffective design of the interaction. In this situation, the core team, outside consultants, and others who are the key source people for the new way need to engage in cultural intervention. Instead of bypassing, the essential requirement is design that makes the meetings effective instruments for change. However, people who are expert at product development are rarely if ever skilled at this type of cultural intervention. Instead, they are more likely to bypass the bypass. Strong starts thus all too easily end in only limited improvement.

Case Study: Implementation of Improved Product Development

Jack, the consultant on total quality development, entered the lobby of the famous XYZ company full of hope. He was there in response to the invitation of Wayne, the head of product development for the X division. Wayne had heard Jack talk at a business seminar and had been impressed. In a long telephone conversation, Jack received the clear message from Wayne that new products were very important to X division, and that the division recognized that its position was eroding and it needed to make improvements. Jack thought, "This promises to be better than many companies I have visited, who only wanted to be entertained for a day so that they learn the latest buzzwords. Others are like the executives who call Dr. Deming and say, 'Come spend a day with us and save us the way you saved the Japanese.'"

Jack's expectations were fulfilled. He had a great day with Wayne and his staff. Jack gave a two-hour overview of total quality development and was briefed on the status of X division and its recent efforts to learn from past mistakes. He met several key people who were clearly very interested in making major improvements. During the next several weeks there were more telephone conversations, and a consulting arrangement was completed. During the next six months, Jack visited X division a total of 13 days. Everything went very well. A core team was formed, and Jack worked with it to define total quality development in the context of X division. At the end of six months, there was a clear document, *The X Way to New Products*. There had been many presentations on the varied aspects of total quality development, and change was in the air.

As Jack reflected, he was optimistic. However, there were some concerns. Although Wayne was very supportive, Jack had never met the X division general manager, or any higher management. Jack remembered the six months that he had spent at the W division of the UVW company. That too had gone very well. Then the group general manager launched a major reorganization that completely blew away the product development improvement activity. There had been similar problems at other companies. Top management priorities had overwhelmed the initiative to improve product development. Jack thought that perhaps he should talk with the division and group general managers to whom Wayne reported. However, Jack did not feel confident that he could be effective with the general managers, neither of whom had a background in product development. Wayne seemed to have things under control. In this case Jack was right (or lucky). The organization remained stable, and other top management priorities did not cause excessive diversion.

During the next visit, Jack had a long talk with Wayne, who was very positive about the progress. Wayne had plenty of praise for Jack, the core team, and—by implication—himself. Then Jack brought up the next step, the preparation of an implementation plan. Wayne became pensive. "Implementation plan? What would that include?" Jack listed the major elements. Wayne replied, "OK. Since you think it is important, I will have Jane, our planner, prepare a document. However, I think that we can get the ball rolling by starting a few small projects. When it works well there, it will naturally spread."

Jack was worried. He knew from experience that an implementation plan was essential. The nucleation and growth approach could not overcome organizational cultural biases against change. Many decisions had to be made. Activities such as training had to be budgeted and arranged. However, Wayne had the ball, and Jack hoped that everything would work out for the best.

During his next several visits, Jack spent much time with two projects that Wayne had identified as leading the way. They were led by the two most promising young project leaders in Wayne's organization. Jack's first meeting with Jim and his staff was for a half day. They were very cordial. Their talk was filled with the language, especially buzzwords and phrases, from *The X Way to New Products*. At first, Jack was pleasantly surprised by their affably progressive attitude. It was really good that Wayne's fast-trackers were getting with the new way so well. However, their somewhat self-congratulatory presentations described minor achievements. To Jack's surprise, he was not asked any questions. However, Jim and his colleagues were so pleasant in their reception of the new way that it seemed ungracious to make an issue of the ineffective productivity of the interaction.

A year and a half after Jack started working with X division, Wayne said that they could go ahead on their own now. Wayne thanked Jack for the great success that Jack had helped him achieve. Now, for the first time, Jack raised the issue that the designs of the interactions with the projects were ineffective. Having recently read some of the writings of Chris Argyris, Jack said that much bypassing had been occurring, and that he had been bypassing the bypass. He did not think that the X division was in a position to capture the great start that had been made with the creation of *The X Way to New Products*. However, Wayne said that Jim always did a great job. Wayne was confident that the product development people of X division could take pride in their great accomplishment.

Two years later, Jack gave a talk at a symposium in the same city as X division. He called Wayne and arranged to spend a day there. Wayne painted a glowing picture of the status of X division. In discussions with some of the core team members, Jack found widespread good practice of some elements of total quality development, while there was little use of others. Older and wiser, they reflected on the cultural barriers that they had not anticipated.

The reader is encouraged to make the connections between this composite case study and the four cultural resistances to improvement of product development that were described in the previous section. The first explicit problem was the lack of an implementation plan. At this time it was clear that Wayne and Jack did not have the same viewpoint, but this was not brought into the open and discussed. This is called *bypassing* by Chris Argyris, and to help us better cope with the difficulties of cultural change, we next turn to his teachings.

Teachings of Chris Argyris

In his many writings, the Harvard professor Chris Argyris has shown great insight into the problems of cultural change (Argyris, 1990 and 1991). He has developed the concept of skilled incompetence, which is very deft actions by individuals and organizations that lead to poor judgments and actions. Many corporate people are "skilled at permitting themselves to be disempowered." This is similar to the sentiment expressed at the Honolulu conference that was mentioned earlier. The managers were too eager to lament their powerlessness. Mr. Tsuchiya urged them to use the power that they do have.

Professor Argyris brings into the light the many self-delusions that make cultural change difficult. We engage in defense mechanisms that make it difficult to get at the real issues. Then we camouflage this behavior with a patina of civility that creates further difficulty in dealing with real issues. Argyris has formed two models of behavior (see Table 9.3, which is adapted from Argyris, 1990).

My experience in industry leads me to believe that the insights of Professor Argyris are powerful and that much help can be obtained from his precepts. The following quotation from Argyris (1990) reveals the meaning of skilled incompetence:

> Most individuals learn Model I theory-in-use early in life. When implemented effectively to deal with issues that are upsetting, embarrassing, or threatening, the result is defensiveness on the part of the players. This defensiveness leads to misunderstandings, distortions, and self-fulfilling and self-sealing processes. These are errors in the sense that human beings do not intend or prefer them.
>
> But the errors are not caused by lack of knowledge or by ignorance. These errors are caused by the skillful implementation of Model I. If incompetence is producing consequences that are counterproductive to our intentions, then the incompetence is skilled.
>
> If the incompetence is due to skillful actions, then we have a clue about why human beings are often unaware when they are acting counterproductively. The incompetence is caused by the very fact that the behavior is skilled. Whenever we are skillful at something, we act automatically and spontaneously. We take our actions for granted. We do not pay much attention to our actions because we produce them in milliseconds. Thus, the price of acting skillfully is unawareness. We could lose our skill if we were required to pay attention to our actions....
>
> Model I theory-in-use is designed to produce defensive consequences and therefore requires defensive reasoning. Model I is also designed to keep individuals unaware of their counterproductive actions, thereby reinforcing Model I and the social virtues that we are taught early in life.
>
> Organizations populated by human beings using Model I will necessarily be full of defenses that become routine because Model I is a defense-producing theory of action. Let us turn to examining the organizational defenses and see how they become part of the routines of the organization....

TABLE 9.3 (From Chris Argyris, *Overcoming Organizational Defenses*. Copyright © 1990 by Allyn and Bacon. Reprinted by permission.)

Model I Social Virtues	Model II Social Virtues
Help and Support	
Give approval and praise to others. Tell others what you believe will make them feel good about themselves. Reduce their feelings of hurt by telling them how much you care, and if possible, agree with them that their challengers acted improperly.	Increase the others' capacity to confront their own ideas, to create a window into their own minds, and to face their unsurfaced assumptions, biases, and fears by acting in these ways toward other people.
Respect for Others	
Defer to other people and do not confront their reasoning or actions.	Attribute to other people a high capacity for engaging in self-reflection and self-examination without becoming so upset that they lose their effectiveness and their sense of self-responsibility and choice. Keep testing this attribution opening.
Strength	
Advocate your position in order to win. Hold your own position in the face of advocacy. Feeling vulnerable is a sign of weakness.	Advocate your position and combine it with inquiry and self-reflection. Feeling vulnerable while encouraging inquiry is a sign of strength.
Honesty	
Tell other people no lies or tell others all you think and feel.	Encourage yourself and other people to say what they know yet fear to say. Minimize what would otherwise be subject to distortion and cover-up of the distortion.
Integrity	
Stick to your principles, values, and beliefs.	Advocate your principles, values, and beliefs in a way that invites inquiry into them and encourages other people to do the same.

Model I governing values (to be in unilateral control, to win and not to lose, and to suppress negative feelings) and action strategies (to advocate, persuade, sell, and use face-saving devices) lead to organizational routines. For example, whenever human beings are faced with any issue that contains significant embarrassment or threat, they act in ways that bypass, as best they can, the embarrassment or threat. In order for the bypass to work, it must be covered up. The basic strategy involves bypass and cover-up.

Because most individuals use these actions, the actions become part of the fabric of everyday life. And because so many individuals use these actions frequently, the actions become organizational norms. The actions come to be viewed as rational, sensible, and realistic.

The results are organizational defensive routines. Organizational defensive routines are actions or policies that prevent individuals or segments of the organization from experiencing embarrassment or threat. Simultaneously, they prevent people from identifying and getting rid of the causes of the potential embarrassment or threat. Organizational defense routines are anti learning, overprotective, and self-sealing.

Professor Argyris (1993) has found that the Model I social virtues have four governing values:

(1) Be in unilateral control.
(2) Strive to win and not to lose.
(3) Suppress negative feelings.
(4) Be as rational as possible.

These values have associated action rules, such as "strive to make evaluations and attributions in ways that do not encourage inquiry into or testing of the validity of the claims." The tension that this behavior creates leads to private conversations that are very critical of *them*." However, these conversations are never revealed. Of course, the large discrepancy between the private conversations and the public conversations is a symptom of a major problem.

Argyris tells (1993) the case of a chief information officer (CIO) who is working with his staff to become more effective. The staff has been criticized by line management. The staff responds:

- Line do not know what they want.
- They make demands with unrealistic deadlines.

- The problems are unfixable because of line management's recalcitrance.

Asked to write out his private thoughts, the CIO cited such reactions as:

- These guys act like a bunch of babies.
- They do not realize how insensitive and opinionated they are.

This is a typical bad situation. Everyone needs help to concentrate on data that can be tested, and followed up with action.

Note that this is similar to the previous description of the relationship between product development and top executives. There is a strong us/them relationship that is self-sealed with the help of untested attributions.

Skilled incompetence plays a major role in making cultural change difficult. Argyris (1990) recommends the following six steps:

(1) Make a diagnosis of the problem.
(2) Connect the diagnosis to the actual behavior of the participants.
(3) Show them how their behavior creates organizational defenses.
(4) Help them to change their behavior.
(5) Change the defensive routine that reinforced the old behavior.
(6) Develop new organizational norms and culture that reinforce the new behavior.

Skilled application of these steps will undoubtedly help to achieve the cultural change that is necessary to fully implement total quality development. Weakening of the defense mechanisms is necessary for the cultural change to succeed.

The reader is encouraged to apply these six steps to the composite case study that preceded this section. How could they be used to plan interventions that would overcome the cultural barriers? One possible approach follows:

(1) Make a diagnosis: Jim and his team are not asking for help, which is what they would do if they were confidently seeking to

maximize their improvement. They are bypassing to minimize potential embarrassment and threat.

(2) Identify the behavior: Not asking for help; emphasizing good news; not having a plan for the consultations.

(3) Show organizational defenses: Everyone senses that Jim and his key leaders want to emphasize good news, rather than maximize learning. Then everyone takes Jim's cue and emphasizes good news, instead of confronting the cultural barriers to improvement.

(4) Help them to change their behavior: But Jack and the core team are product development experts, not behaviorists. Ah, there's the rub. Well, start out with the clear fact that Jim and his team are not asking for help, which makes it difficult to help them. Then suggest going through the *five whys*.[1] This appeals to engineers' desire to rationally deduce root causes. Somewhere along the path of the five whys we can surely focus on the bypassing.

(5) Change the defensive routine: Real improvement beats public relations, but can we sell it? Yes, if we can understand why the team is intent on this particularly virulent form of bypassing. (Many other forms of bypassing occur. The action will have to be tailored to the form.)

(6) Develop new organizational norms: Get Wayne to tell this crew to shape up or ship out? No, that was the old culture. How do we develop organizational norms that maximize improvement?

To utilize the six steps with the help of Model II social virtues certainly seems to be a potentially effective approach. Most product people will find this type of activity quite foreign to them. However, to avoid cultural-change action is to ensure ineffectiveness.

One approach that can help is described by Argyris (1991):

In a paragraph or so, the CEO described a meeting he intended to have with his direct reports to address the problem. Next, he divided the paper in half, and on the right-hand side of the page, he wrote a scenario for the meeting—much like the script for a movie or play—describing what he

---

[1] The "five whys" are an iterative questioning procedure, designed to get at the answers behind the answers.

would say and how his subordinates would likely respond. On the left-hand side of the page, he wrote down any thoughts and feelings that he would be likely to have during the meeting but that he wouldn't express for fear they would derail the discussion.

But instead of holding the meeting, the CEO analyzed this scenario with his direct reports. The case became the catalyst for a discussion in which the CEO learned several things about the way he acted with his management team.

Professor Argyris describes the valuable learning that took place on the part of both the CEO and his direct reports. Then he summarizes:

> In effect, the case study exercise legitimizes talking about issues that people have never been able to address before. Such a discussion can be emotional—even painful. But for managers with the courage to persist, the payoff is great: management teams and entire organizations work more openly and more effectively and have greater options for behaving flexibly and adapting to particular situations.

How did the Model I social virtues cause problems for Jack and the division X people? Most product development people probably find it difficult to use Model II social virtues, and especially difficult to encourage others to become proficient in using them. In planning the interventions that could have been used in the case study, how could Model II social virtues be used? These questions are rhetorical, as Argyris' interventions have been little tried in product development work. It is obvious that Jack had many opportunities to use Model II social virtues. A clear example is the project meetings with no requests for help. Rather than acquiesce in the genial aura of ineffectual goodwill, Jack could have designed an intervention to reduce such bypassing. At the very least, that action would have ended his bypassing of the bypass.

The Law According to Moses

Joel Moses, dean of engineering at MIT, has created some very provocative concepts on organization and ideology (Moses, 1990). He concludes that much dysfunctional behavior and organization are deeply rooted in American ideology and therefore will strongly tend to survive attempts at improvement, such as the implementation of basic concurrent engineering.

Professor Moses describes four forms of organization, two of which are relevant to large-scale purposeful activity:[2]

(1) Layered organization
(2) Tree organization

The tree organization is the familiar one that large corporations use. Organizational charts around the world are drawn in this fashion. The critical issue is actual behavior and actions. In the individualistic tree structure that is used and has strong ideological support in the United States, there is a strong tendency to foster some of the dysfunctions that have been emphasized in this book. Moses explicitly cites the six weaknesses that are identified in the report of the MIT Commission on Industrial Productivity, *Made in America* (Dertouzos et al., 1989), as being the result of American ideology and its favored organizational style. The weakness that most obviously fits Moses' analysis is *failures of cooperation*. Professor Moses also cites 4 of the 10 cash drains of this book as the result of the individualistic tree-structure organization and ideology. With further analysis, we might make the case that the Moses hypothesis influences all of the 10 cash drains. The individualistic tree structure clearly reinforces the cloistered groups of technical specialists cited in this book as a fundamental problem.

The tree structure facilitates communication with your manager and with anyone who reports to you. The tree path impedes other communications. However, the needs of the project often require other communication paths. For example, suppose a team is needed to analyze and design the critical interface between two subsystems. Although the two subsystems interface, they are far apart in the tree organization. This makes it very difficult to organize the needed team. The tree structure tends to funnel the initiative for the needed cooperation to the vice presidential level. This makes it difficult to get onto the agenda. Also, it gives

---

[2] The other two are (1) family and (2) networked systems. The family is very effective for small-scale activities, but cannot be extended to large-scale activities. Adam Smith's view of the market is an example of a networked system.

much opportunity to activate corporate "games." The formation of the needed team is unlikely because the tree structure and its supporting ideology incorporate so much natural resistance. The formation will not occur despite the fact that the interface needs a team, which may consist of only two people. As this exemplifies, the tree structure seriously impedes much communication and cooperation that are necessary for the success of projects.

In contrast, the layered structure naturally includes the needed communication and cooperation. Everyone communicates with others on the same layer, the next higher layer, and the next lower layer. This is much more in keeping with project needs. For example, the needed subsystem interface team is easily formed, so naturally that it is hardly noticed as a team.

Professor Moses traces layered organization to the biblical Moses and to Plato. It was passed down to the present time through feudal societies, which were very layered. The United States never had a feudal society, and so it has no memory of layered organization. Japan and Germany fully left feudal society only in the nineteenth century, so their behavior still has a natural tendency toward cooperation in layered interactions. By contrast, Aristotle favored the tree structure, which became dominant during the Renaissance through St. Thomas Aquinas. Thus, the contest between the two forms of organization and their associated ideologies is very old, with deep-seated attitudes, and the United States has a strong bias toward the individualistic tree structure.

Professor Moses writes in 1990, "The dominant values in individualistic Western ideologies which have a major impact on the firm are individualism, competition, and creativity. Similarly the dominant values for communitarian ideologies are consensus decision making, cooperation, and flexibility." Here Moses refers to competition within the organization. "A tree inherently creates competition among siblings— competition for resources, promotions, and approval. Thus, members of such an organization, who are on the same level, but in different parts of the tree, have difficulty in cooperating." The difficulty of forming an interface team is a perfect example of this.

This book emphasizes moving in the direction from individualism toward cooperation. More explicitly, effective behavior adjusts to the situation. For example, an emphasis on individualism and creativity is helpful at the stage of generating new concepts. Consensus is best in selecting the final concept. Moses believes that the dominant American ideology makes it difficult, but not impossible, to implement the shift from individualism toward cooperation. He feels that such a shift can best be made when the organization feels that it is in a crisis.

The experience of implementing basic concurrent engineering at Xerox in the early 1980s is an example showing that product development teamwork develops in a crisis. However, it does seem to be true that full proficiency in adopting modes over the full spectrum from individualism to cooperation that best match the project requirements does not come easily to most Americans. This also applies to a considerable extent to the British and many other western Europeans.

Professor Moses offers three approaches to overcoming the excessive reliance on one ideology and organizational structure:

(1) Increase trust.
(2) Use group incentives.
(3) Encourage multimodal behavior.

Moses cites some Japanese MIT students whose company advised them before they left to study at MIT to "make nine friends." A conscious effort to develop acquaintances and trust in the workplace helps to overcome failures of cooperation.

Rewarding teams or the entire organization for success is an obvious way to foster cooperation. However, American culture has resisted it, especially in product development. It is plausible that ideology supports the resistance, consistent with Moses' hypothesis. Group rewards deserve to be tried much more extensively.

Moses' third recommendation addresses the clear American tendency to be unimodal in behavior. Americans are competitive in all situations. In contrast, for example, Japanese companies compete on products in the marketplace, while cooperating on methodology. An example of the latter is the cooperative users' group on Taguchi's system of quality engineering in Tokyo. Companies that compete fiercely in the marketplace come together to share experiences that help all of them. Cultural resistance has met attempts to foster similar activities in American cities. As Moses writes, "One needs to convince people that it is quite proper to behave somewhat differently on different occasions. One way to convince people of this is to create realistic situations that require group cooperation, and to have members of the group realize that they do not lose their individuality or creativity as a result of participating in such situations."

We can hope that self-awareness of the tendency to behave in all situations according to the individualistic tree-structure ideology will lead to improvement. Perhaps you can select a recent experience of your own where this tendency has been most destructive. Then prepare a plan for intervention that might have led to more effective behavior. Argyris' six steps listed in this chapter might be used as a basis for the plan. The type of dysfunctional behavior that is described by Moses is perpetuated by the skilled incompetence that Argyris has emphasized.

Be aware of the need for cultural change, and attempt to foster it. It is not easy for engineers, but if we ignore it, we will be ineffective change agents.

Managing Cultural Change

Cultural change is a major challenge in implementing total quality development. Resistance will not readily go away and therefore must be coped with.

The Cultural Gap

The first step in starting cultural change is to identify the cultural gap in the organization. Prepare an inventory of the current culture, and compare it with the goal. The difference is the cultural gap to be overcome. Simply identifying it will get it out into the open, thus at least exposing it to scrutiny. Otherwise, it remains a hidden agenda, perniciously undercutting all attempts at improvement. This step can be followed by planned interventions based on the model of Professor Argyris. His six steps, and the model II social virtues, provide insightful guidance to overcoming organizational defenses.

Step by Step

Any attempts at sudden cultural change are doomed. We might as well ask a psychiatrist to cure a schizophrenic patient overnight. As with any other complex activity, in cultural change there is no silver bullet. It is important to maintain a steady advance, not so fast as to frighten people, but not so slow as to leave everyone feeling relaxed and comfortable. It must be accepted that cultural change will be a little challenging and uncomfortable, except for a few lead users who are in the vanguard. (They will be uncomfortable with the slowness of the pace, which everyone else feels is too fast.)

As we progress through the four implementation quadrants, we bring cultural change along steadily. In the first quadrant (Figure 9.13), the core team (the vanguard 5%) become familiar and comfortable with the principles of total quality development and start implementing parts of it on projects. This will take 6 to 18 months. We then use these initial learnings and successes as the basis for proceeding to the second quadrant. Now most of the key product executives become familiar with total quality development and understand that its implementation must be one of the top three activities for the next two to three years.

At some time during the fourth quadrant, we achieve the first major success (a major product is early and good). Now the culture is ripe for strong affirmation. "Here at the corporation [or division] our engineers practice total quality development. If you want to practice something else, we are sure that you can be a good engineer at some other corporation, and we will be glad to help you identify that corporation." Like the knowledge that one is about to be hanged the next day, this tends to wonderfully concentrate the mind. However, attempts to do this much earlier, at the beginning of the first quadrant, would be highly disruptive.

As with all activities, the top leaders do not want to be too far ahead of the troops, or too far behind. They must maintain a steady and firm pace. Constancy of purpose is required, as Deming has reminded us. During my career of 40 years, I have observed tremendous variance of executive behavior in this regard. Some product executives have seen dealing with the "in" basket each day as their main activity. At the positive end of the spectrum, Frank Pipp was an outstanding leader for improvement at Xerox during the early 1980s. His steady constancy of purpose moved the organization along as rapidly as possible, but he never got so far ahead that he lost contact with the troops.

We manage the pace to be best for cultural change, with actions that are appropriate for the current state of progress. Actions that are appropriate for one stage are not appropriate for another. The ultimatum described a moment ago would not be appropriate for the first quadrant. It would primarily frighten people during that stage. Equally inappropriate would be a statement by the top product executive during the fourth quadrant saying, "You can use total quality development if you want, but we wouldn't want to tell you what to do." This would be serious abdication. Success requires leadership.

SUCCESS

Success breeds success and is the biggest factor for improvement. Successful management will effectively lead the development of new products by the use of total quality development. Success will lead to more confidence, and thus to greater success. The greatest motivation for cultural change is the desire to be more than mere all-stars, but rather to be members of winning teams. The benefits of successful implementation of total quality development are great, as will be described in Chapter 10.

CHAPTER

10

The Reward

- ■ **Shorter Time to Market**
- ■ **Enhanced Customer Satisfaction**
- ■ **Reduced Costs**
- ■ **Variety and Flexibility**
- ■ **Cash Flow**
- ■ **Large Improvement**
- ■ **Continuous Improvement**
- ■ **Yes, It Is for You**
- ■ **Winning Teams**

The reward is simple: Total quality development enables success in the global economy. Anything substantially short of the total quality development that this book describes leads to serious economic problems.

The benefits of total quality development are shorter time to market, enhanced customer satisfaction, and reduced costs; combined, they make for international competitiveness. The ability to complete more product cycles than the competition provides greater product variety, increased flexibility, and increased corporate learning. The lead rapidly grows over the companies that are still stuck in the rut of traditional product development.

SHORTER TIME TO MARKET

Quickness to market is essential in the modern dynamic international economy. It makes our company's products leaders in the eyes of customers. Also, it enables rapid adaptation to changing market conditions. Total quality development delivers new products in a short time because it:

- Reduces rework (of development)
- Minimizes pseudocreativity
- Creates team consensus and commitment

Rework is reduced by the emphasis on problem prevention and disciplined decision making. Early and continuous emphasis on the voice of the customer, together with robust design is the path to problem prevention. The strong attention to the voice of the customer helps us avoid the changes of specifications that plague traditional product development. Robust design minimizes the build-test-fix rework that under traditional development greatly extends the time to market. Robust technologies are adapted to several products with little rework of the development. Disciplined decisions eliminate dysfunctional iteration. Our team adheres to well-made decisions with constancy of purpose.

Pseudocreativity, the excessive emphasis on being new and different (but not better), is reduced by the reusability matrix, the Pugh concept selection process, and competitive benchmarking. These key elements of total quality development focus our creative energies on real improvements that are satisfying to customers.

Team consensus and commitment keep all of our activities coordinated. Unproductive diversions are avoided. The multifunctional team concentrates on the significant issues.

Total quality development greatly reduces time to market.

ENHANCED CUSTOMER SATISFACTION

In the modern economy, customers demand satisfaction. They insist on products with attractive features. Also, the products must work well in the customers' environment and applications. Total quality development results in products that satisfy customers through its emphasis on:

- Listening to the voice of the customer
- Robust design
- Dominant concepts

Clear understanding of the voice of the customer leads to product features that attract customers. Robust designs work well in the wide range of customer uses. The dominant designs that stem from the Pugh concept selection process and competitive benchmarking are inherently superior. They are creative responses to the voice of the customer that enable robustness and low cost.

Total quality development greatly improves customer satisfaction.

REDUCED COSTS

As the economy becomes more global, the omnipresent emphasis on cost is even more demanding. The product with the attractive features and the robust functionality always draws the customers if it also has a competitive price.

Total quality development reduces manufacturing cost and field cost by the emphasis on:

- Competitive benchmarking
- Dominant concepts
- Robust design
- Concurrent engineering

Competitive benchmarking, especially design competitive benchmarking (Chapter 5), keeps us aware of the most cost-effective designs in the world. These provide guidance and motivation that lead to designs that are intrinsically simple and easy to produce and maintain.

The Pugh concept selection process leads to dominant concepts that are low in cost. Early selection gives us time to concentrate on cost-reduction details.

Robust design reduces factory cost and field cost. Factory cost is reduced because there is less scrap, rework, and inspection, and less need for finicky precision. Field costs are reduced by the greater reliability of robust functionality.

Concurrent engineering brings the product functionality people, the production people, and the field-support people together in the decision making. Simply stated, it gives costs an equal emphasis in the early decision making. Design for manufacturability and maintainability, and the presence of production and field-support people on the multifunctional team, help us reduce costs.

Total quality development greatly reduces costs.

VARIETY AND FLEXIBILITY

Product variety and corporate flexibility are increasingly important in international competition. Customers want availability of products having the features that match their needs and desires. The flexible corporation is quick on its feet in adapting to changing market conditions.

Total quality development provides variety and flexibility through:

- Strategy
- Robust technology
- Careful listening to the voice of the customer
- Quick time to market

The integrated product and technology strategies, incorporating the right level of reusability, emphasize product variety. We plan strategies, say, with four products, one every year and a half, rather than one product in four and a half years.

Robust technologies are technologies that are adaptable in several products and thus facilitate product variety. Quick adaptation enables agility in the marketplace.

Careful listening to the voice of the customer leads to a good match between products and the variety of market segments and niches. Strategic QFD helps us plan the product variety that wins customers.

Quick time to market enables flexibility. Fidelity to the voice of the customer enables us quickly to grasp new market conditions and to bring out our new product quickly in response to them.

Total quality development greatly improves product variety and corporate flexibility.

CASH FLOW

Traditional product development is inherently plagued by the 10 cash drains, which deplete huge amounts of money in extra costs and reduced market share. Total quality development eliminates the 10 cash drains and greatly improves the financial position of our company. Positive cash flow is greatly improved.

LARGE IMPROVEMENT

The improvements in all the areas just described will be large, typically 30% to 100% or more. The exact amount will depend upon the situation.

The potential varies some from industry to industry. Also, the potential varies from company to company. If a company already practices some elements of total quality development, then it has captured some of the rewards. It is my judgment that nearly all companies in the United States and western Europe can reduce time to market by at least 30%, and most by 50% (or a factor of 2).

Predictions of the exact amount of improvement are difficult. Kim Clark and Takahiro Fujimoto (1991) made the most comprehensive study of product development performance (limited to the automotive industry). It suggests that major improvements are possible. My interpretation of their data is that schedules can be reduced by 30% or more, product costs by 50%, and people-hours of development effort by 50%. Other, less public, studies during the early 1980s suggested that most companies could improve by factors of 2 or more for schedule and most other metrics.

According to Lewis Veraldi (1988), basic concurrent engineering saved $200 million in the development of the Ford Taurus and gave it best-in-class status on 300 items. The success of the Taurus greatly improved the financial performance of Ford. The implementation of basic concurrent engineering (and similar improvements in manufacturing) at Xerox (Bebb, 1990) reduced product cost by a factor of 2 between 1980 and 1986. Quality was greatly improved; one metric (parts falling out on the assembly line) improved by a factor of more than 15, while another metric (number of product defects after assembly) improved by a factor of 4.

Late in the 1980s, the vanguard at Xerox implemented improvements that brought them close to the total quality development that is the subject of this book. The results have been excellent. Maurice Holmes, president of the Office Document Systems Business Division, summarized the achievements (Holmes, 1993):

> After having established this new process the first product put through it took only 36 months, as per its schedule, and was completed at the end of 1991. In so doing, not only did we achieve the obvious benefits associated with this faster time to market—higher gross margins, higher placements, being perceived as the technology leader (ahead of the competition)—but the predictability, because it was completed to plan, meant that investments

made in marketing the product were not wasted and this saved Xerox millions of dollars.

Competitive benchmarking is the way to determine your organization's potential for improvement. All studies have suggested that major improvements can be made. One has to be careful that a desire to quantify potential gains does not lead to paralysis by analysis. The message from the studies is to have high expectations.

Success is helped by high expectations. David Kearns, then the CEO of Xerox, concluded that the main reason for the success of Japanese companies was higher expectations (Alster, 1987):

> I was riding on an airplane [after one visit to Japan] and I asked myself: What is the difference between Japanese and U.S. businessmen? You've got all of the cultural things we've talked about.... Finally, I wrote down and circled "expectation levels." I really believed that they had expectation levels for success that were so much higher than the U.S. businessmen I dealt with and clearly, from my own experience, inside of my own company. So I felt that clearly we had to change. We had to reset all our expectation levels.

Total quality development has the potential for bringing very large improvements in most cases. Implementation with high expectations brings business success. The vigorous implementation of total quality development will bring great rewards.

CONTINUOUS IMPROVEMENT

After the implementation of total quality development captures the large rewards, further benefit comes from continuous improvement. The implementation of total quality development makes an organization world-class. Continuous improvement *keeps* it world-class.

Continuous improvement is achieved by enhancements to total quality development, which are facilitated by total quality management and the learning organization (Senge, 1990; Argyris, 1991). The greater number of total quality development product cycles increases corporate learning. Study and practice will continue to improve the basic principles of total quality development.

YES, IT IS FOR YOU

Total quality development is useful for any development activity. The emphasis in this book is on hardware products. Total quality development benefits the development of software, packaged goods, and services. It can be applied to wide-ranging activities such as the development of medical services, the development of an organization, the development of a book, and the development of a fund-raising campaign. Think broadly about the potential benefits from your use of total quality development.

WINNING TEAMS

Total quality development makes organizations dynamically competitive, enabling them to sell their products against the competition anywhere in the world. This success supports an ever-rising standard of living, not dependent on tariffs or trade quotas. But while economic success is the ultimate justification for using total quality development, for product people the motivation is more visceral. With total quality development we can be more than just all-stars; we can be members of winning teams.

APPENDIX

A

Signal-to-Noise Ratio

T he evaluation of performance is critical to the rapid optimization of new products and processes, which in turn is essential for achieving good quality and greatly reducing product development time. If performance is evaluated by simply compiling a list of detailed and specific problems, the improvement of the product or process will be ad hoc and diffuse, with quality improvement very uncertain. To be an international leader in quality and rapid development, it is imperative to develop compact metrics for the efficient evaluation of performance.

In defining metrics that measure the output from a system that we describe as performance, we consider both the output that we wish to achieve (ideal customer satisfaction target) and the undesirable output that we would prefer not to have present (variance from the ideal). We want a metric that provides one number that will appropriately encompass both desirable and undesirable performance. We think of the desirable performance as the signal and the undesirable performance as the noise. This is analogous to the original use of the term *signal-to-noise ratio* (SN ratio) in the field of electronic communications.

We want the SN ratio to have several characteristics besides that of being a good measure of performance that takes into account both desirable output and undesirable output. These desired characteristics are:

(1) If several factors, A, B, and C, each individually have an effect on the performance, then we'd like the total effect of all three factors to simply be the sum of the individual effects. This property is called *additivity*.

(2) The maximization of the performance metric should correspond to the minimization of quality loss.

(3) The optimization of the performance metrics should be independent of the adjustment of the performance value. Often, after the design is optimized, we may wish to adjust the performance to some preferred value. This adjustment should not upset the optimization.

To summarize, we want the performance metric to have economic significance and to facilitate optimization procedures.

NOMINAL-IS-BEST CHARACTERISTICS

Many systems have output that can be characterized as "nominal is best": there is some nominal output value that is the preferred value. Any values that are different from the nominal value are less desirable. Examples are production processes. They are intended to create a nominal value for a dimension or some other characteristic. Another example is a power supply. If we have a 24-volt power supply, we very much prefer that it put out 24 volts. Both 23 and 25 volts are much less desirable.

If we measure the performance of a system in several experiments, we can then calculate from the data the mean value and the value of the standard deviation. Suppose you are asked, The standard deviation is 1; do you like it? What will you answer? Of course, there is no way to give a sensible answer with the information that has been provided. First of all, you do not know the dimensions of the quantity. Second, you have no reference point by which to judge the magnitude. If you are told that the mean value is 10, you are likely to think that the standard deviation of 1 is excessive. However, if the mean value is 100, you may think that a standard deviation of 1 is quite good; and if the mean value is 1000, you are almost certain to like the standard deviation of 1. This suggests that the ratio of the mean value divided by the standard deviation is a good performance metric. This ratio causes the dimensions to cancel so that we need not worry about the actual dimensions of the performance measurement. Also, this ratio contains a reference by which we can achieve a reasonable perspective on the magnitude of the standard deviation. Therefore, this ratio seems like a reasonable performance metric.

It also tends to give the property of making the performance metric independent of subsequent adjustment. Consider the data for three different designs that are summarized in Figure A.1. The distinct designs, 1, 2, and 3, have each been tested under several conditions of noise, and the mean value and standard deviation have been calculated for each design. These give the design points that are plotted in Figure A.1. On the basis of the data that are shown in Figure A.1, which design do you prefer?

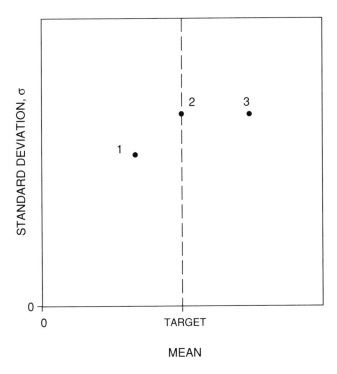

FIGURE A.1. Three design points.

Many people initially think that design 1 is preferable, because it has the smallest standard deviation. However, we see that design 1 happened to be tested under circumstances that gave output much less than the target value. Therefore, we must adjust the system to increase the output so that the mean value for design 1 is as close as possible to the target value.

Usually, adjusting the mean value to the target is quite easily done. In fact, a more significant concern is that engineers are all too ready to adjust the performance to the target in order to make the product look good under one set of conditions. Engineers having demonstrated much ingenuity in this respect, we can be confident that adjustment of the mean to the target will be easily accomplished.

Now, what is going to happen to the standard deviation of design 1 when the mean is adjusted to the target? Adjustment is most conveniently done with an adjustment factor that changes the mean and the standard deviation in the same proportion, keeping their ratio constant. Thus, when the mean for design 1 is adjusted to the target, our most realistic expectation is that the standard deviation will increase to the value plotted as 1′ in Figure A.2. Similarly, the standard deviation for design 3 will be reduced to the value 3′. Thus, we see that the performance for design 3 is actually the best. This leads us to want to take the ratio of mean to standard deviation in optimizing the performance. From the plots in Figures A.1 and A.2, we see that achieving the best ratio of mean divided by the standard deviation will give us the smallest value of standard deviation after the mean has been adjusted to the target value.

By basing the nominal-is-best SN ratio on the ratio of the mean value to the standard deviation, we are creating a performance metric that will remain constant during adjustment to the target if the assumption of constant ratio of mean value to standard deviation is satisfied. Therefore, when performing adjustments to the target, we can check the SN ratio

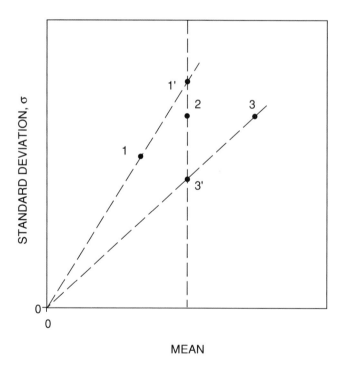

FIGURE A.2. Smallest deviation after adjustment to the target.

over the range of the adjustment. If the experimentally determined SN ratio is almost constant over the range of adjustment, then we can be confident that the optimization by which the standard deviation has been minimized will remain valid even after the mean value has been adjusted to the target. Therefore, after conducting the optimization experiments and plotting the data, we search for an adjustment factor that has the characteristics that are shown in Figure A.3. In Figure A.3, the plotted data show that the SN ratio is constant. This justifies our assumption that the ratio of the mean value to the standard deviation will remain constant during adjustment of the mean value to the target. Also, we see in Figure A.3 that the mean is linear in its relationship with the adjustment factor.

From Figure A.3, we can easily change the value of the adjustment factor to bring the mean to the target without in any way disturbing the optimization that has minimized the value of standard deviation. We can be confident that if we use this adjustment factor to adjust the perfor-

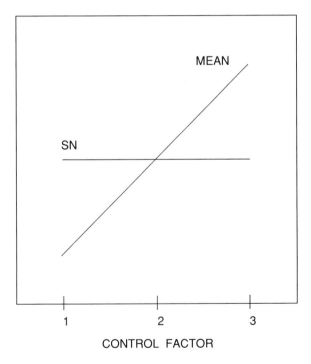

Figure A.3. Characteristics of an adjustment factor.

mance value for each of the designs to the target, the design that we choose as optimum on the basis of SN ratio will actually have the smallest standard deviation. Of course, in actual experimentation, we will not find data that conform to our assumptions as well as is shown in Figure A.3. However, we often find a control factor that has characteristics that are approximately as shown in Figure A.3. Then this control factor will make a good adjustment factor. If the SN ratio changes by an amount greater than we would prefer, we can always compare the new standard deviation after adjustment. This can be done easily by simply taking the new value of the SN ratio. In this way, even if the SN ratio changes by a significant amount, the definition of the SN ratio for a nominal-is-best characteristic will enable us to quickly find the optimum design. Therefore, the SN ratio for the nominal-is-best system is:

$$\text{SN ratio} = 10 \log E \left[\frac{m^2}{\sigma^2} \right]$$

$$= 10 \log \frac{\frac{1}{n}(S_m - V)}{V} \tag{A.1}$$

where

$E =$ expected value

$m =$ mean

$\sigma =$ standard deviation

$S_m =$ square associated with the mean $= (\sum y^2/n)$

$V =$ variance $= 1/n - 1 (\sum y^2 - S_m)$

$y =$ data values that are measured

$n =$ number of data that are measured

Commonly, the n data points are obtained under n different conditions of noise. (*Noise* here refers to undesirable but inevitable deviations from nominal in the parts of the system and in the environment in which the system is used.) The logarithm is used because it usually improves additivity. The multiplier of 10 simply reflects the usual convention in electronics and acoustics of using the unit of decibels. The nominal-is-best SN ratio is used for many engineering systems.

For some performance characteristics, negative values are possible. Then it may happen that the mean value is smaller than the standard deviation. For such situations, it is usually best to take $1/V$ in Equation (A.1).

Many performance characteristics that are simple to consider as nominal-is-best are actually dynamic characteristics (described later in this appendix). For example, a power supply that has an advertised output of 24 V is not expected to produce this output if the input voltage is zero; the output depends on the input. However, over the usual range of input voltage (approximately a constant value), it is reasonable to consider that the output has a fixed target of 24 V. Actual performance characteristics should be carefully analyzed to determine whether they have static target values or are dynamic characteristics.

SMALLER-IS-BETTER CHARACTERISTICS

Many performance measures have zero as the desired value. Examples are background density on a copy, wow on a turntable, and imbalance in car wheels. A little thought suggests that the reason these characteristics have zero as the preferred value is that the characteristics are, themselves, noises. In many cases it is expedient to treat the characteristic as "smaller is better." In this case, the performance metric is simply the variance from zero. In other words, this is the mean square error from zero. (Of course, the term *variance* more specifically means the mean square error from the mean value.) This performance characteristic is given simply by the following equation:

$$SN \, ratio = -10 \log \frac{1}{n} \sum y^2 \qquad (A.2)$$

The negative sign must be used because the metric that is being measured is undesirable. As its value decreases, we want the SN ratio to increase.

Adjustment does not play a role for smaller-is-better characteristics. The objective is to move the performance as close to zero as possible. However, zero is impossible to attain. The concept of adjusting to zero has no relevance during design, although during production we can adjust each unit toward zero if it exceeds the tolerance.

We should consider the possibility that the smaller-is-better characteristic might be best integrated into another type of characteristic. For example, wow might be made the noise in a nominal-is-best characteristic. Background density on a copy is the output noise when the input signal is zero. It would be better to consider the full range of inputs from white to black, rather than concentrate on one value of input. It may be that the smaller-is-better characteristic is seldom, if ever, the best performance metric. However, it is convenient to use for many applications, particularly for initial applications.

BIGGER-IS-BETTER CHARACTERISTICS

"Bigger-is-better" is typical of characteristics such as strength. A little thought will show that the inverse of a bigger-is-better characteristic is simply the smaller-is-better characteristic that we considered in the previous section. Therefore, if we have a bigger-is-better characteristic y, then we can simply take the reciprocal of y as a smaller-is-better characteristic. This directly leads to the following equation for the bigger-is-better SN ratio:

$$\text{SN ratio} = -10 \log \frac{1}{n} \sum \frac{1}{y^2} \qquad (A.3)$$

STATIC CHARACTERISTICS

The three SN ratios that have been described are all *static* characteristics. In other words, the value that we want is a constant, which can be defined before we start the experiments. In many cases, the performance characteristic is not so simple and cannot be represented by a constant value;

it is a *dynamic* characteristic. Dynamic characteristics are described in the following section.

DYNAMIC CHARACTERISTICS

There are four basic types of dynamic characteristics:

(1) Input analog/output analog
(2) Input analog/output digital
(3) Input digital/output analog
(4) Input digital/output digital

Here we will consider only the first case, in which both the input and the output are continuous variables (analog signals). The most important fact about digital signals to keep in mind in creating the appropriate performance characteristics is that digital signals are actually continuous variables (analog signals) coupled with a protocol that distinguishes 0s from 1s.

An example of input analog/output analog dynamic systems is the steering system of an automobile. The intended turning radius is not a constant: it depends on the angle that the driver imparts to the steering wheel (Taguchi, 1986). For such a system we can define the desired performance as a linear relationship between turning radius and steering wheel angle. If all data points lie on a straight line, then the performance is perfect. Define the best straight line as:

$$y_\beta = m + \beta(M - \overline{M}) \qquad (A.4)$$

where

$m =$ mean of y value
$\beta =$ slope of line
$M =$ signal factor
$\overline{M} =$ average value of signal factor

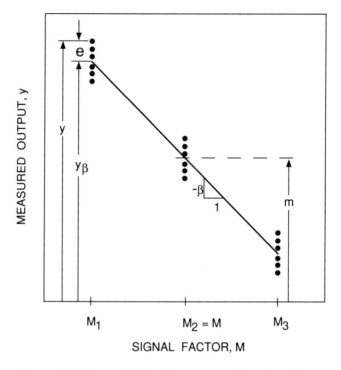

FIGURE A.4. Dynamic SN ratio measures fit to best line.

Actual data will not lie exactly on a straight line. We define the discrepancy from the best straight line as error, e in Figure A.4. The best line is the one that minimizes the sum of the squares of the errors:

$$\sum_{1}^{n} e^2 = \sum \{y - [m + \beta(M - \overline{M})]\}^2 \qquad (A.5)$$

The SN ratio is

$$SN\,ratio = 10\log \frac{\dfrac{1}{\sum (M - \overline{M})^2}(S_\beta - V)}{V}$$

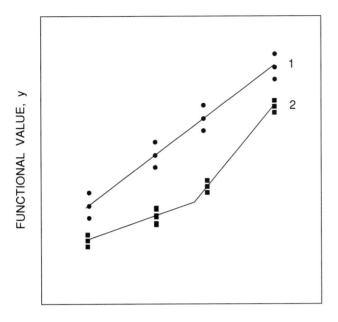

FIGURE A.5. Bilinear fit.

$$S_\beta = \sum \left\{ (M - \overline{M}) \left[\frac{\sum y(M - \overline{M})}{\sum (M - \overline{M})^2} \right] \right\}^2 \tag{A.6}$$

Here n is the total number of data points. Again, the performance evaluations are commonly done while subjecting the system to several noise conditions. For example, Figure A.4 might result from six noise conditions at each of three signal values, for a total of 18 data points.

As was the case for the nominal-is-best static case, the performance must be adjusted to the target after the design values that produced the largest SN value have been selected. Now the straight line must be adjusted to coincide with the design target straight line. Two parameters, m and β, must be adjusted, so two adjustment factors must be found among the design parameters.

In general, that part of performance that will be adjusted will be decided on the basis of what is easy to adjust. In some systems it may be easy to adjust a bilinear response. Then the SN ratio can be based on the best bilinear fit to the data. In Figure A.5, curve 2 has the least dispersion. If it is easy to adjust the bilinear curve to coincide with the target performance, then the design that led to curve 2 should be selected. It should not be penalized by comparing the data with a single straight line. Three adjustment factors are needed.

Dynamic SN ratios are more important and more powerful than static SN ratios. Most devices transform input energy into output energy. The best performance characteristic quantifies the dynamic relationship between output and input, as influenced by noises. Often, the use of a static characteristic is a way station on the road to the development of a powerful dynamic characteristic.

CONCLUSION

Utilization of the SN ratio to concisely measure performance and to focus the activities to optimize the values of the critical parameters is essential in order to achieve strongly improved quality and shorter development time. By combining physics, economics, and deep knowledge of engineering practice, SN ratios are a great advance over common expressions of performance. The reader is encouraged to further study performance evaluation in Taguchi (1986), Taguchi (1987, specifically, Chapters 18, 19, 22, 23, and 24 and Section 40.4), Taguchi and Phadke (1984), and Phadke and Taguchi (1987).

DERIVATION OF DYNAMIC SN RATIO

The best values for m and β are found by differentiating $\sum e^2$ from Equation (A.5) with respect to m and β and setting the derivatives equal to zero:

$$\frac{\partial}{\partial m}\sum e^2 = \frac{\partial}{\partial m}\sum \{y - [m + \beta(M - \overline{M})]\}^2 = 0$$

$$-2\sum \{y - [m + \beta(M - \overline{M})]\} = 0$$

$$\sum y = nm + \beta\sum(M - \overline{M})$$

$$\sum y = nm + 0 \tag{A.7}$$

$$m = \frac{\sum y}{n} \tag{A.8}$$

$$\frac{\partial}{\partial \beta}\sum e^2 = \frac{\partial}{\partial \beta}\sum \{y - [m + \beta(M - \overline{M})]\}^2 = 0$$

$$-2\sum \{y - [m + \beta(M - \overline{M})]\}(M - \overline{M}) = 0$$

$$\sum (y - m)(M - \overline{M}) = \beta\sum(M - \overline{M})^2 \tag{A.9}$$

However,

$$m\sum(M - \overline{M}) = 0$$

Therefore,

$$\beta = \frac{\sum y(M - \overline{M})}{\sum(M - \overline{M})^2} \tag{A.10}$$

$$\sum e^2 = \sum \left\{ y - m - (M - \overline{M})\frac{\sum y(M - \overline{M})}{\sum(M - \overline{M})^2} \right\}^2 \tag{A.11}$$

The average value of $\sum e^2$ per data point is

$$V = \frac{\sum e^2}{n-2} \tag{A.12}$$

There are two adjustable constants, m and β, so the value of $\sum e^2$ for two (or fewer) data points is zero. Therefore, V is the average incremental increase in $\sum e^2$ per additional data point (above two).

Equation (A.12) is the average incremental value of $\sum e^2$ (called the *variance*) for y. What is the variance for M? When e is added to Equation (A.4), the complete equation for y is

$$y = m + \beta(M - \overline{M}) + e \tag{A.13}$$

Solving for M,

$$M = \frac{1}{\beta}(y - m + \beta\overline{M}) - \frac{e}{\beta} \tag{A.14}$$

The first term on the right is the estimate of M based on the measured value y:

$$\hat{M} = \frac{1}{\beta}(y - m + \beta\overline{M}) \tag{A.15}$$

The variance of M is

$$V' = \overline{(M - \hat{M})^2} \tag{A.16}$$

$$V' = \frac{\overline{e^2}}{\beta^2} \tag{A.17}$$

$$V' = \frac{V}{\beta^2} \tag{A.18}$$

The value of β^2 is found from Equation (A.10). However, this experimental determination overestimates the actual value of β^2, because it includes the effect of error. Therefore, a small correction is made:

$$E(S_\beta) = V + \left[\sum (M - \overline{M}^2 \right] \beta^2 \qquad (A.19)$$

$$\beta^2 = \frac{1}{\sum (M - \overline{M})^2} (S_\beta - V) \qquad (A.20)$$

where

$$S_\beta = \beta^2 \sum (M - \overline{M})^2 \qquad (A.21)$$

$$S_\beta = \left[\frac{\sum y(M - \overline{M})}{\sum (M - \overline{M})^2} \right]^2 \sum (M - \overline{M})^2 \qquad (A.22)$$

Combining Equations (A.18) and (A.20) gives

$$V' = \frac{V}{\frac{1}{\sum (M - \overline{M})^2}} (S_\beta - V) \qquad (A.23)$$

The SN ratio is defined by

$$SN\,ratio = 10 \log \frac{1}{V'} \qquad (A.24)$$

$$SN\,ratio = 10 \log \frac{\frac{1}{\sum (M - \overline{M})^2} (S_\beta - V)}{V} \qquad (A.25)$$

Total Quality Development Road Map

This appendix is to help you, the reader, quickly locate any activity in relation to the complete process of total quality development. The first activity is strategy, to determine the products and technologies that are to be developed. Then the technologies are developed to provide the major improvements for each new product concept, as shown in Figure B.1. The products are then developed by a three-phase process, which is further divided into eight subphases, summarized in Figure B.2.

The figure numbers that are displayed in Figure B.2 refer to figures in the main body of this book that describe each subphase in more detail. By referring to these figures, you can see at the next level of detail the complete product development process that is summarized in Figure B.2. Finally, you can see the most detailed level by looking at the textual summaries at the ends of Chapters 4 through 8.

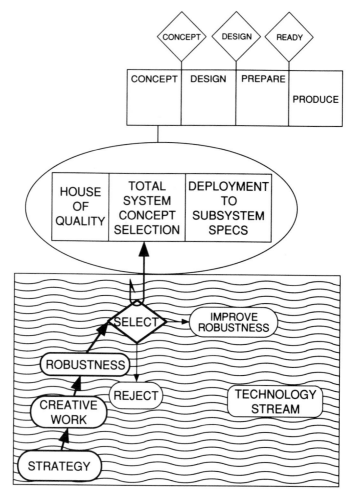

Figure B.1. Technology development—the source for major product concept improvements.

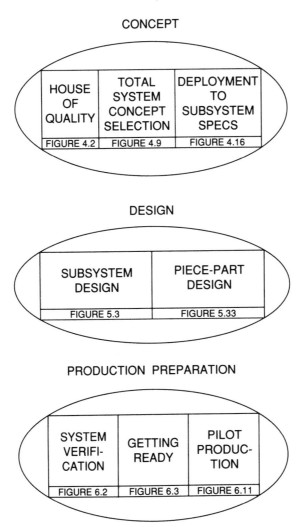

FIGURE B.2. Product development process—three phases and eight subphases.

APPENDIX

C

Summary of QFD
and
Quality Engineering

This appendix summarizes the integration of QFD and Taguchi's quality engineering. It is a road map that enables the reader to quickly survey the entire subject and thus obtain a strong perspective on the interconnections. This appendix can help the reader recognize the context and role of the many activities that are described in the main body of this book and can be read in conjunction with it.

The integration of QFD and quality engineering provides a powerful capability, much of the improvement that comes with total quality development. Together they provide an effective form of system engineering.

The basic unit of quality function deployment combined with quality engineering (QFD/QE) is shown in Figure C.1. The basic unit of Figure C.1 is repeated from one level to the next, with the input to the following level coming from the output from the previous level. This is summarized in Table C.1. The combination of Figure C.1 and Table C.1 can also be displayed as four repetitions of Figure C.1, each corresponding to a level in Table C.1. However, this becomes too large and complex for inclusion in a book.

The combination of Figure C.1 and Table C.1 is really the entire summary of QFD/QE. The reader will be well rewarded by the thorough study of the two together. A concise description of the basic process follows.

The functional requirements, F, are amplified (A) into the detailed product expectations, E_N. The expectations are also deployed from the previous expectations, E_{N-1}. This is described under the heading Step 8—Develop the Product Expectations in Chapter 4, and further clarified under Functional Analysis and QFD in Chapter 5. The deployment of the expectations from E_{N-1} to E_N is done in the QFD matrices, which are summarized in Table C.2.

The functional requirements and the product expectations are used for concept selection, as described in the section Selecting a Winning Concept of Chapter 4. The winning concept includes the product concept, C_H, and the production process concept, C_P, although they are normally selected in more than one selection activity.

The product structure, process structure, and functional structure can all be incorporated in one matrix, or combination of trees, as is sug-

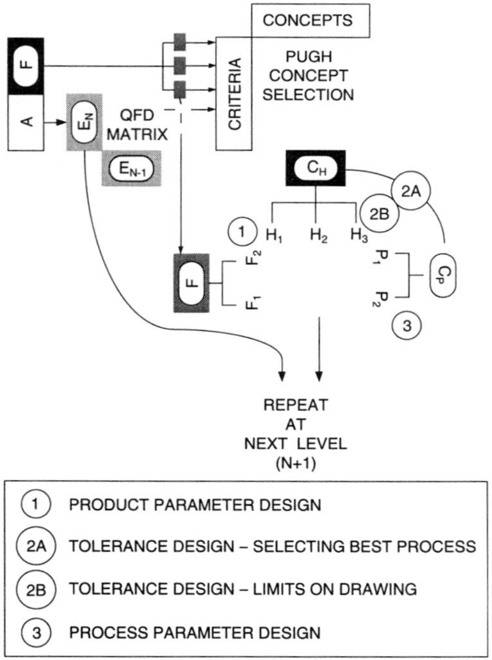
F
A
E_N
QFD MATRIX
E_{N-1}
CRITERIA
CONCEPTS
PUGH CONCEPT SELECTION
C_H
2A
2B
1
H_1 H_2 H_3
F
F_1 F_2
P_1 P_2
C_P
3
REPEAT AT NEXT LEVEL (N+1)
1 PRODUCT PARAMETER DESIGN
2A TOLERANCE DESIGN – SELECTING BEST PROCESS
2B TOLERANCE DESIGN – LIMITS ON DRAWING
3 PROCESS PARAMETER DESIGN

FIGURE C.1 Basic unit of QFD/QE.

TABLE C.1 Legend for Figure C.1

F Function	E_{N-1} Input Expectations	E_N Output Expectations	C_H Hardware (Product) Concept
Total system function	Total system VoC	Product expectations	Total system concept
Subsystem function	Product expectations	SS expectations	SS concept
Part function	SS expectations	Part expectations	Blank-part concept
Part-feature function	Part expectations	Part-feature expectations	Part-feature concept

C_P Process Concept	F_i Functional Variable Contributed to by:	H_i Hardware Characteristics Controlling F_i	P_i Process Variable Controlling H_i
TS assembly concept	Total system	SS interfaces	Assembly
SS assembly concept	Subsystem	Function interfaces	Assembly
Part formation concept	Part	Material	Part formation
Part finishing concept	Part feature	Detailed characteristics	Part finishing

TABLE C.2 EQFD Deployment Through the Levels

Level	Matrix	Input	Output
Total system (TS)	HoQ (Figure 4.7)	VoC	TS expectations
Subsystem (SS)	TS/SS matrix (Figure 4.17)	TS expectations	SS expectations
Piece part (PP)	SS/PP matrix (Figure 5.30)	SS expectations	PP expectations
Part feature (PF)	PP design matrix (Figure 5.38)	PP expectations	PF expectations

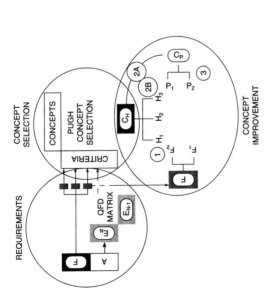

FIGURE C.2 The three major elements of system engineering.

gested by the form of the lower right portion of Figure C.1. This form emphasizes that the process parameters, P, control the product parameters, H, which in turn control the functional parameters, F. However, it is more common to form two matrices, process/product (P/H) and product/function (H/F).

For many of the critical parameters, the structure of Figure C.1 enables the multifunctional team to select the best values. However, for the most critical parmeters, quality engineering is appropriate. *Product parameter design* determines the best values of H that optimize the F/H relationships to provide robust function. *Tolerance design* selects the production processes that provide the least total cost. *Process parameter design* determines the best values of the process parameters, P, that optimize the H/P relationships to provide robust production—that is, consistent units of production.

Table C.2 summarizes the deployment through the levels; see Chapter 3. The series of QFD matrices also deploys from product (part-feature expectations, last row of Table C.2) to process.

The three primary activities of system engineering are explicitly displayed in Figure C.2. This emphasizes that the integration of QFD and quality engineering provides a very effective form of system engineering.

BIBLIOGRAPHY

Adler, Paul S., and Aaron Shenbar. 1990. "Adopting Your Technological Base: The Organizational Challenge." *Sloan Management Review* 32: 25–37.

Allen, Frederick. 1988. "The Letter That Changed the Way We Fly." *Invention and Technology* (Fall): 6–13.

Alster, Norm. 1987. "An American Original Beats Back the Copycats" (interview with David Kearns). *Electronic Business* (October 1): 52–58.

Argyris, Chris. 1990. *Overcoming Organizational Defenses*. Boston: Allyn and Bacon.

_____. 1991. "Teaching Smart People How to Learn." *Harvard Business Review* 69 (May–June): 99–109.

_____. 1993. "Education for Leading-Learning." *Organizational Dynamics* (Winter): 5–17.

Ashley, Steven. 1991. "Rapid Prototyping Systems." *Mechanical Engineering* 113 (no. 4): 34–43.

Bebb, H. Barry. 1990. "Growth of Customer Satisfaction through Implementation of Concurrent Engineering Design Practices." In *Proceedings of the Conference on Concurrent Engineering Design* (sponsored by the Society of Manufacturing Engineers), Ypsilanti, Mich. (June 7–8).

Boothroyd, Geoffrey. 1992. "Simplifying the Process." *Manufacturing Breakthrough* 1: 85–89.

Burchill, Gary. 1993. "Concept Engineering: An Investigation of Time versus Market Orientation in Product Concept Development." Ph.D. dissertation, Sloan School of Management, MIT.

Clark, Kim B., and Takahiro Fujimoto. 1991. *Product Development Performance*. Boston: Harvard Business School Press.

Clausing, Don. 1991. "Flexible Product Development." In *Proceedings of the Conference on Time-Based Competition: Speeding New Product Design and Development*, Vanderbilt University, Nashville (May 16–17).

Clausing, Don. 1992. *Enhanced Quality Function Deployment*. Set of five video tapes. Cambridge, Mass.: MIT Center for Advanced Engineering Study.

Clausing, Don, and Stuart Pugh. 1991. "Enhanced Quality Function Deployment." In *Proceedings of the Design Productivity International Conference*, Honolulu: 15–25.

Deming, W. Edward. 1986. *Out of the Crises*. Cambridge, Mass.: MIT Center for Advanced Engineering Study.

Dertouzos, M. L., R. K. Lester, R. M. Solow, and the MIT Commission on Industrial Productivity. 1989. *Made in America*. Cambridge, Mass.: MIT Press.

Ferguson, Charles H. 1990. "Computers and the Coming of the U.S. Keiretsu." *Harvard Business Review* 68 (July–August): 55–70.

Gomory, Ralph E., and Harold T. Shapiro. 1988. "A Dialogue on Competitiveness." *Issues in Science and Technology* 4 (no. 4): 36–42.

Hauser, John R. 1993. "How Puritan-Bennett Used the House of Quality." *Sloan Management Review* 34: 61–70.

Hauser, John R., and Don Clausing. 1988. "The House of Quality." *Harvard Business Review* 66 (May–June): 63–73.

Henderson, Rebecca M., and Kim B. Clark. 1990. "Architectural Innovation: The Reconfiguration of Existing Product Technologies and the Failure of Established Firms." *Administrative Science Quarterly* 35: 9–30.

Hollins, Bill, and Stuart Pugh. 1990. *Successful Product Design*. London: Butterworth.

Holmes, Maurice. 1993. "Competing on Delivery." *Manufacturing Breakthrough* 2: 29–34.

Hosking, Dian-Marie, and Ian E. Morley. 1991. *A Social Psychology of Organizing*. London: Harvester Wheatsheaf.

Hounshell, David A. 1984. *From the American System to Mass Production, 1800–1932*. Baltimore: Johns Hopkins University Press.

Klein, Robert L. 1990. "New Techniques for Listening to the Voice of the Customer." In *Transactions of the Second Symposium on Quality Function Deployment*, Novi, Mich. (June 18–19): 197–203.

Meyer, Marc H., and James M. Utterback. 1993. "The Product Family and the Dynamics of Core Capability." *Sloan Management Review* 34: 29–47.

Morley, Ian E. 1990. "Building Cross-Functional Design Teams." In *Proceedings of the First International Conference on Integrated Design Management*, London (June 13–14): 100–110.

Moses, Joel. 1990. "Organization and Ideology." MIT discussion paper, November 20.

Nishiguchi, Toshihiro. 1989. "Strategic Dualism: An Alternative in Industrial Societies." Ph.D. dissertation, Faculty of Social Studies, Nuffield College, Oxford University.

Nonaka, Ikujiro, and Hirotaka Takeuchi. 1986. "The New Product Development Game." *Harvard Business Review* 64 (January–February): 137–146.

Pandey, Amitabh, and Don Clausing. 1991. "QFD Implementation Survey Report." Working paper of the Laboratory for Manufacturing and Productivity, MIT, November.

Phadke, Madhav S. 1989. *Quality Engineering Using Robust Design*. Englewood Cliffs, N.J.: Prentice-Hall.

Phadke, Madhav S., and Genichi Taguchi. 1987. "Selection of Quality Characteristics and S/N Ratios for Robust Design." In *Proceeding of the IEEE GLOBECOM-87 Conference*, Tokyo, (November): 1002–1007.

Pipp, Frank. 1990. "Organizational Strategies for Concurrent Engineering in Xerox." Presented at the conference Concurrent Engineering: The Paradigm of the 90's, Colorado Springs, Colo., June 8.

Pugh, Stuart. 1977. "Creativity in Engineering Design–Method, Myth or Magic?" In *Proceedings of the SEFI Conference on Essential Elements in Engineering Education*, Copenhagen (June): 137–146.

_____. 1979. "Give the Designer a Chance—Can He Contribute to Hazard Reductions?" *Product Liability International* 1 (no. 9): 223–225.

_____. 1981. "Concept Selection—A Method That Works." In *Proceedings of the International Conference on Engineering Design (ICED)*, Rome (March): 479–506.

_____. 1983. "The Application of CAD in Relation to Dynamic/Static Product Concepts." In *Proceedings of the International Conference on Engineering Design (ICED)*, Copenhagen (August): 564–571.

_____. 1984. "Further Development of the Hypothesis of Static/Dynamic Product Concepts." In *Proceedings of the International Symposium on Design and Synthesis*, Tokyo (July): 216–221.

_____. 1991. *Total Design*. Reading, Mass.: Addison-Wesley.

Pugh, Stuart, and D. G. Smith. 1974. "Dumper Truck Design Highlights Industrial/Academic Cooperation." *Design Engineering* (August): 27–29.

_____. 1976. "CAD in the Context of Engineering Design—The Designer's Viewpoint." In *Proceedings of the Second International Conference on Computers in Engineering and Building Design*, London: 193–198.

Sachs, Emanuel, Michael Cima, James Bredt, Alain Curodeau, Tailin Fan, and David Brancazio. 1992. "CAD-Casting: Direct Fabrication of Ceramic Shells and Cores by Three-Dimensional Printing." *Manufacturing Review* 5(2): 117–126.

Senge, Peter M. 1990. *The Fifth Discipline: The Art and Practice of the Learning Organization*. New York: Doubleday.

Shiba, Shoji, Alan Graham, and David Walden. 1993. *A New American TQM.* Cambridge, Mass.: Productivity Press.

Shingo, Shigeo. 1985. *A Revolution in Manufacturing: The SMED System.* Stamford, Conn.: Productivity Press.

Sontow, Karsten, and Don Clausing. 1993. "Integration of Quality Function Deployment with Further Methods of Quality Planning." Working paper of the Laboratory for Manufacturing and Productivity, MIT, April.

Stalk, George, Jr. 1988. "Time—The Next Source of Competitive Advantage." *Harvard Business Review* 66 (July–August): 112–125.

Suh, Nam. 1990. *Principles of Design.* New York: Oxford University Press.

Taguchi, Genichi. 1986. *Introduction to Quality Engineering: Designing Quality into Products and Processes.* Tokyo: Asian Productivity Organization. (Available in North America, the United Kingdom, and western Europe from UNIPUB/Kraus International Publications, White Plains, N.Y.)

———. 1987. *Systems of Experimental Design.* White Plains, N.Y.: UNIPUB/Kraus International Publications. Also Dearborn, Mich.: American Supplier Institute.

Taguchi, Genichi, and Don Clausing. 1990. "Robust Quality." *Harvard Business Review* 68 (January–February): 65–75.

Taguchi, Genichi, and Madhav S. Phadke. 1984. "Quality Engineering through Design Optimization." In *Proceedings of the IEEE GLOBECOM-84 Conference,* Atlanta (November): 1106–1113.

Urban, Glen L., and John R. Hauser. 1981. *Design and Marketing of New Products.* Englewood Cliffs, N.J.: Prentice-Hall.

Veraldi, Lewis. 1988. "New Program Management at Ford." Presented at the First Dartmouth Conference on Next Generation Management and Engineering, Hanover, N.H., September 12.

von Hippel, Eric. 1988. *The Sources of Innovation.* New York: Oxford University Press.

Index

ABOUT THE AUTHOR

Don P. Clausing, Ph.D., is Bernard M. Gordon Adjunct Professor of Engineering Innovation and Practice at the Massachusetts Institute of Technology, where he developed and now teaches MIT's course on the improved total design process. An active consultant, he has helped leading companies realize significant improvement in their design processes, and gives workshops and seminars on the topic throughout the U.S. and abroad. With nearly thirty years of industry experience, Dr. Clausing played a major role as principal engineer at Xerox in leading the company's product development process improvement effort. He is credited with introducing quality function deployment (QFD) and the design practices of Stuart Pugh to U.S. industry, as well as being a pioneer in the implementation of Taguchi's system of quality engineering in the United States. He holds a Ph.D. and M.S. in materials science from the California Institute of Technology and a B.S. in mechanical engineering from Iowa State University.